The Condition
of Postmodernity

B

The Condition of Postmodernity

An Enquiry into the Origins of Cultural Change

David Harvey

BLACKWELL
Cambridge MA & Oxford UK

First published 1990

Reprinted 1990 (three times), 1991,
1992 (twice), 1993, 1994, 1995 (twice),
1996, 1997 (twice), 1999 (twice), 2000 (twice)

Blackwell Publishers Inc
350 Main Street
Malden, Massachusetts 02148, USA

Blackwell Publishers Ltd
108 Cowley Road
Oxford OX4 1JF, UK

Library of Congress Cataloging in Publication Data
Harvey, David, 1935–
The condition of postmodernity/David Harvey
p. cm.
Bibliography: p.
Includes index.
ISBN 0–631–16292–5 — ISBN 0–631–16294–1 (pbk)
1. Civilization. Modern–1950– 2. Capitalism. 3. Space and time.
4. Postmodernism. I. Title.
CB428.H38 1989
909.82.—dc19 88–39135
CIP

British Library Cataloguing in Publication Data
A CIP catalogue record for this book is available from the British Library

Typeset in 10.5 on 12pt Garamond
by Setrite
Printed in the United States of America

This book is printed on acid-free paper

Contents

The argument

There has been a sea-change in cultural as well as in political—economic practices since around 1972.

This sea-change is bound up with the emergence of new dominant ways in which we experience space and time.

While simultaneity in the shifting dimensions of time and space is no proof of necessary or causal connection, strong a priori grounds can be adduced for the proposition that there is some kind of necessary relation between the rise of postmodernist cultural forms, the emergence of more flexible modes of capital accumulation, and a new round of 'time—space compression' in the organization of capitalism.

But these changes, when set against the basic rules of capitalistic accumulation, appear more as shifts in surface appearance rather than as signs of the emergence of some entirely new postcapitalist or even postindustrial society.

Preface

I cannot remember exactly when I first encountered the term post-modernism. I probably reacted to it in much the same way as I did to the various other 'isms' that have come and gone over the past couple of decades, hoping that it would disappear under the weight of its own incoherence or simply lose its allure as a fashionable set of 'new ideas.'

But it seemed as if the clamour of postmodernist arguments increased rather than diminished with time. Once connected with poststructuralism, postindustrialism, and a whole arsenal of other 'new ideas,' postmodernism appeared more and more as a powerful configuration of new sentiments and thoughts. It seemed set fair to play a crucial role in defining the trajectory of social and political development simply by virtue of the way it defined standards of social critique and political practice. In recent years it has determined the standards of debate, defined the manner of 'discourse,' and set parameters on cultural, political, and intellectual criticism.

It therefore seemed appropriate to enquire more closely into the nature of postmodernism, not so much as a set of ideas but as a historical condition that required elucidation. I had, however, to undertake a survey of the dominant ideas and, since postmodernism turns out to be a mine-field of conflicting notions, that project turned out to be by no means easy to undertake. The results of that enquiry, set out in Part I, have been boiled down to the bare minimum, though I hope not unreasonably so. The rest of the work examines the political–economic background (again, in a somewhat simplified way) before looking much more closely at the experience of space and time as one singularly important mediating link between the dynamism of capitalism's historical–geographical development and complex processes of cultural production and ideological transformation. In this way it proves possible to make sense of some of the wholly new discourses that have arisen in the Western world over the past few decades.

There are signs, these days, that the cultural hegemony of post-modernism is weakening in the West. When even the developers tell an architect like Moshe Safdie that they are tired of it, then can philosophical thinking be far behind? In a sense it does not matter whether postmodernism is or is not on the way out, since much can be learned from a historical enquiry into the roots of what has been a quite unsettling phase in economic, political, and cultural development.

In writing this book I have had a lot of help and critical encouragement. Vicente Navarro, Erica Schoenberger, Neil Smith, and Dick Walker provided a host of comments either on the manuscript or upon the ideas I was developing. The Roland Park Collective provided a grand forum for intellectual discussion and debate. It was also my good fortune to work with an extremely talented group of graduate students at the Johns Hopkins University, and I would like to thank Kevin Archer, Patrick Bond, Michael Johns, Phil Schmandt, and Eric Swyngedouw for the tremendous intellectual stimulation they provided during my last years there. Jan Bark initiated me into the joys of having someone do the word-processing competently and with good humour while undertaking much of the burden of constructing the index. Angela Newman drew the diagrams, Tony Lee helped with the photography, Sophie Hartley sought out the permissions, and Alison Dickens and John Davey, of Basil Blackwell, provided many helpful editorial comments and suggestions. And Haydee was a wonderful source of inspiration.

Acknowledgements

The author and publisher are grateful to the following for their kind permission to reproduce plates: Alcatel 3.2; Archives Nationales de France 3.3, 3.8; The Art Institute of Chicago, Joseph Winterbotham Collection, © The Art Institute of Chicago. All Rights Reserved. © DACS 1988 3.9; Associated Press 1.21; A. Aubrey Bodine Collection, courtesy of the Peale Museum, Baltimore. 1.22; Jean-François Batellier 1.4; Bildarchiv Photo Marburg 1.20; British Architectural Library/RIBA 3.6; The British Library 3.4; Leo Castelli Gallery, New York, © Robert Rauschenberg, © DACS 1988 (photograph by Rudolph Burckhardt) 1.9; Deutsches Architekturmusuem, Frankfurt am Main, 1.28; P. Dicken, Global Shift 3.1; Equitable Life Assurance Collection of the U.S. 1.5; Fondation Le Corbusier, Paris, © DACS 1988 1.1a; Galerie Bruno Bischofberger, Zurich, 1.6; Lintas Limited, London, 1.10; Lloyds Bank Plc, London, 4.1; Lloyd's of London (photograph by Janet Gill) 1.19; Los Angeles Times 1.18; Mansell Collection 1.7; Metro Pictures, New York, 1.2; Metropolitan Life Insurance Company Archives, New York, 1.1b; Musée National d'Art Moderne, Centre Georges Pompidou, Paris, © ADAGP, Paris, and DACS, London 1988 3.11, 3.12; Musée d'Orsay, Cliché des Musées Nationaux, Paris, 1.8; The Museum of Modern Art, New York, Purchase Fund, © ADAGP, Paris, and DACS, London 1989 3.10; National Portrait Gallery, London 3.5; Roger-Viollet 1.3. All other photographs were kindly provided by the author.

The author and publisher would also like to thank the estate of T.S. Eliot, and the publishers of the *Four Quartets*, Faber and Faber Ltd and Harcourt Brace Jovanovich, for permission to reproduce the extract from *Burnt Norton*, and Heinrich Klotz, *Revision der Moderne: Postmoderne Architektur 1960–1980*, Prestel Verlag München, 1984, for the catalogue description of Charles Moore's *Piazza d'Italia*.

Part I

The passage from modernity to postmodernity in contemporary culture

The fate of an epoch that has eaten of the tree of knowledge is that it must ... recognize that general views of life and the universe can never be the products of increasing empirical knowledge, and that the highest ideals, which move us most forcefully, are always formed only in the struggle with other ideals which are just as sacred to others as ours are to us.   *Max Weber*

1

Introduction

Jonathan Raban's *Soft city,* a highly personalized account of London life in the early 1970s, was published in 1974. It received a fair amount of favourable comment at the time. But its interest to me here is as a historical marker, because it was written at a moment when a certain shifting can be detected in the way in which problems of urban life were being talked about in both popular and academic circles. It presaged a new kind of discourse that would later generate terms like 'gentrification' and 'yuppie' as common descriptors of urban living. It was also written at that cusp in intellectual and cultural history when something called 'postmodernism' emerged from its chrysalis of the anti-modern to establish itself as a cultural aesthetic in its own right.

Unlike most of the critical and oppositional writing about urban life in the 1960s (and I here think primarily of Jane Jacobs, whose book on *The death and life of great American cities* came out in 1961, but also Theodore Roszak), Raban depicts as both vibrant and present what many earlier writers had felt as a chronic absence. To the thesis that the city was falling victim to a rationalized and automated system of mass production and mass consumption of material goods, Raban replied that it was in practice mainly about the production of signs and images. He rejected the thesis of a city tightly stratified by occupation and class, depicting instead a wide-spread individualism and entrepreneurialism in which the marks of social distinction were broadly conferred by possessions and appearances. To the supposed domination of rational planning (see plate 1.1) Raban opposed the image of the city as an 'encyclopaedia' or 'emporium of styles' in which all sense of hierarchy or even homogeneity of values was in the course of dissolution. The city dweller was not, he argued, someone necessarily given over to calculating rationality (as many sociologists presumed). The city was more like a

Plate 1.1 (above) Le Corbusier's Dream for Paris of the 1920s *and (below)*
the achieved design for Stuyvesant Town, New York

theatre, a series of stages upon which individuals could work their own distinctive magic while performing a multiplicity of roles. To the ideology of the city as some lost but longed-for community, Raban responded with a picture of the city as labyrinth, honey-combed with such diverse networks of social interaction oriented to such diverse goals that 'the encyclopaedia becomes a maniacal scrap-book filled with colourful entries which have no relation to each other, no determining, rational or economic scheme.'

My purpose here is not to criticize this particular representation (though it would not, I think, be hard to show that it was a rather particular perception of matters on the part of a young professional newly arrived in London). I do wish to concentrate on how such an interpretation could be so confidently asserted and so well received. For there are a number of things going on in *Soft city* that deserve close attention.

To begin with, the book offers more than a little comfort to those who feared that the city was falling victim to the totalitarianism of planners, bureaucrats, and corporate elites. The city, Raban insists, is much too complicated a place ever to be so disciplined. A labyrinth, an encyclopaedia, an emporium, a theatre, the city is somewhere where fact and imagination simply *have* to fuse. Raban also appealed unbashedly to notions of subjective individualism which had so often been forced underground by the collectivist rhetoric of the 1960s social movements. For the city was also a place where people were relatively free to act as, and become what, they pleased. 'Personal identity had been rendered soft, fluid, endlessly open' to the exercise of the will and the imagination:

> For better or worse, [the city] invites you to remake it, to consolidate it into a shape you can live in. You, too. Decide who you are, and the city will again assume a fixed form around you. Decide what it is, and your own identity will be revealed, like a map fixed by triangulation. Cities, unlike villages and small towns, are plastic by nature. We mould them in our images: they, in their turn, shape us by the resistance they offer when we try to impose our own personal form on them. In this sense, it seems to me that living in a city is an art, and we need the vocabulary of art, of style, to describe the peculiar relation between man and material that exists in the continual creative play of urban living. The city as we imagine it, the soft city of illusion, myth, aspiration, nightmare, is as real, maybe more real, than the hard city one can locate in maps and statistics, in monographs on urban sociology and demography and architecture. (pp. 9–10)

While affirmative in this sense, Raban did not pretend that all was well with urban life. Too many people lost their way in the labyrinth, it was simply too easy for us to lose each other as well as ourselves. And if there was something liberating about the possibility of playing many diverse roles there was also something stressful and deeply unsettling about it. Beneath all that, lay the grumbling threat of inexplicable violence, the inevitable companion of that omni-present tendency for social life to dissolve into total chaos. Inexplicable killings and random urban violence in fact form the opening gambit in Raban's account. The city may be a theatre, but that meant there were opportunities for villains and fools to strut there and turn social life into tragi-comedy, even violent melodrama, particularly if we failed to read the codes right. Although we are 'necessarily dependent on surfaces and appearances' it was not always clear how we could learn to attend to these surfaces with the requisite sympathy and seriousness. This task was rendered doubly difficult by the way creative entrepreneurialism had been harnessed to the task of producing fantasy and disguise, while behind all the churnings of codes and fashions lurked a certain 'imperialism of taste' that stood to re-create in new ways the very hierarchy of values and significations that changing fashions otherwise undermined:

> Signals, styles, systems of rapid, highly conventionalized communication, are the lifeblood of the big city. It is when these systems break down — when we lose our grasp on the grammar of urban life — that [violence] takes over. The city, our great modern form, is soft, amenable to the dazzling and libidinous variety of lives, dreams, interpretations. But the very plastic qualities which make the great city the liberator of human identity also cause it to be especially vulnerable to psychosis and totalitarian nightmare.

There is more than a touch of the French literary critic Roland Barthes's influence in this passage, and sure enough that writer's classic text *Writing degree zero* turns up for favourable mention on more than one occasion. To the degree that Le Corbusier's modernist style of architecture (plate 1.1) is the *bête noire* in Raban's scheme of things, *Soft city* records a moment of fierce tension between one of the great heroes of the modernist movement and someone like Barthes, who was shortly to become one of the central figures of postmodernism. *Soft city,* written at that moment, is a prescient text that should itself be read not as an anti-modernist argument but as a vital affirmation that the postmodernist moment has arrived.

I was recently reminded of Raban's evocative descriptions while visiting an exhibition of Cindy Sherman's photographs (plate 1.2). The photographs depict seemingly different women drawn from many walks of life. It takes a little while to realize, with a certain shock, that these are portraits of the same woman in different guises. Only the catalogue tells you that it is the artist herself who is that woman. The parallel with Raban's insistence upon the plasticity of human personality through the malleability of appearances and surfaces is striking, as is the self-referential positioning of the authors to themselves as subjects. Cindy Sherman is considered a major figure in the postmodern movement.

So what is this postmodernism of which many now speak? Has social life so changed since the early 1970s that we can reasonably talk about living in a postmodern culture, a postmodern age? Or is it simply that trends in high culture have taken, as is their wont, yet another twist, and that academic fashions have also changed with scarcely a ripple of effect or an echo of correspondence in the daily life of ordinary citizens? Raban's book suggests that there is more to matters than the latest intellectual fad imported from Paris or the latest twirl in the New York art market. There is more to it, too, than the shift in architectural style that Jencks (1984) records, though here we approach a realm that has the potential to bring high cultural concerns closer to daily life through the production of built form. Major changes have indeed occured in the qualities of urban life since 1970 or so. But whether such shifts deserve the appellation of 'postmodern' is another question. The answer depends rather directly, of course, on exactly what we might mean by that term. And here we do have to grapple with the latest intellectual fads imported from Paris and twists in the New York art market, because it is out of those ferments that the concept of the 'postmodern' has emerged.

No one exactly agrees as to what is meant by the term, except, perhaps, that 'postmodernism' represents some kind of reaction to, or departure from, 'modernism'. Since the meaning of modernism is also very confused, the reaction or departure known as 'postmodernism' is doubly so. The literary critic Terry Eagleton (1987) tries to define the term as follows:

> There is, perhaps, a degree of consensus that the typical postmodernist artefact is playful, self-ironizing and even schizoid; and that it reacts to the austere autonomy of high modernism by impudently embracing the language of commerce and the commodity. Its stance towards cultural tradition is one of irreverent pastiche, and its contrived depthlessness undermines

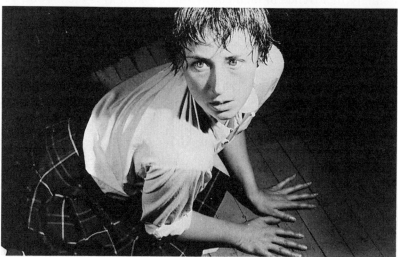

Plate 1.2 Cindy Sherman, Untitled, *1983 and* Untitled #92, *1981.*
Postmodernism and the mask: Cindy Sherman's photographic art uses herself
as a subject in multiple disguises, many of which make overt reference to film
or media images.

all metaphysical solemnities, sometimes by a brutal aesthetics of
squalor and shock.

In more positive vein, the editors of the architectural journal
PRECIS 6 (1987, 7–24) see postmodernism as a legitimate reaction

to the 'monotomy' of universal modernism's vision of the world. 'Generally perceived as positivistic, technocentric, and rationalistic, universal modernism has been identified with the belief in linear progress, absolute truths, the rational planning of ideal social orders, and the standardization of knowledge and production.' Post-modernism, by way of contrast, privileges 'heterogeneity and difference as liberative forces in the redefinition of cultural discourse.' Fragmentation, indeterminacy, and intense distrust of all universal or 'totalizing' discourses (to use the favoured phrase) are the hallmark of postmodernist thought. The rediscovery of pragmatism in philosophy (e. g. Rorty, 1979), the shift of ideas about the philosophy of science wrought by Kuhn (1962) and Feyerabend (1975), Foucault's emphasis upon discontinuity and difference in history and his privileging of 'polymorphous correlations in place of simple or complex casuality,' new developments in mathematics emphasizing indeterminacy (catastrophe and chaos theory, fractal geometry), the re-emergence of concern in ethics, politics, and anthropology for the validity and dignity of 'the other,' all indicate a widespread and profound shift in 'the structure of feeling.' What all these examples have in common is a rejection of 'meta-narratives' (large-scale theoretical interpretations purportedly of universal application), which leads Eagleton to complete his description of postmodernism thus:

> Post-modernism signals the death of such 'metanarratives' whose secretly terroristic function was to ground and legitimate the illusion of a 'universal' human history. We are now in the process of wakening from the nightmare of modernity, with its manipulative reason and fetish of the totality, into the laid-back pluralism of the post-modern, that heterogeneous range of lifestyles and language games which has renounced the nostalgic urge to totalize and legitimate itself. . . . Science and philosophy must jettison their grandiose metaphysical claims and view themselves more modestly as just another set of narratives.

If these depictions are correct, then it would certainly seem as if Raban's *Soft city* is suffused with postmodernist sentiment. But the real import of that has still to be established. Since the only agreed point of departure for understanding the postmodern is in its purported relation to the modern, it is to the meaning of the latter term that I shall first attend.

2

Modernity and modernism

'Modernity,' wrote Baudelaire in his seminal essay 'The painter of modern life' (published in 1863), 'is the transient, the fleeting, the contingent; it is the one half of art, the other being the eternal and the immutable.'

I want to pay very close attention to this conjoining of the ephemeral and the fleeting with the eternal and the immutable. The history of modernism as an aesthetic movement has wavered from one side to the other of this dual formulation, often making it appear as if it can, as Lionel Trilling (1966) once observed, swing around in meaning until it is facing in the opposite direction. Armed with Baudelaire's sense of tension we can, I think, better understand some of the conflicting meanings attributed to modernism, and some of the extraordinarily diverse currents of artistic practice, as well as aesthetic and philosophical judgements offered up in its name.

I shall leave aside, for the moment, the question *why* modern life might be characterized by so much ephemerality and change. But that the condition of modernity is so characterized is not generally disputed. Here, for example, is Berman's (1982, 15) description:

> There is a mode of vital experience − experience of space and time, of the self and others, of life's possibilities and perils − that is shared by men and women all over the world today. I will call this body of experience 'modernity'. To be modern is to find ourselves in an environment that promises adventure, power, joy, growth, transformation of ourselves and the world − and, at the same time, that threatens to destroy everything we have, everything we know, everything we are. Modern environments and experiences cut across all boundaries of geography and ethnicity, of class and nationality, of religion and ideology; in this sense, modernity can be said to unite all

mankind. But it is a paradoxical unity, a unity of disunity; it pours us all into a maelstrom of perpetual disintegration and renewal, of struggle and contradiction, of ambiguity and anguish. To be modern is to be part of a universe in which, as Marx said, 'all that is solid melts into air.'

Berman goes on to show how a variety of writers in different places and at different times (Goethe, Marx, Baudelaire, Dostoevsky, and Biely, among others) confronted and tried to deal with this overwhelming sense of fragmentation, ephemerality, and chaotic change. This same theme has recently been echoed by Frisby (1985) who in a study of three modern thinkers – Simmel, Kracauer, and Benjamin – emphasizes that 'their central concern was with a distinctive experience of time, space and causality as transitory, fleeting, and fortuitous and arbitrary.' While it may be true that both Berman and Frisby are reading into the past a very strong contemporary sensitivity to ephemerality and fragmentation, and therefore, perhaps, overemphasizing that side of Baudelaire's dual formulation, there is abundant evidence to suggest that most 'modern' writers have recognized that the only secure thing about modernity is its insecurity, its penchant, even, for 'totalizing chaos.' The historian Carl Schorske (1981, xix) notes, for example, that in *fin de siècle* Vienna:

High culture entered a whirl of infinite innovation, with each field proclaiming independence of the whole, each part in turn falling into parts. Into the ruthless centrifuge of change were drawn the very concepts by which cultural phenomena might be fixed in thought. Not only the producers of culture, but also its analysts and critics fell victim to the fragmentation.

The poet W. B. Yeats caught this same mood in the lines:

Things fall apart; the centre cannot hold;
Mere anarchy is loosed upon the world.

If modern life is indeed so suffused with the sense of the fleeting, the ephemeral, the fragmentary, and the contingent, then a number of profound consequences follow. To begin with, modernity can have no respect even for its own past, let alone that of any premodern social order. The transitoriness of things makes it difficult to preserve any sense of historical continuity. If there is any meaning to history, then that meaning has to be discovered and defined from within the maelstrom of change, a maelstrom that affects the terms of discussion as well as whatever it is that is being discussed. Modernity, therefore, not only entails a ruthless break with any or all preceding historical conditions, but is characterized by a never-ending process of internal ruptures and fragmentations within itself. An avant-garde has usually played, as Poggioli (1968) and Bürger (1984) record, a vital role in the history of modernism, interrupting any sense of continuity by radical surges, recuperations, and repressions. How to interpret this, how to discover the 'eternal and immutable' elements in the midst of such radical disruptions, becomes a serious problem. Even if modernism always remained committed to discover, as the painter Paul Klee put it, 'the essential character of the accidental,' it now had to do so in a field of continually changing meanings that often seemed to 'contradict the rational experience of yesterday.' Aesthetic practices and judgements fragmented into that kind of 'maniacal scrapbook filled with colourful entries that have no relation to each other, no determining, rational, or economic scheme,' which Raban describes as an essential aspect of urban life.

Where, in all of this, could we look for some sense of coherence, let alone say something cogent about the 'eternal and immutable' that was supposed to lurk within this maelstrom of social change in space and time? Enlightenment thinkers generated a philosophical and even a practical answer to that question. Since this answer has dominated much of the subsequent debate over the meaning of modernity, it merits some closer scrutiny.

Although the term 'modern' has a rather more ancient history, what Habermas (1983, 9) calls the *project* of modernity came into focus during the eighteenth century. That project amounted to an extraordinary intellectual effort on the part of Enlightenment thinkers 'to develop objective science, universal morality and law, and autonomous art according to their inner logic.' The idea was to use the accumulation of knowledge generated by many individuals working freely and creatively for the pursuit of human emancipation and the enrichment of daily life. The scientific domination of nature promised freedom from scarcity, want, and the arbitrariness of natural calamity. The development of rational forms of social organization and rational modes of thought promised liberation from the irrationalities of myth, religion, superstition, release from the arbitrary use of power as well as from the dark side of our own human natures. Only through such a project could the universal, eternal, and the immutable qualities of all of humanity be revealed.

Enlightenment thought (and I here rely on Cassirer's, 1951, account) embraced the idea of progress, and actively sought that break with history and tradition which modernity espouses. It was, above all, a secular movement that sought the demystification and desacralization of knowledge and social organization in order to liberate human beings from their chains. It took Alexander Pope's injunction, 'the proper study of mankind is man,' with great seriousness. To the degree that it also lauded human creativity, scientific discovery, and the pursuit of individual excellence in the name of human progress, Enlightenment thinkers welcomed the maelstrom of change and saw the transitoriness, the fleeting, and the fragmentary as a necessary condition through which the modernizing project could be achieved. Doctrines of equality, liberty, faith in human intelligence (once allowed the benefits of education), and universal reason abounded. 'A good law must be good for everyone,' pronounced Condorcet in the throes of the French Revolution, 'in exactly the same way that a true proposition is true for all.' Such a vision was incredibly optimistic. Writers like Condorcet, Habermas (1983, 9) notes, were possessed 'of the extravagant expectation that the arts and sciences would promote not only the control of natural forces but also understanding of the world and of the self, moral progress, the justice of institutions and even the happiness of human beings.'

The twentieth century – with its death camps and death squads, its militarism and two world wars, its threat of nuclear annihilation and its experience of Hiroshima and Nagasaki – has certainly shattered this optimism. Worse still, the suspicion lurks that the Enlightenment project was doomed to turn against itself and transform the quest for human emancipation into a system of universal oppression in the name of human liberation. This was the daring thesis advanced by Horkheimer and Adorno in their *The dialetic of Enlightenment* (1972). Writing in the shadow of Hitler's Germany and Stalin's Russia, they argued that the logic that hides behind Enlightenment rationality is a logic of domination and oppression. The lust to dominate nature entailed the domination of human beings, and that could only lead, in the end, to 'a nightmare condition of self-domination' (Bernstein, 1985, 9). The revolt of nature, which they posited as the only way out of the impasse, had then to be conceived of as a revolt of human nature against the oppressive power of purely instrumental reason over culture and personality.

Whether or not the Enlightenment project was doomed from the start to plunge us into a Kafkaesque world, whether or not it was bound to lead to Auschwitz and Hiroshima, and whether it has any power left to inform and inspire contemporary thought and action, are crucial questions. There are those, like Habermas, who continue to support the project, albeit with a strong dose of scepticism over aims, a lot of anguishing over the relation between means and ends, and a certain pessimism as to the possibility of realizing such a project under contemporary economic and political conditions. And then there are those – and this is, as we shall see, the core of post-modernist philosophical thought – who insist that we should, in the name of human emancipation, abandon the Enlightenment project entirely. Which position we take depends upon how we explain the 'dark side' of our recent history and the degree to which we attribute it to the defects of Enlightenment reason rather than to a lack of its proper application.

Enlightenment thought, of course, internalized a whole host of difficult problems and possessed not a few troublesome contradictions. To begin with, the question of the relation between means and ends was omni-present, while the goals themselves could never be specified precisely except in terms of some utopian plan that often looked as oppressive to some as it looked emancipatory to others. Further-more, the question of exactly who possessed the claim to superior reason and under what conditions that reason should be exercised as power had to be squarely faced. Mankind will have to be forced to be free, said Rousseau; and the Jacobins of the French Revolution took over in their political practice where Rousseau's philosophical thought had left off. Francis Bacon, one of the precursors of En-lightenment thought, envisaged in his utopian tract *New Atlantis* a house of wise sages who would be the guardians of knowledge, the ethical judges, and the true scientists; while living outside the daily life of the community they would exercise extraordinary moral power over it. To this vision of an elite but collective male, white wisdom, others opposed the image of the unbridled individualism of great thinkers, the great benefactors of humankind, who through their singular efforts and struggles would push reason and civilization willy-nilly to the point of true emancipation. Others argued either that there was some inherent teleology at work (even, perhaps, divinely inspired), to which the human spirit was bound to respond, or that there existed some social mechanism, such as Adam Smith's celebrated hidden hand of the market, that would convert even the most dubious of moral sentiments into a result advantageous to all. Marx, who in many respects was a child of Enlightenment thought, sought to convert utopian thinking – the struggle for human beings to realize their 'species being' as he put it in his early works – into a materialist science by showing how universal human emancipation might emerge from the class-bound and evidently repressive, though contradictory, logic of capitalist development. In so doing he focused on the working class as the agent of human liberation and eman-cipation precisely because it was the dominated class of modern capitalist society. Only when the direct producers were in control of their own destinies, he argued, could we hope to replace domination and repression by a realm of social freedom. But if 'the realm of freedom begins only when the realm of necessity is left behind,' then the progressive side of bourgeois history (particularly its creation of enormous productive powers) had to be fully acknowledged and the positive outcomes of Enlightenment rationality fully appropriated.

The project of modernity has never been without its critics. Edmund Burke made no effort to hide his doubts and disgust at the excesses of the French Revolution. Malthus, rebutting Condorcet's optimism, argued the impossibility of ever escaping the chains of natural scarcity and want. De Sade likewise showed that there might be quite another dimension to human liberation apart from that envisaged in conventional Enlightenment thought. And by the early twentieth century two major, yet quite differently positioned, critics had put their stamp upon the debate. First, there was Max Weber whose overall argument is summarized by Bernstein, a key protagonist in the debate over modernity and its meanings, thus:

> Weber argued that the hope and expectation of the Enlighten- ment thinkers was a bitter and ironic illusion. They maintained a strong necessary linkage between the growth of science, ra- tionality, and universal human freedom. But when unmasked and understood, the legacy of the Enlightenment was the triumph of ... purposive−instrumental rationality. This form of ration- ality affects and infects the entire range of social and cultural life encompassing economic structures, law, bureaucratic administration, and even the arts. The growth of [purpos- ive−instrumental rationality] does not lead to the concrete realization of universal freedom but to the creation of an 'iron cage' of bureaucratic rationality from which there is no escape. (Bernstein, 1985, 5)

If Weber's 'sober warning' reads like the epitaph of Enlightenment reason, then Nietzsche's earlier attack upon its very premises must surely be regarded as its nemesis. It was rather as if Nietzsche plunged totally into the other side of Baudelaire's formulation in order to show that the modern was nothing more than a vital energy, the will to live and to power, swimming in a sea of disorder, anarchy, destruction, individual alienation, and despair. 'Beneath the surface of modern life, dominated by knowledge and science, he discerned vital energies that were wild, primitive and completely merciless' (Bradbury and McFarlane, 1976, 446). All the Enlightenment imagery about civilization, reason, universal rights, and morality was for naught. The eternal and immutable essence of humanity found its proper representation in the mythical figure of Dionysus: 'to be at one and the same time "destructively creative" (i.e. to form the temporal world of individualization and becoming, a process destructive of unity) and "creatively destructive" (i.e. to devour the illusory universe of individualization, a process involving the reaction of unity)' (loc. cit.). The only path to affirmation of self was to act, to manifest will, in this maelstrom of destructive creation and creative destruction even if the outcome was bound to be tragic.

The image of 'creative destruction' is very important to understanding modernity precisely because it derived from the practical dilemmas that faced the implementation of the modernist project. How could a new world be created, after all, without destroying much that had gone before? You simply cannot make an omelette without breaking eggs, as a whole line of modernist thinkers from Goethe to Mao have noted. The literary archetype of such a dilemma is, as Berman (1982) and Lukacs (1969) point out, Goethe's *Faust*. An epic hero prepared to destroy religious myths, traditional values, and customary ways of life in order to build a brave new world out of the ashes of the old, Faust is, in the end, a tragic figure. Synthesizing thought and action, Faust forces himself and everyone else (even Mephistopheles) to extremes of organization, pain, and exhaustion in order to master nature and create a new landscape, a sublime spiritual achievement that contains the potentiality for human liberation from want and need. Prepared to eliminate everthing and everyone who stands in the way of the realization of this sublime vision, Faust, to his own ultimate horror, deploys Mephistopheles to kill a much-loved old couple who live in a small cottage by the sea-shore for no other reason than the fact that they do not fit in with the master plan. 'It appears,' says Berman (1982), 'that the very process of development, even as it transforms the wasteland into a thriving physical and social space, recreates the wasteland inside of the developer himself. This is how the tragedy of development works.'

There are enough modern figures – Haussmann at work in Second Empire Paris and Robert Moses at work in New York after World War II – to make this figure of creative destruction more than a myth (plates 1.3, 1.4). But we here see at work that opposition between the ephemeral and the eternal in a rather different guise. If the modernist has to destroy in order to create, then the only way to represent eternal truths is through a process of destruction that is liable, in the end, to be itself destructive of those truths. Yet we are forced, if we strive for the eternal and immutable, to try and put our

Plate 1.3 Haussmann's creative destruction of Second Empire Paris: the rebuilding of the Place Saint Germain

stamp upon the chaotic, the ephemeral, and the fragmentary. The Nietzschian image of creative destruction and destructive creation bridges the two sides of Baudelaire's formulation in a new way. Interestingly, the economist Schumpeter picked up this very same image in order to understand the processes of capitalist development. The entrepreneur, in Schumpeter's view a heroic figure, was the creative destroyer *par excellence* because the entrepreneur was prepared to push the consequences of technical and social innovation to vital extremes. And it was only through such creative heroism that human progress could be assured. Creative destruction, for Schumpeter, was the progressive leitmotif of benevolent capitalist development. For others, it was simply the necessary condition of twentieth-century progress. Here is Gertrude Stein writing on Picasso in 1938:

As everything destroys itself in the twentieth century and nothing continues, so then the twentieth century has a splendour which is its own and Picasso is of this century, he has that strange quality of an earth that one has never seen and of things destroyed as they have never been destroyed. So then Picasso has his splendour.

Plate 1.4 The boulevard art of Paris, attacking the modernist destruction of the ancient urban fabric: a cartoon by J. F. Batellier in 'Sans Retour, Ni Consigne'

Prophetic words and a prophetic conception this, on the part of both Schumpeter and Stein, in the years before the greatest event in capitalism's history of creative destruction – World War II.

By the beginning of the twentieth century, and particularly after Nietzsche's intervention, it was no longer possible to accord Enlightenment reason a privileged status in the definition of the eternal and immutable essence of human nature. To the degree that Nietzsche had led the way in placing aesthetics above science, rationality, and politics, so the exploration of aesthetic experience – 'beyond good and evil' – became a powerful means to establish a new mythology as to what the eternal and the immutable might be about in the midst of all the ephemerality, fragmentation, and patent chaos of modern life. This gave a new role, and a new impetus, to cultural modernism.

Artists, writers, architects, composers, poets, thinkers, and philosophers had a very special position within this new conception of the modernist project. If the 'eternal and immutable' could no longer be automatically presupposed, then the modern artist had a creative role to play in defining the essence of humanity. If 'creative destruction' was an essential condition of modernity, then perhaps the artist as individual had a heroic role to play (even if the consequences might be tragic). The artist, argued Frank Lloyd Wright – one of the greatest of all modernist architects – must not only comprehend the spirit of his age but also initiate the process of changing it.

We here encounter one of the more intriguing, but to many deeply troubling, aspects to modernism's history. For when Rousseau replaced Descartes's famous maxim 'I think therefore I exist,' with 'I feel therefore I exist,' he signalled a radical shift from a rational and instrumentalist to a more consciously aesthetic strategy for realizing Enlightenment aims. At about the same time, Kant, too, recognized that aesthetic judgement had to be construed as distinct from practical reason (moral judgement) and understanding (scientific knowledge), and that it formed a necessary though problematic bridge between the two. The exploration of aesthetics as a separate realm of cognition was very much an eighteenth-century affair. It arose in part out of the need to come to terms with the immense variety of cultural artefacts, produced under very different social conditions, which increasing trade and cultural contact revealed. Did Ming vases, Grecian urns, and Dresden china all express some common sentiment of beauty? But it also arose out of the sheer difficulty of translating Enlightenment principles of rational and scientific understanding into moral and political principles appropriate for action. It was into this gap that Nietzsche was later to insert his powerful message with such devastating effect, that art and aesthetic sentiments had the power to go beyond good or evil. The pursuit of aesthetic experience as an end in itself became, of course, the hallmark of the romantic movement (as exemplified by, say, Shelley and Byron). It generated that wave of 'radical subjectivism,' of 'untrammelled individualism,' and of 'search for individual self-realization' which, in Daniel Bell's (1978) view, has long put modernist cultural behaviour and artistic practices fundamentally at odds with the protestant ethic. Hedonism fits ill, according to Bell, with the saving and investment which supposedly nourish capitalism. Whatever view we take of Bell's thesis, it is surely true that the romantics paved the way for active aesthetic interventions in cultural and political life. Such interventions were anticipated by writers such as Condorcet and Saint-Simon. The latter insisted, for example, that,

> It is we, artists, who will serve you as avant-garde. What a most
> beautiful destiny for the arts, that of exercising over society a

positive power, a true priestly function, and of marching forcefully in the van of all the intellectual faculties in the epoch of
their greatest development! (quoted in Bell, 1978, 35; cf. Poggioli,
1968, 9)

The problem with such sentiments is that they see the aesthetic
link between science and morality, between knowledge and action, in
such a way as 'never to be threatened by historical evolution' (Raphael,
1981, 7). Aesthetic judgement, as in the cases of Heidegger and
Pound, could just as easily lead to the right as to the left of the
political spectrum. As Baudelaire was very quick to see, if flux and
change, ephemerality and fragmentation, formed the material basis of
modern life, then the definition of a modernist aesthetic depended
crucially upon the artist's positioning with respect to such processes.
The individual artist could contest them, embrace them, try to
dominate them, or simply swim within them, but the artist could
never ignore them. The effect of any one of these positionings was,
of course, to alter the way cultural producers thought about the flux
and change as well as the political terms in which they represented
the eternal and immutable. The twists and turns of modernism as a
cultural aesthetic can largely be understood against the background
of such strategic choices.

I cannot here rehearse the vast and convoluted history of cultural
modernism since its inception in Paris after 1848. But some very
general points need to be made if we are to understand the postmodernist reaction. If we go back to Baudelaire's formulation, for
example, we find him defining the artist as someone who can concentrate his or her vision on ordinary subjects of city life, understand
their fleeting qualities, and yet extract from the passing moment all
the suggestions of eternity it contains. The successful modern artist
was one who could find the universal and the eternal, 'distil the
bitter or heady flavour of the wine of life' from 'the ephemeral, the
fleeting forms of beauty in our day' (Baudelaire, 1981, 435). To the
degree that modernist art managed to do that it became our art,
precisely because 'it is the one art that responds to the scenario of
our chaos' (Bradbury and McFarlane, 1976, 27).

But how to *represent* the eternal and the immutable in the midst of
all the chaos? To the degree that naturalism and realism proved
inadequate (see below p. 262), the artist, architect, and writer had to
find some special way to represent it. Modernism from its very
beginning, therefore, became preoccupied with language, with finding
some special mode of representation of eternal truths. Individual
achievement depended upon innovation in language and in modes of

representation, with the result that the modernist work, as Lunn (1985, 41) observes, 'often wilfully reveals its own reality as a construction or an artifice,' thereby transforming much of art into a 'self-referential construct rather than a mirror of society.' Writers like James Joyce and Proust, poets like Mallarmé and Aragon, painters like Manet, Pissarro, Jackson Pollock, all showed a tremendous preoccupation with the creation of new codes, significations, and metaphorical allusions in the languages they constructed. But if the word was indeed fleeting, ephemeral, and chaotic, then the artist had, for that very reason, to represent the eternal through an instantaneous effect, making 'shock tactics and the violation of expected continuities' vital to the hammering home of the message that the artist sought to convey.

Modernism could speak to the eternal only by freezing time and all its fleeting qualities. For the architect, charged to design and build a relatively permanent spatial structure, this was a simple enough proposition. Architecture, wrote Mies van der Rohe in the 1920s, 'is the will of the age conceived in spatial terms.' But for others the 'spatialization of time' through the image, the dramatic gesture, and instantaneous shock, or simply by montage/collage was more problematic. T. S. Eliot ruminated on the problem in *Four Quartets* this way:

> To be conscious is not to be in time
> But only in time can the moment in the rose-garden,
> The moment in the arbour where the rain beat,
> Be remembered; involved with past and future.
> Only through time time is conquered.

Resort to the techniques of montage/collage provided one means of addressing this problem, since different effects out of different times (old newspapers) and spaces (the use of common objects) could be superimposed to create a simultaneous effect. By exploring simultaneity in this way, 'modernists were accepting the ephemeral and transitory as the locus of their art' at the same time as they were forced collectively to reaffirm the potency of the very conditions against which they were reacting. Le Corbusier recognized the problem in his 1924 tract *The city of tomorrow*. 'People tax me very readily with being a revolutionary,' he complained, but the 'equilibrium they try so hard to maintain is for vital reasons purely ephemeral: it is a balance which has to be perpetually re-established.' Furthermore, the sheer inventiveness of all those 'eager minds likely to disturb' that equilibrium produced the ephemeral and fleeting qualities of aesthetic judgement itself, accelerated changes in aesthetic fashions rather than slowed them down: impressionism, post-impressionism, cubism, fauvism, Dada, surrealism, expressionism, etc. 'The avant-garde,' comments Poggioli in his most lucid study of its history, 'is condemned to conquer, through the influence of fashion, that very popularity it once disdained – and this is the beginning of its end.'

Furthermore, the commodification and commercialization of a market for cultural products during the nineteenth century (and the concomitant decline of aristocratic, state, or institutional patronage) forced cultural producers into a market form of competition that was bound to reinforce processes of 'creative destruction' within the aesthetic field itself. This mirrored and in some instances surged ahead of anything going on in the political–economic sphere. Each and every artist sought to change the bases of aesthetic judgement, if only to sell his or her product. It also depended on the formation of a distinctive class of 'cultural consumers.' Artists, for all their predilection for anti-establishment and anti-bourgeois rhetoric, spent much more energy struggling with each other and against their own traditions in order to sell their products than they did engaging in real political action.

The struggle to produce a *work of art,* a once and for all creation that could find a unique place in the market, had to be an individual effort forged under competitive circumstances. Modernist art has always been, therefore, what Benjamin calls 'auratic art,' in the sense that the artist had to assume an aura of creativity, of dedication to art for art's sake, in order to produce a cultural object that would be original, unique, and hence eminently marketable at a monopoly price. The result was often a highly individualistic, aristocratic, disdainful (particularly of popular culture), and even arrogant perspective on the part of cultural producers, but it also indicated how our reality might be constructed and re-constructed through aesthetically informed activity. It could be, at best, profoundly moving, challenging, upsetting, or exhortatory to many who were exposed to it. Recognizing this feature, certain avant-gardes – Dadaists, early surrealists – tried to mobilize their aesthetic capacities to revolutionary ends by fusing their art into popular culture. Others, like Walter Gropius and Le Corbusier, sought to impose it from above for similar revolutionary purposes. And it was not only Gropius who thought it important to 'bring art back to the people through the production of beautiful things.' Modernism internalized its own maelstrom of ambiguities, contradictions, and pulsating aesthetic changes at the same time as it sought to affect the aesthetics of daily life.

The facts of that daily life had, however, more than a passing influence upon the aesthetic sensibility created, no matter how much the artists themselves proclaimed an aura of 'art for art's sake.' To begin with, as Benjamin (1969) points out in his celebrated essay on 'The work of art in the age of mechanical reproduction,' the changing technical capacity to reproduce, disseminate, and sell books and images to mass audiences, coupled with the invention of first photography and then film (to which we would now add radio and television), radically changed the material conditions of the artists' existence and, hence, their social and political role. And apart from the general consciousness of flux and change which flowed through all modernist works, a fascination with technique, with speed and motion, with the machine and the factory system, as well as with the stream of new commodities entering into daily life, provoked a wide range of aesthetic responses varying from denial, through imitation to speculation on utopian possibilities. Thus, as Reyner Banham (1984) shows, early modernist architects like Mies van der Rohe drew a lot of their inspiration from the purely functional grain elevators then springing up all over the American Midwest. Le Corbusier in his plans and writings took what he saw as the possibilities inherent in the machine, factory, and automobile age and projected them into some utopian future (Fishman, 1982). Tichi (1987, 19) documents how popular American journals like *Good Housekeeping* were depicting the house as 'nothing more than a factory for the production of happiness' as early as 1910, years before Le Corbusier ventured his celebrated (and now much reviled) dictum that the house is a 'machine for modern living.'

It is important to keep in mind, therefore, that the modernism that emerged before the First World War was more of a reaction to the new conditions of production (the machine, the factory, urbanization), circulation (the new systems of transport and communications), and consumption (the rise of mass markets, advertising, mass fashion) than it was a pioneer in the production of such changes. Yet the form the reaction took was to be of considerable subsequent importance. Not only did it provide ways to absorb, reflect upon, and codify these rapid changes, but it also suggested lines of action that might modify or support them. William Morris, for example, reacting against the de-skilling of craft workers through machine and factory production under the command of capitalists, sought to promote a new artisan culture which combined the power of craft tradition with a powerful plea 'for simplicity of design, a cleaning out of all sham, waste and self-indulgence' (Relph, 1987, 99–107). As Relph goes on to point out, the Bauhaus, the highly influential

German design unit founded in 1919, initially took much of its inspiration from the Arts and Crafts Movement that Morris had founded, and only subsequently (1923) turned to the idea that 'the machine is our modern medium of design.' The Bauhaus was able to exercise the influence it did over production and design precisely through its redefinition of 'craft' as the skill to mass-produce goods of an aesthetically pleasing nature with machine efficiency.

These were the sorts of diverse reactions that made of modernism such a complex and often contradictory affair. It was, write Bradbury and McFarlane (1976, 46),

> an extraordinary compound of the futurist and the nihilistic, the revolutionary and the conservative, the naturalistic and the symbolistic, the romantic and the classical. It was the celebration of a technological age and a condemnation of it; an excited acceptance of the belief that the old regimes of culture were over, and a deep despairing in the face of that fear; a mixture of convictions that the new forms were escapes from historicism and the pressures of the time with convictions that they were precisely the living expression of these things.

Such diverse elements and oppositions were composed into quite different brews of modernist sentiment and sensibility in different places and times:

> One can draw maps showing artistic centres and provinces, the international balance of cultural power — never quite the same as, though doubtlessly intricately related to, the balance of political and economic power. The maps change as the aesthetics change: Paris is surely, for Modernism, the outright dominant centre, as the fount of bohemia, tolerance and the *émigré* life-style, but we can sense the decline of Rome and Florence, the rise and then fall of London, the phase of dominance of Berlin and Munich, the energetic bursts from Norway and Finland, the radiation out of Vienna, as being essential stages in the shifting geography of Modernism, charted by the movement of writers and artists, the flow of thought waves, the explosions of significant artistic production.' (Bradbury and McFarlane, 1976, 102)

This complex historical geography of modernism (a tale yet to be fully written and explained) makes it doubly difficult to interpret exactly what modernism was about. The tensions between internationalism and nationalism, between globalism and parochialist ethnocentrism, between universalism and class privileges, were never far from the surface. Modernism at its best tried to confront the tensions, but at its worst either swept them under the rug or exploited them (as did the United States in its appropriation of modernist art after 1945) for cynical, political advantage (Guilbaut, 1983). Modernism look quite different depending on where one locates oneself and when. For while the movement as a whole had a definite internationalist and universalist stance, often deliberately sought for and conceived, it also clung fiercely to the idea of 'an elite international avant-garde art held in a fructifying relationship with a strong-felt sense of place' (ibid., p. 157). The particularities of place — and I here think not only of the village-like communities in which artists typically moved but also of the quite different social, economic, political, and environmental conditions that prevailed in, say, Chicago, New York, Paris, Vienna, Copenhagen, or Berlin — therefore put a distinctive stamp on the diversity of the modernist effort (see Part III, below).

It also seems that modernism, after 1848, was very much an urban phenomenon, that it existed in a restless but intricate relationship with the experience of explosive urban growth (several cities surging above the million mark by the end of the century), strong rural—to—urban migration, industrialization, mechanization, massive re-orderings of built environments, and politically based urban movements, of which the revolutionary uprisings in Paris in 1848 and 1871 were a clear but ominous symbol. The pressing need to confront the psychological, sociological, technical, organizational, and political problems of massive urbanization was one of the seed-beds in which modernist movements flourished. Modernism was 'an art of cities' and evidently found 'its natural habitat in cities,' and Bradbury and McFarlane pull together a variety of studies of individual cities to support the point. Other studies, such as T. J. Clark's magnificent work on the art of Manet and his followers in Second Empire Paris, or Schorske's equally brilliant synthesis of cultural movements in *fin de siècle* Vienna, confirm how important the urban experience was in shaping the cultural dynamics of diverse modernist movements. And it was, after all, in response to the profound crisis of urban organization, impoverishment, and congestion that a whole wing of modernist practice and thinking was directly shaped (see Timms and Kelley, 1985). There is a strong connecting thread from Haussmann's re-shaping of Paris in the 1860s through the 'garden city' proposals of Ebenezer Howard (1898), Daniel Burnham (the 'White City' constructed for the Chicago World's Fair of 1893 and the Chicago Regional Plan of 1907), Garnier (the linear industrial city of 1903), Camillo Sitte and Otto Wagner (with quite different plans to transform *fin de siècle* Vienna), Le Corbusier (*The city of tomorrow* and the *Plan Voisin* proposal for Paris of 1924), Frank Lloyd Wright (the Broadacre project of 1935) to the large-scale urban renewal efforts undertaken in the 1950s and 1960s in the spirit of high modernism. The city, remarks de Certeau (1984, 95) 'is simultaneously the machinery and the hero of modernity.'

Georg Simmel put a rather special gloss on the connection in his extraordinary essay 'The metropolis and mental life,' published in 1911. Simmel there contemplated how we might respond to and internalize, psychologically and intellectually, the incredible diversity of experiences and stimuli to which modern urban life exposed us. We were, on the one hand, liberated from the chains of subjective dependence and thereby allowed a much greater degree of individual liberty. But this was achieved at the expense of treating others in objective and instrumental terms. We had no choice except to relate to faceless 'others' via the cold and heartless calculus of the necessary money exchanges which could co-ordinate a proliferating social division of labour. We also submit to a rigorous disciplining in our sense of space and time, and surrender ourselves to the hegemony of calculating economic rationality. Rapid urbanization, furthermore, produced what he called a 'blasé attitude,' for it was only by screening out the complex stimuli that stemmed from the rush of modern life that we could tolerate its extremes. Our only outlet, he seems to say, is to cultivate a sham individualism through pursuit of signs of status, fashion, or marks of individual eccentricity. Fashion, for example, combines 'the attraction of differentiation and change with that of similarity and conformity'; the 'more nervous an epoch is, the more rapidly. will its fashions change, because the need for the attraction of differentiation, one of the essential agents of fashion, goes hand in hand with the languishing of nervous energies' (quoted in Frisby, 1985, 98).

My purpose here is not to judge Simmel's vision (though the parallels and contrasts with Raban's more recent postmodernist essay are most instructive) but to see it as one representation of a connection between the urban experience and modernist thought and practice. The qualities of modernism seem to have varied, albeit in an interactive way, across the spectrum of the large polyglot cities that emerged in the second half of the nineteenth century. Indeed, certain kinds of modernism achieved a particular trajectory through the capitals of the world, each flourishing as a cultural arena of a particular sort. The geographical trajectory from Paris to Berlin, Vienna, London, Moscow, Chicago, and New York could be reversed as well as short-cut depending upon which sort of modernist practice one has in mind.

If, for example, we were to look solely at the diffusion of those material practices from which intellectual and aesthetic modernism drew so much of its stimulus — the machines, the new transport and communication systems, skyscrapers, bridges, and engineering wonders of all kinds, as well as the incredible instability and insecurity that accompanied rapid innovation and social change — then the United States (and Chicago in particular) should probably be regarded as the catalyst of modernism after 1870 or so. Yet, in this case, the very lack of 'traditionalist' (feudal and aristocratic) resistance, and the parallel popular acceptance of broadly modernist sentiments (of the sort that Tichi documents), made the works of artists and intellectuals rather less important as the avant-garde cutting edge of social change. Edward Bellamy's populist novel of a modernist utopia, *Looking backwards*, gained rapid acceptance and even spawned a political movement in the 1890s. Edgar Allan Poe's work, on the other hand, achieved very little initial honour in its own land even if he was regarded as one of the great modernist writers by Baudelaire (whose Poe translations, to this day very popular, were illustrated by Manet as early as the 1860s). Louis Sullivan's architectural genius likewise remained largely buried in the extraordinary ferment of Chicago's modernization. Daniel Burnham's highly modernist conception of rational urban planning tended to get lost in his penchant for ornamentation of buildings and classicism of individual building design. The fierce class and traditional resistances to capitalist modernization in Europe, on the other hand, made the intellectual and aesthetic movements of modernism much more important as a cutting edge of social change, giving to the avantgarde a political and social role broadly denied them in the United States until after 1945. Hardly suprisingly, the history of intellectual and aesthetic modernism is much more Euro-centered, with some of the less progressive or class-divided urban centres (such as Paris and Vienna) generating some of the greatest ferments.

It is invidious, but nevertheless useful, to impose upon this complex history some relatively simple periodizations, if only to help understand what kind of modernism the postmodernists are reacting against. The Enlightenment project, for example, took it as axiomatic that there was only one possible answer to any question. From this it followed that the world could be controlled and rationally ordered if we could only picture and represent it rightly. But this presumed that there existed a single correct mode of representation which, if we could uncover it (and this was what scientific and mathematical endeavours were all about), would provide the means to Enlightenment ends. This was a way of thinking that writers as diverse as Voltaire, d'Alembert, Diderot, Condorcet, Hume, Adam Smith,

Saint-Simon, Auguste Comte, Matthew Arnold, Jeremy Bentham, and John Stuart Mill all had in common.

But after 1848 the idea that there was only one possible mode of representation began to break down. The categorical fixity of Enlightenment thought was increasingly challenged, and ultimately replaced by an emphasis upon divergent systems of representation. In Paris, writers like Baudelaire and Flaubert and painters like Manet began to explore the possibility of different representational modes in ways that resembled the discovery of the non-Euclidean geometries which shattered the supposed unity of mathematical language in the nineteenth century. Tentative at first, the idea exploded from 1890 onwards into an incredible diversity of thought and experimentation in centres as different as Berlin, Vienna, Paris, Munich, London, New York, Chicago, Copenhagen, and Moscow, to reach its apogee shortly before the First World War. Most commentators agree that this furore of experimentation resulted in a qualitative transformation in what modernism was about somewhere between 1910 and 1915. (Virginia Woolf preferred the earlier date and D. H. Lawrence the later.) In retrospect, as Bradbury and McFarlane document convincingly, it is not hard to see that some kind of radical transformation did indeed occur in these years. Proust's *Swann's way* (1913), Joyce's *Dubliners* (1914), Lawrence's *Sons and lovers* (1913), Mann's *Death in Venice* (1914), Pound's 'Vorticist manifesto' of 1914 (in which he likened pure language to efficient machine technology) are some of the marker texts published at a time that also witnessed an extraordinary efflorescence in art (Matisse, Picasso, Brancusi, Duchamp, Braque, Klee, de Chirico, Kandinsky, many of whose works turned up in the famous Armory Show in New York in 1913, to be seen by more than 10,000 visitors a day), music (Stravinsky's *The rite of spring* opened to a riot in 1913 and was paralleled by the arrival of the atonal music of Schoenberg, Berg, Bartok, and others), to say nothing of the dramatic shift in linguistics (Saussure's structuralist theory of language, in which the meaning of words is given by their relation to other words rather than by their reference to objects, was conceived in 1911) and in physics, consequent upon Einstein's generalization of the theory of relativity with its appeal to, and material justification of, non-Euclidean geometries. Equally significant, as we shall later see, was the publication of F. W. Taylor's *The principles of scientific management* in 1911, two years before Henry Ford set in motion the first example of assembly-line production in Dearborn, Michigan.

It is hard not to conclude that the whole world of representation and of knowledge underwent a fundamental transformation during this short space of time. How and why it did so is the quintessential question. In Part III we shall explore the thesis that the simultaneity derived from a radical change in the experience of space and time in Western capitalism. But there are some other elements in the situation which deserve note.

The changes were certainly affected by the loss of faith in the ineluctability of progress, and by the growing unease with the categorical fixity of Enlightenment thought. The unease in part derived from the turbulent path of class struggle, particularly after the revolutions of 1848 and the publication of *The communist manifesto*. Before then, thinkers in the Enlightenment tradition, such as Adam Smith or Saint-Simon, could reasonably argue that once the shackles of feudal class relations had been thrown off, a benevolent capitalism (organized either through the hidden hand of the market or through the power of association made much of by Saint-Simon) could bring the benefits of capitalist modernity to all. This was a thesis vigorously rejected by Marx and Engels, and it became less tenable as the century wore on and the class disparities produced within capitalism became more and more evident. The socialist movement increasingly challenged the unity of Enlightenment reason and inserted a class dimension into modernism. Was it the bourgeoisie or the workers' movement which was to inform and direct the modernist project? And whose side were the cultural producers on?

There could be no simple answer to that question. To begin with, propagandistic and directly political art that integrated with a revolutionary political movement was hard to make consistent with the modernist canon for individualistic and intensely 'auratic' art. To be sure, the idea of an artistic avant-garde could, under certain circumstances, be integrated with that of a political avant-garde party. From time to time communist parties have striven to mobilize 'the forces of culture' as part of their revolutionary programme, while some of the avant-garde artistic movements and artists (Léger, Picasso, Aragon, etc.) actively supported the communist cause. Even in the absence of any explicit political agenda, however, cultural production had to have political effects. Artists, after all, relate to events and issues around them, and construct ways of seeing and representing which have social meanings. In the halcyon days of modernist innovation before World War I, for example, the kind of art produced celebrated universals even in the midst of multiple perspectives. It was expressive of alienation, antagonistic to all sense of hierarchy (even of the subject, as cubism showed), and frequently critical of 'bourgeois' consumerism and life-styles. Modernism was during that phase very much on the side of a democratizing spirit and progressive universalism, even when at its most 'auratic' in conception. Between the wars, on the other hand, artists were more and more forced by events to wear their political commitments on their sleeves.

The shift in modernism's tone also stemmed from the need to confront head-on the sense of anarchy, disorder, and despair that Nietzsche had sown at a time of astonishing agitation, restlessness, and instability in political–economic life – an instability which the anarchist movement of the late nineteenth century grappled with and contributed to in important ways. The articulation of erotic, psychological, and irrational needs (of the sort that Freud identified and Klimt represented in his free-flowing art) added another dimension to the confusion. This particular surge of modernism, therefore, had to recognize the impossibility of representing the world in a single language. Understanding had to be constructed through the exploration of multiple perspectives. Modernism, in short, took on multiple perspectivism and relativism as its epistemology for revealing what it still took to be the true nature of a unified, though complex, underlying reality.

Whatever may have constituted this singular underlying reality and its 'eternal presence' remained obscure. From this standpoint Lenin, for one, inveighed against the errors of relativism and multiple perspectivism in his criticisms of Mach's 'idealist' physics, and tried to emphasize the political as well as the intellectual dangers to which formless relativism surely pointed. There is a sense in which the outbreak of the First World War, that vast inter-imperialist struggle, vindicated Lenin's argument. Certainly, a strong case can be made that 'modernist subjectivity ... was simply unable to cope with the crisis into which Europe in 1914 was plunged' (Taylor, 1987, 127).

The trauma of world war and its political and intellectual responses (some of which we shall take up more directly in Part III) opened the way to a consideration of what might constitute the essential and eternal qualities of modernity that lay on the nether side of Baudelaire's formulation. In the absence of Enlightenment certitudes as to the perfectibility of man, the search for a myth appropriate to modernity became paramount. The surrealist writer Louis Aragon, for example, suggested that his central aim in *Paris peasant* (written in the 1920s) was to elaborate a novel 'that would present itself as mythology,' adding, 'naturally, a mythology of the modern.' But it also seemed possible to build metaphorical bridges between ancient and modern myths. Joyce chose Ulysses, while Le Corbusier, according to Frampton (1980), always sought 'to resolve the dichotomy between the Engineer's Aesthetic and Architecture, to inform utility with the hierarchy of myth' (a practice he increasingly emphasized in his creations at Chandigarh and Ronchamp in the 1960s). But who or what was it that was being mythologized? This was the central question that characterized the so-called 'heroic' period of modernism.

Modernism in the inter-war years may have been 'heroic' but it was also fraught with disaster. Action was plainly needed to rebuild the war-torn economies of Europe as well as to solve all the problems of the political discontents associated with capitalist forms of burgeoning urban—industrial growth. The fading of unified Enlightenment beliefs and the emergence of perspectivism left open the possibility of informing social action with some aesthetic vision, so that the struggles between the different currents of modernism became of more than just passing interest. What is more, the cultural producers knew it. Aesthetic modernism was important, and the stakes were high. The appeal to 'eternal' myth became even more imperative. But that search turned out to be as confused as it was dangerous. 'Reason coming to terms with its mythical origins, becomes bewilderingly tangled with myth ... myth is already enlightenment and enlightenment relapses into mythology' (Huyssens, 1984).

The myth either had to redeem us from 'the formless universe of contingency' or, more programmatically, to provide the impetus for a new project for human endeavour. One wing of modernism appealed to the image of rationality incorporated in the machine, the factory, the power of contemporary technology, or the city as a 'living machine.' Ezra Pound had already advanced the thesis that language should conform to machine efficiency and, as Tichi (1987) has observed, modernist writers as diverse as Dos Passos, Hemingway, and William Carlos Williams modelled their writing on exactly that proposition. Williams specifically held, for example, that a poem is nothing more or less than ' a machine made of words.' And this was the theme that Diego Rivera celebrated so vigorously in his extraordinary Detroit murals and which became the leitmotif of many progressive mural painters in the United States during the depression (plate 1.5).

'Truth is the significance of fact,' said Mies van der Rohe, and a host of cultural producers, particularly those working in and around the influential Bauhaus movement of the 1920s, set out to impose rational order ('rational' defined by technological efficiency and machine production) for socially useful goals (human emancipation, emancipation of the proletariat, and the like). 'By order bring about freedom,' was one of Le Corbusier's slogans, and he emphasized that freedom and liberty in the contemporary metropolis depended crucially upon the imposition of rational order. Modernism in the inter-

Plate 1.5 The myth of the machine dominated modernist as well as realist art in the inter-war years: Thomas Hart Benton's 1929 mural 'Instruments of Power' is a typical exemplar.

war period took a strongly positivist turn and, through the intensive efforts of the Vienna Circle, established a new style of philosophy which was to become central to social thought after World War II. Logical positivism was as compatible with the practices of modernist architecture as it was with the advance of all forms of science as avatars of technical control. This was the period when houses and cities could be openly conceived of as 'machines for living in'. It was during these years also that the powerful Congress of International Modern Architects (CIAM) came together to adopt its celebrated Athens Charter of 1933, a charter that for the next thirty years or so was to define broadly what modernist architectural practice was to be about.

Such a limited vision of the essential qualities of modernism was open to easy enough perversion and abuse. There are strong objections even within modernism (think of Chaplin's *Modern Times*) to the idea that the machine, the factory, and the rationalized city provide a sufficiently rich conception to define the eternal qualities of modern life. The problem for 'heroic' modernism was, quite simply, that once the machine myth was abandoned, any myth could be lodged into that central position of the 'eternal truth' presupposed in the modernist project. Baudelaire himself, for example, had dedicated his essay 'The *Salon* of 1846' to the bourgeois who sought to 'realize the idea of the future in all its diverse forms, political, industrial, and artistic.' An economist like Schumpeter would surely have applauded that.

The Italian futurists were so fascinated by speed and power that they embraced creative destruction and violent militarism to the point where Mussolini could become their hero. De Chirico lost interest in modernist experimentation after World War I and sought a commercialized art with roots in classical beauty mingled with powerful horses and narcissistic pictures of himself dressed up in historic costumes (all of which were to earn him the approval of Mussolini). Pound too, with his thirst for machine efficiency of language and his admiration of the avant-gardist warrior poet capable of dominating a 'witless multitude,' became deeply attached to a political regime (Mussolini's) that could ensure that the trains ran on time. Albert Speer, Hitler's architect, may have actively attacked modernism's aesthetic principles in his resurrection of classicist themes, but he was to take over many modernist techniques and put them to nationalist ends with the same ruthlessness that Hitler's engineers showed in taking over the practices of Bauhaus design in their construction of the death camps (see, for example, Lane's, 1985, illuminating study, *Architecture and politics in Germany, 1918–1945*). It proved possible to combine up-to-date scientific engineering practices, as incorporated in the most extreme forms of technical—bureaucratic and machine rationality, with a myth of Aryan superiority and the blood and soil of the Fatherland. It was exactly in this way that a virulent form of 'reactionary modernism' came to have the purchase it did in Nazi Germany, suggesting that this whole episode, while modernist in certain senses, owed more to the weakness of Enlightenment thought than it did to any dialectal reversal or progression to a 'natural' conclusion (Herf, 1984, 233).

This was a period when the always latent tensions between internationalism and nationalism, between universalism and class politics, were heightened into absolute and unstable contradiction. It was hard to remain indifferent to the Russian revolution, the rising power of socialist and communist movements, the collapse of economies and governments, and the rise of fascism. Politically committed art took over one wing of the modernist movement. Surrealism, constructivism, and socialist realism all sought to mythologize the proletariat in their respective ways, and the Russians set about inscribing that in space, as did a whole succession of socialist governments in Europe, through the creation of buildings like the celebrated Karl Marx-Hof in Vienna (designed not only to house workers but also to be a bastion of military defence against any rural conservative assault mounted against a socialist city). But the configurations were unstable. No sooner had doctrines of socialist realism been enunciated as a rejoinder to 'decadent' bourgeois modernism and fascist nationalism, than popular front politics on the part of many communist parties led to a swing back to nationalist art and culture as a means to unite proletarian with wavering middle-class forces in the united front against fascism.

Many artists of the avant-garde tried to resist such direct social referencing and cast their net far and wide for more universal mythological statements. T. S. Eliot created a virtual melting pot of imagery and languages drawn from every corner of the earth in *The Waste Land*, and Picasso (amongst others) plundered the world of primitive (particularly African) art during some of his more creative phases. During the inter-war years there was something desperate about the search for a mythology that could somehow straighten society out in such troubled times. Raphael (1981, xii) captures the dilemmas in his trenchant but sympathetic critique of Picasso's *Guernica:*

> The reasons for which Picasso was compelled to resort to signs and allegories should now be clear enough: his utter political helplessness in the face of a historical situation which he set out to record; his titanic effort to confront a particular historical event with an allegedly eternal truth; his desire to give hope and comfort and to provide a happy ending, to compensate for the terror, the destruction, and inhumanity of the event. Picasso did not see what Goya had already seen, namely, that the course of history can be changed only by historical means and only if men shape their own history instead of acting as the automaton of an earthly power or an allegedly eternal idea.

Unfortunately, as Georges Sorel (1974) suggested in his brilliant *Reflections on violence*, first published in 1908, it was possible to invent myths that might have a consuming power over class politics. Syndicalism of the sort that Sorel promoted originated as a participatory movement of the left, deeply antagonistic to all forms of state power, but evolved into a corporatist movement (attractive to someone like Le Corbusier in the 1930s) that became a powerful organizing tool of the fascist right. In so doing it was able to appeal to certain myths of a hierarchically ordered but nevertheless participatory and exclusive community, with clear identity and close social bonding, replete with its own myths of origin and omnipotence. It is instructive to note how heavily fascism drew upon classical

references (architecturally, politically, historically) and built mythological conceptions accordingly. Raphael (1981, 95) suggests an
interesting reason: the Greeks 'were always conscious of the national
character of their mythology, whereas the Christians always ascribed
to theirs a value independent of space and time.' The German philosopher Heidegger likewise in part based his allegiance to the
principles (if not the practices) of Nazism on his rejection of a
universalizing machine rationality as an appropriate mythology for
modern life. He proposed, instead, a counter-myth of rootedness in
place and environmentally-bound traditions as the only secure foundation for political and social action in a manifestly troubled world
(see Part III). The aestheticization of politics through the production
of such all-consuming myths (of which Nazism was but one) was the
tragic side of the modernist project that became more and more
salient as the 'heroic' era came crashing to an end in World War II.

If the modernism of the inter-war years was 'heroic' but fraught
with disaster, the 'universal' or 'high' modernism that became hegemonic after 1945 exhibited a much more comfortable relation to the
dominant power centres in society. The contested search for an
appropriate myth appeared to abate in part, I suspect, because the
international power system – organized, as we shall see in Part II,
along Fordist–Keynesian lines under the watchful eye of US hegemony – itself became relatively stable. High modernist art, architecture, literature, etc. became establishment arts and practices in a
society where a corporate capitalist version of the Enlightenment
project of development for progress and human emancipation held
sway as a political–economic dominant.

The belief 'in linear progress, absolute truths, and rational planning
of ideal social orders' under standardized conditions of knowledge
and production was particularly strong. The modernism that resulted
was, as a result, 'positivistic, technocentric, and rationalistic' at the
same time as it was imposed as the work of an elite avant-garde of
planners, artists, architects, critics, and other guardians of high taste.
The 'modernization' of European economies proceeded apace, while
the whole thrust of international politics and trade was justified as
bringing a benevolent and progressive 'modernization process' to a
backward Third World.

In architecture, for example, the ideas of the CIAM, of Le
Corbusier, and of Mies van der Rohe, held sway in the struggle to
revitalize war-torn or ageing cities (reconstruction and urban renewal), to reorganize transport systems, build factories, hospitals,
schools, state works of all kinds, and last, but not least, to build
adequate housing for a potentially restless working class. It is easy in

retrospect to argue that the architecture that resulted merely produced impeccable images of power and prestige for publicity-conscious corporations and governments, while producing modernist housing projects for the working class that became 'symbols of alienation and dehumanization' on the other (Huyssens, 1984, 14; Frampton, 1980). But it is also arguable that some kind of large-scale planning and industrialization of the construction industry, coupled with the exploration of techniques for high-speed transportation and high-density development, were necessary if capitalistic solutions were to be found to the dilemmas of postwar development and political—economic stabilization. In many of these respects high modernism succeeded only too well.

Its real nether side lay, I would suggest, in its subterranean celebration of corporate bureaucratic power and rationality, under the guise of a return to surface worship of the efficient machine as a sufficient myth to embody all human aspirations. In architecture and planning, this meant the eschewing of ornament and personalized design (to the point where public housing tenants were not allowed to modify their environments to meet personal needs, and the students living in Le Corbusier's Pavillon Suisse had to fry every summer because the architect refused, for aesthetic reasons, to let blinds be installed). It also meant a prevailing passion for massive spaces and perspectives, for uniformity and the power of the straight line (always superior to the curve, pronounced Le Corbusier). Giedion's *Space, time and architecture,* first published in 1941, became the aesthetic bible of this movement. The great modernist literature of Joyce, Proust, Eliot, Pound, Lawrence, Faulkner — once judged as subversive, incomprehensible, or shocking — was taken over and canonized by the establishment (in universities and the major literary reviews).

Guilbaut's (1983) account of *How New York stole the idea of modern art* is instructive here, not least because of the multiple ironies that the story reveals. The traumas of World War II and the experience of Hiroshima and Nagasaki were, like the traumas of World War I, hard to absorb and represent in any realist way, and the turn to abstract expressionism on the part of painters like Rothko, Gottlieb, and Jackson Pollock consciously reflected that need. But their works became central for quite other reasons. To begin with, the fight against fascism was depicted as a fight to defend Western culture and civilization from barbarism. Explicitly rejected by fascism, international modernism became, in the United States, 'confounded with culture more broadly and abstractly defined.' The trouble was that international modernism had exhibited strong socialist, even propagandist, tendencies in the 1930s (through surrealism, construc-

tivism, and socialist realism). The de-politicization of modernism
that occurred with the rise of abstract expressionism ironically presaged its embrace by the political and cultural establishment as an
ideological weapon in the cold war struggle. The art was full enough
of alienation and anxiety, and expressive enough of violent fragmentation and creative destruction (all of which were surely appropriate
to the nuclear age) to be used as a marvellous exemplar of US commitment to liberty of expression, rugged individualism and creative
freedom. No matter that McCarthyite repression was dominant, the
challenging canvases of Jackson Pollock proved that the United
States was a bastion of liberal ideals in a world threatened by communist totalitarianism. Within this twist there existed another even
more devious turn. 'Now that America is recognized as the center
where art and artists of all the world must meet,' wrote Gottlieb and
Rothko in 1943, 'it is time for us to accept cultural values on a truly
global plane.' In so doing they sought a myth that was 'tragic and
timeless.' What that appeal to myth in practice allowed was a quick
passage from 'nationalism to internationalism and then from internationalism to universalism' (cited in Guilbout, 1983 p. 174). But in
order to be distinguishable from the modernism extant elsewhere
(chiefly Paris), a 'viable new aesthetic' had to be forged out of
distinctively American raw materials. What was distinctively American
had to be celebrated as the essence of Western culture. And so it was
with abstract expressionism, along with liberalism, Coca-Cola and
Chevrolets, and suburban houses full of consumer durables. Avant-
garde artists, concludes Guilbaut (p. 200), 'now politically "neutral"
individualists, articulated in their works values that were subsequently
assimilated, utilized, and co-opted by politicians, with the result that
artistic rebellion was transformed into aggressive liberal ideology.'

I think it very important, as Jameson (1984a) and Huyssens (1984)
insist, to recognize the significance of this absorption of a particular
kind of modernist aesthetic into official and establishment ideology,
and its use in relation to corporate power and cultural imperialism. It
meant that, for the first time in the history of modernism, artistic
and cultural, as well as 'progressive' political revolt had to be directed
at a powerful version of modernism itself. Modernism lost its appeal
as a revolutionary antidote to some reactionary and 'traditionalist'
ideology. Establishment art and high culture became such an exclusive
preserve of a dominant elite that experimentation within its frame
(with, for example, new forms of perspectivism) became increasingly
difficult, except in relatively new aesthetic fields such as film (where
modernist works like Orson Welles's *Citizen Kane* became classics).
Worse still, it seemed that establishment art and high culture could

do nothing more than monumentalize corporate and state power or the 'American dream' as self-referential myths, projecting a certain emptiness of sensibility on that side of Baudelaire's formulation that dwelt upon human aspirations and eternal truths.

It was in this context that the various counter-cultural and anti-modernist movements of the 1960s sprang to life. Antagonistic to the oppressive qualities of scientifically grounded technical−bureaucratic rationality as purveyed through monolithic corporate, state, and other forms of institutionalized power (including that of bureau-cratized political parties and trade unions), the counter-cultures explored the realms of individualized self-realization through a distinc-tive 'new left' politics, through the embrace of anti-authoritarian gestures, iconoclastic habits (in music, dress, language, and life-style), and the critique of everyday life. Centred in the universities, art institutes, and on the cultural fringes of big-city life, the move-ment spilled over into the streets to culminate in a vast wave of rebelliousness that crested in Chicago, Paris, Prague, Mexico City, Madrid, Tokyo, and Berlin in the global turbulence of 1968. It was almost as if the universal pretensions of modernity had, when com-bined with liberal capitalism and imperialism, succeeded so well as to provide a material and political foundation for a cosmopolitan, trans-national, and hence global movement of resistance to the hegemony of high modernist culture. Though a failure, at least judged in its own terms, the movement of 1968 has to be viewed, however, as the cultural and political harbinger of the subsequent turn to post-modernism. Somewhere between 1968 and 1972, therefore, we see postmodernism emerge as a full-blown though still incoherent move-ment out of the chrysalis of the anti-modern movement of the 1960s.

3

Postmodernism

Over the last two decades 'postmodernism' has become a concept to be wrestled with, and such a battleground of conflicting opinions and political forces that it can no longer be ignored. 'The culture of the advanced capitalist societist,' announce the editors of *PRECIS* 6 (1987), 'has undergone a profound shift in the *structure of feeling*.' Most, I think, would now agree with Huyssens's (1984) more cautious statement:

> What appears on one level as the latest fad, advertising pitch and hollow spectacle is part of a slowly emerging cultural transformation in Western societies, a change in sensibility for which the term 'post-modern' is actually, at least for now, wholly adequate. The nature and depth of that transformation are debatable, but transformation it is. I don't want to be misunderstood as claiming that there is a wholesale paradigm shift of the cultural, social, and economic orders; any such claim clearly would be overblown. But in an important sector of our culture there is a noticeable shift in sensibility, practices and discourse formations which distinguishes a post-modern set of assumptions, experiences and propositions from that of a preceding period.

With respect to architecture, for example, Charles Jencks dates the symbolic end of modernism and the passage to the postmodern as 3.32 p.m. on 15 July 1972, when the Pruitt–Igoe housing development in St Louis (a prize-winning version of Le Corbusier's 'machine for modern living') was dynamited as an uninhabitable environment for the low-income people it housed. Thereafter, the ideas of the CIAM, Le Corbusier, and the other apostles of 'high modernism' increasingly gave way before an onslaught of diverse possibilities, of which those set forth in the influential *Learning from Las Vegas* by Venturi, Scott Brown, and Izenour (also published in 1972) proved to be but one powerful cutting edge. The point of that work, as its title implies, was to insist that architects had more to learn from the study of popular and vernacular landscapes (such as those of suburbs and commercial strips) than from the pursuit of some abstract, theoretical, and doctrinaire ideals. It was time, they said, to build for people rather than for Man. The glass towers, concrete blocks, and steel slabs that seemed set fair to steamroller over every urban landscape from Paris to Tokyo and from Rio to Montreal, denouncing all ornament as crime, all individualism as sentimentality, all romanticism as kitsch, have progressively given way to ornamented tower blocks, imitation mediaeval squares and fishing villages, custom-designed or vernacular housing, renovated factories and warehouses, and rehabilitated landscapes of all kinds, all in the name of procuring some more 'satisfying' urban environment. So popular has this quest become that no less a figure than Prince Charles has weighed in with vigorous denunciations of the errors of postwar urban redevelopment and the developer destruction that has done more to wreck London, he claims, then the Luftwaffe's attacks in World War II.

In planning circles we can track a similar evolution. Douglas Lee's influential article 'Requiem for large-scale planning models' appeared in a 1973 issue of the *Journal of the American Institute of Planners* and correctly predicted the demise of what he saw as the futile efforts of the 1960s to develop large-scale, comprehensive, and integrated planning models (many of them specified with all the rigour that computerized mathematical modelling could then command) for metropolitan regions. Shortly thereafter, the *New York Times* (13 June 1976) described as 'mainstream' the radical planners (inspired by Jane Jacobs) who had mounted such a violent attack upon the soulless sins of modernist urban planning in the 1960s. It is nowadays the norm to seek out 'pluralistic' and 'organic' strategies for approaching urban development as a 'collage' of highly differentiated spaces and mixtures, rather than pursuing grandiose plans based on fuctional zoning of different activities. 'Collage city' is now the theme and 'urban revitalization' has replaced the vilified 'urban renewal' as the key buzz-word in the planners' lexicon. 'Make no little plans,' Daniel Burnham wrote in the first wave of modernist planning euphoria at the end of the nineteenth century, to which a postmodernist like Aldo Rossi can now more modestly reply: 'To what, then, could I have aspired in my craft? Certainly to small things, having seen that the possibility of great ones was historically precluded.'

Shifts of this sort can be documented across a whole range of diverse fields. The postmodern novel, McHale (1987) argues, is characterized by a shift from an 'epistemological' to an 'ontological' dominant. By this he means a shift from the kind of perspectivism that allowed the modernist to get a better bearing on the meaning of a complex but nevertheless singular reality, to the foregrounding of questions as to how radically different realities may coexist, collide, and interpenetrate. The boundary between fiction and science fiction has, as a consequence, effectively dissolved, while postmodernist characters often seem confused as to which world they are in, and how they should act with respect to it. Even to reduce the problem of perspective to autobiography, says one of Borges' characters, is to enter the labyrinth: 'Who was I? Today's self, bewildered, yesterday's, forgotten; tomorrow's, unpredictable?' The question marks tell it all.

In philosophy, the intermingling of a revived American pragmatism with the post-Marxist and poststructuralist wave that struck Paris after 1968 produced what Bernstein (1985, 25) calls 'a rage against humanism and the Enlightenment legacy.' This spilled over into a vigorous denunciation of abstract reason and a deep aversion to any project that sought universal human emancipation through mobilization of the powers of technology, science, and reason. Here, also, no less a person that Pope John Paul II has entered the fray on the side of the postmodern. The Pope 'does not attack Marxism or liberal secularism because they are the wave of the future,' says Rocco Buttiglione, a theologian close to the Pope, but because the 'philosophies of the twentieth century have lost their appeal, their time has already passed.' The moral crisis of our time is a crisis of Enlightenment thought. For while the latter may indeed have allowed man to emancipate himself 'from community and tradition of the Middle Ages in which his individual freedom was submerged,' the Enlightenment affirmation of 'self without God' in the end negated itself because reason, a means, was left, in the absence of God's truth, without any spiritual or moral goal. If lust and power are 'the only values that don't need the light of reason to be discovered,' then reason had to become a mere instrument to subjugate others (*Baltimore Sun*, 9 September 1987). The postmodern theological project is to reaffirm God's truth without abandoning the powers of reason.

With such illustrious (and centrist) figures as the Prince of Wales and Pope John Paul II resorting to postmodernist rhetoric and argumentation, there can be little doubt as to the breadth of change that has occurred in 'the structure of feeling' in the 1980s. Yet there is still abundant confusion as to what the new 'structure of feeling' might entail. Modernist sentiments may have been undermined, deconstructed, surpassed, or bypassed, but there is little certitude as to the coherence or meaning of the systems of thought that may have replaced them. Such uncertainty makes it peculiarly difficult to evaluate, interpret, and explain the shift that everyone agrees has occurred.

Does postmodernism, for example, represent a radical break with modernism, or is it simply a revolt within modernism against a certain form of 'high modernism' as represented, say, in the architecture of Mies van der Rohe and the blank surfaces of minimalist abstract expressionist painting? Is postmodernism a style (in which case we can reasonably trace its precursors back to Dada, Nietzsche, or even, as Kroker and Cook (1986) prefer, to St Augustine's *Confessions* in the fourth century) or should we view it strictly as a periodizing concept (in which case we debate whether it originated in the 1950s, 1960s, or 1970s)? Does it have a revolutionary potential by virtue of its opposition to all forms of meta-narratives (including Marxism, Freudianism, and all forms of Enlightenment reason) and its close attention to 'other worlds' and to 'other voices' that have for too long been silenced (women, gays, blacks, colonized peoples with their own histories)? Or is it simply the commercialization and domestication of modernism, and a reduction of the latter's already tarnished aspirations to a *laissez-faire*, 'anything goes' market eclecticism? Does it, therefore, undermine or integrate with neo-conservative politics? And do we attach its rise to some radical restructuring of capitalism, the emergence of some 'postindustrial' society, view it, even, as the 'art of an inflationary era' or as the 'cultural logic of late capitalism' (as Newman and Jameson have proposed)?

We can, I think, begin to get a grip on these difficult questions by casting an eye over the schematic differences between modernism and postmodernism as laid out by Hassan (1975, 1985; see table 1.1). Hassan sets up a series of stylistic oppositions in order to capture the ways in which postmodernism might be portrayed as a reaction to the modern. I say 'might' because I think it dangerous (as does Hassan) to depict complex relations as simple polarizations, when almost certainly the true state of sensibility, the real 'structure of feeling' in both the modern and postmodern periods, lies in the manner in which these stylistic oppositions are synthesized. Nevertheless, I think Hassan's tabular schema provides a useful starting point.

There is much to contemplate in this schema, drawing as it does on fields as diverse as linguistics, anthropology, philosophy, rhetoric, political science, and theology. Hassan is quick to point out how the dichotomies are themselves insecure, equivocal. Yet there is much

Table 1.1 Schematic differences between modernism and postmodernism

modernism	postmodernism
romanticism/Symbolism	paraphysics/Dadaism
form (conjunctive, closed)	antiform (disjunctive, open)
purpose	play
design	chance
hierarchy	anarchy
mastery/logos	exhaustion/silence
art object/finished work	process/performance/happening
distance	participation
creation/totalization/synthesis	decreation/deconstruction/antithesis
presence	absence
centring	dispersal
genre/boundary	text/intertext
semantics	rhetoric
paradigm	syntagm
hypotaxis	parataxis
metaphor	metonymy
selection	combination
root/depth	rhizome/surface
interpretation/reading	against interpretation/misreading
signified	signifier
lisible (readerly)	scriptible (writerly)
narrative/*grande histoire*	anti-narrative/*petite histoire*
master code	idiolect
symptom	desire
type	mutant
genital/phallic	polymorphous/androgynous
paranoia	schizophrenia
origin/cause	difference-difference/trace
God the Father	The Holy Ghost
metaphysics	irony
determinacy	indeterminacy
transcendence	immanence

Source: Hassan (1985, 123–4)

here that captures a sense of what the differences might be. 'Modernist' town planners, for example, do tend to look for 'mastery' of the metropolis as a 'totality' by deliberately designing a 'closed form,' whereas postmodernists tend to view the urban process as uncontrollable and 'chaotic,' one in which 'anarchy' and 'change' can 'play' in entirely 'open' situations. 'Modernist' literary critics do tend to look at works as examples of a 'genre' and to judge them by the 'master code' that prevails within the 'boundary' of the genre, whereas the 'postmodern' style is simply to view a work as a 'text' with its own particular 'rhetoric' and 'idiolect,' but which can in principle be compared with any other text of no matter what sort. Hassan's oppositions may be caricatures, but there is scarcely an arena of present intellectual practice where we cannot spot some of them at work. In what follows I shall try and take up a few of them in the richer detail they deserve.

I begin with what appears to be the most startling fact about postmodernism: its total acceptance of the ephemerality, fragmentation, discontinuity, and the chaotic that formed the one half of Baudelaire's conception of modernity. But postmodernism responds to the fact of that in a very particular way. It does not try to transcend it, counteract it, or even to define the 'eternal and immutable' elements that might lie within it. Postmodernism swims, even wallows, in the fragmentary and the chaotic currents of change as if that is all there is. Foucault (1983, xiii) instructs us, for example, to 'develop action, thought, and desires by proliferation, juxtaposition, and disjunction,' and 'to prefer what is positive and multiple, difference over uniformity, flows over unities, mobile arrangements over systems. Believe that what is productive is not sedentary but nomadic.' To the degree that it does try to legitimate itself by reference to the past, therefore, postmodernism typically harks back to that wing of thought, Nietzsche in particular, that emphasizes the deep chaos of modern life and its intractability before rational thought. This does not imply, however, that postmodernism is simply a version of modernism; real revolutions in sensibility can occur when latent and dominated ideas in one period become explicit and dominant in another. Nevertheless, the continuity of the condition of fragmentation, ephemerality, discontinuity, and chaotic change in both modernist and postmodernist thought is important. I shall make much of it in what follows.

Embracing the fragmentation and ephemerality in an affirmative fashion implies a whole host of consequences that bear directly on Hassan's oppositions. To begin with, we find writers like Foucault and Lyotard explicitly attacking any notion that there might be a meta-language, meta-narrative, or meta-theory through which all things can be connected or represented. Universal and eternal truths, if they exist at all, cannot be specified. Condemning meta-narratives (broad interpretative schemas like those deployed by Marx or Freud) as 'totalizing,' they insist upon the plurality of 'power-discourse' formations (Foucault), or of 'language games' (Lyotard). Lyotard in fact defines the postmodern simply as 'incredulity towards meta-narratives.'

Foucault's ideas – particularly as developed in his early works – deserve attention since they have been a fecund source for post-modernist argument. The relation between power and knowledge is there a central theme. But Foucault (1972, 159) breaks with the notion that power is ultimately located within the state, and abjures us to 'conduct an *ascending* analysis of power, starting, that is, from its infinitesimal mechanisms, which each have their own history, their own trajectory, their own techniques and tactics, and then see how these mechanisms of power have been – and continue to be – invested, colonized, utilized, involuted, transformed, displaced, extended, etc. by ever more general mechanisms and by forms of global domination.' Close scrutiny of the micro-politics of power relations in different localities, contexts, and social situations leads him to conclude that there is an intimate relation between the systems of knowledge ('discourses') which codify techniques and practices for the exercise of social control and domination within particular localized contexts. The prison, the asylum, the hospital, the university, the school, the psychiatrist's office, are all examples of sites where a dispersed and piecemeal organization of power is built up independently of any systematic strategy of class domination. What happens at each site cannot be understood by appeal to some overarching general theory. Indeed the only irreducible in Foucault's scheme of things is the human body, for that is the 'site' at which all forms of repression are ultimately registered. So while there are, in Foucault's celebrated dictum, 'no relations of power without resistances' he equally insists that no utopian scheme can ever hope to escape the power–knowledge relation in non-repressive ways. He here echoes Max Weber's pessimism as to our ability to avoid the 'iron cage' of repressive bureaucratic–technical rationality. More particularly, he interprets Soviet repression as the inevitable outcome of a utopian revolutionary theory (Marxism) which appealed to the same techniques and knowledge systems as those embedded in the capitalist system it sought to replace. The only way open to 'eliminate the fascism in our heads' is to explore and build upon the open qualities of human discourse, and thereby intervene in the way knowledge is produced and constituted at the particular sites where a localized power-discourse prevails. Foucault's work with homosexuals and prisoners was not aimed at producing reforms in state practices, but dedicated to the cultivation and enhancement of localized resistance to the institutions, techniques, and discourses of organized repression.

Foucault evidently believed that it was only through such a multi-faceted and pluralistic attack upon localized practices of repression that any global challenge to capitalism might be mounted without replicating all the multiple repressions of capitalism in a new form. His ideas appeal to the various social movements that sprang into existence during the 1960s (feminists, gays, ethnic and religious groupings, regional autonomists, etc.) as well as to those disillusioned with the practices of communism and the politics of communist parties. Yet it leaves open, particularly so in the deliberate rejection of any holistic theory of capitalism, the question of the path whereby such localized struggles might add up to a progressive, rather than regressive, attack upon the central forms of capitalist exploitation and repression. Localized struggles of the sort that Foucault appears to encourage have not generally had the effect of challenging capitalism, though Foucault might reasonably respond that only struggles fought in such a way as to challenge all forms of power-discourse might have such a result.

Lyotard, for his part, puts a similar argument, though on a rather different basis. He takes the modernist preoccupation with language and pushes it to extremes of dispersal. While 'the social bond is linguistic,' he argues, it 'is not woven with a single thread' but by an 'indeterminate number' of 'language games.' Each of us lives 'at the intersection of many of these' and we do not necessarily establish 'stable language combinations and the properties of the ones we do establish are not necessarily communicable.' As a consequence, 'the social subject itself seems to dissolve in this dissemination of language games.' Interestingly, Lyotard here employs a lengthy metaphor of Wittgenstein's (the pioneer of the theory of language games), to illuminate the condition of postmodern knowledge: 'Our language can be seen as an ancient city: a maze of little streets and squares, of old and new houses, and of houses with additions from different periods; and this surrounded by a multitude of new boroughs with straight regular streets and uniform houses.'

The 'atomization of the social into flexible networks of language games' suggests that each of us may resort to a quite different set of codes depending upon the situation in which we find ourselves (at home, at work, at church, in the street or pub, at a memorial service, etc.). To the degree that Lyotard (like Foucault) accepts that 'knowledge is the principal force of production' these days, so the problem is to define the locus of that power when it is evidently 'dispersed in clouds of narrative elements' within a heterogeneity of language games. Lyotard (again like Foucault) accepts the potential open qualities of ordinary conversations in which rules can bend and shift so as 'to encourage the greatest flexibility of utterance.' He makes much of the seeming contradiction between this openness and the rigidities with which institutions (Foucault's 'non-discursive domains') circumscribe what is or is not admissible within their boundaries. The realms of law, of the academy, of science and bureaucratic government, of military and political control, of electoral politics, and corporate power, all circumscribe what can be said and how it can be said in important ways. But the 'limits the institution imposes on potential language "moves" are never established once and for all,' they are 'themselves the stakes and provisional results of language strategies, within the institution and without.' We ought not, therefore, to reify institutions prematurely, but to recognize how the differentiated performance of language games creates institutional languages and powers in the first place. If 'there are many different language games − a heterogeneity of elements' we have then also to recognize that they can 'only give rise to institutions in patches − local determinism.'

Such 'local determinisms' have been understood by others (e.g. Fish, 1980) as 'interpretative communities,' made up of both producers and consumers of particular kinds of knowledge, of texts, often operating within a particular institutional context (such as the university, the legal system, religious groupings), within particular divisions of cultural labour (such as architecture, painting, theatre, dance), or within particular places (neighbourhoods, nations, etc.) Individuals and groups are held to control mutually within these domains what they consider to be valid knowledge.

To the degree that multiple sources of oppression in society and multiple foci of resistance to domination can be identified, so this kind of thinking has been taken up in radical politics, even imported into the heart of Marxism itself. We thus find Aronowitz arguing in *The crisis of historical materialism* that 'the multiple, local, autonomous struggles for liberation occurring throughout the post-modern world make all incarnations of master discourses absolutely illegitimate' (Bove, 1986, 18). Aronowitz is here seduced, I suspect, by the most liberative and therefore most appealing aspect of postmodern thought − its concern with 'otherness.' Huyssens (1984) particularly castigates the imperialism of an enlightened modernity that presumed to speak for others (colonized peoples, blacks and minorities, religious groups, women, the working class) with a unified voice. The very title of Carol Gilligan's *In a different voice* (1982) — a feminist work which challenges the male bias in setting out fixed stages in the moral development of personality — illustrates a process of counter-attack upon such universalizing presumptions. The idea that all groups have a right to speak for themselves, in their own voice, and have that voice accepted as authentic and legitimate is essential to the pluralistic stance of postmodernism. Foucault's work with marginal and interstitial groups has influenced a whole host of researchers, in fields as diverse as criminology and anthropology, into new ways to reconstruct and represent the voices and experiences of their subjects. Huyssens, for his part, emphasizes the opening given in postmodernism to understanding difference and otherness, as well as the liberatory potential it offers for a whole host of new social movements (women, gays, blacks, ecologists, regional autonomists, etc.). Curiously, most movements of this sort, though they have definitely helped change 'the structure of feeling,' pay scant attention to postmodernist arguments, and some feminists (e.g. Hartsock, 1987) are hostile for reasons that we will later consider.

Interestingly, we can detect this same preoccupation with 'otherness' and 'other worlds' in postmodernist fiction. McHale, in emphasizing the pluralism of worlds that coexist within postmodernist fiction, finds Foucault's concept of a *heterotopia* a perfectly appropriate image to capture what that fiction is striving to depict. By heterotopia, Foucault means the coexistence in 'an impossible space' of a 'large number of fragmentary possible worlds' or, more simply, incommensurable spaces that are juxtaposed or superimposed upon each other. Characters no longer contemplate how they can unravel or unmask a central mystery, but are forced to ask, 'Which world is this? What is to be done in it? Which of myselves is to do it?' instead. The same shift can be detected in the cinema. In a modernist classic like *Citizen Kane* a reporter seeks to unravel the mystery of Kane's life and character by collecting multiple reminiscences and perspectives from those who had known him. In the more postmodernist format of the contemporary cinema we find, in a film like *Blue Velvet*, the central character revolving between two quite incongruous worlds — that of a conventional 1950s small-town America with its high school, drugstore culture, and a bizarre, violent, sex-crazed underworld of drugs, dementia, and sexual perversion. It seems impossible that these two worlds should exist in the same space, and the central character moves between them, unsure which is the true reality, until the two worlds collide in a terrible denouement. A postmodernist painter like David Salle likewise tends to 'collage together incompatible source materials as an alternative to choosing between them' (Taylor, 1987, 8; see plate 1.6). Pfeil (1988) even goes so far as to depict the total field of postmodernism as 'a distilled representation of the whole antagonistic, voracious world of otherness.'

But to accept the fragmentation, the pluralism, and the authenticity of other voices and other worlds poses the acute problem of communication and the means of exercising power through command thereof. Most postmodernist thinkers are fascinated by the new possibilities for information and knowledge production, analysis, and transfer. Lyotard (1984), for example, firmly locates his arguments in the context of new technologies of communication and, drawing upon Bell's and Touraine's theses of the passage to a 'postindustrial' information-based society, situates the rise of postmodern thought in the heart of what he sees as a dramatic social and political transition in the languages of communication in advanced capitalist societies. He looks closely at the new technologies for the production, dissemination and use of that knowledge as a 'principal force of production.' The problem, however, is that knowledge can now be coded in all kinds of ways, some of which are more accessible than others. There is more than a hint in Lyotard's work, therefore, that modernism has changed because the technical and social conditions of communication have changed.

Postmodernists tend to accept, also, a rather different theory as to what language and communication are all about. Whereas modernists had presupposed that there was a tight and identifiable relation between what was being said (the signified or 'message') and how it was being said (the signifier or 'medium'), poststructuralist thinking sees these as 'continually breaking apart and re-attaching in new combinations.' 'Deconstructionism' (a movement initiated by Derrida's reading of Martin Heidegger in the late 1960s) here enters the picture as a powerful stimulus to postmodernist ways of thought. Deconstructionism is less a philosophical postion than a way of thinking about and 'reading' texts. Writers who create texts or use words do so on the basis of all the other texts and words they have encountered, while readers deal with them in the same way. Cultural life is then viewed as a series of texts intersecting with other texts, producing more texts (including that of the literary critic, who aims to produce another piece of literature in which texts under consideration are intersecting freely with other texts that happen to have affected his or her thinking). This intertextual weaving has a life of its own. Whatever we write conveys meanings we do not or could not possibly intend, and our words cannot say what we mean. It is vain to try and master

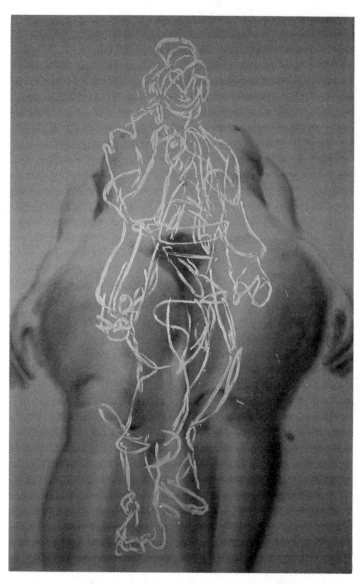

Plate 1.6 The collision and superimposition of different ontological worlds is a major characteristic of postmodern art. David Salle's 'Tight as Houses', 1980, illustrates the idea.

a text because the perpetual interweaving of texts and meanings is beyond our control. Language works through us. Recognizing that, the deconstructionist impulse is to look inside one text for another, dissolve one text into another, or build one text into another.

Derrida considers, therefore, collage/montage as the primary form of postmodern discourse. The inherent heterogeneity of that (be it in painting, writing, architecture) stimulates us, the receivers of the text or image, 'to produce a signification which could be neither univocal nor stable.' Both producers and consumers of 'texts' (cultural artefacts) participate in the production of significations and meanings (hence Hassan's emphasis upon 'process,' 'performance,' 'happening,' and 'participation' in the postmodernist style). Minimizing the authority of the cultural producer creates the opportunity for popular participation and democratic determinations of cultural values, but at the price of a certain incoherence or, more problematic, vulnerability to mass-market manipulation. However this may be, the cultural producer merely creates raw materials (fragments and elements), leaving it open to consumers to recombine those elements in any way they wish. The effect is to break (deconstruct) the power of the author to impose meanings or offer a continuous narrative. Each cited element says Derrida, 'breaks the continuity or the linearity of the discourse and leads necessarily to a double reading: that of the fragment perceived in relation to its text of origin; that of the fragment as incorporated into a new whole, a different totality.' Continuity is given only in 'the trace' of the fragment as it moves from production to consumption. The effect is to call into question all the illusions of fixed systems of representation (Foster, 1983, 142).

There is more than a hint of this sort of thinking within the modernist tradition (directly from surrealism, for example) and there is a danger here of thinking of the meta-narratives in the Enlightenment tradition as more fixed and stable than they truly were. Marx, as Ollman (1971) observes, deployed his concepts relationally, so that terms like value, labour, capital, are 'continually breaking apart and re-attaching in new combinations' in an open-ended struggle to come to terms with the totalizing processes of capitalism. Benjamin, a complex thinker in the Marxist tradition, worked the idea of collage/montage to perfection, in order to try and capture the many-layered and fragmented relations between economy, politics, and culture without ever abandoning the standpoint of a totality of practices that constitute capitalism. Taylor (1987, 53–65) likewise concludes, after reviewing the historical evidence of its use (particularly by Picasso), that collage is a far from adequate indicator of difference between modernist and postmodernist painting.

But if, as the postmodernists insist, we cannot aspire to any unified representation of the world, or picture it as a totality full of connections and differentiations rather than as perpetually shifting fragments, then how can we possibly aspire to act coherently with respect to the world? The simple postmodernist answer is that since coherent representation and action are either repressive or illusionary (and therefore doomed to be self-dissolving and self-defeating), we should not even try to engage in some global project. Pragmatism (of the Dewey sort) then becomes the only possible philosophy of action. We thus find Rorty (1985, 173), one of the major US philosophers in the postmodern movement, dismissing 'the canonical sequence of philosophers from Descartes to Nietzsche as a distraction from the history of concrete social engineering which made the contemporary North American culture what it is now, with all its glories and all its dangers.' Action can be conceived of and decided only within the confines of some local determinism, some interpretative community, and its purported meanings and anticipated effects are bound to break down when taken out of these isolated domains, even when coherent within them. We similarly find Lyotard (1984, 66) arguing that 'consensus has become an outmoded and suspect value' but then adding, rather surprisingly, that since 'justice as a value is neither outmoded nor suspect' (how it could remain such a universal, untouched by the diversity of language games, he does not tell us), we 'must arrive at an idea and practice of justice that is not linked to that of consensus.'

It is precisely this kind of relativism and defeatism that Habermas seeks to combat in his defence of the Enlightenment project. While Habermas is more than willing to admit what he calls 'the deformed realization of reason in history' and the dangers that attach to the simplified imposition of some meta-narrative on complex relations and events, he also insists that 'theory can locate a gentle, but obstinate, a never silent although seldom redeemed claim to reason, a claim that must be recognized de facto whenever and wherever there is to be consensual action.' He, too, turns to the question of language, and in *The theory of communicative action* insists upon the dialogical qualities of human communication in which speaker and hearer are necessarily oriented to the task of reciprocal understanding. Out of this, Habermas argues, consensual and normative statements do arise, thus grounding the role of universalizing reason in daily life. It is this that allows 'communicative reason' to operate 'in history as an avenging force.' Habermas's critics are, however, more numerous than his defenders.

The portrait of postmodernism I have so far sketched in seems to depend for its validity upon a particular way of experiencing, inter-preting, and being in the world. This brings us to what is, perhaps, the most problematic facet of postmodernism, its psychological pre-suppositions with respect to personality, motivation, and behaviour. Preoccupation with the fragmentation and instability of language and discourses carries over directly, for example, into a certain conception of personality. Encapsulated, this conception focuses on schizophrenia (not, it should be emphasized, in its narrow clinical sense), rather than on alienation and paranoia (see Hassan's schema). Jameson (1984b) explores this theme to very telling effect. He uses Lacan's de-scription of schizophrenia as a linguistic disorder, as a breakdown in the signifying chain of meaning that creates a simple sentence. When the signifying chain snaps, then 'we have schizophrenia in the form of a rubble of distinct and unrelated signifiers.' If personal identity is forged through 'a certain temporal unification of the past and future with the present before me,' and if sentences move through the same trajectory, then an inability to unify past, present, and future in the sentence betokens a similar inability to 'unify the past, present and future of our own biographical experience or psychic life.' This fits, of course, with postmodernism's preoccupation with the signifier rather than the signified, with participation, performance, and hap-pening rather than with an authoritative and finished art object, with surface appearances rather than roots (again, see Hassan's schema). The effect of such a breakdown in the signifying chain is to reduce experience to 'a series of pure and unrelated presents in time.' Offer-ing no counterweight, Derrida's conception of language colludes in the production of a certain schizophrenic effect, thus, perhaps, ex-plaining Eagleton's and Hassan's characterization of the typical post-modernist artefact as schizoid. Deleuze and Guattari (1984, 245), in their supposedly playful exposition *Anti-Oedipus*, hypothesize a re-lationship between schizophrenia and capitalism that prevails 'at the deepest level of one and the same economy, one and the same production process,' concluding that 'our society produces schizos the same way it produces Prell shampoo or Ford cars, the only difference being that the schizos are not saleable.'

A number of consequences follow from the domination of this motif in postmodernist thought. We can no longer conceive of the individual as alienated in the classical Marxist sense, because to be alienated presupposes a coherent rather than a fragmented sense of self from which to be alienated. It is only in terms of such a centred sense of personal identity that individuals can pursue projects over time, or think cogently about the production of a future significantly better than time present and time past. Modernism was very much about the pursuit of better futures, even if perpetual frustration of that aim was conducive to paranoia. But postmodernism typically strips away that possibility by concentrating upon the schizophrenic circumstances induced by fragmentation and all those instabilities (including those of language) that prevent us even picturing coherently, let alone devising strategies to produce, some radically different future. Modernism, of course, was not without its schizoid moments – particularly when it sought to combine myth with heroic modernity – and there has been a sufficient history of the 'deformation of reason' and of 'reactionary modernisms' to suggest that the schizophrenic circumstance, though for the most part dominated, was always latent within the modernist movement. Nevertheless, there is good reason to believe that 'alienation of the subject is displaced by fragmentation of the subject' in postmodern aesthetics (Jameson, 1984a, 63). If, as Marx insisted, it takes the alienated individual to pursue the Enlightenment project with a tenacity and coherence sufficient to bring us to some better future, then loss of the alienated subject would seen to preclude the conscious construction of alternative social futures.

The reduction of experience to 'a series of pure and unrelated presents' further implies that the 'experience of the present becomes powerfully, overwhelmingly vivid and "material": the world comes before the schizophrenic with heightened intensity, bearing the mysterious and oppressive charge of affect, glowing with hallucinatory energy' (Jameson, 1984b, 120). The image, the appearance, the spectacle can all be experienced with an intensity (joy or terror) made possible only by their appreciation as pure and unrelated presents in time. So what does it matter 'if the world thereby momentarily loses its depth and threatens to become a glossy skin, a stereoscopic illusion, a rush of filmic images without density?' (Jameson, 1984b). The immediacy of events, the sensationalism of the spectacle (political, scientific, military, as well as those of entertainment), become the stuff of which consciousness is forged.

Such a breakdown of the temporal order of things also gives rise to a peculiar treatment of the past. Eschewing the idea of progress, postmodernism abandons all sense of historical continuity and memory, while simultaneously developing an incredible ability to plunder history and absorb whatever it finds there as some aspect of the present. Postmodernist architecture, for example, takes bits and pieces from the past quite eclectically and mixes them together at will (see chapter 4). Another example, taken from painting, is given by Crimp (1983, 44–5). Manet's *Olympia*, one of the seminal paintings of the early modernist movement, was modelled on Titian's

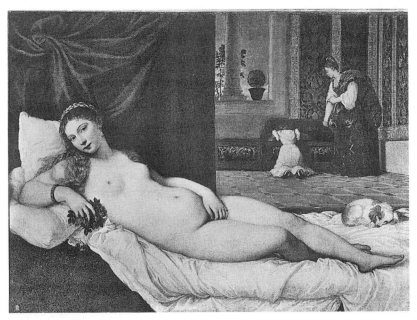

Plate 1.7 The Venus d'Urbino *by Titian provided the inspiration for Manet's* Olympia *of 1863.*

Venus (plates 1.7; 1.8). But the manner of its modelling signalled a self-conscious break between modernity and tradition, and the active intervention of the artist in that transition (Clark, 1985). Rauschenberg, one of the pioneers of the postmodernist movement, deployed images of Velazquez's *Rokeby Venus* and Rubens's *Venus at her toilet* in a series of paintings in the 1960s (plate 1.9). But he uses these images in a very different way, simply silk-screening a photographic original onto a surface that contains all kinds of other features (trucks, helicopters, car keys). Rauschenberg simply *reproduces,* whereas Manet *produces,* and it is this move, says Crimp, 'that requires us to think of Rauschenberg as a post-modernist.' The modernist 'aura' of the artist as producer is dispensed with. 'The fiction of the creating subject gives way to frank confiscation, quotation, excerption, accumulation and repetition of already existing images.'

This sort of shift carries over into all other fields with powerful implications. Given the evaporation of any sense of historical continuity and memory, and the rejection of meta-narratives, the only role left for the historian, for example, is to become, as Foucault

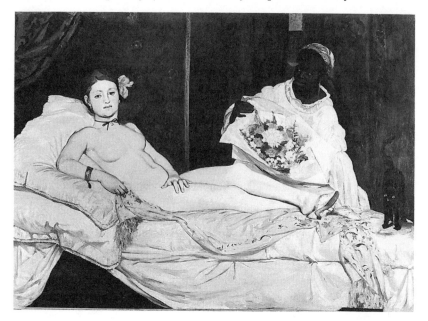

Plate 1.8 Manet's pioneering modernist work Olympia *re-works the ideas of Titian.*

insisted, an archaeologist of the past, digging up its remnants as Borges does in his fiction, and assembling them, side by side, in the museum of modern knowledge. Rorty (1979, 371), in attacking the idea that philosophy can ever hope to define some permanent epistemological framework for enquiry, likewise ends up insisting that the only role of the philosopher, in the midst of the cacophony of cross-cutting conversations that comprise a culture, is to 'decry the notion of having a view while avoiding having a view about having views.' 'The essential trope of fiction,' we are told by the post-modernist writers of it, is a 'technique that requires suspension of belief as well as of disbelief' (McHale, 1987, 27–33). There is, in postmodernism, little overt attempt to sustain continuity of values, beliefs, or even disbeliefs.

This loss of historical continuity in values and beliefs, taken together with the reduction of the work of art to a text stressing discontinuity and allegory, poses all kinds of problems for aesthetic and critical judgement. Refusing (and actively 'deconstructing') all authoritative or supposedly immutable standards of aesthetic judgement, postmodernism can judge the spectacle only in terms of how

Plate 1.9 Rauschenberg's pioneering postmodernist work Persimmon *(1964),
collages many themes including direct reproduction of Rubens's* Venus at her
toilet.

spectacular it is. Barthes proposes a particularly sophisticated version
of that strategy. He distinguishes between *pleasure* and *'jouissance'*
(perhaps best translated as 'sublime physical and mental bliss') and
suggests we strive to realize the second, more orgasmic effect (note

the connection to Jameson's description of schizophrenia) through a
particular mode of encounter with the otherwise lifeless cultural
artefacts that litter our social landscape. Since most of us are not
schizoid in the clinical sense, Barthes defines a kind of 'mandarin
practice' that allows us to achieve '*jouissance*' and to use that experience as a basis for aesthetic and critical judgements. This means
identification with the act of writing (creation) rather than reading
(reception). Huyssens (1984, 38—45) reserves his sharpest irony for
Barthes, however, arguing that he reinstitutes one of the tiredest
modernist and bourgeois distinctions: that 'there are lower pleasures
for the rabble, i.e. mass culture, and then there is *nouvelle cuisine* of
the pleasure of the text, *jouissance*.' This reintroduction of the high-
brow/low-brow disjunction avoids the whole problem of the potential
debasement of modern cultural forms by their assimilation to pop
culture through pop art. 'The euphoric American appropriation of
Barthes's *jouissance* is predicated on ignoring such problems and on
enjoying, not unlike the 1984 yuppies, the pleasures of writerly
connoisseurism and textual gentrification.' Huyssens's image, as
Raban's descriptions in *Soft city* suggest, may be more than a little
appropriate.

The other side to the loss of temporality and the search for
instantaneous impact is a parallel loss of depth. Jameson (1984a;
1984b) has been particularly emphatic as to the 'depthlessness' of
much of contemporary cultural production, its fixation with appearances, surfaces, and instant impacts that have no sustaining power
over time. The image sequences of Sherman's photographs are of
exactly that quality, and as Charles Newman remarked in a *New York
Times* review on the state of the American novel (*NYT*, 17 July
1987):

> The fact of the matter is that a sense of diminishing control,
> loss of individual autonomy and generalized helplessness has
> never been so instantaneously recognizable in our literature —
> the flattest possible characters in the flattest possible landscapes
> rendered in the flattest possible diction. The presumption seems
> to be that American is a vast fibrous desert in which a few
> laconic weeds nevertheless manage to sprout in the cracks.

'Contrived depthlessness' is how Jameson describes postmodern
architecture, and it is hard not to give credence to this sensibility as
the overhelming motif in postmodernism, offset only by Barthes's
attempts to help us to the moment of *jouissance*. Attention to surfaces
has, of course, always been important to modernist thought and

practice (particulary since the cubists), but it has always been paralleled by the kind of question that Raban posed about urban life: how can we build, represent, and attend to these surfaces with the requisite sympathy and seriousness in order to get behind them and identify essential meanings? Postmodernism, with its resignation to bottomless fragmentation and ephemerality, generally refuses to contemplate that question.

The collapse of time horizons and the preoccupation with instantaneity have in part arisen through the contemporary emphasis in cultural production on events, spectacles, happenings, and media images. Cultural producers have learned to explore and use new technologies, the media, and ultimately multi-media possibilities. The effect, however, has been to re-emphasize the fleeting qualities of modern life and even to celebrate them. But it has also permitted a *rapprochement*, in spite of Barthes's interventions, between popular culture and what once remained isolated as 'high culture.' Such a *rapprochement* has been sought before, though nearly always in a more revolutionary mode, as movements like Dada and early surrealism, constructivism, and expressionism tried to bring their art to the people as part and parcel of a modernist project of social transformation. Such avant-gardist movements possessed a strong faith in their own aims as well as immense faith in new technologies. The closing of the gap between popular culture and cultural production in the contemporary period, while strongly dependent on new technologies of communication, seems to lack any avant-gardist or revolutionary impulse, leading many to accuse postmodernism of a simple and direct surrender to commodification, commercialization, and the market (Foster, 1985). However this may be, much of postmodernism is consciously anti-auratic and anti-avant-garde and seeks to explore media and cultural arenas open to all. It is no accident that Sherman, for example, use photography and evokes pop images as if from film stills in the poses she assumes.

This raises the most difficult of all questions about the postmodern movement, namely its relationship with, and integration into, the culture of daily life. Although much of the discussion of it proceeds in the abstract, and therefore in the not very accessible terms that I have been forced to use here, there are innumerable points of contact between producers of cultural artefacts and the general public: architecture, advertising, fashion, films, staging of multi-media events, grand spectacles, political campaigns, as well as the ubiquitous television. It is not always clear who is influencing whom in this process.

Venturi et al. (1972, 155) recommend that we learn our architectural aesthetics from the Las Vegas strip or from much-maligned suburbs like Levittown, simply because people evidently like such environments. 'One does not have to agree with hard hat politics,' they go on to say, 'to support the rights of the middle-middle class to their own architectural aesthetics, and we have found that Levittown-type aesthetics are shared by most members of the middle-middle class, black as well as white, liberal as well as conservative.' There is absolutely nothing wrong, they insist, with giving people what they want, and Venturi himself was even quoted in the *New York Times* (22 October 1972), in an article fittingly entitled 'Mickey Mouse teaches the architects,' saying 'Disney World is nearer to what people want than what architects have ever given them.' Disneyland, he asserts, is 'the symbolic American utopia.'

There are those, however, who see such a concession of high culture to Disneyland aesthetics as a matter of necessity rather than choice. Daniel Bell (1978, 20), for example, depicts postmodernism as the exhaustion of modernism through the institutionalization of creative and rebellious impulses by what he calls 'the cultural mass' (the millions of people working in broadcast media, films, theatre, universities, publishing houses, advertising and communications industries, etc. who process and influence the reception of serious cultural products and produce the popular materials for the wider mass-culture audience). The degeneration of high-brow authority over cultural taste in the 1960s, and its replacement by pop art, pop culture, ephemeral fashion, and mass taste is seen as a sign of the mindless hedonism of capitalist consumerism.

Iain Chambers (1986; 1987) interprets a similar process rather differently. Working-class youth in Britain found enough money in their pockets during the postwar boom to participate in the capitalist consumer culture, and actively used fashion to construct a sense of their own public identities, even defined their own pop-art forms, in the face of a fashion industry that sought to impose taste through advertising and media pressures. The consequent democratization of taste across a variety of sub-cultures (from inner-city macho male to college campuses) is interpreted as the outcome of a vital struggle that pitched the rights of even the relatively underprivileged to shape their own identities in the face of a powerfully organized commercialism. The urban-based cultural ferments that began in the early 1960s and continue to this very day lie, in Chambers's view, at the root of the postmodern turn:

Post modernism, whatever form its intellectualizing might take, has been fundamentally anticipated in the metropolitan cultures of the last twenty years: among the electronic signifiers of cinema, television and video, in recording studios and record players, in fashion and youth styles, in all those sounds, images and diverse histories that are daily mixed, recycled and 'scratched' together on that giant screen which is the contemporary city.

It is hard, also, not to attribute some kind of shaping role to the proliferation of television use. After all, the average American is now reputed to watch television for more than seven hours a day, and television and video ownership (the latter now covering at least half of all US households) is now so widespread throughout the capitalist world that some effects must surely be registered. Postmodernist concerns with surface, for example, can be traced to the necessary format of television images. Television is also, as Taylor (1987, 103– 5) points out, 'the first cultural medium in the whole of history to present the artistic achievements of the past as a stitched-together collage of equi-important and simultaneously existing phenomena, largely divorced from geography and material history and transported to the living rooms and studios of the West in a more or less uninterrupted flow.' It posits a viewer, furthermore, 'who shares the medium's own perception of history as an endless reserve of equal events.' It is hardly surprising that the artist's relation to history (the peculiar historicism we have already noted) has shifted, that in the era of mass television there has emerged an attachment to surfaces rather than roots, to collage rather than in-depth work, to super-imposed quoted images rather than worked surfaces, to a collapsed sense of time and space rather than solidly achieved cultural artefact. And these are all vital aspects of artistic practice in the post-modern condition.

To point to the potency of such a force in shaping culture as a total way of life is not necessarily to lapse, however, into a simple-minded technological determinism of the 'television causes post-modernism' variety. For television is itself a product of late capitalism and, as such, has to be seen in the context of the promotion of a culture of consumerism. This directs our attention to the production of needs and wants, the mobilization of desire and fantasy, of the politics of distraction as part and parcel of the push to sustain sufficient buoyancy of demand in consumer markets to keep capitalist production profitable. Charles Newman (1984, 9) sees much of the postmodernist aesthetic as a response to the inflationary surge of late capitalism. 'Inflation,' he argues, 'affects the ideas exchange just as surely as it does commercial markets.' Thus 'we are witness to continual internecine warfare and spasmodic changes in fashion, the simultaneous display of all past styles in their infinite mutations, and the continuous circulation of diverse and contradictory intellectual elites, which signal the reign of the cult of creativity in all areas of behaviour, an unprecedented non-judgemental receptivity to Art, a tolerance which finally amounts to indifference.' From this standpoint, Newman concludes, 'the vaunted fragmentation of art is no longer an aesthetic choice: it is simply a cultural aspect of the economic and social fabric.'

This would certainly go some way to explain the postmodernist thrust to integrate into popular culture through the kind of frank, even crass, commercialization that modernists tended to eschew by their deep resistance to the idea (though never quite the fact) of commodification of their production. There are those however, who attribute the exhaustion of high modernism precisely to its absorption as the formal aesthetics of corporate capitalism and the bureaucratic state. Postmodernism then signals nothing more than a logical extension of the power of the market over the whole range of cultural production. Crimp (1987, 85) waxes quite acerbic on this point:

> What we have seen in the last several years is the virtual takeover of art by big corporate interests. For whatever role capital played in the art of modernism, the current phenomenon is new precisely because of its scope. Corporations have become the major patrons of art in every respect. They form huge collections. They fund every major museum exhibition .... Auction houses have become lending institutions, giving a completely new value to art as collateral. And all of this affects not only the inflation of value of old masters but art production itself.... [The corporations] are buying cheap and in quantity, counting on the escalation of the value of young artists.... The return to painting and sculpture of a traditional cast is the return to commodity production, and I would suggest that, whereas traditionally art had an ambiguous commodity status, it now has a thoroughly unambiguous one.

The growth of a museum culture (in Britain a museum opens every three weeks, and in Japan over 500 have opened up in the last fifteen years) and a burgeoning 'heritage industry' that took off in the early 1970s, add another populist (though this time very middle-class) twist to the commercialization of history and cultural forms. 'Post-modernism and the heritage industry are linked,' says Hewison (1987, 135), since 'both conspire to create a shallow screen that intervenes between our present lives and our history.' History becomes a 'contemporary creation, more costume drama and re-enactment than critical discourse.' We are, he concludes, quoting Jameson, 'condemned to seek History by way of our own pop images and simulacra of that history which itself remains for ever out of reach.' The house is viewed no longer as a machine but as 'an antique for living in.'

The invocation of Jameson brings us, finally, to his daring thesis that postmodernism is nothing more than the cultural logic of late capitalism. Following Mandel (1975), he argues that we have moved into a new era since the early 1960s in which the production of culture 'has become integrated into commodity production generally: the frantic urgency of producing fresh waves of ever more novel seeming goods (from clothes to airplanes), at ever greater rates of turnover, now assigns an increasingly essential structural function to aesthetic innovation and experimentation.' The struggles that were once exclusively waged in the arena of production have, as a consequence, now spilled outwards to make of cultural production an arena of fierce social conflict. Such a shift entails a definite change in consumer habits and attitudes as well as a new role for aesthetic definitions and interventions. While some would argue that the counter-cultural movements of the 1960s created an environment of unfulfilled needs and repressed desires that postmodernist popular cultural production has merely set out to satisfy as best it can in commodity form, others would suggest that capitalism, in order to sustain its markets, has been forced to produce desire and so titillate individual sensibilities as to create a new aesthetic over and against traditional forms of high culture. In either case, I think it important to accept the proposition that the cultural evolution which has taken place since the early 1960s, and which asserted itself as hegemonic in the early 1970s, has not occurred in a social, economic, or political vacuum. The deployment of advertising as 'the official art of capitalism' brings advertising strategies into art, and art into advertising strategies (as a comparison of David Salle's painting and an advertisement for Citizen Watches (plates 1.6 and 1.10) illustrates). It is interesting, therefore, to ruminate upon the stylistic shift that Hassan sets up in relation to the forces that emanate from mass-consumer culture: the mobilization of fashion, pop art, television and other forms of media image, and the variety of urban life styles that have become part and parcel of daily life under capitalism. Whatever else we do with the concept, we should not read postmodernism as some autonomous artistic current. Its rootedness in daily life is one of its most patently transparent features.

The portrait of postmodernism I have here constructed, with the

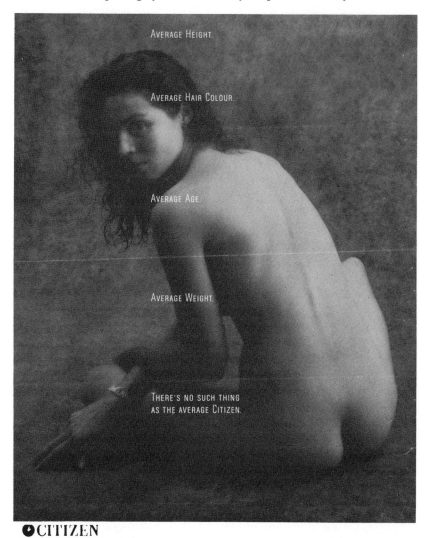

Plate 1.10 An advertisement for Citizen Watches engages directly with the postmodernist techniques of superimposition of ontologically different worlds that bear no necessary relation to each other (compare the David Salle painting of plate 1.6). The watch being advertised is almost invisible.

help of Hassan's schema, is certainly incomplete. It is equally certainly rendered fragmentary and ephemeral by the sheer plurality and elusiveness of cultural forms wrapped in the mysteries of rapid flux and change. But I think I have said enough as to what constitutes the general frame of that 'profound shift in the structure of feeling' that separates modernity from postmodernity to begin upon the task of unravelling its origins and speculatively constructing an interpretation of what it might betoken for our future. Nevertheless, I think it helpful to round out this portrait with a more detailed look at how postmodernism is manifest in contemporary urban design, because a closer focus helps reveal the fine-grained textures rather than the broad brush strokes of which the postmodernist condition is constructed in daily life. This is, then, the task I shall take up in the next chapter.

Note

The illustrations used in this chapter have been criticized by some feminists of a postmodern persuasion. They were deliberately chosen because they allowed comparison across the supposed pre-modern, modern and postmodern divides. The classical Titian nude is actively reworked in Manet's modernist Olympia. Rauschenberg simply reproduces through postmodern collage, David Salle superimposes different worlds, and the Citizen's Watch advertisement (the most outrageous of the lot but which appeared in the weekend magazine supplements of several quality newspapers in Britain for an extended period) is a slick use of the same postmodern technique for purely commercial purposes. All the illustrations make use of a woman's body to inscribe their particular message. The additional point I sought to make is that the subordination of women, one of the many 'troublesome contradictions' in bourgeois Enlightenment practices (see p. 14 above and p. 252 below), can expect no particular relief by appeal to postmodernism. I thought the illustrations made the point so well that no further elaboration was necessary. But, in some circles at least, these particular pictures were not worth their usual thousand words. Nor, it seems, should I have relied upon postmodernists appreciating their own technique of telling even a slightly different story by way of the illustrations as compared to the text. (*June, 1991.*)

4

Postmodernism in the city: architecture and urban design

In the field of architecture and urban design, I take postmodernism broadly to signify a break with the modernist idea that planning and development should focus on large-scale, metropolitan-wide, technologically rational and efficient urban *plans*, backed by absolutely no-frills architecture (the austere 'functionalist' surfaces of 'international style' modernism). Postmodernism cultivates, instead, a conception of the urban fabric as necessarily fragmented, a 'palimpsest' of past forms superimposed upon each other, and a 'collage' of current uses, many of which may be ephemeral. Since the metropolis is impossible to command except in bits and pieces, urban *design* (and note that postmodernists design rather than plan) simply aims to be sensitive to vernacular traditions, local histories, particular wants, needs, and fancies, thus generating specialized, even highly customized architectural forms that may range from intimate, personalized spaces, through traditional monumentality, to the gaiety of spectacle. All of this can flourish by appeal to a remarkable eclecticism of architectural styles.

Above all, postmodernists depart radically from modernist conceptions of how to regard space. Whereas the modernists see space as something to be shaped for social purposes and therefore always subservient to the construction of a social project, the postmodernists see space as something independent and autonomous, to be shaped according to aesthetic aims and principles which have nothing necessarily to do with any overarching social objective, save, perhaps, the achievement of timeless and 'disinterested' beauty as an objective in itself.

It is useful to consider the meaning of such a shift for a variety of reasons. To begin with, the built environment constitutes one element in a complex of urban experience that has long been a vital crucible for the forging of new cultural sensibilities. How a city looks and how its spaces are organized forms a material base upon which a range of possible sensations and social practices can be thought about, evaluated, and achieved. One dimension of Raban's *Soft city* can be rendered more or less hard by the way the built environment is shaped. Conversely, architecture and urban design have been the focus of considerable polemical debate concerning the ways in which aesthetic judgements can or should be incorporated in spatially fixed form, and with what effects on daily life. If we experience architecture as communication, if, as Barthes (1975, 92) insists, 'the city is a discourse and this discourse is truly a language,' then we ought to pay close attention to what is being said, particularly since we typically absorb such messages in the midst of all the other manifold distractions of urban life.

Prince Charles's 'kitchen cabinet' of advisers on matters to do with architecture and urban design includes the architect Leon Krier. Krier's complaints against modernism, as published (long-hand for special effect) in 1987 in *Architectural Design Profile* (no. 65) are of direct interest since they now inform public debate in Britain at both the highest and the most general level. The central problem for Krier is that modernist urban planning works mainly through mono-functional zoning. As a result, circulation of people between zones by way of artificial arteries becomes the central preoccupation of the planner, generating an urban pattern that is, in Krier's judgement, 'anti-ecological' because it is wasteful of time, energy, and land:

> The *symbolic poverty* of current architecture and townscape is a direct result and expression of functionalist monotony as legislated by functional zoning practices. The principal modern building types and planning models such as the Skyscraper, the Groundscraper, the Central Business District, the Commercial Strip, the Office Park, the Residential Suburb, etc. are invariably horizontal or vertical *over*concentrations of single uses in one urban zone, in one building programme, or under one roof.

Krier contrasts this situation with the 'good city' (by its nature ecological) in which 'the totality of urban functions' are provided within 'compatible and pleasant walking distances.' Recognizing that such an urban form 'cannot grow by extension in width and height' but only 'through multiplication,' Krier seeks a city form made up of 'complete and finite urban communities,' each constituting an independent urban quarter within a large family of urban quarters, that in turn make up 'cities within a city.' Only under such conditions will it be possible to recuperate the *'symbolic richness'* of traditional urban forms based on 'the propinquity and dialogue of the greatest

possible variety and hence on the expression of true variety as
evidenced by the meaningful and truthful articulation of public spaces,
urban fabric, and skyline.'

Krier, like some other European postmodernists, seeks the active
restoration and re-creation of traditional 'classical' urban values. This
means either restoration of an older urban fabric and its rehabilitation
to new uses, or the creation of new spaces that express the traditional
visions with all the cunning that modern technologies and materials
will allow. While Krier's project is only one out of many possible
directions that postmodernists could cultivate – quite at odds, for
example, with Venturi's admiration for Disneyland, the Las Vegas
strip, and suburban ornamentation – it does harp upon a certain
conception of modernism as its reactive beginning point. It is useful,
therefore, to consider to what degree and why the sort of modernism Krier decries became so dominant a feature of postwar urban
organization.

The political, economic, and social problems that faced the advanced
capitalist countries in the wake of World War II were as extensive as
they were severe. International peace and prosperity had somehow
to be built upon a programme that met the aspirations of peoples
who had given massively of their lives amd energies in a struggle
generally depicted (and justified) as a struggle for a safer world, a
better world, a better future. Whatever else that meant, it did not
mean a return to the prewar conditions of slump and unemployment,
of hunger marches and soup-kitchens, of deteriorating slums and
penury, and to the social unrest and political instability to which
such conditions could all too easily lend themselves. Postwar politics,
if they were to remain democratic and capitalistic, had to address
questions of full employment, decent housing, social provision, welfare, and broad-based opportunity to construct a better future (see
Part II).

While the tactics and conditions differed from place to place (in,
for example, the extent of war-time destruction, the acceptable degree
of centralization in political control, or the level of commitment to
state welfarism), the trend was everywhere to look to the war-time
experience of mass production and planning as means to launch
upon a vast programme of reconstruction and reorganization. It was
almost as if a new and revivified version of the Enlightenment
project sprang, phoenix-like, out of the death and destruction of
global conflict. The reconstruction, re-shaping, and renewal of the
urban fabric became an essential ingredient within this project. This
was the context in which the ideas of the CIAM, of Le Corbusier, of

Mies van der Rohe, of Frank Lloyd Wright, and the like, could gain
the kind of purchase they did, less as a controlling force of ideas over
production than as a theoretical framework and justification for what
practical-minded engineers, politicians, builders, and developers
were in many cases engaged upon out of sheer social, economic, and
political necessity.

Within this general framework all kinds of solutions were explored.
Britain, for example, adopted quite stringent town and country planning legislation. The effect was to restrict suburbanization and to
substitute planned new-town development (on the Ebenezer Howard
model) or high-density infilling or renewal (on the Le Corbusier
model) in its stead. Under the watchful eye and sometimes strong
hand of the state, procedures were devised to eliminate slums, build
modular housing, schools, hospitals, factories, etc. through the
adoption of the industrialized construction systems and rational planning procedures that modernist architects had long proposed. And
all this was framed by a deep concern, expressed again and again in
legislation, for the rationalization of spatial patterns and of circulation
systems so as to promote equality (at least of opportunity), social
welfare, and economic growth.

While many other European countries pursued variants of the
British solution, the United States pushed towards urban reconstruction of a rather different sort. Rapid and weakly controlled suburbanization (the answer to every demobilized soldier's dream, as the
rhetoric of the time had it) was privately developed but heavily
subsidized by government-backed housing finance and direct public
investments in highway construction and other infrastructures. The
deterioration of the inner cities consequent upon the flight outwards of
both jobs and people then provoked a powerful and again government-
subsidized strategy of urban renewal through massive clearance and
reconstruction of older city centres. It was in this context that someone like Robert Moses – the 'power broker,' as Caro (1974) depicts
him, of metropolitan redevelopment in New York – was able to
insert himself in between the sources of public funds and the requirements of private developers to such powerful effect, and to reshape
the whole New York metropolitan region through high-way construction, bridge building, park provision, and urban renewal.
The US solution, though different in form, nevertheless also relied
heavily upon mass production, industrialized construction systems,
and a sweeping conception of how a rationalized urban space might
emerge when linked, as Frank Lloyd Wright had envisaged in his
Broadacre project of the 1930s, through individualized means of
transportation using publicly provided infrastructures.

It would, I think, be both erroneous and unjust to depict these 'modernist' solutions to the dilemmas of postwar urban development and redevelopment as unalloyed failures. War-torn cities were rapidly reconstructed, and populations housed under much better conditions than was the case in the inter-war years. Given the technologies available at the time and the obvious scarcity of resources, it is hard to see how much of that could have been achieved except through some variant of what was actually done. And while some solutions turned out to be much more successful (in the sense of yielding widespread public satisfaction, as did Le Corbusier's Unité d'Habitation in Marseilles) than others (and I note the postmodernist penchant for always and only citing the bad ones), the overall effort was reasonably successful in reconstituting the urban fabric in ways that helped preserve full employment, improve material social provision, contribute to welfare goals, and generally help preserve a capitalist social order that was plainly threatened in 1945. Nor is it true to say that modernist styles were hegemonic for purely ideological reasons. The standardization and assembly-line uniformity of which postmodernists were later to complain were as omni-present in the Las Vegas strip and Levittown (hardly built to modernist specifications) as they were in Mies van der Rohe's buildings. Both labour and conservative governments pursued modernist projects in postwar Britain, though it is curious that the left is now largely blamed for them when it was the conservatives, by cutting corners on costs of low-income housing in particular, who perpetrated many of the worst examples of instant slums and alienated living conditions. The dictates of costs and efficiency (particularly important in relation to the less affluent populations served), coupled with organizational and technological constraints, surely played as important a role as ideological concern for style.

Nevertheless, it did indeed become fashionable in the 1950s to laud the virtues of the international style, to vaunt its capacities to create a new species of human being, to view it as the expressive arm of an interventionist bureaucratic state apparatus that, in conjunction with corporate capital, was reckoned to be the guardian of all further advances in human welfare. Some of the ideological claims were grandiose. But the radical transformations in the social and physical landscapes of capitalist cities often had little to do with such claims. To begin with, speculative land and property development (to gain land rent and to build profitably, quickly, and cheaply) were dominant forces in a development and construction industry that was a major branch of capital accumulation. Even when contained by planning regulations or oriented around public investments, corporate capital still had a great deal of power. And where corporate capital was in command (especially in the United States), it could happily appropriate every modernist trick in the architect's book to continue that practice of building monuments that soared ever higher as symbols of corporate power. Monuments like the *Chicago Tribune* building (built from a design chosen by competition between many of the great modernist architects of the period) and the Rockefeller Center (with its extraordinary enshrining of the credo of John D. Rockefeller) are part of a continuous history of celebrating supposedly sacrosanct class power that brings us in more recent times to the Trump Tower or the postmodernist monumentalism of Philip Johnson's AT & T building (see plates 1.11, 1.12, 1.13). It is completely wrong, I think, to lay all the blame for the urban ills of postwar development at the modern movement's door, without regard to the political–economic tune to which postwar urbanization was dancing. The postwar surge in modernist sentiment was, however, widespread, and could be so at least in part because of the considerable variety of on-the-ground neo-modernist constructs to which the postwar reconstruction gave rise.

It is useful here, I think, to go back and look at Jane Jacobs's attack upon all of this in *The death and life of great American cities*, published in 1961, not only because it was one of the earliest, most articulate, and most influential of the anti-modernist tracts, but because it sought to define a whole mode of approach to understanding urban life. While the 'pointmen' of her wrath were Ebenezer Howard and Le Corbusier, she in fact aimed her barbs at a whole range of targets from city planners, federal policy makers, and financiers, to the editors of Sunday supplements and women's magazines. Surveying the urban scene as it had been reconstituted since 1945, she saw:

> Low income projects that become worse centers of delinquency, vandalism and general social hopelessness than the slums they were supposed to replace. Middle income housing projects which are truly marvels of dullness and regimentation, sealed against any buoyancy or vitality of city life. Luxury housing projects that mitigate their inanity, or try to, with vapid vulgarity. Cultural centers that are unable to support a good bookstore. Civic centers that are avoided by everyone but bums, who have fewer choices of loitering place than others. Commercial centers that are lackluster imitations of standardized suburban chain-store shopping. Promenades that go from no place to nowhere and have no promenaders. Expressways that eviscerate great

Plate 1.11 The modernist monumentalism of the Rockefeller Center

cities. This is not the rebuilding of cities. This is the sacking of cities.

This 'Great Blight of Dullness' (see plate 1.14) arose in her judgement, from a profound misunderstanding of what cities are about. 'Processes are of the essence,' she argued, and it is upon the social processes of interaction that we should focus. And when we look at these on the ground, in 'healthy' city environments, we find an

Plate 1.12 Trump Tower: one of the most recent architectural celebrations of personal power to grace the skyline of New York City

intricate system of *organized* rather than disorganized complexity, a vitality and energy of social interaction that depend crucially upon diversity, intricacy, and the capacity to handle the unexpected in controlled but creative ways. 'Once one thinks about city processes, it follows that one must think of catalysts of these processes, and this too is of the essence.' There were, she noted, some market processes at work which tended to counter a 'natural' human affinity for

Plate 1.13 The modernism of Trump Tower (left) battles the postmodernism of Phillip Johnson's AT&T building (right) for position on the New York skyline.

diversity and produce a stifling conformity of land uses. But that problem was seriously compounded by the way planners declared themselves enemies of diversity, fearing chaos and complexity because they saw it as disorganized, ugly, and hopelessly irrational. 'It is curious,' she complained, 'that city planning neither respects spontaneous self-diversification among city populations nor contrives to

Plate 1.14 The 'Great Blight of Dullness' of which Jane Jacobs complained is well represented in this typical example of public housing in Baltimore.

provide for it. It is curious that city designers seem neither to recognize this force of self-diversification nor to be attracted by the esthetic problems of expressing it.'

On the surface, at least, it would seem that postmodernism is precisely about finding ways to express such an aesthetics of diversity. But it is important to consider how it does so. In that way we can uncover the deep limitations (which the more reflective postmodernists recognize) as well as the superficial advantages of many postmodernist efforts.

Jencks (1984), for example, argues that postmodern architecture has its roots in two significant technological shifts. First, contemporary communications have collapsed the 'usual space and time boundaries' and produced both a new internationalism and strong internal differentiations within cities and societies based on place, function, and social interest. This 'produced fragmentation' exists in a context of transport and communications technologies that have the capacity to handle social interaction across space in a highly differentiated manner. Architecture and urban design have therefore been presented with new and more wide-ranging opportunities to diversify spatial form than was the case in the immediate postwar period. Dispersed, decentralized, and deconcentrated urban forms are now much more technologically feasible than they once were. Second, new technologies (particularly computer modelling) have dissolved the need to conjoin mass production with mass repetition, and permitted the flexible mass production of 'almost personalized products' expressive of a great variety of styles. 'The results are closer to nineteenth century handicraft than to the regimented super-blocks of 1984.' By the same token a whole new range of building materials, some of which permit of almost exact imitation of much older styles (from oak beams to weathered brick) can now be procured quite cheaply. To give the new technologies prominence in this way is not to interpret the postmodern movement as technologically determined. But Jencks does suggest that the context in which architects and urban planners now operate has altered in ways that liberate them from some of the more powerful constraints that existed in the immediate postwar period.

The postmodern architect and urban designer can, as a consequence, more easily accept the challenge to communicate with different client groups in personalized ways, while tailoring products to different situations, functions, and 'taste cultures.' They are, says Jencks, very concerned with 'signs of status, history, commerce, comfort, ethnic domain, signs of being neighbourly' and willing to cater to all and every taste, such as those of Las Vegas or Levittown — tastes that the modernists tended to dismiss as common and banal. In principle, therefore, postmodern architecture is anti-avant-gardist (unwilling to impose solutions, as the high modernists, the bureaucratic planners, and the authoritarian developers tended — and still tend — to do).

It is by no means clear, however, that a simple turn to populism is sufficient to answer Jane Jacobs's complaints. Rowe and Koetter in their *Collage city* (the very title of which indicates sympathy with the postmodernist thrust) worry that 'the architectural proponents of populism are all for democracy and all for freedom: but they are characteristically unwilling to speculate as to the necessary conflicts of democracy with law, of the necessary collisions of freedom with justice.' By surrendering to an abstract entity called 'the people,' the populists cannot recognize how manifold the people happens to be, and consequently 'how much in need of protection from each other its components happen to stand.' The problems of minorities and the underprivileged, or of the diverse counter-cultural elements that so intrigued Jane Jacobs, get swept under the rug unless some very democratic and egalitarian system of community-based planning can be devised that meets the needs of rich and poor alike. This pre-supposes, however, a series of well-knit and cohesive urban com-munities as its starting point in an urban world that is always in flux and transition.

This problem is compounded by the degree to which the different 'taste cultures' and communities express their desires through dif-ferentiated political influence and market power. Jencks concedes, for example, that postmodernism in architecture and urban design tends to be shamelessly market-oriented because that is the primary language of communication in our society. Although market inte-gration plainly carries with it the danger of pandering to the rich and the private consumer rather than to the poor and to public needs, that is in the end, Jencks holds, a situation the architect is powerless to change.

Such a cavalier response to lop-sided market power scarcely favours an outcome that meets Jacobs's objections. To begin with, it is just as likely to replace the planner's zoning with a market-produced zoning of ability to pay, an allocation of land to uses based on the principles of land rent rather than the kind of principles of urban design that someone like Krier plainly has in mind. In the short run, a transition from planned to market mechanisms may temporarily mix up uses into interesting configurations, but the speed of gentri-fication and the monotony of the result (see plate 1.15) suggests that in many instances the short run is very short indeed. Market and land-rent allocation of this kind have already re-shaped many urban landscapes into new patterns of conformity. Free-market populism, for example, puts the middle classes into the enclosed and protected spaces of shopping malls (plate 1.16) and atria (plate 1.17), but it does nothing for the poor except to eject them into a new and quite nightmarish postmodern landscape of homelessness (see plate 1.18).

The pursuit of the consumption dollars of the rich has led, how-ever, to much greater emphasis upon product differentiation in urban design. By exploring the realms of differentiated tastes and aesthetic preferences (and doing whatever they could to stimulate those tasks), architects and urban designers have re-emphasized a powerful aspect of capital accumulation: the production and consumption of what Bourdieu (1977; 1984) calls 'symbolic capital.' The latter can be defined as 'the collection of luxury goods attesting the taste and distinction of the owner.' Such capital is, of course, transformed money capital which 'produces its proper effect inasmuch, and only inasmuch, as it conceals the fact that it originates in "material" forms of capital.' The fetishism (direct concern with surface appearances that conceal underlying meanings) is obvious, but it is here deployed

Plate 1.15 The signs of rehabilitation and gentrification often assume almost exactly the same serial monotony as the modernism they were supposed to replace: rehabilitation in Baltimore is everywhere signalled by the standard coach lamp hanging outside the house.

deliberately to conceal, through the realms of culture and taste, the real basis of economic distinctions. Since 'the most successful ideological effects are those which have no words, and ask no more than complicitous silence,' the production of symbolic capital serves ideological functions because the mechanisms through which it contributes

Plate 1.16 Baltimore's Gallery at Harbor Place is typical of the innumerable interior shopping malls that have been constructed since around 1970.

'to the reproduction of the established order and the perpetuation of domination remain hidden.'

It is instructive to put Krier's search for symbolic richness in the context of Bourdieu's theses. The search to communicate social distinctions through the acquisition of all manner of symbols of status has long been a central facet of urban life. Simmel produced some brilliant analyses of this phenomenon at the turn of the century, and a whole series of researchers (such as Firey in 1945 and Jager in

Plate 1.17 This atrium in the IBM building on Madison Avenue, New York, attempts a garden atmosphere within a secure space sealed off from a dangerous, heavily built-up and polluted city outside.

1986) have returned again and again to consideration of it. But I think it is fair to say that the modernist push, partly for practical, technical, and economic, but also for ideological reasons, did go out of its way to repress the significance of symbolic capital in urban life. The inconsistency of such a forced democratization and egalitarianism of taste with the social distinctions typical of what, after all, remained a class-bound capitalist society, undoubtedly created a climate of repressed demand if not repressed desire (some of which was expressed in the cultural movements of the 1960s). This repressed desire pro-

Plate 1.18 Homelessness in Los Angeles creates an entirely new form of unwanted and proscribed popular architecture.

bably did play an important role in stimulating the market for more diversified urban environments and architectural styles. This is the desire, of course, that many postmodernists seek to satisfy, if not titillate shamelessly. 'For the middle class suburbanite,' Venturi et al. observe, 'living not in an antebellum mansion, but in a smaller version lost in a large space, identity must come through symbolic treatment of the form of the house, either by styling provided by the developer (for instance, split-level Colonial) or through a variety of symbolic ornaments applied thereafter by the owner.'

The trouble here is that taste is a far from static category. Symbolic capital remains capital only to the degree that the whims of fashion sustain it. Struggles exist among the taste makers, as Zukin shows in an excellent work on *Loft living*, which examines the roles of 'capital and culture in urban change' by way of a study of the evolution of a real-estate market in the Soho district of New York. Powerful forces, she shows, established new criteria of taste in art as well as in urban living, and profited well off both. Conjoining the idea of symbolic capital with the search to market Krier's symbolic richness has much to tell us, therefore, about such urban phenomena as gentrification, the production of community (real, imagined, or simply packaged for sale by producers), the rehabilitation of urban landscapes, and the recuperation of history (again, real, imagined, or simply reproduced as pastiche). It also helps us to comprehend the present fascination with embellishment, ornamentation, and decoration as so many codes and symbols of social distinction. I am not at all sure that this is what Jane Jacobs had in mind when she launched her criticism of modernist urban planning.

Paying attention to the needs of the 'heterogeneity of urban villagers and taste cultures,' however, takes architecture away from the ideal of some unified meta-language and breaks it down into highly differentiated discourses. 'The *"langue"* (total set of communicational sources) is so heterogeneous and diverse that any singular *"parole"* (individual selection) will reflect this.' Although he does not use the phrase, Jencks could easily have said that the language of architecture dissolves into highly specialized language games, each appropriate in its own way to a quite different interpretative community.

The result is fragmentation, often consciously embraced. The Office for Metropolitan Architecture group is described in the *Postmodern visions* catalogue (Klotz, 1985), for example, as understanding 'the perceptions and experiences of the present as symbolic and associative, a fragmentary collage, with the Big City providing the ultimate metaphor.' The group produces graphic and architectural work 'characterized by the collage of fragments of reality and splinters of experience enriched by historical references.' The metropolis is conceived of as 'a system of anarchic and archaic signs and symbols that is constantly and independently self-renewing.' Other architects strive to cultivate the labyrinthine qualities of urban environments by interweaving interiors and exteriors (as in the ground plan of the new skyscrapers between Fifth and Sixth Avenues in Mid-Town Manhattan or the AT & T and IBM complex on Madison Avenue − see plate 1.17), or simply through the creation of an interior sense of inescapable complexity, an interior maze like that of the museum in the re-shaped Gare d'Orsay in Paris, the new Lloyds Building in London, or the Bonaventure Hotel in Los Angeles, the confusions of which have been dissected by Jameson (1984b). Postmodern built environments typically seek out and deliberately replicate themes that Raban so strongly emphasized in *Soft city*: an emporium of styles, an encyclopaedia, a 'maniacal scrap-book filled with colourful entries.'

The multivalency of architecture which results, in turn generates a tension that renders it 'radically schizophrenic by necessity.' It is interesting to see how Jencks, the chief chronicler of the post-modern movement in architecture, invokes the schizophrenia that many others identify as a general characteristic of the postmodern mind-set. Architecture, he argues, must embody a double coding, 'a popular traditional one which like spoken language is slow-changing, full of clichés and rooted in family life,' and a modern one rooted in a 'fast-changing society, with its new functional tasks, new materials, new technologies and ideologies' as well as quick-changing art and fashion. We here encounter Baudelaire's formulation but in a new historicist guise. Postmodernism abandons the modernist search for inner meaning in the midst of present turmoil, and asserts a broader base for the eternal in a constructed vision of historical continuity and collective memory. Again, it is important to see exactly how this is done.

Krier, as we have seen, seeks to recuperate classical urban values directly. The Italian architect Aldo Rossi puts a different argument:

> Destruction and demolition, expropriation and rapid changes in use as a result of speculation and obsolescense, are the most recognizable signs of urban dynamics. But beyond all else, the images suggest the interrupted destiny of the individual, of his often sad and difficult participation in the destiny of the collective. This vision in its entirety seems to be reflected with a quality of permanence in urban monuments. Monuments, signs of the collective will as expressed through the principles of architecture, offer themselves as primary elements, fixed points in the urban dynamic. (Rossi, 1982, 22)

Plate 1.19 Quinlan Terry's Richmond Riverside Panorama in London illustrates a postmodern tendency to revive past urban forms – in this case eighteenth century classicism. Such replications, without a hint of irony or parody, create simulacra which are hard to distinguish from well-restored versions of the original.

Here we encounter the tragedy of modernity once more, but this time stabilized by the fixed points of monuments that incorporate and preserve a 'mysterious' sense of collective memory. The preservation of myth through ritual 'constitutes a key to understanding the meaning of monuments and, moreover, the implications of the founding of cities and of the transmission of ideas in an urban context.' The task of the architect, in Rossi's view, is to participate 'freely' in the production of 'monuments' expressive of collective memory, while also recognizing that what constitutes a monument is itself a mystery which is 'above all to be found in the secret and ceaseless will of its collective manifestations.' Rossi grounds his understanding of that in the concept of *'genre de vie'* – that relatively permanent way of life that ordinary people construct for themselves under certain ecological, technological, and social conditions. This concept, drawn from the work of the French geographer Vidal de la Blache, provides Rossi with a sense of what collective memory represents. The fact that Vidal found the concept of *genre de vie* appropriate to interpret relatively slow-changing peasant societies, but began, towards the end of his life, to doubt its applicability to the rapidly changing landscapes of capitalist industrialization (see his *Geographie de l'est* published in 1916), escapes Rossi's attention. The problem, under conditions of rapidly unfolding industrial change, is to prevent his theoretical posture lapsing into the aesthetic production of myth through architecture, and thereby falling into the very trap that 'heroic' modernism encountered in the 1930s. Not surprisingly, Rossi's architecture has been heavily criticized. Umberto Eco describes it as 'frightening', while others point to what they see as its fascist overtones (plate 1.20).

Rossi at least has the virtue of taking the problem of historical reference seriously. Other postmodernists simply make gestures towards historical legitimacy by extensive and often eclectic quotation of past styles. Through films, television, books, and the like, history and past experience are turned into a seemingly vast archive 'instantly retrievable and capable of being consumed over and over again at the push of a button.' If, as Taylor (1987, 105) puts it, history can be seen 'as an endless reserve of equal events,' then architects and urban designers can feel free to quote them in any kind of order they wish. The postmodern penchant for jumbling together all manner of references to past styles is one of its more pervasive characteristics. Reality, it seems, is being shaped to mimic media images.

But the outcome of inserting such a practice into the contemporary socio-economic and political context is more than a little quirky. Since around 1972, for example, what Hewison (1987) calls 'the

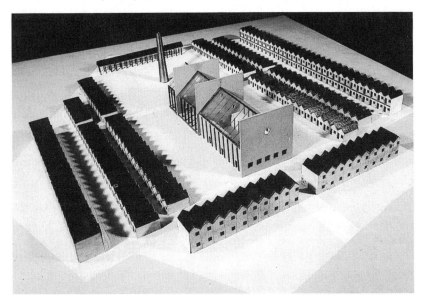

Plate 1.20 Aldo Rossi's design for student accommodation in Chieti yields a very different sort of impression within the eclecticism of postmodern architecture.

heritage industry' has suddenly become big business in Britain. Museums, country houses, reconstructed and rehabilitated urban landscapes that echo past forms, directly produced copies of past urban infrastructures, have become part and parcel of a vast transformation of the British landscape to the point where, in Hewison's judgement, Britain is rapidly turning from the manufacture of goods to the manufacturing of heritage as its principal industry. Hewison explains the impulse behind it all in terms a bit reminiscent of Rossi:

> The impulse to preserve the past is part of the impulse to preserve the self. Without knowing where we have been, it is difficult to know where we are going. The past is the foundation of individual and collective identity, objects from the past are the source of significance as cultural symbols. Continuity between past and present creates a sense of sequence out of aleatory chaos and, since change is inevitable, a stable system of ordered meaning enables us to cope with both innovation and decay. The nostalgic impulse is an important agency in adjustment to crisis, it is a social emollient and reinforces national identity when confidence is weakened or threatened.

Hewison is, I think, here revealing something of great potential importance because it is indeed the case that the preoccupation with identity, with personal and collective roots, has become far more pervasive since the early 1970s because of widespread insecurity in labour markets, in technological mixes, credit systems, and the like (see Part II). The television series *Roots*, which traced the history of a black American family from African origins to the present day, sparked a wave of family history research and interest thoughout the whole Western world.

It has, unfortunately, proved impossible to separate postmodernism's penchant for historical quotation and populism from the simple task of catering, if not pandering, to nostalgic impulses. Hewison sees a relation between the heritage industry and postmodernism. 'Both conspire to create a shallow screen that intervenes between our present lives, our history. We have no understanding of history in depth, but instead are offered a contemporary creation, more costume drama and re-enactment than critical discourse.'

The same judgement may be made of the way postmodernist architecture and design quotes the vast range of information and images of urban and architectural forms to be found in different parts of the world. We all of us, says Jencks, carry around with us a *musée imaginaire* in our minds, drawn from experience (often touristic) of other places, and knowledge culled from films, television, exhibitions, travel brochures, popular magazines, etc. It is inevitable, he says, that all of these get run together. And it is both exciting and healthy that this should be so. 'Why, if one can afford to live in different ages and cultures, restrict oneself to the present, the locale? Eclecticism is the natural evolution of a culture with choice.' Lyotard echoes that sentiment exactly. 'Eclecticism is the degree zero of contemporary general culture: one listens to reggae, watches a western, eats McDonald's food for lunch and local cuisine for dinner, wears Paris perfume in Tokyo and 'retro' clothes in Hong Kong.'

The geography of differentiated tastes and cultures is turned into a pot-pourri of internationalism that is in many respects more startling, perhaps because more jumbled, than high internationalism ever was. When accompanied by strong migration streams (not only of labour but also of capital) this produces a plethora of 'Little' Italies, Havanas, Tokyos, Koreas, Kingstons, and Karachis as well as Chinatowns, Latino *barrios*, Arab quarters, Turkish zones, and the like. Yet the effect, even in a city like San Francisco where minorities collectively make up the majority, is to draw a veil over real geography through construction of images and reconstructions, costume dramas, staged ethnic festivals, etc.

The masking arises not only out of the postmodernist penchant for eclectic quotation, but also out of an evident fascination with surfaces. Jameson (1984b), for example, regards the reflecting glass surfaces of the Bonaventure Hotel as serving to 'repel the city outside' much as reflector sunglasses prevent the seer being seen, thus permitting the hotel 'a peculiar and placeless dissociation' from its neighbourhood. The contrived columns, ornamentation, extensive quotations from different styles (in time and space) give much of postmodern architecture that sense of 'contrived depthlessness' of which Jameson complains. But the masking nevertheless confines conflict between, for example, the historicism of being rooted in place and the internationalism of style drawn from the *musée imaginaire*, between function and fantasy, between the producer's aim to signify and the consumer's willingness to take the message.

Behind all this eclecticism (particularly of historical and geographical quotation) it is hard to spot any particular purposeful design. Yet there do seem to be effects which are themselves so purposeful and widespread that in restrospect it is hard not to attribute a simple set of orchestrating principles. Let me illustrate with one example.

'Bread and circuses' is an ancient and well-tried formula for social control. It has frequently been consciously deployed to pacify restless or discontented elements in a population. But spectacle can also be an essential aspect of revolutionary movement (see, for example, Ozouf's, 1988, study of festivals as a means to express revolutionary will in the French Revolution). Did not even Lenin, after all, refer to revolution as 'the festival of the people'? The spectacle has always been a potent political weapon. How has urban spectacle been deployed these last few years?

In US cities, urban spectacle in the 1960s was constituted out of the mass oppositional movements of the time. Civil rights demonstrations, street riots, and inner city uprisings, vast anti-war demonstrations, and counter-cultural events (rock concerts in particular) were grist for the seething mill of urban discontent that whirled around the base of modernist urban renewal and housing projects. But since around 1972, the spectacle has been captured by quite different forces, and been put to quite different uses. The evolution of urban spectacle in a city like Baltimore is both typical and instructive.

In the wake of the riots that erupted after the assassination of Martin Luther King in 1968 (plate 1.21), a small group of influential politicians, professionals, and business leaders got together to see if there was some way to bring the city together. The urban renewal

Plate 1.21 Riots, burnings, and looting were an all-too-frequent urban spectacle in the inner cities of the United States in the 1960s. Baltimore in April 1968, after the assassination of Martin Luther King, was one of many examples.

effort of the 1960s had created a highly functional and strongly modernist downtown of offices, plazas and occasionally spectacular architecture such as the Mies van der Rohe building of One Charles Center (plates 1.22 and 1.23). But the riots threatened the vitality of downtown and the viability of investments already made. The leaders sought a symbol around which to build the idea of the city as a community, a city which could believe in itself sufficiently to over-come the divisions and the siege mentality with which the common citizenry approached downtown and its public spaces. 'Spawned by the necessity to arrest the fear and disuse of downtown areas caused by the civic unrest in the late 1960s,' said a later Department of Housing and Urban Development report, 'the Baltimore City Fair was orig-inated . . . as way to promote urban redevelopment.' The fair set out to celebrate the neighbourhood and ethnic diversity in the city, even went out of its way to promote ethnic (as opposed to racial) identity. There were 340,000 visitors to the fair in the first year (1970), but by 1973 that number had swelled to nearly two million. Bigger, but step

Plate 1.22 Baltimore urban renewal of the 1960s in the modernist style: the Federal Building in Hopkins Plaza

by step inexorably less 'neighbourly' and more commercial (even the ethnic groups began to profit from the sale of ethnicity), the fair became the lead item in drawing larger and larger crowds to the downtown area on a regular basis, to see all manner of staged spectacles. It was a short step from that to an institutionalized commercialization of a more or less permanent spectacle in the construction of Harbor Place (a waterfront development reputed now to draw in more people than Disneyland), a Science Center, an Aquarium, a Convention Center, a marina, innumerable hotels, pleasure citadels of all kinds. Judged by many as an outstanding success (though the impact upon city poverty, homelessness, health care, education provision, has been negligible and perhaps even nega-tive), such a form of development required a wholly different archi-tecture from the austere modernism of the downtown renewal that

Plate 1.23 Baltimore urban renewal modernism: the Mies van der Rohe building of One Charles Centre

had dominated in the 1960s. An architecture of spectacle, with its sense of surface glitter and transitory participatory pleasure, of display and ephemerality, of *jouissance*, became essential to the success of a project of this sort (plates 1.24, 1.25, 1.26).

Baltimore was not alone in the construction of such new urban spaces. Boston's Faneuil Hall, San Francisco's Fisherman's Wharf (with Ghirardelli Square), New York's South Street Seaport, San Antonio's Riverwalk, London's Covent Garden (soon to be followed by Docklands), Gateshead's Metrocentre, to say nothing of the fabled West Edmonton Mall, are just the fixed aspects of organized spectacles that include more transitory events such as the Los Angeles Olympic Games, the Liverpool Garden Festival, and the re-staging of almost every imaginable historical event (from the Battle of Hastings to that of Yorktown). Cities and places now, it seems, take

Plate 1.24 Baltimore goes to the City Fair: a collage of scenes of a managed and controlled urban spectacle (by Apple Pie Graphics)

much more care to create a positive and high quality image of place, and have sought an architecture and forms of urban design that respond to such need. That they should be so pressed, and that the result should be a serial repetition of successful models (such as Baltimore's Harbor Place), is understandable, given the grim history of deindustrialization and restructuring that left most major cities in the advanced capitalist world with few options except to compete with each other, mainly as financial, consumption, and entertainment centres. Imaging a city through the organization of spectacular urban spaces became a means to attract capital and people (of the right sort) in a period (since 1973) of intensified inter-urban competition and urban entrepreneurialism (see Harvey, 1989).

While we shall return to a closer examination of this phenomenon in Part III, it is important here to note how architecture and urban design have responded to these new-felt urban needs. The projection

Plate 1.25 Harbor Place attempts a postmodernist atmosphere of leisure sprawled around modernist scenes of urban renewal.

of a definite image of place blessed with certain qualities, the organization of spectacle and theatricality, have been achieved through an eclectic mix of styles, historical quotation, ornamentation, and the diversification of surfaces (in Baltimore, Scarlett Place exemplifies the idea in somewhat bizarre form, see plate 1.27). All of these tendencies are exhibited in Moore's Piazza d'Italia in New Orleans. We here see the combination of many of the elements that have been so far described within one singular and quite spectacular project (plate 1.28). The description in the *Post-modern visions* catalogue (Klotz, 1985) is most revealing:

> In an area of New Orleans requiring redevelopment Charles Moore has created the public Piazza d'Italia for the local Italian population. Its form and architectonic language have brought the social and communicative functions of a European and,

Plate 1.26 The pavilions of Harbor Place are reputed to bring as many visitors to Baltimore as to Disneyland.

more specifically, Italian piazza to the southern United States.

Within the context of a new block of buildings covering a substantial area and featuring relatively regular, smooth, and angular windows, Moore has inserted a large circular piazza that represents a kind of negative form and is therefore all the more surprising when one enters through the barrier of the surrounding architecture. A small temple stands at the entrance and heralds the historical formal language of the piazza, which is framed by fragmented colonnades. At the center of the arrangement is a fountain basin, the 'Mediterranean' bathing the boot of Italy, which extends down from the 'Alps.' The placement of Sicily at the center of the piazza pays tribute to the fact that the Italian population of the area is dominated by immigrants from that island.

The arcades, placed in front of the convex facades of the building around the piazza, make ironic reference to the five orders of classical column (Doric, Ionic, Corinthian, Tuscan, and Composite) by placing them in a subtly colored continuum, indebted somewhat to Pop Art. The bases of the fluted columns are formed like pieces of a fragmented architrave, more a nega-

Plate 1.27 Scarlett Place of Baltimore brings together historical preservation (the nineteenth-century Scarlett Seed Warehouse is incorporated into the far left-hand corner) and the postmodernist urge for quotation, in this case from a Mediterranean hilltop village (note the modernist public housing in the background).

tive form than a fully three-dimensional architectural detail. Their elevation is faced in marble, and their cross section is like a slice of cake. The columns are separated from their Corinthian capitals by rings of neon tubing, which give them colorful luminous necklaces at night. The arched arcade at the top of the Italian boot also has neon lights on its facade. Other capitals take on a precise, angular form and are placed like Art Deco brooches beneath the architrave, while other columns present further variations, their fluting created by jets of water.

All of this brings the dignified vocabulary of classical architecture up to date with Pop Art techniques, a post-modernist palette, and theatricality. It conceives of history as a continuum of portable accessories, reflecting the way the Italians themselves have been 'transplanted' to the New World. It presents a nostalgic picture of Italy's renaissance and baroque palaces and its piazzas, but at the same time there is a sense of dislocation. After all, this is not realism, but a façade, a stage set, a fragment inserted into a new and modern context. The Piazza d'Italia is a

Plate 1.28 Charles Moore's Piazza d'Italia in New Orleans is frequently cited as one of the classic pieces of postmodernist architecture.

piece of architecture as well as a piece of theater. In the tradition of the Italian 'res publica,' it is a place for the public to gather; yet at the same time, it does not take itself too seriously, and it can be a place for games and amusement. The alienated features of the Italian homeland act as ambassadors in the New World, thus reaffirming the neighborhood population's identity in a district of New Orleans that threatens to become a slum. This piazza must count as one of the most important and striking examples of post-modernist building in the world. It has been the mistake of many publications to show the piazza in isolation; however, the model here shows the successful integration of this theatrical event into its context of modern buildings.

But if architecture is a form of communication, the city a discourse, then what can such a structure, inserted into the urban fabric of New Orleans, possibly say or mean? The postmodernists themselves will probably answer that it depends at least as much, if not more, on what is in the eye of the beholder, as it does on the thoughts of the producer. Yet there is a certain facile naivety in such an answer. For there is much too much coherence between the imagery of city life laid out in books such as Raban's *Soft city* and the system of architectural production and urban design here described for there to be nothing in particular beneath the surface glitter. The example of spectacle suggests certain dimensions of social meaning, and Moore's Piazza d'Italia is hardly innocent in what it sets out to say and how it says it. We there see the penchant for fragmentation, the eclecticism of styles, the peculiar treatments of space and time ('history as a continuum of portable accessories'). There is alienation understood (shallowly) in terms of emigration and slum formation, that the architect tries to recuperate through construction of a place where identity might be reclaimed even in the midst of commercialism, pop art, and all the accoutrements of modern life. The theatricality of effect, the striving for *jouissance* and schizophrenic effect (in Jencks's sense) are all consciously present. Above all, postmodern architecture and urban design of this sort convey a sense of some search for a fantasy world, the illusory 'high' that takes us beyond current realities into pure imagination. The matter of postmodernism, the catalogue to the *Post-modern visions* exhibition (Klotz, 1985) forthrightly declares, is 'not just function but fiction.'

Charles Moore represents only one strain of practice within the eclectic umbrella of postmodernism. The Piazza d'Italia would hardly earn the approval of Leon Krier, whose instincts for classical revival are so strong as sometimes to put him outside the postmodernist appellation altogether, and it looks very odd when juxtaposed with an Aldo Rossi design. Furthermore, the eclecticism and pop imagery that lie at the heart of the line of thinking that Moore represents have come in for strong criticism, precisely because of their lack of theoretical rigour and their populist conceptions. The strongest line of argument now comes from what is called 'deconstructivism.' In part of a reaction against the way that much of the postmodern movement had entered into the mainstream and generated a popularized architecture that is lush and indulgent, deconstructivism seeks to regain the high ground of elite and avant-garde architectural practice by active deconstruction of the modernism of the Russian constructivists of the 1930s. The movement in part acquires its interest because of its deliberate attempt to fuse the deconstructionist thinking from literary theory with postmodernist architectural practices that often seem to have developed according to a logic all their own. It shares with modernism a concern to explore pure form and space, but does so in such a way as to conceive of a building not as a unified whole but as 'disparate "texts" and parts that remain distinct and unaligned, without achieving a sense of unity,' and which are, therefore, susceptible to 'several asymmetrical and irreconcilable' readings. What deconstructivism has in common with much of post-modernism, however, is its attempt to mirror 'an unruly world subject to carooming moral, political and economic system.' But it does so in such a way as to be 'disorienting, even confusing' and so break down 'our habitual ways of perceiving form and space.' Frag-mentation, chaos, disorder, even within seeming order, remain central themes (Goldberger, 1988; Giovannini, 1988).

Fiction, fragmentation, collage, and eclecticism, all suffused with a sense of ephemerality and chaos, are, perhaps, the themes that do-minate in today's practices of architecture and urban design. And there is, evidently, much in common here with practices and thinking in many other realms such as art, literature, social theory, psy-chology, and philosophy. How is it, then, that the prevailing mood takes the form it does? To answer that question with any power requires that we first take stock of the mundane realities of capitalist modernity and postmodernity, and see what clues might lie there as to the possible functions of such fictions and fragmentations in the reproduction of social life.

5

Modernization

Modernism is a troubled and fluctuating aesthetic response to conditions of modernity produced by a particular process of modernization. A proper interpretation of the rise of postmodernism, therefore, ought to grapple with the nature of modernization. Only in that way will we be able to judge whether postmodernism is a different reaction to an unchanging modernization process, or whether it reflects or presages a radical shift in the nature of modernization itself, towards, for example, some kind of 'postindustrial' or even 'postcapitalist' society.

Marx provides one of the earliest and most complete accounts of capitalist modernization. I think it useful to begin with that not only because Marx was, as Berman argues, one of the great early modernist writers, combining all the breadth and vigour of Enlightenment thought with a nuanced sense of the paradoxes and contradictions to which capitalism is prone, but also because the theory of capitalist modernization that he offers makes for particularly compelling reading when set against the cultural theses of postmodernity.

In *The communist manifesto* Marx and Engels argue that the bourgeoisie has created a new internationalism via the world market, together with 'subjection of nature's forces to man, machinery, application of chemistry to agriculture and industry, steam navigation, railways, electric telegraphs, clearing of whole continents for cultivation, canalization of rivers, whole populations conjured out of the ground.' It has done this at great cost: violence, destruction of traditions, oppression, reduction of the valuation of all activity to the cold calculus of money and profit. Furthermore:

Constant revolutionizing of production, uninterrupted disturbance of all social relations, everlasting uncertainty and agitation, distinguish the bourgeois epoch from all earlier times. All fixed, fast-frozen relationships, with their train of venerable ideas and opinions, are swept away, all new-formed ones become obsolete before they can ossify. All that is solid melts into air, all that is holy is profaned, and men at last are forced to face with sober sense the real conditions of their lives and their relations with their fellow men. (Marx and Engels, 1952, 25)

The sentiments certainly match those of Baudelaire and, as Berman points out, Marx here unlooses a rhetoric that defines the underside of all modernist aesthetics. But what is special about Marx is the way he dissects the origin of this general condition.

Marx begins *Capital,* for example, with an analysis of commodities, those everyday things (food, shelter, clothing, etc.) which we daily consume in the course of reproducing ourselves. Yet the commodity is, he avers, 'a mysterious thing' because it simultaneously embodies both a use value (it fulfils a particular want or need) and an exchange value (I can use it as a bargaining chip to procure other commodities). This duality always renders the commodity ambiguous for us; shall we consume it or trade it away? But as exchange relations proliferate and price-fixing markets form, so one commodity typically crystallizes out as money. With money the mystery of the commodity takes on a new twist, because the use value of money is that it represents the world of social labour and of exchange value. Money lubricates exchange but above all it becomes the means by which we typically compare and assess, both before and after the fact of exchange, the value of all commodities. Plainly, since the way we put value on things is important, an analysis of the money form and the consequences that flow from its use are of paramount interest.

The advent of a money economy, Marx argues, dissolves the bonds and relations that make up 'traditional' communities so that 'money becomes the real community.' We move from a social condition, in which we depend directly on those we know personally, to one in which we depend on impersonal and objective relations with others. As exchange relations proliferate, so money appears more and more as 'a power external to and independent of the producers,' so what 'originally appears as a means to promote production becomes a relation alien' to them. Money concerns dominate producers. Money and market exchange draws a veil over, 'masks' social relationships between things. This condition Marx calls 'the fetishism of commodities.' It is one of Marx's most compelling insights, for it poses the problem of how to interpret the real but nevertheless superficial relationships that we can readily observe in the market place in appropriate social terms.

The conditions of labour and life, the sense of joy, anger, or frustration that lie behind the production of commodities, the states of mind of the producers, are all hidden to us as we exchange one object (money) for another (the commodity). We can take our daily breakfast without a thought for the myriad people who engaged in its production. All traces of exploitation are obliterated in the object (there are no finger marks of exploitation in the daily bread). We cannot tell from contemplation of any object in the supermarket what conditions of labour lay behind its production. The concept of fetishism explains how it is that under conditions of capitalist modernization we can be so objectively dependent on 'others' whose lives and aspirations remain so totally opaque to us. Marx's meta-theory seeks to tear away that fetishistic mask, and to understand the social relations that lie behind it. He would surely accuse those postmodernists who proclaim the 'impenetrability of the other' as their creed, of overt complicity with the fact of fetishism and of indifference towards underlying social meanings. The interest of Cindy Sherman's photographs (or any postmodern novel for that matter) is that they focus on masks without commenting directly on social meanings other than on the activity of masking itself.

But we can take the analysis of money deeper still. If money is to perform its functions effectively, Marx argues, it must be replaced by mere symbols of itself (coins, tokens, paper currency, credit), which lead it to be considered as a mere symbol, an 'arbitrary fiction' sanctioned by 'the universal consent of mankind.' Yet it is through these 'arbitrary fictions' that the whole world of social labour, of production and hard daily work, get represented. In the absence of social labour, all money would be worthless. But it is only through money that social labour can be represented at all.

The magical powers of money are compounded by the way owners 'lend their tongues' to commodities by hanging a price ticket on them, appealing to 'cabalistic signs' with names like pounds, dollars, francs. So even though money is the signifier of the value of social labour, the perpetual danger looms that the signifier will itself become the object of human greed and of human desire (the hoarder, the avaricious miser, etc.). This probability turns to certainty once we recognize that money, on the one hand a 'radical leveller' of all other forms of social distinction, is itself a form of social power that can be appropriated as 'the social power of private persons.' Modern society, Marx concludes, 'soon after its birth, pulled Plutus by the hair of his head from the bowels of the earth, greets gold as its Holy Grail, as the glittering incarnation of the very pinciple of its own life.' Does postmodernism signal a reinterpretation or reinforcement of the role of money as *the* proper object of desire? Baudrillard depicts post-modern culture as an 'excremental culture,' and money=excrement in both Baudrillard's and Freud's view (some hints of that sentiment can be found in Marx). Postmodern concerns for the signifier rather than the signified, the medium (money) rather than the message (social labour), the emphasis on fiction rather than function, on signs rather than things, on aesthetics rather than ethics, suggest a rein-forcement rather than a transformation of the role of money as Marx depicts it.

As commodity producers seeking money, however, we are depen-dent upon the needs and capacity of others to buy. Producers con-sequently have a permanent interest in cultivating 'excess and in-temperance' in others, in feeding 'imaginary appetites' to the point where ideas of what constitutes social need are replaced by 'fantasy, caprice, and whim.' The capitalist producer increasingly 'plays the pimp' between the consumers and their sense of need, excites in them 'morbid appetites, lies in wait for each of [their] weaknesses – all so that he can demand the cash for this service of love.' Pleasure, leisure, seduction, and erotic life are all brought within the range of money power and commodity production. Capitalism therefore 'produces sophistication of needs and of their means on the one hand, and a bestial barbarization, a complete, unrefined, and abstract simplicity of need, on the other' (Marx, 1964, 148). Advertising and commercialization destroy all traces of production in their imagery, reinforcing the fetishism that arises automatically in the course of market exchange.

Furthermore, money, as the supreme representation of social power in capitalist society, itself becomes the object of lust, greed, and desire. Yet here, too, we encounter double meanings. Money confers the privilege to exercise power over others – we can buy their labour time or the services they offer, even build systematic relations of domination over exploited classes simply through control over money power. Money, in fact, fuses the political and the econ-omic into a genuine political economy of overwhelming power re-lations (a problem that micro-theorists of power like Foucault system-atically avoid and which macro-social theorists like Giddens – with his strict division between allocative and authoritative sources of power – cannot grasp). The common material languages of money and commodities provide a universal basis within market capitalism for linking everyone into an identical system of market valuation and so procuring the reproduction of social life through an objectively grounded system of social bonding. Yet within these broad constraints, we are 'free,' as it were, to develop our own personalities and relationships in our own way, our own 'otherness,' even to forge group language games, provided, of course, that we have enough money to live on satisfactorily. Money is a 'great leveller and cynic,' a powerful underminer of fixed social relations, and a great 'democratizer'. As a social power that can be held by individual persons it forms the basis for a wide-ranging individual liberty, a liberty that can be deployed to develop ourselves as free-thinking individuals without reference to others. Money unifies precisely *through* its capacity to accommodate individualism, otherness, and extraordinary social fragmentation.

But by what process is the capacity for fragmentation latent in the money form transformed into a necessary feature of capitalist modernization?

Participation in market exchange presupposes a certain division of labour as well as a capacity to separate (alienate) oneself from one's own product. The result is an estrangement from the product of one's own experience, a fragmentation of social tasks and a separation of the subjective meaning of a process of production from the objective market valuation of the product. A highly organized technical and social division of labour, though by no means unique to capitalism, is one of the founding principles of capitalist modernization. This forms a powerful lever to promote economic growth and the accumulation of capital, particularly under conditions of market exchange in which individual commodity producers (protected by private property rights) can explore the possibilities of specialization within an open economic system. This explains the power of economic (free market) liberalism as a founding doctrine for capitalism. It is precisely in such a context that possessive individualism and creative entrepreneurialism, innovation, and speculation, can flourish, even though this also means a proliferating fragmentation of tasks and responsibilities, and a necessary transformation of social relations to the point where producers are forced to view others in purely instrumental terms.

But there is much more to capitalism than commodity production and market exchange. Certain historical conditions – in particular, the existence of wage labour – are required before profit-seeking – launching money into circulation in order to gain more money – can become *the* basic way for social life to be reproduced. Based on the violent separation of the mass of the direct producers from control over the means of production, the emergence of wage labour – persons who have to sell labour power in order to live – is the 'result of many revolutions, of the extinction of a whole series of older forms of production' (*Capital*, 1: 166–7). The sense of a radical, total, and violent rupture with the past — another of the basic elements of modernist sensibility — is omni-present in Marx's account of the origins of capitalism.

But Marx takes matters much further. The conversion of labour into wage labour means 'the separation of labour from its product, of subjective labour power from the objective conditions of labour' (*Capital*, 1: 3). This is a very different kind of market exchange. Capitalists when they purchase labour power necessarily treat it in instrumental terms. The labourer is viewed as a 'hand' rather than as a whole person (to use Dickens's satirical comment in *Hard Times*), and the labour contributed is a 'factor' (notice the reification) of production. The purchase of labour power with money gives the capitalist certain rights to dispose of the labour of others without necessary regard for what the others might think, need, or feel. The omni-presence of this class relation of domination, offset only to the degree that the labourers actively struggle to assert their rights and express their feelings, suggests one of the founding principles upon which the very idea of 'otherness' is produced and reproduced on a continuing basis in capitalist society. The world of the working class becomes the domain of that 'other,' which is necessarily rendered opaque and potentially unknowable by virtue of the fetishism of market exchange. And I should also add parenthetically that if there are already those in society (women, blacks, colonized peoples, minorities of all kinds) who can readily be conceptualized as the other, then the conflation of class exploitation with gender, race, colonialism, ethnicity, etc. can proceed apace with all manner of invidious results. Capitalism did not invent 'the other' but it certainly made use of and promoted it in highly structured ways.

Capitalists can deploy their rights strategically to impose all kinds of conditions upon the labourer. The latter is typically alienated from the product, from command over the process of producing it, as well as from the capacity to realize the value of the fruit of his or her efforts — the capitalist appropriates that as profit. The capitalist has the power (though by no means arbitrary or total) to mobilize the powers of co-operation, division of labour, and machinery as powers of capital over labour. The result is an organized detail division of labour within the factory, which reduces the labourer to a fragment of a person. 'The absurd fable of Menenius Agrippa, which makes man a mere fragment of his own body, becomes realized' (*Capital*, 1: 340). We here encounter the principle of the division of labour at work in a quite different guise. Whereas the division of labour in society 'brings into contact independent commodity producers, who acknowledge no other authority but that of competition, of the coercion exerted by the pressure of their mutual interests,' the 'division of labour within the workshop implies the undisputed authority of the capitalist over men, that are but parts of a mechanism that belongs to him.' Anarchy in the social division of labour is replaced by the despotism — enforced through hierarchies of authority and close supervision of tasks — of the workshop and the factory.

This enforced fragmentation, which is both social and technical within a single labour process, is further emphasized by the loss of control over the instruments of production. This turns the labourer effectively into an 'appendage' of the machine. Intelligence (knowledge, science, technique) is objectified in the machine, thus separating manual from mental labour and diminishing the application of intelligence on the part of the direct producers. In all of these respects, the individual labourer is 'made poor' in individual productive powers 'in order to make the collective labourer, and through him capital rich in social productive power' (*Capital*, 1: 341). This process does not stop with the direct producers, with the peasants pulled off the land, the women and children forced to give of their labour in the factories and mines. The bourgeoisie 'has pitilessly torn asunder the motley feudal ties that bound man to his "natural superiors," and has left remaining no other nexus between man and man than callous "cash payment." ... [It] has stripped of its halo every occupation hitherto honoured and looked up to with reverent awe. It has converted the physician, the lawyer, the priest, the poet, the man of science, into its paid wage labourers' (*The communist manifesto*, 45).

How is it, then, that the 'bourgeoisie cannot exist without constantly revolutionizing the instruments of production, and thereby the relations of production?' The answer Marx provides in *Capital* is both thorough and convincing. The 'coercive laws' of market competition force all capitalists to seek out technological and organizational changes that will enhance their own profitability *vis-à-vis* the social average, thus entraining all capitalists in leap-frogging processes of innovation that reach their limit only under conditions of massive labour surpluses. The need to keep the labourer under control in the workplace, and to undercut the bargaining power of the labourer in the market (particularly under conditions of relative labour scarcity and active class resistance), also stimulates capitalists to innovate. Capitalism is necessarily technologically dynamic, not because of the mythologized capacities of the innovative entrepreneur (as Schumpeter was later to argue) but because of the coercive laws of competition and the conditions of class struggle endemic to capitalism.

The effect of continuous innovation, however, is to devalue, if not destroy, past investments and labour skills. *Creative destruction* is embedded within the circulation of capital itself. Innovation exacerbates instability, insecurity, and in the end, becomes the prime force pushing capitalism into periodic paroxysms of crisis. Not only does the life of modern industry become a series of periods of moderate activity, prosperity, over-production, crisis, and stagnation, 'but the uncertainty and instability to which machinery subjects the employment, and consequently the conditions of existence, of the operatives become normal.' Furthermore:

> All means for the development of production transform themselves into means of domination over, and exploitation of, the producers; they mutilate the labourer into a fragment of a man, degrade him to the level of an appendage of a machine, destroy every remnant of charm in his work and turn it into a hated toil; they estrange from him the intellectual potentialities of the labour-process in the same proportion as science is incorporated in it as an independent power; they distort the conditions under which he works, subject him during the labour-process to a despotism the more hateful for its meanness; they transform his life-time into working-time, and drag his wife and child beneath the wheels of the Juggernaut of capital. (*Capital*, 1: 604)

The struggle to maintain profitability sends capitalists racing off to explore all kinds of other possibilities. New product lines are opened up, and that means the creation of new wants and needs. Capitalists are forced to redouble their efforts to create new needs in others, thus emphasizing the cultivation of imaginary appetites and the role of fantasy, caprice and whim. The result is to exacerbate insecurity and instability, as masses of capital and workers shift from one line of production to another, leaving whole sectors devastated, while the perpetual flux in consumer wants, tastes, and needs becomes a permanent locus of uncertainty and struggle. New spaces are necessarily opened up as capitalists seek new markets, new sources of raw materials, fresh labour power, and new and more profitable sites for production operations. The drive to relocate to more advantageous places (the geographical movement of both capital and labour) periodically revolutionizes the international and territorial division of labour, adding a vital geographical dimension to the insecurity. The resultant transformation in the experience of space and place is matched by revolutions in the time dimension, as capitalists strive to reduce the turnover time of their capital to 'the twinkling of an eye' (see below, Part III). Capitalism, in short, is a social system internalizing rules that ensure it will remain a permanently revolutionary and disruptive force in its own world history. If, therefore, 'the only secure thing about modernity is insecurity,' then it is not hard to see from where that insecurity derives.

Yet, Marx insists, there is a single unitary principle at work that underpins and frames all of this revolutionary upheaval, fragmentation, and perpetual insecurity. The principle resides in what he calls, most abstractly, 'value in motion' or, more simply, the circulation of capital restlessly and perpetually seeking new ways to garner profits. By the same token, there are higher-order co-ordinating systems that seem to have the power − though in the end Marx will insist that this power is itself transitory and illusory − to bring order to all this chaos and set the path of capitalist modernization on a more stable terrain. The credit system, for example, embodies a certain power to regulate money uses; money flows can be switched so as to stabilize relations between production and consumption, to arbitrate between current expenditures and future needs, and to shift surpluses of capital from one line of production or region to another on a rational basis. But here, too, we immediately encounter a central contradiction because credit creation and disbursement can never be separated from speculation. Credit is, according to Marx, always to be accounted for as 'fictitious capital,' as some kind of money bet on production that does not yet exist. The result is a permanent tension between what Marx calls 'the financial system' (credit paper, fictitious capital, financial instruments of all kinds) and its 'monetary base' (until recently attached to some tangible commodity such as gold or silver). This contradiction is founded on a particular paradox: money has to take some tangible form (gold, coin, notes, entries in a ledger, etc.) even though it is a general representation of all social labour. The question of which of the diverse tangible representations is 'real' money typically erupts at times of crisis. Is it better to hold stocks and share certificates, notes, gold, or cans of tuna, in the midst of a depression? It also follows that whoever controls the tangible form (the gold producers, the state, the banks who issue credit) that is most 'real' at a given time, has enormous social influence, even if, in the last instance, it is the producers and exchangers of commodities in aggregate who effectively define 'the value of money' (a paradoxical term which we all understand, but which technically signifies 'the value of value'). Control over the rules of money formation is, as a consequence, a strongly contested terrain of struggle which generates considerable insecurity and uncertainty as to the 'value of value.' In speculative booms, a financial system which starts out by appearing as a sane device for regulating the incoherent tendencies of capitalist production, ends up becoming 'the main lever for overproduction and over-speculation.' The fact that postmodernist architecture regards itself as being about *fiction* rather than *function* appears, in the light of the reputations of the financiers, property developers, and speculators that organize construction, more than a little apt.

The state, constituted as a coercive system of authority that has a monopoly over institutionalized violence, forms a second organizing principle through which a ruling class can seek to impose its will not only upon its opponents but upon the anarchical flux, change, and uncertainty to which capitalist modernity is always prone. The tools vary from regulation of money and legal guarantees of fair market contracts, through fiscal interventions, credit creation, and tax redistributions, to provision of social and physical infrastructures, direct control over capital and labour allocations as well as over wages and prices, the nationalization of key sectors, restrictions on working-class power, police surveillance, and military repression and the like. Yet the state is a territorial entity struggling to impose its will upon a fluid and spatially open process of capital circulation. It has to contest within its borders the factional forces and fragmenting effects of widespread individualism, rapid social change, and all the ephemerality that typically attaches to capital circulation. It also depends on taxation and credit markets, so that states can be disciplined by the circulation process at the same time as they can seek to promote particular strategies of capital accumulation.

To do so effectively the state must construct an alternative sense of community to that based on money, as well as a definition of public interests over and above the class and secretarian interests and struggles that are contained within its borders. It must, in short, legitimize itself. It is, therefore, bound to engage to some degree in the *aestheticization of politics*. This issue is addressed in Marx's classic study of *The eighteenth brumaire of Louis Bonaparte*. How is it, he there asks, that even at the height of revolutionary ferment, the revolutionaries themselves 'anxiously conjure up the spirits of the past to their service and borrow from them names, battle cries and costumes in order to present the new scene of world history in this time-honoured disguise and borrowed language'? The 'awakening of the dead in [bourgeois] revolutions served the purpose of glorifying the new struggles, not of parodying the old; of magnifying the given task in imagination, not fleeing from its solution in reality; of finding once more the spirit of revolution, not of making its ghost walk about again.' The invocation of myth may have played a key role in past revolutions, but here Marx strives to deny what Sorel was later to affirm. 'The social revolution of the nineteenth century cannot draw .its poetry from the past,' Marx argues, 'but only from the future.' It must strip off 'all superstition in regard to the past,' else 'the tradition of all the dead generations weighs like a nightmare on the brain of the living' and converts the cathartic tragedy of revolution into the ritual of farce. In pitting himself so mercilessly against the power of myth and the aestheticization of politics, Marx in effect affirms their remarkable powers to stifle progressive working-class revolutions. Bonapartism was, for Marx, a form of 'caesarism' (with all its classical allusions) that could, in the person of Louis Bonaparte assuming the mantle of his uncle, block the revolutionary aspirations of the progressive bourgeoisie and the working class alike. Thus did Marx come to terms with the aesthetization of politics that fascism later achieved in far more virulent form.

The tension between the fixity (and hence stability) that state regulation imposes, and the fluid motion of capital flow, remains a crucial problem for the social and political organization of capitalism. This difficulty (to which we shall return in Part II) is modified by the way in which the state stands itself to be disciplined by internal forces (upon which it relies for its power) and external conditions – competition in the world economy, exchange rates, and capital movements, migration, or, on occasion, direct political interventions on the part of superior powers. The relation between capitalist development and the state has to be seen, therefore, as mutually determining rather then unidirectional. State power can, in the end, be neither more nor less stable than the political economy of capitalist modernity will allow.

There are, however, many positive aspects to capitalist modernity. The potential command over nature that arises as capitalism 'rends the veil' over the mysteries of production holds a tremendous potential for reducing the powers of nature-imposed necessities over our lives. The creation of new wants and needs can alert us to new cultural possibilities (of the sort that avant-garde artists were later to explore). Even the 'variation of labour, fluency of function, universal mobility of the labourer' demanded by modern industry, holds the potential to replace the fragmented worker 'by the fully developed individual, fit for a variety of labours, ready to face any change of production, and to whom the different functions he performs, are but so many modes of giving free scope to his own natural and acquired powers' (*Capital*, 1:458). The reduction of spatial barriers and the formation of the world market not only allows a generalized access to the diversified products of different regions and climes, but also puts us into direct contact with all the peoples of the earth.

Above all, revolutions in productive force, in technology and science, open up new vistas for human development and self-realization.

It is particularly useful to look at these conceptions in relation to 'heroic' modernism's jousting with mythology. The latter, Marx argues, 'controls and fashions the forces of nature in the imagination and through the imagination; it disappears therefore when real control over these forces is established.' Mythology is, in short, a humanly constructed, intermediate, and historically determined link, which disappears when human beings acquire the the capacity to make their history according to conscious choice and design (Raphael, 1981, 89). Revolutions in technology rendered possible by the division of labour and the rise of the materialist sciences had the effect of demystifying the processes of production (aptly called 'mysteries' and 'arts' in the pre-modern period) and opening up the capacity to liberate society from scarcity and the more oppressive aspects of nature-imposed necessity. This was the good side of capitalist modernization. The problem, however, was to liberate us from the fetishisms of market exchange and to demystify (and by extension demythologize) the social and historical world in exactly the same way. This was the scientific task that Marx set himself in *Capital*. But it is always possible, particularly in the face of the uncertainties and fragmentations to which capitalism is prone (economic crises for example), to re-mythologize, to seek once again to control and fashion the social forces in imagination and through imagination, under conditions where all semblance of control over these forces seems to be lost. The struggle to create a 'de-mythologized' art and science of history (both perfectly feasible projects in Marx's view) has to be seen as part and parcel of this broader social struggle. But that battle (for which Marx believed he had prepared a powerful foundation) could be won only through the transition to an all-encompassing and powerful socialism, which would render appropriation of the natural and social world through myth redundant and irrelevant. Meanwhile, the tension between the mystifications, fetishisms, and mythological constructions of the older order, and the penchant for revolutionizing our conceptions of the world has to be appreciated as central to intellectual, artistic, and scientific life.

It is out of the tension between the negative and positive qualities of capitalism that new ways to define our species being can be constructed:

Thus capital creates the bourgeois society, and the universal appropriation of nature as well as of the social bond itself by the members of society. Hence the great civilizing influence of capital; its production of a stage of society in comparison to which all earlier ones appear as mere *local developments* of humanity and as *nature-idolatry*. For the first time nature becomes purely an object for humankind, purely a matter of utility; ceases to be recognized as a power for itself; and the theoretical discovery of its autonomous laws appears merely as a ruse so as to subjugate it to human needs. ... Capital drives beyond national barriers and prejudices as much as beyond nature worship, as well as [beyond] all traditional, confined, complacent, encrusted satisfactions of present needs, and reproduction of old ways of life. It is destructive towards all of this, and constantly revolutionizes it, tearing down all the barriers which hem in the development of the forces of production, the expansion of needs, the all-sided development of production, and the exploitation and exchange of natural and mental forces. (*Grundrisse*, 410)

There is more than a hint of the Enlightenment project in passages of this sort. And Marx gives us plenty of advice on how we might fuse all the sporadic though widespread resistances, discontents, and struggles against the oppressive, destructive, fragmenting, and destabilizing aspects of life under capitalism so as to master the maelstrom and become collective creators of our own history according to conscious plan. 'The realm of freedom actually begins only where labour which is determined by necessity and mundane considerations ceases. ... Beyond it begins that development of human energy which is an end in itself, the true realm of freedom.'

What Marx depicts, therefore, are social processes at work under capitalism conducive to individualism, alienation, fragmentation, ephemerality, innovation, creative destruction, speculative development, unpredictable shifts in methods of production and consumption (wants and needs), a shifting experience of space and time, as well as a crisis-ridden dynamic of social change. If these conditions of capitalist modernization form the material context out of which both modernist and postmodernist thinkers and cultural producers forge their aesthetic sensibilities, principles, and practices, it seems reasonable to conclude that the turn to postmodernism does not reflect any fundamental *change* of social condition. The rise of postmodernism either represents a departure (if such there is) in ways of thinking about what could or should be done about that social condition, or else (and this is the proposition we explore in considerable depth in

Part II) it reflects a shift in the way in which capitalism is working these days. In either case, Marx's account of capitalism, if correct, provides us with a very solid basis for thinking about the general relations between modernization, modernity, and the aesthetic movements that draw their energies from such conditions.

6

POSTmodernISM or
postMODERNism?

How, then, should postmodernism in general be evaluated? My preliminary assessment would be this. That in its concern for difference, for the difficulties of communication, for the complexity and nuances of interests, cultures, places, and the like, it exercises a positive influence. The meta-languages, meta-theories, and meta-narratives of modernism (particularly in its later manifestations) did tend to gloss over important differences, and failed to pay attention to important disjunctions and details. Postmodernism has been particularly important in acknowledging 'the multiple forms of otherness as they emerge from differences in subjectivity, gender and sexuality, race and class, temporal (configurations of sensibility) and spatial geographic locations and dislocations' (Huyssens, 1984, 50). It is this aspect of postmodernist thought that gives it a radical edge, so much so that traditional neo-conservatives, such as Daniel Bell, fear rather than welcome its accommodations with individualism, commercialism, and entrepreneuralism. Such neo-conservatives would, after all, hardly welcome Lyotard's (1980, 66) assertion that 'the temporary contract is in practice supplanting permanent institutions in the professional, emotional, sexual, cultural, family, and international domains, as well as in political affairs.' Daniel Bell plainly regrets the collapse of solid bourgeois values, the erosion of the work ethic in the working class, and sees contemporary trends less as a turn towards a vibrant postmodernist future and more as an exhaustion of modernism that surely harbingers a social and political crisis in years to come.

Postmodernism also ought to be looked at as mimetic of the social, economic, and political practices in society. But since it is mimetic of different facets of those practices it appears in very different guises. The superimposition of different worlds in many a postmodern novel, worlds between which an uncommunicative 'otherness' prevails in a space of coexistence, bears an uncanny relationship to the increasing ghettoization, disempowerment, and isolation of poverty and minority populations in the inner cities of both Britain and the United States. It is not hard to read a post-modern novel as a metaphorical transect across the fragmenting social landscape, the sub-cultures and local modes of communication, in London, Chicago, New York, or Los Angeles. Since most social indicators suggest a strong increase in actual ghettoization since 1970, it is useful to think of postmodern fiction as perhaps mimetic of that fact.

But the increasing affluence, power, and authority emerging at the other end of the social scale produces an entirely different ethos. For while it is hard to see that working in the postmodern AT&T building by Philip Johnson is any different from working in the modernist Seagram building by Mies van der Rohe, the image projected to the outside is different. 'AT&T insisted they wanted something other than just another glass box,' said the architect. 'We were looking for something that projected the company's image of nobility and strength. No material does that better than granite' (even though it was double the cost of glass). With luxury housing and corporate headquarters, aesthetic twists become an expression of class power. Crimp (1987) takes it further:

> The present condition of architecture is one in which architects debate academic, abstract aesthetics while they are in fact in the thrall of the real-estate developers who are ruining our cities and turning working class people out of their homes.... Philip Johnson's new skyscraper ... is a developer building, with a few applied geegaws, thrust upon a neighborhood that is not particularly in need of another skyscraper.

Invoking the memory of Hitler's architect Albert Speer, Crimp goes on to attack the postmodernist mask of what he sees as a new authoritarianism in the direction of city forms.

I have chosen these two examples to illustrate how important it is to think through exactly what kinds of social practice, what sets of social relations, are being reflected in different aesthetic movements. Yet this account is surely incomplete because we have yet to establish – and this will be the subject of enquiry in Parts II and III of this study – exactly what postmodernism might be mimetic of. Further-more, it is just as surely dangerous to presuppose that postmodernism is solely mimetic rather than an aesthetic intervention in politics, economy, and social life in its own right. The strong injection of *fiction* as well as *function* into common sensibility, for example, must have consequences, perhaps unforeseen, for social action. Even Marx insisted, after all, that what distinguishes the worst of architects from the best of bees is that the architect erects stuctures in the imagination before giving them material form. Changes in the way we imagine, think, plan, and rationalize are bound to have material consequences. Only in these very broad terms of the conjoining of mimesis and aesthetic intervention can the broad range of postmodernism make sense.

Yet postmodernism sees itself rather more simply: for the most part as a wilful and rather chaotic movement to overcome all the supposed ills of modernism. But in this regard I think postmodernists exaggerate when they depict the modern as grossly as they do, either caricaturing the whole modernist movement to the point where, as even Jencks admits, 'modern architecture bashing has become a form of sadism that is getting far too easy,' or isolating one wing of modernism for criticism (Althusserianism, modern brutalism, or whatever) as if that was all there was. There were, after all, many cross-currents within modernism, and postmodernists echo some of them quite explicitly (Jencks, for example, looks back to the period 1870−1914, even to the confusions of the 1920s, while including Le Corbusier's monastery at Ronchamp as an important precursor of one aspect of postmodernism). The meta-narratives that the post-modernists decry (Marx, Freud, and even later figures like Althusser) were much more open, nuanced, and sophisticated than the critics admit. Marx and many of the Marxists (I think of Benjamin, Thomp-son, Anderson, as diverse examples) have an eye for detail, frag-mentation, and disjunction that is often caricatured out of existence in postmodern polemics. Marx's account of modernization is exceedingly rich in insights into the roots of modernist as well as postmodernist sensibility.

It is equally wrong to write off the material achievements of modernist practices so easily. Modernists found a way to control and contain an explosive capitalist condition. They were effective for example, in the organization of urban life and the capacity to build space in such a way as to contain the intersecting processes that have made for a rapid urban change in twentieth-century capitalism. If there is a crisis implicit in all of that, it is by no means clear that it is the modernists, rather than the capitalists, who are to blame. There are, indeed, some extraordinary successes in the modernist pantheon (I note the British school building and design programme in the early 1960s that solved some of the acute housing problems of education within tight budget constraints). While some housing projects were indeed dismal failures, others were not, particularly when compared with the slum conditions from which many people came. And it turns out that the social conditions in Pruitt–Igoe – that great symbol of modernist failure – were much more at the heart of the problem than pure architectural form. The blaming of physical form for social ills has to rest on the most vulgar kind of environmental determinism that few would be prepared tó accept in other circumstances (though I note with distress that another member of Prince Charles's 'kitchen cabinet' is the geographer Alice Coleman, who regularly mistakes correlation between bad design and anti-social behaviour with causation). It is interesting to note, therefore, how the tenant population in Le Corbusier's 'habitat for living' at Firminy-le-Vert has organized into a social movement to prevent its destruction (not, I should add, out of any particular loyalty to Le Corbusier but more simply because it happens to be their home). As even Jencks admits, postmodernists have taken over all of the great achievements of the modernists in architectural design, though they have certainly altered aesthetics and appearances in at least superficial ways.

I also conclude that there is much more continuity than difference between the broad history of modernism and the movement called postmodernism. It seems more sensible to me to see the latter as a particular kind of crisis within the former, one that emphasizes the fragmentary, the ephemeral, and the chaotic side of Baudelaire's formulation (that side which Marx so admirably dissects as integral to the capitalist mode of production) while expressing a deep scepticism as to any particular prescriptions as to how the eternal and immutable should be conceived of, represented, or expressed.

But postmodernism, with its emphasis upon the ephemerality of *jouissance*, its insistence upon the impenetrability of the other, its concentration on the text rather than the work, its penchant for deconstruction bordering on nihilism, its preference for aesthetics over ethics, takes matters too far. It takes them beyond the point where any coherent politics are left, while that wing of it that seeks a shameless accommodation with the market puts it firmly in the tracks of an entrepreneurial culture that is the hallmark of reactionary neoconservativism. Postmodernist philosophers tell us not only to accept but even to revel in the fragmentations and the cacophony of voices through which the dilemmas of the modern world are understood. Obsessed with deconstructing and delegitimating every form of argument they encounter, they can end only in condemning their own validity claims to the point where nothing remains of any basis for reasoned action. Postmodernism has us accepting the reifications and partitionings, actually celebrating the activity of masking and cover-up, all the fetishisms of locality, place, or social grouping, while denying that kind of meta-theory which can grasp the political— economic processes (money flows, international divisions of labour, financial markets, and the like) that are becoming ever more univer- salizing in their depth, intensity, reach and power over daily life.

Worst of all, while it opens up a radical prospect by acknowledging the authenticity of other voices, postmodernist thinking immedi- ately shuts off those other voices from access to more universal sources of power by ghettoizing them within an opaque otherness, the specificity of this or that language game. It thereby disempowers those voices (of women, ethnic and racial minorities, colonized peoples, the unemployed, youth, etc.) in a world of lop-sided power relations. The language game of a cabal of international bankers may be impenetrable to us, but that does not put it on a par with the equally impenetrable language of inner-city blacks from the stand- point of power relations.

The rhetoric of postmodernism is dangerous for it avoids con- fronting the realities of political economy and the circumstances of global power. The silliness of Lyotard's 'radical proposal' that opening up the data banks to everyone as a prologue to radical reform (as if we would all have equal power to use that opportunity) is instructive, because it indicates how even the most resolute of postmodernists is faced in the end with either making some univer- salizing gesture (like Lyotard's appeal to some pristine concept of justice) or lapsing, like Derrida, into total political silence. Meta- theory cannot be dispensed with. The postmodernists simply push it underground where it continues to function as a 'now unconcious effectivity' (Jameson 1984b).

I find myself agreeing, therefore, with Eagleton's repudiation of Lyotard, for whom 'there can be no difference between truth, au- thority and rhetorical seductiveness; he who has the smoothest tongue or the raciest story has the power.' The eight-year reign of a charis- matic story-teller in the White House suggests that there is more than a little continuity to that political problem, and that post- modernism comes dangerously close to complicity with the aesthe- ticizing of politics upon which it is based. This takes us back to a very basic question. If both modernity and postmodernity derive their aesthetic from some kind of struggle with the *fact* of fragment- ation, ephemerality, and chaotic flux, it is, I would suggest, very important to establish why such a fact should have been so pervasive an aspect of modern experience for so long a period of time, and why the intensity of that experience seems to have picked up so powerfully since 1970. If the only thing certain about modernity is uncertainty, then we should, surely, pay considerable attention to the social forces that produce such a condition. It is to these social forces that I now turn.

Part II

The political—economic transformation of late twentieth-century capitalism

The interval between the decay of the old and the formation and establishment of the new, constitutes a period of transition, which must always necessarily be one of uncertainty, confusion, error, and wild and fierce fanaticism.   *John Calhoun*

7

Introduction

If there has been some kind of transformation in the political economy of late twentieth-century capitalism, then it behoves us to
establish how deep and fundamental the change might be. Signs and
tokens of radical changes in labour processes, in consumer habits, in
geographical and geopolitical configurations, in state powers and
practices, and the like, abound. Yet we still live, in the West, in a
society where production for profit remains the basic organizing
principle of economic life. We need some way, therefore, to represent
all the shifting and churning that has gone on since the first major
post-war recession of 1973, which does not lose sight of the fact that
the basic rules of a capitalist mode of production continue to operate
as invariant shaping forces in historical–geographical development.

The language (and therefore the hypothesis) that I shall explore is
one in which we view recent events as a transition in the *regime of
accumulation* and its associated *mode of social and political regulation*.
In representing matters this way, I am resorting to the language of a
certain school of thought known as the 'regulation school.' Their
basic argument, pioneered by Aglietta (1979) and advanced by Lipietz
(1986), Boyer (1986a; 1986b), and others, can briefly be summarized.
A regime of accumulation 'describes the stabilization over a long
period of the allocation of the net product between consumption and
accumulation; it implies some correspondence between the transformation of both the conditions of production and the conditions
of reproduction of wage earners.' A particular system of accumulation
can exist because 'its schema of reproduction is coherent.' The problem, however, is to bring the behaviours of all kinds of individuals
– capitalists, workers, state employees, financiers, and all manner of
other political–economic agents – into some kind of configuration
that will keep the regime of accumulation functioning. There must
exist, therefore, 'a materialization of the regime of accumulation

taking the form of norms, habits, laws, regulating networks and so on that ensure the unity of the process, i.e. the appropriate consistency of individual behaviours with the schema of reproduction. This body of interiorized rules and social processes is called *the mode of regulation*' (Lipietz, 1986, 19).

This kind of language is useful, in the first instance, as a heuristic device. It focuses our attention upon the complex interrelations, habits, political practices, and cultural forms that allow a highly dynamic, and consequently unstable, capitalist system to acquire sufficient semblance of order to function coherently at least for a certain period of time.

There are two broad areas of difficulty within a capitalist economic system that have to be successfully negotiated if that system is to remain viable. The first arises out of the anarchic qualities of price-fixing markets, and the second derives from the need to exert sufficient control over the way labour power is deployed to guarantee the addition of value in production and, hence, positive profits for as many capitalists as possible.

Price-fixing markets, to take up the first problem, typically provide innumerable and highly decentralized signals that allow producers to co-ordinate output decisions with the needs, wants, and desires of consumers (subject, of course, to the budget and cost constraints that affect both parties to any market transaction). But Adam Smith's celebrated 'hidden hand' of the market has never been sufficient in itself to guarantee stable growth for capitalism, even when the background institutions (private property, enforceable contracts, appropriate management of money) have been functioning properly. Some degree of collective action — usually state regulation and intervention — is needed to compensate for the market failures (such as unpriced damages to the natural and social environment), to prevent excessive concentrations of market power, or to check the abuse of monopoly privilege where such cannot be avoided (in fields such as transport and communications), to provide collective goods (defence, education, social and psysical infrastructures) that cannot be produced and sold through the market, and to guard against runaway failures due to speculative surges, aberrant market signals, and the potentially negative interplay between entrepreneurial expectations and market signals (the problem of self-fulfilling prophecies in market performance). In practice, collective pressures exercised by the state or other institutions (religious, political, trade union, business community, and cultural organizations) together with the exercise of dominant market power by large corporations and other powerful institutions, affect capitalism's dynamic in vital ways. The pressures can be direct (such as mandated wage and price controls) or indirect (such as subliminal advertising that persuades us to new concepts of our basic needs and desires in life), but the net effect is to shape the trajectory and form of capitalist development in ways that cannot be understood simply by analysis of market transactions. Furthermore, social and psychological propensities, such as individualism and the drive for personal fulfillment through self-expression, the search for security and collective identity, the need to acquire self-respect, status, or some other mark of individual identity, all play a role in shaping modes of consumption and life-styles. One only has to contemplate the whole complex of forces implicated in the proliferation of mass automobile production, ownership, and use to recognize the vast range of social, psychological, political, as well as more conventionally understood economic meanings which attach to one of the key growth sectors of twentieth-century capitalism. The virtue of 'regulation school' thinking is that it insists we look at the total package of relations and arrangements that contribute to the stabilization of output growth and aggregate distribution of income and consumption in a particular historical period and place.

The second arena of general difficulty in capitalist societies concerns the conversion of men and women's capacity to do active work into a labour process whose fruits can be appropriated by capitalists. Labour of any kind requires a certain concentration, self-discipline, habituation to different instruments of production, and knowledge of the potentialities of various raw materials for conversion into useful products. Commodity production under conditions of wage labour, however, locates much of the knowledge, decisions as to technique, as well as disciplinary apparatus, outside the control of the person who actually does the work. The habituation of wage labourers to capitalism was a long-drawn-out (and not particularly happy) historical process, that has to be renewed with the addition of each new generation of workers into the labour force. The disciplining of labour power to the purposes of capital accumulation – a process I shall generally refer to as 'labour control' – is a very intricate affair. It entails, in the first instance, some mix of repression, habituation, co-optation and co-operation, all of which have to be organized not only within the workplace but throughout society at large. The socialization of the worker to conditions of capitalist production entails the social control of physical and mental powers on a very broad basis. Education, training, persuasion, the mobilization of certain social sentiments (the work ethic, company loyalty, national or local pride) and psychological propensities (the search for identity through work, individual initiative, or social solidarity) all play a role and are plainly mixed in with the formation of dominant ideologies cultivated by the mass media, religious and educational institutions, the various arms of the state apparatus, and asserted by simple articulation of their experience on the part of those who do the work. Here, too, the 'mode of regulation' becomes a useful way to conceptualize how the problems of organizing labour power for purposes of capital accumulation are worked out in particular places and times.

I broadly accept the view that the long postwar boom, from 1945 to 1973, was built upon a certain set of labour control practices, technological mixes, consumption habits, and configurations of political—economic power, and that this configuration can reasonably be called Fordist—Keynesian. The break up of this system since 1973 has inaugurated a period of rapid change, flux, and uncertainty. Whether or not the new systems of production and marketing, characterized by more flexible labour processes and markets, of geographical mobility and rapid shifts in consumption practices, warrant the title of a new regime of accumulation, and whether the revival of entrepreneurialism and of neo-conservatism, coupled with the cultural turn to postmodernism, warrant the title of a new mode of regulation, is by no means clear. There is always a danger of confusing the transitory and the ephemeral with more fundamental transformations in political—economic life. But the contrasts between present political—economic practices and those of the postwar boom period are sufficiently strong to make the hypothesis of a shift from Fordism to what might be called a 'flexible' regime of accumulation a telling way to characterize recent history. And while I shall, for didactic purposes, emphasize the contrasts in what follows, I shall return to the evaluative question of how fundamental the changes really are by way of general conclusion.

8

Fordism

The symbolic initiation date of Fordism must, surely, be 1914, when
Henry Ford introduced his five-dollar, eight-hour day as recompense for workers manning the automated car-assembly line he had
established the year before at Dearborn, Michigan. But the manner
of general implantation of Fordism was very much more complicated
than that.

Ford's organizational and technological innovations were, in many
respects, a simple extension of well-established trends. The corporate
form of business organization, for example, had been perfected by
the railroads throughout the nineteenth century, and had already
spread, particularly after the wave of mergers, trust and cartel formation at the end of the century, to many industrial sectors (one
third of US manufacturing assets were subject to merger in the years
1898–1902 alone). Ford likewise did little more than rationalize old
technologies and a pre-existing detail division of labour, though by
flowing the work to a stationary worker he achieved dramatic gains
in productivity. F. W. Taylor's *The principles of scientific management* – an influential tract which described how labour productivity
could be radically increased by breaking down each labour process
into component motions and organizing fragmented work tasks according to rigorous standards of time and motion study – had, after
all, been published in 1911. And Taylor's thinking had a long ancestry,
going back via Gilbreth's experiments of the 1890s to the works of
mid-nineteenth-century writers like Ure and Babbage, which Marx
had found so revealing. The separation between management, conception, control, and execution (and all that this meant in terms of
hierarchical social relations and de-skilling within the labour process)
was also already well under way in many industries. What was
special about Ford (and what ultimately separates Fordism from
Taylorism), was his vision, his explicit recognition that mass pro-

duction meant mass consumption, a new system of the reproduction of labour power, a new politics of labour control and management, a new aesthetics and psychology, in short, a new kind of rationalized, modernist, and populist democratic society.

The Italian communist leader, Antonio Gramsci, languishing in one of Mussolini's jails some two decades later, drew exactly that implication. Americanism and Fordism, he noted in his *Prison notebooks*, amounted to 'the biggest collective effort to date to create, with unprecedented speed, and with a consciousness of purpose unmatched in history, a new type of worker and a new type of man.' The new methods of work 'are inseparable from a specific mode of living and of thinking and feeling life.' Questions of sexuality, the family, forms of moral coercion, of consumerism, and of state action were, in Gramsci's view, all bound up with the search to forge a particular kind of worker 'suited to the new type of work and productive process.' Yet, even two decades after Ford's opening gambit, Gramsci judged that 'this elaboration is still only in its initial phase and therefore (apparently) idyllic.' Why, then, did it take so long for Fordism to mature into a fully-fledged regime of accumulation?

Ford believed that the new kind of society could be built simply through the proper application of corporate power. The purpose of the five-dollar, eight-hour day was only in part to secure worker compliance with the discipline required to work the highly productive assembly-line system. It was coincidentally meant to provide workers with sufficient income and leisure time to consume the mass-produced products the corporations were about to turn out in ever vaster quantities. But this presumed that workers knew how to spend their money properly. So in 1916, Ford sent an army of social workers into the homes of his 'privileged' (and largely immigrant) workers to ensure that the 'new man' of mass production had the right kind of moral probity, family life, and capacity for prudent (i.e. non-alcoholic) and 'rational' consumption to live up to corporate needs and expectations. The experiment did not last too long, but its very existence was a prescient signal of the deep social, psychological, and political problems that Fordism was to pose.

So strongly did Ford believe in corporate power to regulate the economy as a whole, that he increased wages with the onset of the great depression in the belief that this would boost effective demand, revive the market, and restore business confidence. But the coercive laws of competition proved too powerful for even the mighty Ford, and he was forced to lay off workers and cut wages. It took Roosevelt and the New Deal to try and save capitalism by doing through state intervention what Ford had tried to do alone. Ford tried to pre-empt that outcome in the 1930s by pushing his workers to supply the greater part of their own subsistence requirements. They ought, he argued, to cultivate vegetables in their spare time in their own gardens (a practice followed to great effect in Britain during World War II). In insisting that 'self-help is the only means of combating the economic depression' Ford here reinforced the kind of controlled, back-to-the-land utopianism that characterized Frank Lloyd Wright's plans for Broadacre City. But even here we can detect interesting signs of future configurations, since it was the suburbanization and deconcentration of population and industry (rather than the self-help) implicit in Wright's modernist conception that was to become a major element in stimulating effective demand for Ford's products in the long postwar boom after 1945.

How the Fordist system was put into place is, in fact, a long and complicated story, stretching over nearly half a century. It depended on myriad individual, corporate, institutional, and state decisions, many of them unwitting political choices or knee-jerk responses to the crisis tendencies of capitalism, particularly as manifest in the great depression of the 1930s. The subsequent war-time mobilization also implied large-scale planning as well as thorough rationalizations of the labour process in spite of worker resistance to assembly-line production and capitalist fears of centralized control. It was hard for either capitalists or workers to refuse rationalizations which improved efficiency at a time of all-out war effort. Furthermore, confusions of ideological and intellectual practices complicated matters. Both left and right wings of the political spectrum evolved their own version of rationalized state planning (with all its modernist accoutrements) as a solution to the ills to which capitalism was so plainly heir, particularly as manifest in the 1930s. This was the kind of confused political and intellectual history that had Lenin lauding Taylorist and Fordist production technology while the unions in Western Europe refused it, Le Corbusier appearing as an apostle of modernity while consorting with authoritarian regimes (Mussolini for a while, and then the Vichy regime in France), Ebenezer Howard forging utopian plans inspired by the anarchism of Geddes and Kropotkin only to be appropriated by capitalist developers, and Robert Moses beginning the century as a political 'progressive' (inspired by the utopian socialism depicted in Edward Bellamy's *Looking backwards*) and ending up as the 'power broker' who 'took the meat axe' to the Bronx in the name of the automobilization of America (see, e.g. Caro, 1974).

There were, it seems, two major impediments to the spread of

Fordism in the inter-war years. To begin with, the state of class relations throughout the capitalist world was hardly conducive to the easy acceptance of a production system that rested so heavily upon the socialization of the worker to long hours of purely routinized labour, demanding little in the way of traditional craft skills, and conceding almost negligible control to the worker over the design, pace, and scheduling of the production process. Ford had relied almost exclusively on immigrant labour to set up his assembly-line production system, but the immigrants learned, and native American workers were hostile. The turnover in Ford's labour force proved impressively high. Taylorism was likewise fiercely resisted in the 1920s, and some commentators, such as Richard Edwards (1979), insist that worker opposition roundly defeated the implantation of such techniques in most industries, in spite of capitalist domination of labour markets, the continued flow of immigrant labour, and the capacity to mobilize labour reserves from rural (and sometimes black) America. In the rest of the capitalist world, labour organization and craft traditions were simply too strong, and immigration too weak, to permit Fordism or Taylorism any easy purchase on production, even though the general principles of scientific management were widely accepted and applied. In this regard, Henri Fayol's *Administration industrielle et générale* (published in 1916) proved a much more influential text in Europe than did Taylor's. With its emphasis upon organizational structures and hierarchical ordering of authority and information flow, it gave rise to a rather different version of rationalized management compared to Taylor's preoccupation with simplifying the horizontal flow of production processes. Mass-production assembly-line technology, spottily implanted in the United States, was very weakly developed in Europe before the mid-1930s. The European car industry, with the exception of Fiat's plant in Turin, remained for the most part a highly skilled craft industry (though corporately organized) producing up-market cars for elite consumers, and was only lightly touched by assembly-line procedures for the mass production of cheaper models before World War II. It took a major revolution in class relations — a revolution that began in the 1930s but which came to fruition only in the 1950s — to accommodate the spread of Fordism to Europe.

The second major barrier to be overcome lay in the modes and mechanisms of state intervention. A new mode of regulation had to be devised to match the requirements of Fordist production and it took the shock of savage depression and the near-collapse of capitalism in the 1930s to push capitalist societies to some new conception of how state powers should be conceived of and deployed. The crisis appeared fundamentally as a lack of effective demand for product, and it was in those terms that the search for solutions began. With the benefit of hindsight, of course, we can more clearly see all of the dangers posed by national socialist movements. But in the light of the evident failure of democratic governments to do anything other than seem to compound the difficulties of an across-the-board economic collapse, it is not hard to see the attraction of a political solution in which workers were disciplined to new and more efficient production systems, and excess capacity was absorbed in part through productive expenditures on much needed infrastructures for both production and consumption (the other part being allocated to wasteful military expenditures). Not a few politicians and intellectuals (I cite the economist Schumpeter as an example) thought the kinds of solutions being explored in Japan, Italy, and Germany in the 1930s (stripped of their appeals to mythology, militarism, and racism) were along the right lines, and supported Roosevelt's New Deal because they saw it precisely in that light. The democratic stasis of the 1920s (albeit class-bound) had to be overcome, many agreed, by a modicum of state authoritarianism and interventionism, for which very little precedent (save that of Japan's industrialization, or the Bonapartist interventions of Second Empire France) could be found. Disillusioned by the inability of democratic governments to undertake what he considered essential tasks of modernization, Le Corbusier turned first to syndicalism, and later to authoritarian regimes, as the only political forms capable of facing up to the crisis. The problem, as an economist like Keynes saw it, was to arrive at a set of scientific managerial strategies and state powers that would stabilize capitalism, while avoiding the evident repressions and irrationalities, all the warmongering and narrow nationalism that national socialist solutions implied. It is in such a context of confusion that we have to understand the highly diversified attempts within different nation states to arrive at political, institutional and social arrangements that could accommodate the chronic incapacities of capitalism to regulate the essential conditions for its own reproduction.

The problem of the proper configuration and deployment of state powers was resolved only after 1945. This brought Fordism to maturity as a fully-fledged and distinctive regime of accumulation. As such, it then formed the basis for a long postwar boom that stayed broadly intact until 1973. During that period, capitalism in the advanced capitalist countries achieved strong but relatively stable rates of economic growth (see figure 2.1 and table 2.1). Living standards rose (figure 2.2), crisis tendencies were contained, mass democracy was preserved and the threat of inter-capitalist wars kept remote.

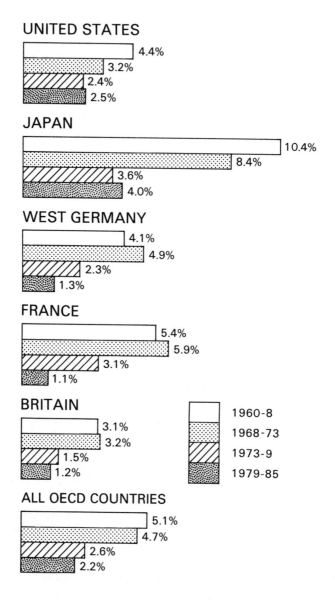

Figure 2.1 Annual rates of economic growth in selected advanced capitalist countries and the OECD as a whole for selected time periods, 1960–1985 (Source: OECD)

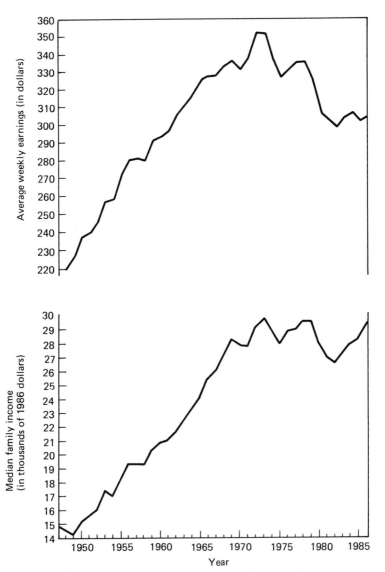

Figure 2.2 Real wages and family incomes in the USA, 1947–1986
(Sources: *Historical Statistics of the United States and Economic Reports to the President*)

Fordism became firmly connected with Keynesianism, and capitalism indulged in a splurge of internationalist world-wide expansions that drew a host of de-colonized nations into its net. How such a system

Table 2.1   *Average rates of growth for the advanced capitalist countries over various time periods since 1820*

	Annual percentage rates of change		
	Output	Output per capita	Exports
1820–1870	2.2	1.0	4.0
1870–1913	2.5	1.4	3.9
1913–1950	1.9	1.2	1.0
1950–1973	4.9	3.8	8.6
1973–1979	2.6	1.8	5.6
1979–1985	2.2	1.3	3.8

Sources: Maddison, 1982 (1820–1973) and OECD (1973–85)

came to be is a dramatic story that deserves at least cursory scrutiny if we are better to understand the transitions that have occurred since 1973.

The postwar period saw the rise of a series of industries based on technologies that had matured in the inter-war years and been pushed to new extremes of rationalization in World War II. Cars, ship-building, and transport equipment, steel, petrochemicals, rubber, consumer electrical goods, and construction became the propulsive engines of economic growth, focused on a series of grand production regions in the world economy – the Midwest of the United States, the Ruhr–Rhinelands, the West Midlands of Britain, the Tokyo–Yokohama production region. The privileged workforces in these regions formed one pillar of a rapidly expanding effective demand. The other pillar rested on state-sponsored reconstruction of war-torn economies, suburbanization particularly in the United States, urban renewal, geographical expansion of transport and communications systems, and infrastructural development both within and outside the advanced capitalist world. Co-ordinated by way of in-terlinked financial centres – with the United States and New York at the apex of the hierarchy – these core regions of the world economy drew in massive supplies of raw materials from the rest of the non-communist world, and reached out to dominate an increasingly homogeneous mass world market with their products.

The phenomenal growth that occurred in the postwar boom depended, however, on a series of compromises and repositionings on the part of the major actors in the capitalist development process. The state had to take on new (Keynesian) roles and build new institutional powers; corporate capital had to trim its sails in certain respects in order to move more smoothly in the track of secure profitability; and organized labour had to take on new roles and functions with respect to performance in labour markets and in production processes. The tense but nevertheless firm balance of power that prevailed between organized labour, large corporate capital, and the nation state, and which formed the power basis for the postwar boom, was not arrived at by accident. It was the outcome of years of struggle.

The defeat of the resurgent radical working-class movements of the immediate postwar period, for example, prepared the political ground for the kinds of labour control and compromise that made Fordism possible. Armstrong, Glyn, and Harrison (1984, chapter 4) provide a detailed account of how the attack upon traditional (craft-oriented) and radical forms of labour organizing was mounted both in the occupied territories of Japan, West Germany, and Italy and in the supposedly 'free' territories of Britain, France, and the Low Countries. In the United States, where the Wagner Act of 1933 had given the unions power in the market place (with explicit recognition that collective bargaining rights were essential to the resolution of the effective demand problem) in return for sacrificing powers in the realm of production, the unions found themselves under virulent attack in the postwar years for communist infiltration, and were ultimately brought under strict legal discipline through the Taft–Hartley Act of 1952 (an act put through at the height of the McCarthyite period) (Tomlins, 1985). With their principal adversary under control, capitalist class interests could resolve what Gramsci earlier called the problem of 'hegemony' and establish a seemingly new basis for those class relations conducive to Fordism.

How deeply these new class relations penetrated is a matter of some dispute and in any case evidently varied a great deal from one country or even region to another. In the United States, for example, the unions won considerable power in the sphere of collective bargaining in the mass-production industries of the Midwest and North-East, preserved some shop-floor control over job specifications, security and promotions, and wielded an important (though never determinant) political power over such matters as social security benefits, the minimum wage, and other facets of social policy. But they acquired and maintained these rights in return for adopting a collaborative stance with respect to Fordist production techniques and cognate corporate strategies to increase productivity. Burawoy, in his *Manufacturing consent*, illustrates how deeply co-operative sentiments ran within the work-force, though modified by all kinds of 'games' of resistance to any excessive incursions of capitalist power on the shop floor (with respect, for example, to the pace of work). He thus broadly confirms with American data the profile of the co-operation stance of *The affluent worker* compiled by Goldthorpe in Britain. Yet there has been a sufficient record of sudden eruptions of discontent, even among affluent workers (in, for example, the General Motors plant at Lordstown shortly after it opened, or among the affluent car workers that Goldthorpe studied) to suggest that this may be more of a surface adaptation than a total reconstruction of worker attitudes with respect to assembly-line production. The perpetual problem of habituating the worker to such routinized, de-skilled and degraded systems of work, as Braverman (1974) forcefully argues, can never be completely overcome. Nevertheless, bureaucratized trade union organizations were increasingly corralled (sometimes through the exercise of repressive state power) into the corner of swapping real wage gains for co-operation in disciplining workers to the Fordist production system.

The roles of the other partners in the general, if often tacit, social contract that reigned over the postwar boom were similarly well defined. Large corporate power was deployed to assure steady growth in investments that enhanced productivity, guaranteed growth, and raised living standards while ensuring a stable basis for gaining profits. This implied a corporate commitment to steady but powerful processes of technological change, mass fixed capital investment, growth of managerial expertise in both production and marketing, and the mobilization of economies of scale through standardization of product. The strong centralization of capital that had been such a conspicuous feature of US capitalism since 1900 allowed the curbing of inter-capitalist competition within an all-powerful US economy and the emergence of oligopolistic and monopoly pricing and planning practices. Scientific management of all facets of corporate activity (not only production, but also personnel relations, on-the-job training, marketing, product design, pricing strategies, planned obsolescence of equipment and product) became the hallmark of bureaucratic corporate rationality. The decisions of corporations became hegemonic in defining the paths of mass consumption growth, presuming, of course, that the other two partners in the grand coalition did whatever was necessary to keep effective demand at levels sufficient to absorb the steady growth of capitalist output. The massing of workers in large-scale factories always posed, however, the threat of stronger labour organization and enhanced working-class power — hence the importance of the political attack upon radical elements within the labour movement after 1945. Nevertheless, corporations grudgingly accepted union power, particularly when the unions undertook to control their membership and collaborate with management in plans to raise productivity in return for wage gains that stimulated effective demand in the way that Ford had originally envisaged.

The state, for its part, assumed a variety of obligations. To the degree that mass production requiring heavy investment in fixed capital in turn required relatively stable demand conditions to be profitable, so the state strove to curb business cycles through an appropriate mix of fiscal and monetary policies in the postwar period. Such policies were directed towards those areas of public investment – in sectors like transportation, public utilities, etc. – that were vital to the growth of both mass production and mass consumption, and which would also guarantee relatively full employment. Governments likewise moved to provide a strong underpinning to the social wage through expenditures covering social security, health care, education, housing, and the like. In addition, state power was deployed, either directly or indirectly, to affect wage agreements and the rights of workers in production.

The forms of state interventionism varied greatly across the advanced capitalist countries. Table 2.2 illustrates, for example, the variety of postures taken by different governments in Western Europe in relation to wage contract regotiations. Similar qualitative as well as quantitative differences can be found in the patterning of public expenditures, the organization of welfare systems (kept very much within the corporation in the Japanese case, for example), and the degree of active as opposed to tacit state involvement in economic decisions. Patterns of labour unrest, shop-floor organizing and union activism likewise varied considerably from state to state (Lash and Urry, 1987). But what is remarkable is the way in which national governments of quite different ideological complexions – Gaullist in France, the Labour Party in Britain, Christian Democrats in West Germany, etc. – engineered both stable economic growth and rising material living standards through a mix of welfare statism, Keynesian economic management, and control over wage relations. Fordism depended, evidently, upon the nation state taking – much as Gramsci predicted – a very special role within the overall system of social regulation.

Postwar Fordism has to be seen, therefore, less as a mere system of mass production and more as a total way of life. Mass production meant standardization of product as well as mass consumption; and that meant a whole new aesthetic and a commodification of culture that many neo-conservatives, such as Daniel Bell, were later to see as

Table 2.2   The organization of wage bargaining in four countries,
1950—1975

	France	Britain	Italy	West Germany
Unions				
Membership	low	high blue-collar	variable	moderate
Organization	weak with political factionalism	fragmented between industries and trades	periodic with mass movements	structured and unified
Owners	divided among tendencies and organizations	weak collective organization	private—public rivalry	powerful and organized
State	widespread interventions and regulation of work and wages through tripartite accords	voluntary collective bargaining with state-set norms after mid-1960s	periodic legislative intervention depending on class struggle	very weak role

Source: after Boyer, 1986b, table 1

detrimental to the preservation of the work ethic and other supposed capitalist virtues. Fordism also built upon and contributed to the aesthetic of modernism — particularly the latter's penchant for functionality and efficiency — in very explicit ways, while the forms of state interventionism (guided by principles of bureaucratic—technical rationality), and the configuration of political power that gave the system its coherence, rested on notions of a mass economic democracy welded together through a balance of special-interest forces.

Postwar Fordism was also very much an international affair. The long postwar boom was crucially dependent upon a massive expansion of world trade and international investment flows. Slow to develop outside the United States before 1939, Fordism became more firmly implanted in both Europe and Japan after 1940 as part of the war effort. It was consolidated and expanded in the postwar period, either directly through policies imposed in the occupation (or, more paradoxically, in the French case, because the communist-led unions saw Fordism as the only way to assure national economic autonomy in the face of the American challenge) or indirectly through the Marshall Plan and subsequent US direct investment. The latter, which had sputtered along in the inter-war years as US corporations sought market outlets overseas to overcome the limits of internal effective demand, sprang to life after 1945. This opening up of foreign investment (chiefly in Europe) and trade permitted surplus productive capacity in the United States to be absorbed elsewhere, while the progress of Fordism internationally meant the formation of global mass markets and the absorption of the mass of the world's population, outside the communist world, into the global dynamics of a new kind of capitalism. Furthermore, uneven development within the world economy meant the experience of already muted business cycles as so many local and broadly compensating oscillations within a fairly stable growth of world demand. At the input end, the opening up of foreign trade meant the globalization of the supply of often cheaper raw materials (particularly energy supplies). The new internationalism also brought a whole host of other activities in its wake – banking, insurance, services, hotels, airports, and ultimately tourism. It carried with it a new international culture and relied heavily upon new-found capacities to gather, evaluate, and disseminate information.

All of this was secured under the hegemonic umbrella of the United States' financial and economic power backed by military domination. The Bretton Woods agreement of 1944 turned the dollar into the world's reserve currency and tied the world's economic development firmly into US fiscal and monetary policy. The United States acted as the world's banker in return for an opening up of the world's commodity and capital markets to the power of the large corporations. Under this umbrella, Fordism spread unevenly as each state sought its own mode of management of labour relations, monetary and fiscal policy, welfare and public investment strategies, limited internally only by the state of class relations and externally only by its hierarchical position in the world economy and by the fixed exchange rate against the dollar. The international spread of Fordism occurred, therefore, within a particular frame of international political–economic regulation and a geopolitical configuration in which the United States dominated through a very distinctive system of military alliances and power relations.

Not everyone was included in the benefits of Fordism, and there were, to be sure, abundant signs of discontent even at the system's apogee. To begin with, Fordist wage bargaining was confined to certain sectors of the economy and certain nation states where stable demand growth could be matched by large-scale investment in mass-production technology. Other sectors of high risk production still depended on low wages and weak job security. And even Fordist sectors could rest upon a non-Fordist base of sub-contracting. Labour markets therefore tended to divide into what O'Connor (1973) called a 'monopoly' sector, and a much more diverse 'competitive' sector in which labour was far from privileged. The resultant inequalities produced serious social tensions and strong social movements on the part of the excluded — movements that were compounded by the way in which race, gender, and ethnicity often determined who had access to privileged employment and who did not. The inequalities were particularly hard to sustain in the face of rising expectations, fed in part by all the artifice applied to need-creation and the pro-duction of a new kind of consumerist society. Denied access to privileged work in mass production, large segments of the work-force were equally denied access to the much-touted joys of mass consumption. This was a sure formula for discontent. The civil rights movement in the United States spilled over into a revolutionary rage that shook the inner cities. The surge of women into low-paying jobs was accompanied by an equally vigorous feminist movement. And the shock of discovery of awesome poverty in the midst of growing affluence (as exposed in Michael Harrington's *The other America*) spawned strong counter-movements of discontent with the supposed benefits of Fordism.

While the division between a predominantly white, male, and highly unionized work-force and 'the rest' was useful in some ways from the standpoint of labour control, it also had its drawbacks. It meant a rigidity in labour markets that made it hard to re-allocate labour from one line of production to another. The exclusionary power of the unions strengthened their capacity to resist de-skilling, authoritarianism, hierarchy, and loss of control in the workplace. The penchant for using those powers depended on political traditions, modes of organization (the shop steward movement in Britain being particularly powerful), and the willingness of workers to trade in their rights in production for greater market power. Labour strug-gles did not disappear, as unions often found themselves forced to respond to grass-roots discontent. But the unions also found themselves increasingly under attack from the outside, from excluded minorities, women and the underprivileged. To the degree they served their members' narrow interests and dropped more radical socialist concerns, they were in danger of being reduced in the public eye to fragmented special-interest groups pursuing self-serving rather than general aims.

The state bore the brunt of the increasing discontent, sometimes culminating in civil disorders on the part of the excluded. At the very minimum the state had to try and guarantee some kind of adequate social wage for all, or to engage in redistributive policies or legal actions that would actively remedy the inequalities, address the relative impoverishment and lack of inclusion of minorities. Increasingly, the legitimation of state power depended on the ability to spread the benefits of Fordism over all and to find ways to deliver adequate health care, housing and educational services on a massive scale but in a humane and caring way. Qualitative failures on that score were the butt of innumerable criticisms, but in the end it was probably the quantitative failure that provoked the most serious dilemmas. The ability to provide collective goods depended upon continuous acceleration in the productivity of labour in the corporate sector. Only in that way could Keynesian welfare statism be made fiscally viable.

On the consumer side, there was more than a little criticism of the blandness of the quality of life under a regime of standardized mass consumption. The quality of service provision through a non-discriminating system of state administration (based on technical–scientific bureaucratic rationality) also came in for heavy criticism. Fordism and Keynesian state managerialism became associated with an austere functionalist aesthetic (high modernism) in the field of rationalized design. The critics of suburban blandness and downtown monolithic monumentality (like Jane Jacobs) became, as we have seen, a vociferous minority that articulated a whole host of cultural discontents. The counter-cultural critiques and practices of the 1960s therefore paralleled movements of the excluded minorities and the critique of depersonalized bureaucratic rationality. All these threads of opposition began to fuse into a strong cultural–political movement at the very moment when Fordism as an economic system appeared to be at its apogee.

To this must be added all the Third World discontents at a modernization process that promised development, emancipation from want, and full integration into Fordism, but which delivered destruction of local cultures, much oppression, and various forms of capitalist domination in return for rather meagre gains in living standards and services (e.g. public health) for any except a very affluent indigenous elite that chose to collaborate actively with international capital. Movements towards national liberation – sometimes socialist but more often bourgeois–nationalist – focused many of these discontents in ways that sometimes appeared quite threatening to global Fordism. The geopolitical hegemony of the United States was threatened and the USA, which began the postwar era by using anti-communism and militarism as a vehicle for geopolitical and economic stabilization, soon found itself facing the problem of 'guns or butter' in its own fiscal economic policy.

But in spite of all the discontents and all the manifest tensions, the centrepieces of the Fordist regime held firm at least until 1973, and in the process did indeed manage to keep a postwar boom intact that favoured unionized labour, and to some degree spread the 'benefits' of mass production and consumption even further afield. Material living standards rose for the mass of the population in the advanced capitalist countries, and a relatively stable environment for corporate profits prevailed. It was not until the sharp recession of 1973 shattered that framework that a process of rapid, and as yet not well understood, transition in the regime of accumulation began.

9

From Fordism to flexible
accumulation

In retrospect, it seems there were signs of serious problems within Fordism as early as the mid-1960s. By then, the West European and Japanese recoveries were complete, their internal market saturated, and the drive to create export markets for their surplus output had to begin (figure 2.3). And this occurred at the very moment when the success of Fordist rationalization meant the relative displacement of more and more workers from manufacturing. The consequent slackening of effective demand was offset in the United States by the war on poverty and the war in Vietnam. But declining corporate productivity and profitability after 1966 (figure 2.4) meant the beginnings of a fiscal problem in the United States that would not go away except at the price of an acceleration in inflation, which began to undermine the role of the dollar as a stable international reserve currency. The formation of the Eurodollar market, and the credit crunch of 1966–7, were indeed prescient signals of the United States' diminished power to regulate the international financial system. It was at about this time too that import substitution policies in many Third World countries (particularly Latin America), coupled with the first big push by multinationals into offshore manufacturing (particularly in South-East Asia), brought a wave of competitive Fordist industrialization to entirely new environments, where the social contract with labour was either weakly enforced or non-existent. International competition thereafter intensified as Western Europe and Japan, joined by a whole host of newly industrializing countries, challenged United States hegemony within Fordism to the point where the Bretton Woods agreement cracked and the dollar was devalued. Floating and often highly volatile exchange rates thereafter replaced the fixed exchange rates of the postwar boom (figure 2.5).

More generally, the period from 1965 to 1973 was one in which the

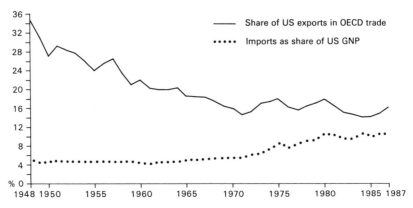

Figure 2.3 US share in OECD trade and manufacturing imports as a percentage of GNP in the USA, 1948—1987 (Sources: OECD, Historical Statistics of the United States and Economic Reports to the President).

inability of Fordism and Keynesianism to contain the inherent contradictions of capitalism became more and more apparent. On the surface, these difficulties could best be captured by one word: rigidity. There were problems with the rigidity of long-term and large-scale fixed capital investments in mass-production systems that precluded much flexibility of design and presumed stable growth in invariant consumer markets. There were problems of rigidities in labour markets, labour allocation, and in labour contracts (especially in the so-called 'monopoly' sector). And any attempt to overcome these rigidities ran into the seemingly immovable force of deeply entrenched working-class power — hence the strike waves and labour disruptions of the period 1968—72. The rigidities of state commitments also became more serious as entitlement programmes (social security, pension rights, etc.) grew under pressure to keep legitimacy at a time when rigidities in production restricted any expansion in the fiscal basis for state expenditures. The only tool of flexible response lay in monetary policy, in the capacity to print money at whatever rate appeared necessary to keep the economy stable. And so began the inflationary wave that was eventually to sink the postwar boom. Behind all these specific rigidities lay a rather unwieldy and seemingly fixed configuration of political power and reciprocal relations that bound big labour, big capital, and big government into what increasingly appeared as a dysfunctional embrace of such narrowly defined vested interests as to undermine rather than secure capital accumulation.

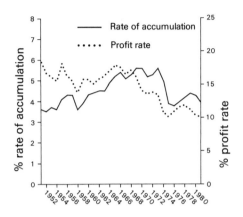

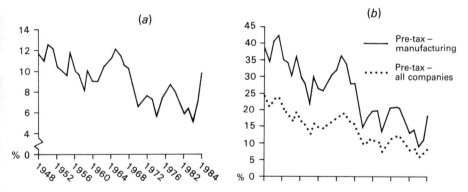

Figure 2.4 Business accumulation and profit rates in the advanced capitalist countries, 1950–1982 (after Armstrong, Glyn and Harrison) and profit rates as (a) percentage of the replacement cost of capital stock and (b) percentage of national income in the USA, 1948–1984
(Source: *Pollin, 1986*)

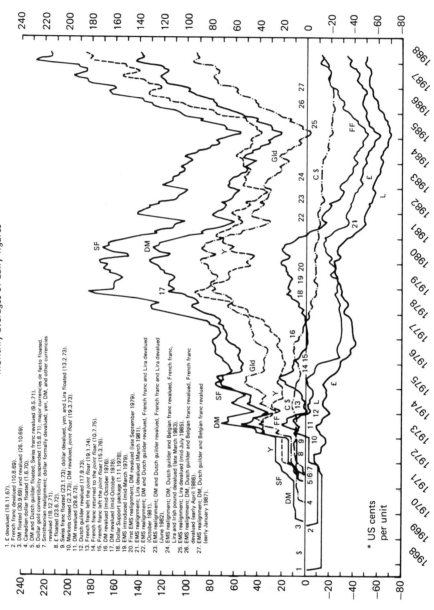

Percentage deviations with respect to dollar parties of October 1967
monthly averages of daily figures*

1. £ devalued (18.11.67).
2. French franc devalued (10.8.69).
3. DM floated (30.9.69) and revalued (26.10.69).
4. Canadian dollar floated (1.6.70).
5. DM and Dutch guilder floated; Swiss franc revalued (9.5.71).
6. Dollar gold convertibility suspended (15.8.71); major currencies de facto floated.
7. Smithsonian realignment; dollar formally devalued; yen, DM, and other currencies revalued (18.12.71).
8. £ floated (23.6.72).
9. Swiss franc floated (23.1.73); dollar devalued, yen, and Lira floated (13.2.73).
10. Markets closed (2.3.73); DM revalued, *joint float* (19.3.73).
11. DM revalued (29.6.73).
12. Dutch guilder revalued (17.9.73).
13. French franc left the *joint float* (19.1.74).
14. French franc returned to the *joint float* (10.7.75).
15. French franc left the *joint float* (15.3.76).
16. DM revalued (mid-October 1976).
17. DM revalued (mid-October 1978).
18. Dollar Support package (1.11.1978).
19. EMS introduced (mid-March 1979).
20. First EMS realignment; DM revalued (late September 1979).
21. EMS realignment; Lira devalued (March 1981).
22. EMS realignment; DM and Dutch guilder revalued, French franc and Lira devalued (October 1981).
23. EMS realignment; DM and Dutch guilder revalued, French franc and Lira devalued (June 1982).
24. EMS realignment; DM, Dutch guilder and Belgian franc revalued, French franc, Lira and Irish pound devalued (late March 1983).
25. EMS realignment; Lira devalued (mid-July 1985).
26. EMS realignment; DM, Dutch guilder and Belgian franc revalued, French franc devalued (early April 1986).
27. EMS realignment; DM, Dutch guilder and Belgian franc revalued (early January 1987).

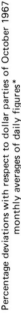

* US cents
per unit

Figure 2.5 Exchange rates of major currencies against the dollar
(Source: OECD Economic Outlook, June 1988.)

The momentum of the postwar boom was maintained through the period 1969–73 by an extraordinarily loose monetary policy on the part of both the United States and Britain. The capitalist world was awash with excess funds, and with few diminished productive outlets for investment, that meant strong inflation. The attempt to put a brake on rising inflation in 1973 exposed a lot of excess capacity in Western economies, triggering first of all a world-wide crash in property markets (see figure 2.6) and severe difficulties for financial institutions. To that were added the effects of OPEC's decision to raise oil prices, and the Arab decision to embargo oil exports to the West in the 1973 Arab–Israeli War. This (1) changed the relative cost of energy inputs dramatically, and pushed all segments of the economy to seek out ways to economize on energy use through technological and organizational change, and (2) led to a recycling problem of surplus petro-dollars, that exacerbated the already brewing instability in the world's financial markets. The strong deflation of 1973–5 further indicated that state finances were over-extended in relation to resources, creating a deep fiscal and legitimation crisis. The technical bankruptcy of New York City in 1975 — with one of the largest public budgets in the world — was illustrative of the seriousness of the problem. At the same time, corporations found themselves with a lot of unusable excess capacity (chiefly idle plant and equipment) under conditions of intensifying competition (figure 2.7). This forced them into a period of rationalization, restructuring, and intensification of labour control (if they could overcome or bypass union power). Technological change, automation, the search for new product lines and market niches, geographical dispersal to zones of easier labour control, mergers, and steps to acccelerate the turnover time of their capital surged to the fore of corporate strategies for survival under general conditions of deflation.

The sharp recession of 1973, exacerbated by the oil shock evidently shook the capitalist world out of the suffocating torpor of 'stagflation' (stagnant output of goods and high inflation of prices), and set in motion a whole set of processes that undermined the Fordist compromise. The 1970s and 1980s have consequently been a troubled period of economic restructuring and social and political readjustment (figure 2.8). In the social space created by all this flux and uncertainty, a series of novel experiments in the realms of industrial organization as well as in political and social life have begun to take shape. These experiments may represent the early stirrings of the passage to an entirely new regime of accumulation, coupled with a quite different system of political and social regulation.

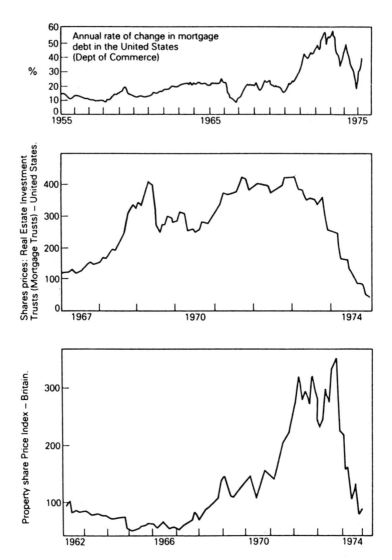

Figure 2.6 Some indices of the property boom and crash in Britain and the United States, 1955–1975. Top: *Annual rate of change in mortgage debt in the United States (Department of Commerce Data)* Middle: *Share prices of real estate investment trusts in the United States* (Source: *Fortune Magazine*) Bottom: *Property share price index in Britain* (Source: *Investors Chronicle*)

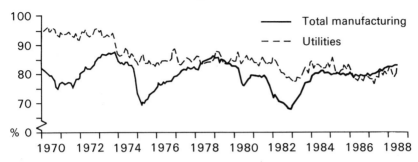

Figure 2.7 Capacity utilization in the United States, 1970–1988
(Source: *Federal Reserve Board*)

Flexible accumulation, as I shall tentatively call it, is marked by a direct confrontation with the rigidities of Fordism. It rests on flexibility with respect to labour processes, labour markets, products, and patterns of consumption. It is characterized by the emergence of entirely new sectors of production, new ways of providing financial services, new markets, and, above all, greatly intensified rates of commercial, technological, and organizational innovation. It has entrained rapid shifts in the patterning of uneven development, both between sectors and between geographical regions, giving rise, for example, to a vast surge in so-called 'service-sector' employment as well as to entirely new industrial ensembles in hitherto underdeveloped regions (such as the 'Third Italy', Flanders, the various silicon valleys and glens, to say nothing of the vast profusion of activities in newly industrializing countries). It has also entailed a new round of what I shall call 'time–space compression' (see Part III) in the capitalist world — the time horizons of both private and public decision-making have shrunk, while satellite communication and declining transport costs have made it increasingly possible to spread those decisions immediately over an ever wider and variegated space.

These enhanced powers of flexibility and mobility have allowed employers to exert stronger pressures of labour control on a workforce in any case weakened by two savage bouts of deflation, that saw unemployment rise to unprecedented postwar levels in advanced capitalist countries (save, perhaps, Japan). Organized labour was undercut by the reconstruction of foci of flexible accumulation in regions lacking previous industrial traditions, and by the importation back into the older centres of the regressive norms and practices established in these new areas. Flexible accumulation appears to imply relatively high levels of 'structural' (as opposed to 'frictional')

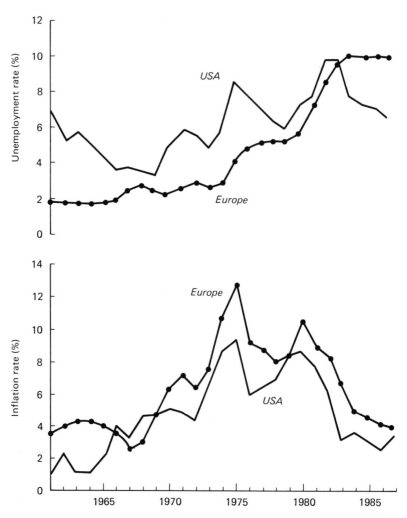

Figure 2.8 Unemployment and inflation rates in Europe and the USA, 1961–1987
(Source: OECD)

Figure 2.9 (a) Index of non-farm hourly earnings, (b) percentage unemployed, (c) percentage of jobless receiving unemployment benefits and (d) median family incomes in the USA, 1974–1987
(Sources: Bureau of Labor Statistics and Economic Reports to the President)

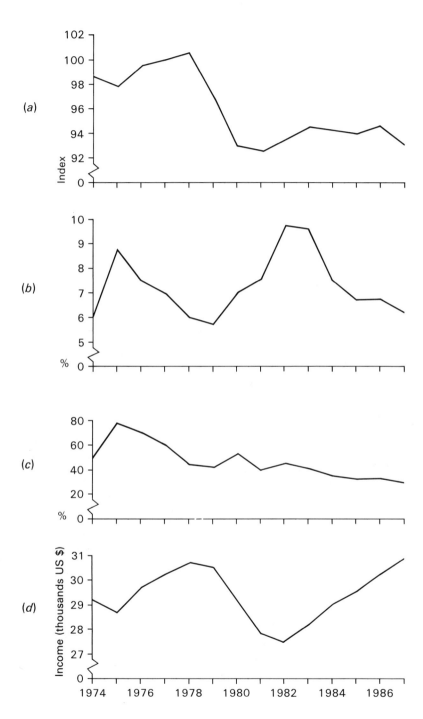

(a)

(b)

(c)

(d)

unemployment, rapid destruction and reconstruction of skills, modest (if any) gains in the real wage, (see figures 2.2 and 2.9) and the roll-back of trade union power — one of the political pillars of the Fordist regime.

The labour market has, for example, undergone a radical restructuring. Faced with strong market volatility, heightened competition, and narrowing profit margins, employers have taken advantage of weakened union power and the pools of surplus (unemployed or underemployed) labourers to push for much more flexible work regimes and labour contracts. It is hard to get a clear overall picture, because the very purpose of such flexibility is to satisfy the often highly specific needs of each firm. Even for regular employers, systems such as 'nine-day fortnights,' or work schedules that average a forty-hour week over the year but oblige the employee to work much longer at periods of peak demand, and compensate with shorter hours at periods of slack, are becoming much more common. But more important has been the apparent move away from regular employment towards increasing reliance upon part-time, temporary or sub-contracted work arrangements.

The result is a labour market structure of the sort depicted in figure 2.10, taken, as are the following quotations, from the Institute of Personnel Management's *Flexible patterns of work* (1986). The *core* — a steadily shrinking group according to accounts emanating from both sides of the Atlantic — is made up of employees 'with full time, permanent status and is central to the long term future of the organization.' Enjoying greater job security, good promotion and re-skilling prospects, and relatively generous pension, insurance, and other fringe benefit rights, this group is nevertheless expected to be adaptable, flexible, and if necessary geographically mobile. The potential costs of laying off core employees in time of difficulty may, however, lead a company to sub-contract even high level functions (varying from design to advertising and financial management), leaving the core group of managers relatively small. The *periphery* encompasses two rather different sub-groups. The first consists of 'full-time employees with skills that are readily available in the labour market, such as clerical, secretarial, routine and lesser skilled manual work.' With less access to career opportunities, this group tends to be characterized by high labour turnover 'which makes work force reductions relatively easy by natural wastage.' The second peripheral group 'provides even greater numerical flexibility and includes part-timers, casuals, fixed term contract staff, temporaries, sub-contractors and public subsidy trainees, with even less job security than the first peripheral group.' All the evidence points to a very

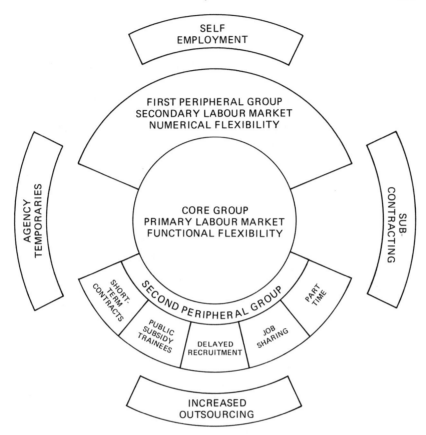

Figure 2.10 Labour market structures under conditions of flexible accumulation
(Source: Flexible Patterns of Work, *ed. C. Curson, Institute of Personnel Management*)

significant growth in this category of employees in the last few years.

Such flexible employment arrangements do not by themselves engender strong worker dissatisfaction, since flexibility can sometimes be mutually beneficial. But the aggregate effects, when looked at from the standpoint of insurance coverage and pension rights, as well as wage levels and job security, by no means appear positive from the standpoint of the working population as a whole. The most radical shift has been either towards increased sub-contracting (70 per cent of British firms surveyed by the National Economic Development Council reported an increase in sub-contracting between

1982 and 1985) or towards temporary rather than part-time work. This follows a long-established pattern in Japan where, even under Fordism, small business sub-contracting acted as a buffer to protect large corporations from the cost of market fluctuations. The current trend in labour markets is to reduce the number of 'core' workers and to rely increasingly upon a work force that can quickly be taken on board and equally quickly and costlessly be laid off when times get bad. In Britain, 'flexible wokers' increased by 16 per cent to 8.1 million between 1981 and 1985 while permanent jobs decreased by 6 per cent to 15.6 million (*Financial Times*, 27 February 1987). Over roughly the same time period, nearly one third of the ten million new jobs created in the USA were thought to be in the 'temporary' category (*New York Times*, 17 March 1988).

This has not, evidently, changed very radically the problems that arose in the 1960s of segmented or 'dual' labour markets, but has re-shaped them according to a rather different logic. While it is true that the declining significance of union power has reduced the singular power of white male workers in monopoly sector markets, it does not follow that those excluded from those labour markets, such as blacks, women, ethnic minorities of all kinds, have achieved sudden parity (except in the sense that many traditionally privileged white male workers have been marginalized alongside them). While some women and some minorities have gained access to more privileged positions, the new labour market conditions have for the most part re-emphasized the vulnerability of disadvantaged groups (as we shall shortly see in the case of women).

The transformation in labour market structure has been paralleled by equally important shifts in industrial organization. Organized sub-contracting, for example, opens up opportunities for small business formation, and in some instances permits older systems of domestic, artisanal, familial (patriarchal), and paternalistic ('godfather', 'guv'nor' or even mafia-like) labour systems to revive and flourish as centrepieces rather than as appendages of the production system. The revival of 'sweatshop' forms of production in cities such as New York and Los Angeles, Paris and London, became a matter for commentary in the mid-1970s and has proliferated rather than shrunk during the 1980s. The rapid growth of 'black,' 'informal,' or 'underground' economies has also been documented throughout the advanced capitalist world, leading some to suggest that there is a growing convergence between 'third world' and advanced capitalist labour systems. Yet the rise of new and the revival of older forms of industrial organization (often dominated by new immigrant groups in large cities, such as the Filipinos, South Koreans, Vietnamese, and Taiwanese in Los Angeles, or the Bangladeshis and Indians in East London) represents rather different things in different places. Sometimes it indicates the emergence of new survival strategies for the unemployed or wholly discriminated against (such as Haitian immigrants in Miami or New York), while in others it is more simply immigrant groups looking for an entry into a capitalist system, organized tax-dodging, or the attraction of high profit from illegal trade that lies at its basis. But in all such cases, the effect is to transform the mode of labour control and employment.

Working-class forms of organization (such as the trade unions), for example, depended heavily upon the massing of workers within the factory for their viability, and find it peculiarly difficult to gain any purchase within family and domestic labour systems. Paternalistic systems are dangerous territories for labour organizing because they are more likely to corrupt union power (if it is present) than union power is likely to liberate employees from 'godfather' domination and paternalistic welfarism. Indeed, one of the signal advantages of embracing such ancient forms of labour process and of petty-capitalist production is that they undermine working-class organization and transform the objective basis for class struggle. Class consciousness no longer derives from the straight class relation between capital and labour, and moves onto a much more confused terrain of inter-familial conflicts and fights for power within a kinship or clan-like system of hierarchically ordered social relations. Struggling against capitalist exploitation in the factory is very different from struggling against a father or uncle who organizes family labour into a highly disciplined and competitive sweatshop that works to order for multi-national capital (table 2.3).

The effects are doubly obvious when we consider the transformed role of women in production and labour markets. Not only do the new labour market structures make it much easier to exploit the labour power of women on a part-time basis, and so to substitute lower-paid female labour for that of more highly paid and less easily laid-off core male workers, but the revival of sub-contracting and domestic and family labour systems permits a resurgence of patriarchal practices and homeworking. This revival parallels the enhanced capacity of multinational capital to take Fordist mass-production systems abroad, and there to exploit extremely vulnerable women's labour power under conditions of extremely low pay and negligible job security (see Nash and Fernandez-Kelly, 1983). The Maquiladora programme that allows US managers and capital ownership to remain north of the Mexican border, while locating factories employing mainly young women south of the border, is a particularly dramatic

Table 2.3 Different forms of labour process and production organization

Type of production	Form	Basis of exploitation	Politics of production
Self-employed	consultants, artisans and informal sector	exchange of goods and services	individualist and market-led anti-monopoly or state regulation
Co-operative	collectives and co-operatives	internal agreements external exchange	negotiation
Patriarchy	small family firms (sweatshops)	kinship based on age and sex	kitchen politics
Communal paternalism	large domestic firms (sweated labour)	community based on norms, customs, and force	politics of face and status
Bureaucratic paternalism	corporate and state managerial systems	calculating rationality, loyalty, and seniority	career ladder and competition within organizations
Patrimonial	hierarchically ordered empires in production, trade, or finance	power relations and exchange of favours (traditional privilege)	bargaining, mutual gain, and dynastic struggles
Proletarian	capitalist firm and factory system	buying and selling of labour power and control over labour process and means of production	market competition, collective action, bargaining, and class struggle

Source: after Deyo, 1987

example of a practice that has become widespread in many of the less developed and newly-industrializing countries (the Philippines, South Korea, Brazil, etc.). The transition to flexible accumulation has in fact been marked by a revolution (by no means progressive) in the role of women in labour markets and labour processes during a period when the women's movement has fought for both greater awareness and improved conditions for what is now more than 40 per cent of the labour force in many of the advanced capitalist countries.

New techniques and organizational forms in production have spelled danger for traditionally organized businesses, sparking a wave of bankruptcies, plant closures, deindustrialization, and restructuring, that has put even the most powerful corporations at risk. The organizational form and managerial technique appropriate to high volume, standardized mass production were not always easy to convert to flexible system production with its emphasis upon problem solving, rapid and often highly specialized responses, and adaptability of skills to special purposes. Where production could be standardized, it proved hard to stop its moving to take advantage of low-paid labour power in the third world, creating there what Lipietz (1986) calls 'peripheral Fordism.' The Penn Central bankruptcy of 1976 and the Chrysler bail-out of 1981 indicated the seriousness of the problem in the United States. Not only did the list of the *Fortune* 500 top corporations in that country undergo considerable modification, their role in the economy also changed – their global employment remained stationary after 1970 (with a net loss in the United States) compared to the doubling of employment that had occurred in their plants from 1954 to 1970. On the other hand, new business formation in the United States picked up dramatically, doubling in the period between 1975 and 1981 (a deep recession year). Many of the new small businesses inserted themselves into the matrix of sub-contracting skilled tasks or consultancy.

The economies of scale sought under Fordist mass production have, it seems, been countered by an increasing capacity to manufacture a variety of goods cheaply in small batches. Economies of scope have beaten out economies of scale. By 1983, for example, *Fortune* reported that 'seventy-five per cent of all machine parts today are produced in batches of fifty or less.' Fordist enterprises could, of course, adopt the new technologies and labour processes (a practice dubbed 'neo-Fordist' by some), but in many instances competitive pressures and the struggle for better labour control led either to the rise of entirely new industrial forms or to the integration of Fordism with a whole network of sub-contracting and 'outsourcing' to give greater flexibility in the face of heightened competition and greater risk. Small-batch production and sub-contracting certainly had the virtues of bypassing the rigidities of the Fordist system and satisfying a far greater range of market needs, including quick-changing ones.

Such flexible production systems have permitted, and to some degree depended upon, an acceleration in the pace of product innovation together with the exploration of·highly specialized and small-scale market niches. Under conditions of recession and heightened competition, the drive to explore such possibilities became fundamental to survival. Turnover time — always one of the keys to capitalist profitability — stood to be reduced dramatically by deployment of the new technologies in production (automation, robots) and new organizational forms (such as the 'just-in-time' inventory-flows delivery system, which cuts down radically on stocks required to keep production flow going). But accelerating turnover time in production would have been useless unless the turnover time in consumption was also reduced. The half-life of a typical Fordist product was, for example, from five to seven years, but flexible accumulation has more than cut that in half in certain sectors (such as textile and clothing industries), while in others — such as the so-called 'thought-ware' industries (e.g. video games and computer software programmes) — the half-life is down to less than eighteen months. Flexible accumulation has been accompanied on the consumption side, therefore, by a much greater attention to quick-changing fashions and the mobilization of all the artifices of need inducement and cultural transformation that this implies. The relatively stable aesthetic of Fordist modernism has given way to all the ferment, instability, and fleeting qualities of a postmodernist aesthetic that celebrates difference, ephemerality, spectacle, fashion, and the commodification of cultural forms.

These shifts on the consumption side, coupled with changes in production, information gathering and financing, seem to underly a remarkable proportionate surge in service employment since the early 1970s. To some degree, this trend could be detected much earlier, perhaps as a consequence of rapid increases in efficiency in much of manufacturing industry through Fordist rationalization and of the evident difficulty of making similar productivity gains in service provision. But the rapid contraction in manufacturing employment after 1972 (table 2.4) has highlighted a rapid growth of service employment, not so much in retailing, distribution, transportation, and personal services (which have remained fairly stable or even lost ground), as in producer services, finance, insurance, and real estate, and certain other sectors such as health and education (see

Table 2.4 Structure of civilian employment in selected advanced
capitalist countries, 1960–1981, illustrating the rise of the
service economy

	Percentage of employed population in:								
	Agriculture			*Industry*			*Services*		
	1960	*1973*	*1981*	*1960*	*1973*	*1981*	*1960*	*1973*	*1981*
Australia	10.3	7.4	6.5	39.9	35.5	30.6	49.8	57.1	62.8
Canada	13.3	6.5	5.5	33.2	30.6	28.3	53.5	62.8	66.2
France	22.4	11.4	8.6	37.8	39.7	35.2	39.8	48.9	56.2
W. Germany	14.0	7.5	5.9	48.8	47.5	44.1	37.3	45.0	49.9
Italy	32.8	18.3	13.4	36.9	39.2	37.5	30.2	42.5	49.2
Japan	30.2	13.4	10.0	28.5	37.2	35.3	41.3	49.3	54.7
Spain	42.3	24.3	18.2	32.0	36.7	35.2	25.7	39.0	46.6
Sweden	13.1	7.1	5.6	42.0	36.8	31.3	45.0	56.0	63.1
UK	4.1	2.9	2.8	48.8	42.6	36.3	47.0	54.5	60.9
USA	8.3	4.2	3.5	33.6	33.2	30.1	58.1	62.6	66.4
OECD	21.7	12.1	10.0	35.3	36.4	33.7	43.0	51.5	56.3

Source: OECD Labour Force Statistics

Walker, 1985; also Noyelle and Stanback, 1984; Daniels, 1985). The exact interpretation (or indeed even basic definitions of what is meant by a service) to be put on this is a matter of considerable controversy. Some of the expansion can be attributed, for example, to the growth of sub-contracting and consultancy which permits activities formerly internalized within manufacturing firms (legal, marketing, advertising, typing, etc.) to be hived off to separate enterprises. It may also be, as we shall see in Part III, that the need to accelerate turnover time in consumption has led to a shift of emphasis from production of goods (most of which, like knives and forks, have a substantial lifetime) to the production of events (such as spectacles that have an almost instantaneous turnover time). Whatever the full explanation may be, any account of the transformation of advanced capitalist economies since 1970 has to look carefully at this marked shift in occupational structure.

All of this has put a premium on 'smart' and innovative entrepreneurialism, aided and abetted by all of the accoutrements of swift, decisive, and well-informed decision-making. The enhanced capacity for geographical dispersal, small-scale production, and the pursuit of custom-markets has not necessarily led, however, to any diminution of corporate power. Indeed, to the degree that information and the ability to make swift decisions in a highly uncertain, ephemeral, and competitive environment become crucial to profits, the well organized corporation has marked competitive advantages over small business. 'Deregulation' (another of the political buzz-words of the era of flexible accumulation) has often meant increased monopolization (after a phase of intensified competition) in sectors such as airlines, energy, and financial services. At one end of the business scale, flexible accumulation has been conducive to massive mergers and corporate diversifications. US companies spent $22 billion acquiring each other in 1977, but by 1981 that had risen to $82 billion, cresting in 1985 at an extraordinary $180 billion. Though mergers and acquisitions declined in 1987, in part as a response to the stock market crash, the total value still stood at $165.8 billion for 2,052 transactions (according to W.T. Grimm, a merger consultant group). Yet in 1988 the merger mania kept going. In the United States merger deals worth than $198 billion were completed in the first three-quarters of the year, while in Europe, de Benedetti of Olivetti's attempt to take over the Union Générale of Belgium, a bank which controlled about one third of that country's productive assets indicated the global spread of merger mania. Most of those employed by the *Fortune* 500 top companies in the USA now work in lines of activity that have nothing to do with the primary line of business with which their company is identified. 'The duty of management is to make money, not steel' announced James Roderick, Chairman of US Steel, in 1979, and he promptly launched into a campaign of acquisitions and expansions to diversify that company's activities. At the other end of the scale, small businesses, patriarchal and artisanal organizational structures have also flourished. Even self-employment, which had declined steadily in the United States after 1950, underwent, according to Reich's (1983) account, substantial revival after 1972, expanding by more than 25 per cent in less than a decade (a trend which encompassed everything from casual work by the unemployed to highly paid consultants, designers, craft workers and specialists). New systems of co-ordination have been put in place either through an intricate variety of sub-contracting arrangements (that connect small firms to large-scale, often multinational, operations) through the formation of new production ensembles in which agglomeration economies have become of increased significance, or through the domination and integration of small businesses under the aegis of powerful financial or marketing organizations (Benetton, for example, engages in no production directly, but simply operates as a powerful marketing machine, which transmits commands to a wide array of independent producers).

What this suggests is that the tension that has always prevailed within capitalism between monopoly and competition, between centralization and decentralization of economic power, is being worked out in fundamentally new ways. This does not necessarily imply, however, that capitalism is becoming more 'disorganized' as Offe (1985) and Lash and Urry (1987) suggest. For what is most interesting about the current situation is the way in which capitalism is becoming ever more tightly organized *through* dispersal, geographical mobility, and flexible responses in labour markets, labour processes, and consumer markets, all accompanied by hefty doses of institutional, product, and technological innovation.

The tighter organization and imploding centralization have in fact been achieved by two parallel developments of the greatest importance. First, accurate and up-to-date information is now a very highly valued commodity. Access to, and control over, information, coupled with a strong capacity for instant data analysis, have become essential to the centralized co-ordination of far-flung corporate interests. The capacity for instantaneous response to changes in exchange rates, fashions and tastes, and moves by competitors is more essential to corporate survival than it ever was under Fordism. The emphasis on information has also spawned a wide array of highly specialized business services and consultancies capable of providing up-to-the-minute information on market trends and the kind of instant data analyses useful in corporate decision-making. It has also created a situation in which vast profits stand to be made on the basis of privileged access to information, particularly in financial and currency markets (witness the proliferating 'insider trading' scandals of the 1980s that struck both New York and London). But this is, in a sense, only the illegal tip of an iceberg where privileged access to information of any sort (such as scientific and technical know-how, government policies, and political shifts) becomes an essential aspect of successful and profitable decision-making.

Access to scientific and technical know-how has always been important in the competitive struggle, but here, too, we can see a renewal of interest and emphasis, because in a world of quick-changing tastes and needs and flexible production systems (as opposed to the relatively stable world of standardized Fordism), access to the latest technique, the latest product, the latest scientific discovery implies the possibility of seizing an important competitive advantage. Knowledge itself becomes a key commodity, to be produced and sold to the highest bidder, under conditions that are themselves increasingly organized on a competitive basis. Universities and re-search institutes compete fiercely for personnel as well as for being first in patenting new scientific discoveries (whoever gets first to the antidote for the Aids virus will surely profit handsomely, as the agree-ment reached between US researchers and France's Pasteur Institute over the sharing of information and royalties clearly recognized). Organized knowledge production has expanded remarkably over the past few decades, at the same time as it has been increasingly put upon a commercial basis (witness the uncomfortable transitions in many university systems in the advanced capitalist world from guar-dianship of knowledge and wisdom to ancillary production of know-ledge for corporate capital). The celebrated Stanford Silicon Valley or the MIT—Boston Route 128 'high-tech' industry connections are configurations that are quite new and special to the era of flexible accumulation (even though, as David Noble points out in *America by design*, many US universities were set up and promoted by corporate capital from their very inception).

Control over information flow and over the vehicles for pro-pagation of popular taste and culture have likewise become vital weapons in competitive struggle. The startling concentration of econ-omic power in book publishing (where 2 per cent of the publishers control 75 per cent of the books published in the USA), the media and the press cannot be explained simply in terms of the production conditions conducive to mergers in those fields. It has a lot to do with the power of other large corporations, as expressed through their controls over mechanisms of distribution and advertising ex-penditures. The latter have grown markedly since the 1960s, and eat up even larger proportions of corporate budgets because, in a highly competitive world, it is not simply products but the corporate image itself that becomes essential, not only to marketing but also for raising capital, pursuing mergers, and gaining leverage over the pro-duction of knowledge, government policy, and the promotion of cultural values. Corporate sponsorship of the Arts (Exhibition spon-sored by —), of universities, and of philanthropic projects is the prestige end of a scale of activities that include everything from lavish brochures and company reports, public relations stunts, and even scandals that constantly keep the company name in the public eye.

The second development — and this has been far more important than the first — was the complete reorganization of the global financial system and the emergence of greatly enhanced powers of financial co-ordination. Again, there has been a dual movement, on the one hand towards the formation of financial conglomerates and brokers of extraordinary global power, and, on the other hand, a rapid proliferation and decentralization of financial activities and flows through the creation of entirely new financial instruments and markets. In the United States, this meant the deregulation of a financial system that had been rigorously circumscribed ever since the reforms of the 1930s. The US *Hunt Commission Report* of 1971 was the first explicit recognition of the need for reforms as a condition of survival and growth of the capitalist economic system. After the traumas of 1973, the pressure for financial deregulation gathered pace in the 1970s and had engulfed all of the world's financial centres by 1986 (London's celebrated 'big bang' reforms of that year drove home the point). Deregulation and financial innovation − both long and complicated processes − had by then become a condition of survival of any world financial centre within a highly integrated global system co-ordinated through instantaneous telecommunications. The formation of a global stock market, of global commodity (even debt) futures markets, of currency and interest rate swaps, together with an accelerated geographical mobility of funds, meant, for the first time, the formation of a single world market for money and credit supply (figure 2.11).

The structure of this global financial system is now so complicated that it surpasses most people's understanding. The boundaries between distinctive functions like banking, brokerage, financial services, housing finance, consumer credit, and the like have become increasingly porous at the same time as new markets in commodity, stock, currency, or debt futures have sprung up, discounting time future into time present in baffling ways. Computerization and electronic communications have pressed home the significance of instantaneous international co-ordination of financial flows. 'Banking,' said the *Financial Times* (8 May 1987), 'is rapidly becoming indifferent to the constraints of time, place and currency.' It is now the case that 'an English buyer can get a Japanese mortgage, an American can tap his New York bank account through a cash machine in Hong Kong and a Japanese investor can buy shares in a London-based Scandinavian bank whose stock is denominated in sterling, dollars, Deutsche Marks and Swiss francs.' This 'bewildering' world of high finance encloses an equally bewildering variety of cross-cutting activities, in which banks borrow massively short-term from other banks, insurance companies and pension funds assemble such vast pools of investment funds as to function as dominant 'market makers', while industrial, merchant, and landed capital become so integrated into financial operations and structures that it becomes increasingly difficult to tell where commercial and industrial interests begin and strictly financial interests end.

This confusion has been particularly associated with the growth of

Hours GMT

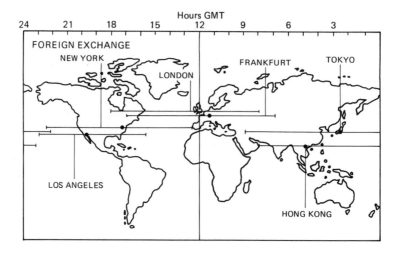

Hours GMT

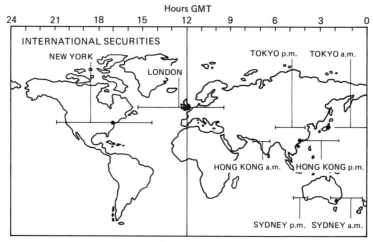

Hours GMT

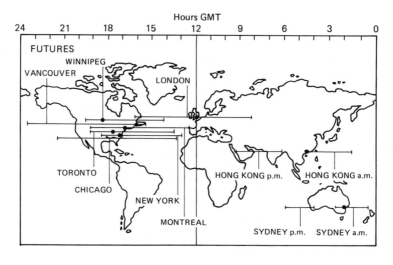

what is now called 'paper entrepreneurialism.' Tremendous emphasis has been put in recent years on finding ways other than straight production of goods and services to make profits. The techniques vary from sophisticated 'creative accounting' through careful monitoring of international markets and political conditions by multinationals, so that they can profit from relative shifts in currency values or interest rates, to straight corporate raiding and asset-stripping of rival or even totally unrelated corporations. The 'merger and takeover mania' of the 1980s was part and parcel of this emphasis upon paper entrepreneurialism, for although there were some instances where such activities could indeed be justified in terms of rationalization or diversification of corporate interests, the thrust was more often than not to gain paper profits without troubling with actual production. Small wonder, as Robert Reich (1983) observes, that 'paper entrepreneurialism now preoccupies some of America's best minds, attacks some of its most talented graduates, employs some of its most creative and original thinking, and spurs some of its most energetic wheeling and dealing.' Over the last fifteen years, he reports, the most sought after and most lucrative jobs to be had in US business lay not in the management of production but in the legal and financial spheres of corporate action.

Awash with liquidity, and perturbed by an indebtedness that has spiralled out of control since 1973, the world's financial system has, however, eluded any collective control on the part of even the most powerful advanced capitalist states. The formation of the so-called 'Eurodollar' financial market out of surplus US dollars in the mid 1960s is symptomatic of the problem. Quite uncontrolled by any national government, this market in 'stateless' money expanded from $50 billion in 1973 to nearly $2 *trillion* by 1987, thus approaching the size of the money aggregates within the United States. The volume of Eurodollars increased at a rate of around 25 per cent per year in the 1970s, compared to a 10 per cent increase in money supply within the USA and a 4 per cent growth rate in the volume of foreign trade. The debt of third world countries likewise mushroomed out of control (see figure 2.12). It does not take much imagination to see that such imbalances portend severe stresses and strains within the global capitalist system. Prophets of doom (like the Wall Street investment banker Felix Rohatyn) now abound, and even *The Economist* and the *Wall Street Journal* sounded sombre warnings

Figure 2.11 Twenty-four hour trading patterns in global financial markets (courtesy of Nigel Thrift)

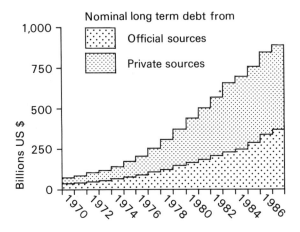

Figure 2.12 Growth of debt of lesser developed countries, 1970—1987 (Source: *World Bank Debt Tables*)

of impending financial disaster well before the stock market crash of October 1987.

The new financial systems put into place since 1972 have changed the balance of forces at work in global capitalism, giving much more autonomy to the banking and financial system relative to corporate, state, and personal financing. Flexible accumulation evidently looks more to finance capital as its co-ordinating power than did Fordism. This means that the potentiality for the formation of independent and autonomous monetary and financial crises is much greater than before, even though the financial system is better able to spread risks over a broader front and shift funds rapidly from failing to profitable enterprises, regions, and sectors. Much of the flux, instability, and gyrating can be directly attributed to this enhanced capacity to switch capital flows around in ways that seem almost oblivious of the constraints of time and space that normally pin down material activities of production and consumption.

The increasing powers of co-ordination lodged within the world's financial system have emerged to some degree at the expense of the power of the nation state to control capital flow and, hence, its own fiscal and monetary policy. The breakdown, in 1971, of the Bretton Woods agreement to fix the price of gold and the convertibility of the dollar was an acknowledgement that the United States no longer had the power to control world fiscal and monetary policy single-handedly. The adoption of a flexible exchange rate system in 1973 (in response to massive speculative currency movements against the dollar) signalled the complete abolition of Bretton Woods. Since that time all nation states have been at the mercy of financial disciplining, either through the effects of capital flow (witness the turnaround in French socialist government policy in the face of strong capital flight after 1981), or by direct institutional disciplining. Britain's concession under a Labour government to austerity measures dictated by the International Monetary Fund in order to gain access to credit in 1976 was a simple acknowledgement of external financial power over internal politics (there was more to matters, evidently, than a simple conspiracy of the 'gnomes of Zurich' that had been so castigated by the Wilson government of the decade before). There had, of course, always been a delicate balance between financial and state powers under capitalism, but the breakdown of Fordism–Keynesianism evidently meant a shift towards the empowerment of finance capital *vis-à-vis* the nation state. The significance of all this becomes even more apparent when put into the context of the rapid reduction in transportation and communications costs that rested on containerization, jumbo-jet cargo transport, and satellite communications, which allowed production and design instructions to be communicated instantaneously anywhere around the world. Industry that had traditionally been tied by locational constraints to raw material sources or markets could become much more footloose. From the mid-1970s onwards a vast literature emerged trying to keep track of the new international division of labour, shifting principles of location, and proliferating mechanisms of co-ordination both within trans-national corporations as well as between different sectoral commodity and product markets. Newly industrializing countries (NICs) such as the South-East Asian 'gang of four' (Hong Kong, Singapore, Taiwan, and South Korea) began to make serious inroads into the markets for certain products (textiles, electronics, etc.) in the advanced capitalist countries, and were soon joined by a host of other NICs (Hungary, India, Egypt) and those countries that had earlier pursued import substitution strategies (Brazil, Mexico) in a locational re-shuffle of the world's industrial production.

Some of the power shifts since 1972 within the global political economy of advanced capitalism have been truly remarkable. United States dependence on foreign trade (historically always rather small – in the range of 4–5 per cent of gross domestic product) doubled in the period 1973–80 (see table 2.5). Imports from developing countries increased almost tenfold, and foreign imports (particularly from Japan) surged to claim a major share of US markets in areas as diverse as silicon chips, televisions and videos, numerically controlled

Table 2.5   *Dependence on foreign trade for selected advanced capitalist countries*

	Exports and imports as per cent of GNP			
	1960	*1970*	*1980*	*1986*
US				
exports	4.37	5.35	10.0	7.0
imports	4.36	5.00	10.5	10.2
UK				
exports	20.9	23.1	27.7	26.2
imports	22.3	22.2	25.3	27.0
Japan				
exports	10.8	10.8	13.7	11.7
imports	10.3	9.5	14.6	7.6
W. Germany				
exports	17.9	21.2	26.3	30.0
imports	16.4	19.1	27.0	24.9
Italy				
exports	12.1	15.4	21.7	20.4
imports	12.4	15.0	24.4	18.7

Source: OECD

machine tools, shoes, textiles and cars. The balance of payments in goods and services for the United States rapidly moved that country from a net global creditor to the status of the world's largest debtor (see figure 2.13). Meanwhile the financial power of Japan grew, turning Tokyo into one of the world's most important financial centres (topping New York for the first time in 1987) simply because of the vast quantities of surplus funds controlled by the Japanese banks. The latter displaced the Americans as the largest holders of international assets in 1985, and by 1987 held $1.4 trillion compared with the $630 billion held by Americans. The four largest banks in the world (in asset terms) are now Japanese.

These shifts have been accompanied and in part ushered in by the rise of an aggressive neo-conservatism in North America and much of Western Europe. The electoral victories of Thatcher (1979) and Reagan (1980) are often viewed as a distinctive rupture in the politics of the postwar period. I understand them more as consolidations of

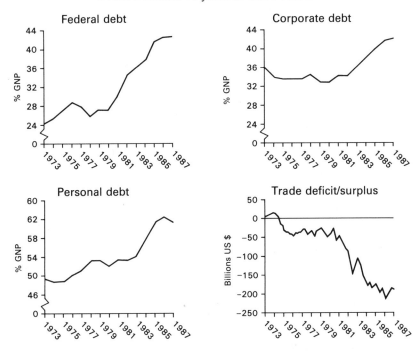

Figure 2.13 Growth of federal, personal and corporate debt in the United States and deterioration in US trade balance, 1973–1987 (Source: Department of Commerce and Federal Reserve Board)

what was already under way throughout much of the 1970s. The crisis of 1973–5 was in part born out of a confrontation with the accumulated rigidities of government policies and practices built up during the Fordist–Keynesian period. Keynesian policies had appeared inflationary as entitlements grew and fiscal capacities stagnated. Since it had always been part of the Fordist political consensus that redistributions should be funded out of growth, slackening growth inevitably meant trouble for the welfare state and the social wage. The Nixon and Heath governments both recognized the problem in the period 1970–4, sparking struggles with organized labour and retrenchment in state expenditures. The Labour and Democratic governments that subsequently came to power bowed to the same imperatives, though ideologically predisposed in quite different directions. Their corporatist approach to solving the problem may have been different (relying on voluntary compliance and union enforcement of wages and prices policies) but the objectives had to be the same. As soon as political choices were seen as a trade-off between growth or equity, there was no question which way the wind would blow for even the most dedicated of reformist governments. The gradual withdrawal of support for the welfare state (see figure 2.9), and the attack upon the real wage and organized union power, that began as an economic necessity in the crisis of 1973—5, were simply turned by the neo-conservatives into a governmental virtue. The image of strong governments administering powerful doses of unpalatable medicine to restore the health of ailing economies became widespread.

To the degree that heightened international competition under conditions of flagging growth forced all states to become more 'entrepreneurial' and concerned to maintain a favourable business climate, so the power of organized labour and of other social movements had to be curbed. Though the politics of resistance may have varied — with tangible results, as Therborn's (1984) comparative study of European states shows — austerity, fiscal retrenchment, and erosion of the social compromise between big labour and big government became watchwords in every state in the advanced capitalist world. Although, therefore, states retain considerable power to intervene in labour contracts, what Jessop (1982, 1983) calls 'the accumulation strategy' of each capitalist nation state has become more strictly circumscribed.

On the reverse side of the coin, governments ideologically committed to non-intervention and fiscal conservatism have been forced by events to be more rather than less interventionist. Laying aside the degree to which the evident insecurities of flexible accumulation create a climate conducive to authoritarianism of the Thatcher—Reagan type, financial instability and the massive problems of internal and external indebtedness have forced periodic interventions in unstable financial markets. The deployment of Federal Reserve power to ameliorate the Mexican debt crisis of 1982, and the US Treasury's agreement to broker what might amount to a $20 billion write-off of Mexican debt held by US banks in 1987, are two examples of this new kind of interventionism in international markets. The decision to nationalize the failing Continental Illinois Bank in 1984, and the massive outlays of the US Federal Deposit and Insurance Corporation (FDIC) to absorb the rising costs of bank failure (see figure 2.14) and the similar drain on the resources of the Federal Savings and Loan Insurance Corporation that required a $10 billion re-capitalization effort in 1987 to guard against the fact that some 20 per cent of the nation's 3,100 thrift institutions were technically insolvent, illustrates the scale of the problem (the estimated bail-out required to deal with the savings and loan crisis stood at $50 to $100 billion by

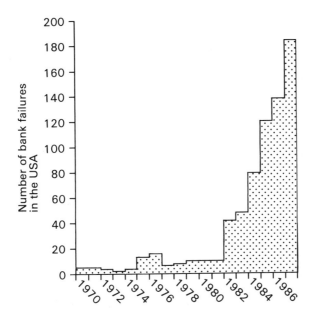

Figure 2.14 Bank Failures in the USA, 1970–1987
(Source: *Federal Deposit and Insurance Corporation*)

September 1988). So exercised did William Isaacs, Chairman of the FDIC, become that he felt obliged to warn the American Bankers Association as early as October 1987 that the USA 'might be headed towards nationalization of banking,' if they could not stem their losses. Operations in international currency markets to stabilize exchange rates come no cheaper – the New York Federal Reserve reported spending more than $4 billion in the two months after the stock market crash of October 1987 to keep the dollar exchange rate relatively orderly, and the Bank of England sold £24 billion in 1987 in order to keep the British pound from rising too fast and too far. The role of the state as a lender or operator of last resort has, evidently, become more rather than less crucial.

But, by the same token, we now see that it is also possible for nation states (South Africa, Peru, Brazil, etc.) to default on their international financial obligations, forcing inter-state negotiations on debt repayments. It is also, I suspect, no accident that the first economic summit between the major capitalist powers occurred in 1975, and that the pursuit of international co-ordinations – either through the IMF or through the pursuit of collective agreements to intervene in currency markets — has intensified ever since, becoming even more emphatic in the wake of the 1987 stock market crash. There has been, in short, a struggle to win back for the collectivity of capitalist states some of the power they have individually lost over the past two decades. This trend was institutionalized in 1982, when the IMF and the World Bank were designated as the central authority for exercising the collective power of capitalist nation states over international financial negotiations. Such power is usually deployed to force curbs on public expenditure, cuts in real wages, and austerity in fiscal and monetary policy, to the point of provoking a wave of so-called 'IMF riots' from São Paulo to Kingston, Jamaica, and from Peru to the Sudan and Egypt since 1976 (see Walton, 1987, for a complete list).

There are many other signs of continuity rather than rupture with the Fordist era. The massive government deficits in the United States, mainly attributable to defence, have been fundamental to whatever economic growth there has been in world capitalism in the 1980s, suggesting that Keynesian practices are by no means dead. Neither does the commitment to 'free-market' competition and deregulation entirely fit with the wave of mergers, corporate consolidations, and the extraordinary growth of interlinkages between supposedly rival firms of different national origin. Arenas of conflict between the nation state and trans-national capital have, however, opened up, undermining the easy accommodation between big capital and big government so typical of the Fordist era. The state is now in a much more problematic position. It is called upon to regulate the activities of corporate capital in the national interest at the same time as it is forced, also in the national interest, to create a 'good business climate' to act as an inducement to trans-national and global finance capital, and to deter (by means other than exchange controls) capital flight to greener and more profitable pastures.

While the history may have varied substantially from one country to another, there is strong evidence that the modalities and targets of, as well as the capacity for, state intervention have changed substantially since 1972 throughout the capitalist world, no matter what the ideological complexion of the government in power (the recent experience of the French and Spanish socialists further helps substantiate the point). This does not mean, however, that state interventionism has generally diminished, for in some respects — particularly regarding labour control — state intervention is more crucial now than it ever was.

This brings us, finally, to the even thornier problem of the ways in which norms, habits, and political and cultural attitudes have shifted since 1970, and the degree to which such shifts integrate with the transition from Fordism to flexible accumulation. Since the political success of neo-conservatism can hardly be attributed to its overall economic achievements (its strong negatives of high unemployment, weak growth, rapid dislocation, and spiralling indebtedness are offset only by control of inflation), several commentators have attributed its rise to a general shift from the collective norms and values, that were hegemonic at least in working-class organizations and other social movements of the 1950s and 1960s, towards a much more competitive individualism as the central value in an entrepreneurial culture that has penetrated many walks of life. This heightened competition (in labour markets as well as amongst entrepreneurs) has, of course, proved destructive and ruinous to some, yet it has undeniably generated a burst of energy that many, even on the left, compare favourably with the stifling orthodoxy and bureaucracy of state control and monopolistic corporate power. It has also permitted substantial redistributions of income to be achieved, which have advantaged, for the most part, the already privileged. Entrepreneurialism now characterizes not only business action, but realms of life as diverse as urban governance, the growth of informal sector production, labour market organization, research and development, and it has even reached into the nether corners of academic, literary, and artistic life.

While the roots of this transition are evidently deep and complicated, their consistency with a transition from Fordism to flexible accumulation is reasonably clear even if the direction (if any) of causality is not. To begin with, the more flexible motion of capital emphasizes the new, the fleeting, the ephemeral, the fugitive, and the contingent in modern life, rather than the more solid values implanted under Fordism. To the degree that collective action was thereby made more difficult — and it was indeed a central aim of the drive for enhanced labour control to render it thus — so rampant individualism fits into place as a necessary, though not a sufficient, condition for the transition from Fordism to flexible accumulation. It was, after all, mainly through the burst of new business formation, innovation, and entrepreneurialism that many of the new systems of production were put into place. But, as Simmel (1978) long ago suggested, it is also at such times of fragmentation and economic insecurity that the desire for stable values leads to a heightened emphasis upon the authority of basic institutions — the family, religion, the state. And there is abundant evidence of a revival of support for such institutions and the values they represent throughout the Western world since about 1970. Such connections are, at least, plausible, and they ought, therefore, to be given more careful scrutiny. The immediate task at hand is to outline an interpretation of the roots of such a major transition in capitalism's dominant regime of accumulation.

10

Theorizing the transition

To the degree that we are witnessing a historical transition, still far from complete and in any case, like Fordism, bound to be partial in certain important respects, so we have encountered a series of theoretical dilemmas. Can we grasp theoretically the logic, if not the necessity, of the transition? To what degree do past and present theoretical formulations of the dynamics of capitalism have to be modified in the light of the radical reorganizations and restructurings taking place in both productive forces and social relations? And can we represent the current regime sufficiently well to get some grip on the probable course and implications of what appears to be an ongoing revolution?

The transition from Fordism to flexible accumulation has, in fact, posed serious difficulties for theories of any sort. Keynesians, monetarists, neo-classical partial equilibrium theorists, appear just as befuddled as everyone else. The transition has also posed serious dilemmas for Marxists. In the face of such difficulties, many commentators have abandoned any pretence of theory, and simply resorted to data-chasing to keep pace with the rapid shifts. But here too there are problems – what data are key indicators rather than contingent series? The only general point of agreement is that something significant has changed in the way capitalism has been working since about 1970.

The first difficulty is to try to encapsulate the nature of the changes we are looking at. In tables 2.6, 2.7, and 2.8 I summarize three recent accounts of the transition. The first, a rather celebratory account by Halal (1986) of the new capitalism, emphasizes the positive and liberatory elements of the new entrepreneurialism. The second, by Lash and Urry (1987), emphasizes power relations and politics in relation to economy and culture. The third, by Swyngedouw (1986), provides much more detail on transformations in technology and the

Table 2.6   The new capitalism according to Halal

	The old capitalism (Industrial paradigm)	The new capitalism (Post-industrial paradigm)
Frontier of progress	hard growth	smart growth
Organization	mechanistic structure	market networks
Decision-making	authoritarian command	participative leadership
Institutional values	financial goals	multiple goals
Management focus	operational management	strategic management
Economic macro-system	profit-centered big business	democratic free enterprise
World system	capitalism versus socialism	hybrids of capitalism and socialism

Source: Halal, 1986

labour process while appreciating how the regime of accumulation and its modes of regulation have shifted. In each case, of course, the opposition is used as a didactic tool to emphasize the differences rather than the continuities, and none of the authors argue that matters are anywhere near as cut and dried as these schemas suggest. The schemas indicate, however, some overlaps but also some differences which are instructive, since they suggest rather different mechanisms of causation. Halal appears closer to Schumpeter's theory of entrepreneurial innovation as the driving force of capitalism, and tends to interpret Fordism and Keynesianism as an unfortunate interlude in capitalist progress. Lash and Urry see the evolution in part as the collapse of the material conditions for a powerful collective working-class politics, and attempt to probe the economic, cultural, and political roots of that collapse. By the very use of the terms 'organized' and 'disorganized' to characterize the transition, they emphasize more the disintegration than the coherence of contemporary capitalism, and therefore avoid confronting the possibility of a tran-

Table 2.7 Contrast between organized and disorganized capitalism according to Lash and Urry

Organized capitalism	Disorganized capitalism
concentration and centralization of industrial banking, and commercial capital in regulated national markets	de-concentration of rapidly increasing corporate power away from national markets. Increasing internationalization of capital and in some cases separation of industrial from bank capital
increasing separation of ownership from control and emergence of complex managerial hierarchies	continued expansion of managerial strata articulating their own individual and political agendas quite distinct from class politics
growth of new sectors of managerial, scientific, technological intelligentsia and of middle-class bureaucracy	relative/absolute decline in blue-collar working class
growth of collective organizations and bargaining within regions and nation states	decline in effectiveness of national collective bargaining
close articulation of state and large monopoly capital interests and rise of class-based welfare statism	increasing independence of large monopolies from state regulation and diverse challenges to centralized state bureaucracy and power
expansion of economic empires and control of overseas production and markets	industrialization of third world and competitive de-industrialization of core countries which turn to specialization in services
incorporation of diverse class interests within a national agenda set through negotiated compromises and bureaucratic regulation	outright decline of class-based politics and institutions

Table 2.7 cont.

Organized capitalism	Disorganized capitalism
hegemony of technical—scientific rationality	cultural fragmentation and pluralism coupled with undermining of traditional class or national identities
concentration of capitalist relations within relatively few industries and regions	dispersal of capitalist relations across many sectors and regions
extractive-manufacturing industries dominant sources of employment	decline of extractive-manufacturing industries and rise of organizational and service industries
strong regional concentration and specialization in extractive-manufacturing sectors	dispersal, diversification of the territorial—spatial division of labour
search for economies of scale through increasing plant (work-force) size	decline in plant size through geographical dispersal, increased sub-contracting, global production systems
growth of large industrial cities dominating regions through provision of centralized services (commercial and financial)	decline of industrial cities and deconcentration from city centres into peripheral or semi-rural areas resulting in acute inner city problems
cultural-ideological configuration of 'modernism'	cultural-ideological configurations of 'postmodernism'

Source: after Lash and Urry (1987)

sition in the regime of accumulation. Swyngedouw, on the other hand, by emphasizing changes in the mode of production and of industrial organization, locates the transition in the mainstream of Marxian political economy while clearly accepting the regulation school's language.

I am more partial to Swyngedouw's interpretation. But if the language of the regulation school has survived better than most, it is, I suspect, because of its rather more pragmatic orientation. There is,

Table 2.8 Contrast between Fordism and flexible accumulation according to Swyngedouw

Fordist production (based on economies of scale)	Just-in-time production (based on economies of scope)
A THE PRODUCTION PROCESS	
mass production of homogeneous goods	small batch production
uniformity and standardization	flexible and small batch production of a variety of product types
large buffer stocks and inventory	no stocks
testing quality ex-post (rejects and errors detected late)	quality control part of process (immediate detection of errors)
rejects are concealed in buffer stocks	immediate reject of defective parts
loss of production time because of long set-up times, defective parts, inventory bottlenecks, etc.	reduction of lost time, diminishing 'the porosity of the working day'
resource driven	demand driven
vertical and (in some cases) horizontal integration	(quasi-) vertical integration sub-contracting
cost reductions through wage control	learning-by-doing integrated in long-term planning
B LABOUR	
single task performance by worker	multiple tasks
payment per rate (based on job design criteria)	personal payment (detailed bonus system)
high degree of job specialization	elimination of job demarcation
no or only little on the job training	long on the job training
vertical labour organization	more horizontal labour organization
no learning experience	on the job learning

Table 2.8 cont.

Fordist production (based on economies of scale)	Just-in-time production (based on economies of scope)
emphasis on diminishing worker's responsibility (disciplining of labour force)	emphasis on worker's co-responsibility
no job security	high employment security for core workers (life-time employment). No job security and poor labour conditions for temporary workers

C SPACE

functional spatial specialization (centralization/decentralization)	spatial clustering and agglomeration
spatial division of labour	spatial integration
homogenization of regional labour markets (spatially segmented labour markets)	labour market diversification (in-place labour market segmentation)
world-wide sourcing of components and sub-contractors	spatial proximity of vertically quasi-integrated firms.

D STATE

regulation	deregulation/re-regulation
rigidity	flexibility
collective bargaining	division/individualization, local or firm-based negotiations
socialization of welfare (the welfare state)	privatization of collective needs and social security
international stability through multi-lateral agreements	international destabilization; increased geopolitical tensions
centralization	decentralization and sharpened interregional/intercity competition
the 'subsidy' state/city	the 'entrepreneurial' state/city
indirect intervention in markets through income and price policies	direct state intervention in markets through procurement

Table 2.8 cont.

Fordist production (based on economies of scale)	Just-in-time production (based on economies of scope)
national regional policies	'territorial' regional policies (third party form)
firm financed research and development	state financed research and development
industry-led innovation	state-led innovation
E IDEOLOGY	
mass consumption of consumer durables: the consumption society	individualized consumption: 'yuppie'-culture
modernism	postmodernism
totality/structural reform	specificity/adaptation
socialization	individualization the 'spectacle' society

Source: Swyngedouw (1986)

within the regulation school, little or no attempt to provide any detailed understanding of the mechanisms and logic of transitions. This, it seems to me, is a serious lack. To plug the gap requires going back to basics and dealing with the underlying logic of capitalism in general. And it was, of course, Marx's peculiar virtue to have built a theory of capitalism in general through an analysis of capitalism under the broadly competitive and *laissez-faire* mode of regulation to be found in Britain in the mid-nineteenth century. Let us go back, therefore, to Marx's 'invariant elements and relations' of a capitalist mode of production and see to what degree they are omni-present beneath all the surface froth and evanescence, the fragmentations and disruptions, so characteristic of present political economy.

Since flexible accumulation is still a form of capitalism we can expect a number of basic propositions to hold. I have tried to summarize these propositions elsewhere, and so I shall simply extract some very basic elements of the argument laid out in *The limits to capital* (Harvey, 1982). I shall refer, in particular, to three basic features of any capitalist mode of production.

1　Capitalism is growth-oriented. A steady rate of growth is essential for the health of a capitalist economic system, since it is only through growth that profits can be assured and the accumulation of capital be sustained. This implies that capitalism has to prepare the ground for, and actually achieve an expansion of, output and a growth in real values, no matter what the social, political, geopolitical, or ecological consequences. To the degree that virtue is made of necessity, it is a corner-stone of capitalism's ideology that growth is both inevitable and good. Crisis is then defined as lack of growth.

2　Growth in real values rests on the exploitation of living labour in production. This is not to say that labour gets little, but that growth is always predicated on a gap between what labour gets and what it creates. This implies that labour control, both in production and in the market place, is vital for the perpetuation of capitalism. Capitalism is founded, in short, on a class relation between capital and labour. Since labour control is essential to capitalist profit, so, too, is the dynamic of class struggle over labour control and market wage fundamental to the trajectory of capitalist development.

3　Capitalism is necessarily technologically and organizationally dynamic. This is so in part because the coercive laws of competition push individual capitalists into leap-frogging innovations in their search for profit. But organizational and technological change also play a key role in modifying the dynamics of class struggle, waged from both sides, in the realm of labour markets and labour control. Furthermore, if labour control is fundamental to the production of profits and becomes a broader issue for the mode of regulation, so technological and organizational innovation in the regulatory system (such as the state apparatus, political systems of incorporation and representation, etc.) becomes crucial to the perpetuation of capitalism. The ideology that 'progress' is both inevitable and good derives in part from this necessity.

What Marx was able to show was that these three necessary conditions of a capitalist mode of production were inconsistent and contradictory and that the dynamic of capitalism was necessarily, therefore, crisis-prone. There was, in his analysis, no way in which the combination of these three necessary conditions could produce steady and unproblematic growth. In particular, the crisis tendencies of capitalism would produce periodic phases of overaccumulation, defined as a condition in which idle capital and idle labour supply could exist side by side with no apparent way to bring these idle resources together to accomplish socially useful tasks. A generalized condition of overaccumulation would be indicated by idle productive capacity, a glut of commodities and an excess of inventories, surplus money capital (perhaps held as hoards), and high unemployment. The conditions that prevailed in the 1930s and have emerged periodically since 1973 have to be regarded as typical manifestations of the tendency towards overaccumulation.

The Marxist argument is, then, that the tendency towards overaccumulation can never be eliminated under capitalism. It is a never-ending and eternal problem for any capitalist mode of production. The only question, therefore, is how the overaccumulation tendency can be expressed, contained, absorbed, or managed in ways that do not threaten the capitalist social order. We here encounter the heroic side of bourgeois life and politics, in which real choices have to be made if the social order is not to dissolve into chaos. Let us look at some of these choices.

1 *Devaluation* of commodities, of productive capacity, of money value, perhaps coupled with outright destruction, provides one way of dealing with surpluses of capital. In simple terms, devaluation means the 'writing down' or 'writing off' of the value of capital equipment (plant and machinery in particular), the cut-rate disposal of surplus stocks of goods (or their outright destruction, such as the famous Brazilian coffee-burning episode in the 1930s), or the inflationary erosion of money power coupled with burgeoning defaults on loan obligations. Labour power can similarly be devalued and even destroyed (rising rates of exploitation, falling real incomes, unemployment, more deaths on the job, poorer health and lower life expectancy, etc.). The great depression saw plenty of devaluation of both capital and labour power, and World War II saw even more. There are plenty of examples, and abundant evidence for devaluation as a response to overaccumulation since 1973. But devaluation extracts a political price and hurts large segments of the capitalist class as well as workers and the various other social classes comprising modern complex capitalist society. Some shake-out might seem a good thing, but uncontrolled bankruptcies and massive devaluation exposes the irrational side of capitalist rationality in far too brutal a way for it to be sustainable for long without eliciting some kind of revolutionary (right or left) response. Nevertheless, controlled devaluation through managed deflationary policies is one very important and by no means uncommon option for dealing with overaccumulation.

2 *Macro-economic control*, through institutionalization of some system of regulation, can contain the overaccumulation problem, perhaps for a considerable period of time. It was, of course, the

virtue of the Fordist—Keynesian regime that a balance of forces, however tenuous, could be created through which the mechanisms causing the overaccumulation problem — the pace of technological and organizational change together with the struggle over labour control — could be kept sufficiently under control so as to assure steady growth. But it took a major crisis of overaccumulation to connect Fordist production with a Keynesian mode of state regulation before some kind of steady macro-economic growth could be assured for any extended period. The rise of a particular regime of accumulation has to be seen, then as now, as the outcome of a whole host of political and economic decisions, by no means always consciously directed towards this or that specific end, provoked by persistent manifestations of the overaccumulation problem.

3 *Absorption of overaccumulation* through temporal and spatial displacement provides, in my judgement, a much richer and long-lasting, but also much more problematic, terrain upon which to try and control the overaccumulation problem. The argument here is rather complicated in its details, so I shall again draw upon accounts published elsewhere (Harvey 1982, 1985c).

(a) Temporal displacement entails either a switch of resources from meeting current needs to exploring future uses, or an acceleration in turnover time (the speed with which money outlays return profit to the investor) so that speed-up this year absorbs excess capacity from last year. Excess capital and surplus labour can, for example, be absorbed by switching from current consumption to long-term public and private investments in plant, physical and social infrastructures, and the like. Such investments mop up surpluses in the present only to return their value equivalent over a long time period in the future (this was the principle that lay behind the public works programmes used to combat the slump conditions in the 1930s in many advanced capitalist countries). The capacity to make the switch depends, however, upon the availability of credit and the capacity for 'fictitious capital formation.' The latter is defined as capital that has a nominal money value and paper existence, but which at a given moment in time has no backing in terms of real productive activity or physical assets as collateral. Fictitious capital is converted into real capital to the degree that investments are made that lead to an appropriate increase in useful assets (e.g. plant and machinery that can be profitably deployed) or commodities (goods and services which can be profitably sold). For this reason temporal displacement into future uses is a short-run palliative to the overaccumulation problem unless, that is, there is continuous displacement via continuously accelerating rates of fictitious capital formation and expanding volumes of longer-term investment. All of this depends upon some continuous and state-backed dynamic growth in indebtedness. Keynesian policies after 1945 in the advanced capitalist countries in part had such an effect.

Absorption of surpluses through accelerations in turnover time − a strong feature in the recent period of flexible accumulation − poses a different kind of theoretical problem. Heightened competition certainly provokes individual firms to speed up their turnover time (those firms with the faster turnover time tend to gain excess profits thereby, and so survive more easily). But only under certain conditions does this produce an aggregate acceleration of turnover time so as to permit aggregate absorption of surpluses. Even then, this is, at best, a short-run palliative, unless it proves possible to accelerate social turnover time continuously year by year (a solution that would surely imply strong write-offs of past assets in any case, since speed-up usually entails new technologies which displace the old).

(b) Spatial displacement entails the absorption of excess capital and labour in geographical expansion. This 'spatial fix' (as I have elsewhere called it) to the overaccumulation problem entails the production of new spaces within which capitalist production can proceed (through infrastructural investments, for example), the growth of trade and direct investments, and the exploration of new possibilities for the exploitation of labour power. Here, too, the credit system and fictitious capital formation, backed by state fiscal, monetary, and, where necessary, military power, become vital mediating influences. And it also follows that the manner of prior occupation of the spaces into which capitalism expands, and the degrees of resistance encountered there, can have profound consequences. In some spaces there has been a history of fierce resistance to the implantation of Western capital (e.g. China), whereas in other spaces (e.g. Japan or the more recent cases of Hong Kong, Singapore, or Taiwan), dominant or even subordinate classes have aggressively inserted themselves into what they saw as a superior economic system. If continuous geographical expansion of capitalism were a real possibility, there could be a relatively permanent solution to the overaccumulation problem. But to the degree that the progressive implantation of capitalism across the face of the earth extends the space within which the overaccumulation problem can arise, so geographical expansion can at best be a short-run solution to the overaccumulation problem. The long-run outcome will almost certainly be heightened international and inter-regional competition, with the least advantaged countries and regions suffering the severest consequences.

(c) Time-space displacements, of course, have a double power with respect to absorption of the overaccumulation problem, and in practice, and particularly to the degree that fictitious capital formation (and, usually, state involvement) is essential to both temporal and spatial displacement, it is the combination of the temporal and spatial strategies that counts. Lending money (often raised on, say, London or New York capital markets through fictitious capital formation) to Latin America to build long-term infrastructures or to purchase capital equipment which will help to generate output for many years to come, is a typical and powerful form of absorption of overaccumulation.

How, then, did Fordism solve the inherent overaccumulation tendencies of capitalism? Before World War II it lacked the appropriate regulatory apparatus to do very much more than engage in some tentative pursuits of temporal and spatial displacement (mainly *within* countries, though overseas direct investment on the part of US corporations did begin in the 1920s), and was therefore forced, for the most part, into savage devaluation of the sort achieved in the 1930s and 1940s. Since 1945 − and largely as a consequence of detailed war-time planning to stabilize the post-war economic order − there emerged a fairly coherent accumulation strategy built around control of devaluation and the absorption of overaccumulation by other means. Devaluation through violent swings in the business cycle was brought under control and reduced to the kind of steady devaluation through planned obsolescence that posed relatively minor problems. On the other hand, a strong system of macro-economic control was instituted which controlled the pace of technological and organizational change (mainly through corporate monopoly power), kept the class struggle within bounds (through collective bargaining and state intervention), and kept mass production and mass consumption roughly in balance through state management. But this mode of regulation would not have been anywhere near as successful as it evidently was, had it not been for the strong presence of both temporal and spatial displacements, albeit under the watchful eye of the interventionist state.

By 1972, for example, we find *Business Week* complaining that the US economy was sitting atop a mountain of debt (though from current heights it all looks like a mole-hill now; see figure 2.13). Keynesian debt-financing, initially intended as a short-term management tool to control business cycles, had, predictably, become sucked into an attempt to absorb overaccumulation by continuous expansion of fictitious capital formation and consequent expansion of the debt burden. Steady expansion of long-term investments, orchestrated by the state proved a useful way, at least up until the mid-1960s, to absorb any excess capital or labour. Spatial displacement (combined, of course, with long-term indebtedness) was an even more powerful influence. Within the United States the radical transformation of metropolitan economies (through the suburbanization of both manufacturing and residences), as well as the expansion into the South and West, absorbed vast quantities of excess capital and labour. Internationally, the reconstruction of the economies of Western Europe and Japan, accelerating flows of foreign direct investment, and the enormous growth in world trade played a critical role in absorbing surpluses. Planning for postwar 'peace with prosperity' in World War II emphasized the need for a global strategy for capital accumulation within a world where trade and investment barriers were to be steadily reduced and colonial subservience replaced by an open system of growth, advancement, and co-operation within a decolonized capitalist world system. Even though some facets of this programme were to prove ideological and illusory, enough of its content was realized to make a spatial revolution in global trading and investment entirely possible.

It was primarily through spatial and temporal displacement that the Fordist regime of accumulation resolved the overaccumulation problem during the long postwar boom. The crisis of Fordism can to some degree be interpreted, therefore, as a running out of those options to handle the overaccumulation problem. Temporal displacement was piling debt upon debt to the point where the only viable government strategy was to monetize it away. This was done, in effect, by printing so much money as to trigger an inflationary surge, which radically reduced the real value of past debts (the thousand dollars borrowed ten years ago has little value after a phase of high inflation). Turnover time could not easily be accelerated without destroying the value of fixed capital assets. New geographical centres of accumulation – the US South and West, Western Europe and Japan, and then a range of newly-industrializing countries – were created. As these Fordist production systems came to maturity, they became new and often highly competitive centres of overaccumulation. Spatial competition intensified between geographically distinct Fordist systems, with the most efficient regimes (such as the Japanese) and lower labour-cost regimes (such as those found in third world countries where notions of a social contract with labour were either lacking or weakly enforced) driving other centres into paroxysms of devaluation through deindustrialization. Spatial competition intensified, particularly after 1973, as the capacity to resolve the overaccumulation problem through geographical displacement ran out. The crisis of Fordism was, therefore, as much a geographical and geopolitical crisis as it was a crisis of indebtedness, class struggle, or corporate stagnation within any particular nation state. It was simply that the mechanisms evolved for controlling crisis tendencies were finally overwhelmed by the power of the underlying contradictions of capitalism. There seemed to be no option except to fall back into devaluation of the sort that occurred in the period 1973—5 or 1980—2 as the primary means of dealing with the tendency towards overaccumulation. Unless, that is, some other and superior regime of capitalist production could be created which would assure a solid basis for further accumulation on a global scale.

Flexible accumulation here seems to fit as a simple recombination of the two basic strategies which Marx defined for procuring profit (surplus value). The first, termed *absolute* surplus value, rests on the extension of the working day relative to the wage needed to guarantee working-class reproduction at a given standard of living. The shift towards longer working hours coupled with an overall reduction in the standard of living either by erosion of the real wage or by the shift of corporate capital from high-wage to low-wage regions captures one facet of flexible capital accumulation.

Many of the standardized production systems built up under Fordism have, for this reason, shifted to the periphery, creating 'peripheral Fordism.' Even the new production systems have tended to shift, once standardized, from their innovative hearths to third world locations (Atari's 1984 move from Silicon Valley to South-East Asia's low-wage labour power is a case in point). Under the second strategy, termed *relative* surplus value, organizational and technological change is set in motion to gain temporary profits for innovative firms and more generalized profits as costs of goods that define the standard of living of labour are reduced. Here, too, the proliferating violence of investments, which cut employment and labour costs in every industry from coal mining and steel production to banking and financial services, has been a highly visible aspect of capital accumulation in the 1980s. Yet reliance on this strategy brings to the fore the significance of highly skilled labour powers with the capacity to understand, implement, and manage the new but much more flexible patterns of technological innovation and market orientation. A highly privileged, and to some degree empowered, stratum within the labour force emerges as capitalism depends more and more on mobilizing the powers of intellectual labour as a vehicle for further accumulation.

In the end, of course, it is the particular manner in which absolute and relative strategies combine and feed off each other that counts. Interestingly, the deployment of new technologies has so freed surpluses of labour power as to make the revival of absolute strategies for procuring surplus value more feasible even in the advanced capitalist countries. What is, perhaps, more unexpected is the way in which new production technologies and co-ordinating forms of organization have permitted the revival of domestic, familial, and paternalistic labour systems, which Marx tended to assume would either be driven out of business or reduced to such conditions of gross exploitation and dehumanizing toil as to be intolerable under advanced capitalism. The revival of the sweatshops in New York and Los Angeles, of home work and 'telecommuting', as well as the burgeoning growth of informal sector labour practices throughout the advanced capitalist world, does indeed represent a rather sobering vision of capitalism's supposedly progressive history. Under conditions of flexible accumulation, it seems as if alternative labour systems can exist side by side within the same space in such a way as to enable capitalist entrepreneurs to choose at will between them (see table 2.3). The same shirt designs can be produced by large-scale factories in India, co-operative production in the 'Third Italy,' sweatshops in New York and London, or family labour systems in Hong Kong. Eclecticism in labour practices seem almost as marked in these times as the eclecticism of postmodern philosophies and tastes.

Yet there is, in spite of the difference of context and the specificities of the example used, something quite compelling and relevant about Marx's account of the logic of capitalist organization and accumulation. Re-reading his account in *Capital* strikes home with a certain jolt of recognition. We there read of the ways in which the factory system can intersect with domestic, workshop, and artisanal systems of manufacture, of how an industrial reserve army is mobilized as a counter-weight to workers' power with respect to both labour control and wage rates, of the ways in which intellectual powers and new technologies are deployed to disrupt the organized power of the working class, of how capitalists try to foster the spirit of competition amongst workers, while all the time demanding flexibility of disposition, of location, and of approach to tasks. We are also forced to consider how all of this creates opportunities as well as dangers and difficulties for working-class people precisely because education, flexibility, and geographical mobility, once acquired, become harder for capitalists to control.

Even though present conditions are very different in many respects, it is not hard to see how the invariant elements and relations that Marx defined as fundamental to any capitalist mode of production still shine through, and in many instances with an even greater luminosity than before, all the surface froth and evanescence so characteristic of flexible accumulation. Is the latter, then, anything more than a jazzed-up version of the same old story of capitalism as usual? That would be too simple a judgement. It treats of capitalism a-historically, as a non-dynamic mode of production, when all the evidence (including that explicitly laid out by Marx) is that capitalism is a constantly revolutionary force in world history, a force that perpetually re-shapes the world into new and often quite unexpected configurations. Flexible accumulation appears, at least, to be a new configuration and, as such, it requires that we scrutinize its manifestations with the requisite care and seriousness, using, nevertheless, the theoretical tools that Marx devised.

11

Flexible accumulation – solid transformation or temporary fix?

I have argued that there has certainly been a sea-change in the surface appearance of capitalism since 1973, even though the underlying logic of capitalist accumulation and its crisis-tendencies remain the same. We need to consider, however, whether the shifts in surface appearance betoken the birth of a new regime of accumulation, capable of containing the contradictions of capitalism for the next generation, or whether they betoken a series of temporary fixes, thus constituting a transitional moment of grumbling crisis in the configuration of late twentieth-century capitalism. The question of flexibility has already been the focus of some debate. Three broad positions seem now to be emerging.

The first position, primarily espoused by Piore and Sabel (1984) and accepted in principle by several subsequent writers, is that the new technologies open up the possibility for a reconstitution of labour relations and of production systems on an entirely different social, economic, and geographical basis. Piore and Sabel see a parallel between the current conjuncture and the missed opportunity of the mid-nineteenth century, when large-scale and eventually monopoly capital ousted the small firm and the innumerable small-scale co-operative ventures that had the potential to solve the problem of industrial organization along decentralized and democratically controlled lines (the figure of Proudhon's anarchism looms large). Much is made of the 'Third Italy' as an example of these new forms of worker-co-operative organizations which, armed with new decentralized technologies of command and control, can successfully integrate with, and even subvert, the dominant and repressive forms of labour organization characteristic of corporate and multinational capital. Not everyone shares this rosy vision of the forms of industrial organization (see, for example, Murray, 1987). There is much that is regressive and repressive about the new practices. Nevertheless, many share the sense that we are at some kind of 'second industrial divide' (to appropriate the title of Piore and Sabel's book), and that new forms of labour organization and new locational principles are radically transforming the face of late twentieth-century capitalism. The revival of interest in the role of small business (a highly dynamic sector since 1970), the rediscovery of sweatshops and of informal activities of all kinds, and the recognition that these are playing an important role in contemporary economic development even in the most advanced of industrialized countries, and the attempt to track the rapid geographical shifts in employment and economic fortunes, have produced a mass of information that seems to support this vision of a major transformation in the way late twentieth-century capitalism is working. A vast literature has indeed emerged, from both left and right ends of the political spectrum, that tends to depict the world as if it is in the full flood of such a radical break in all these dimensions of socio-economic and political life that none of the old ways of thinking and doing apply any more.

The second position sees the idea of flexibility as an 'extremely powerful term which legitimizes an array of political practices' (chiefly reactionary and anti-worker), but without any strong empirical or materialist grounding in the actual facts of organization of late twentieth-century capitalism. Pollert (1988), for example, factually challenges the idea of flexibility in labour markets and labour organ-ization, and concludes that the 'discovery of the "flexible workforce" is part of an ideological offensive which celebrates pliability and casualization, and makes them seem inevitable.' Gordon (1988) similarly challenges the idea of hyper-geographical mobility of capital as far beyond what the facts of international trade (parti-cularly between the advanced capitalist countries and the less deve-loped countries) will support. Gordon is particularly concerned to combat the idea of the supposed powerlessness of the nation state (and of worker movements operating within that framework) to exercise any degree of control over capital mobility. Sayer (1989) likewise disputes the accounts of the new forms of accumulation in new industrial spaces as put forward by Scott (1988) and others on the grounds that they emphasize relatively insignificant and per-ipheral changes. Pollert, Gordon and Sayer all argue that there is nothing new in the capitalist search for increased flexibility or lo-cational advantage, and that the substantive evidence for any radical change in the way capitalism is working is either weak or faulty. Those who promote the idea of flexibility, they suggest, are either consciously or inadvertently contributing to a climate of opinion — an ideological condition — that renders working-class movements less rather than more powerful.

I do not accept this position. The evidence for increased flexibility (sub-contracting, temporary and self-employment, etc.) throughout the capitalist world is simply too overwhelming to make Pollert's counter-examples credible. I also find it surprising that Gordon, who earlier made a reasonably strong case that the suburbanization of industry away from the city centres was in part motivated by a desire to increase labour control, should reduce the question of geographical mobility to a matter of volumes and directions of international trade. Nevertheless, such criticisms introduce a number of important correctives in the debate. The insistence that there is nothing essentially new in the push towards flexibility, and that capitalism has periodically taken these sorts of paths before, is certainly correct (a careful reading of Marx's *Capital* sustains the point). The argument that there is an acute danger of exaggerating the significance of any trend towards increased flexibility and geographical mobility, blinding us to how strongly implanted Fordist production systems still are, deserves careful consideration. And the ideological and political consequences of overemphasizing flexibility in the narrow sense of production technique and labour relations are serious enough to make sober and careful evaluations of the degree of flexibility imperative. If, after all, workers are convinced that capitalists can move or shift to more flexible work practices even when they cannot, then the stomach for struggle will surely be weakened. But I think it equally dangerous to pretend that nothing has changed, when the facts of deindustrialization and of plant relocation, of more flexible manning practices and labour markets, of automation and product innovation, stare most workers in the face.

The third position, which defines the sense in which I use the idea of a transition from Fordism to flexible accumulation here, lies somewhere in between these two extremes. Flexible technologies and organizational forms have not become hegemonic everywhere (but then neither did the Fordism that preceded them). The current conjuncture is characterized by a mix of highly efficient Fordist production (often nuanced by flexible technology and output) in some sectors and regions (like cars in the USA, Japan, or South Korea) and more traditional production systems (such as those of Singapore, Taiwan, or Hong Kong) resting on 'artisanal,' paternalistic, or patriarchal (familial) labour relations, embodying quite different mechanisms of labour control. The latter systems have undoubtedly grown (even within the advanced capitalist countries) since 1970, often at the expense of the Fordist factory assembly line. This shift has important implications. Market coordinations (often of the sub-contracting sort) have expanded at the expense of direct corporate planning within the system of surplus value production and appropriation. The nature and composition of the global working class has also changed, as have the conditions of consciousness formation and political action. Unionization and traditional 'left politics' become very hard to sustain in the face, for example, of the patriarchal (family) production systems characteristic of South-East Asia, or of immigrant groups in Los Angeles, New York, and London. Gender relations have similarly become much more complicated, at the same time as resort to a female labour force has become much more widespread. By the same token, the social basis for ideologies of entrepreneurialism, paternalism, and privatism has increased.

We can, I think, trace back many of the surface shifts in economic behaviour and political attitudes to a simple change in balance between Fordist and non-Fordist systems of labour control, coupled with a disciplining of the former either through competition with the latter (forced restructurings and rationalizations), widespread unemployment or through political repression (curbs on union power) and geographical relocations to 'peripheral' countries or regions and back into industrial heartlands in a 'see-saw' motion of uneven geographical development (Smith, 1984).

I do not see this shift to alternative systems of labour control (with all its political implications) as irreversible, but interpret it as a rather traditional response to crisis. The devaluation of labour power has always been the instinctive response of capitalists to falling profits. The generality of that conceals, however, some contradictory movements. New technologies have empowered certain privileged layers, at the same time as alternative production and labour control systems open up the way to high remuneration of technical, managerial, and entrepreneurial skills. The trend, further exaggerated by the shift to services and the enlargement of 'the cultural mass', has been to increasing inequalities of income (figure 2.15), perhaps presaging the rise of a new aristocracy of labour as well as the emergence of an ill-remunerated and broadly disempowered under-class (Dahrendorf, 1987; Wilson, 1987). This, however, poses serious problems of sustaining effective demand and raises the spectre of a crisis of under-consumption — the kind of manifestation of crisis that Fordism—Keynesianism proved most adept at avoiding. I do not, therefore, see the neo-conservative monetarism that attaches to flexible modes of accumulation and the overall devaluation of labour power through enhanced labour control as offering even a short-term solution to the crisis-tendencies of capitalism. The budget deficit of the United States has, I think, been very important to the stabilization of capitalism these last few years, and if that proves unsustainable, then the path of capitalist accumulation world-wide will be rocky indeed.

What does seem special about the period since 1972 is the extra-

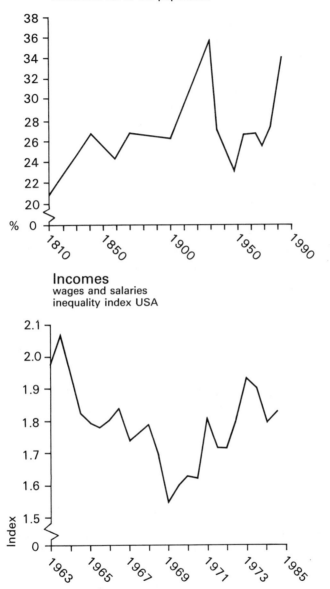

Assets
percentage of US assets owned by
wealthiest 1% of the population

Incomes
wages and salaries
inequality index USA

*Figure 2.15 Inequality of asset ownership (1810–1987) and in incomes
(1963–1985) in the United States
(*Sources*: Historical Statistics of the United States, Economic Reports to the
President, Harrison and Bluestone, 1988)*

ordinary efflorescence and transformation in financial markets (see figures 2.12, 2.13, and 2.14). There have been phases of capitalist history — from 1890 to 1929, for example — when 'finance capital' (however defined) seemed to occupy a position of paramount importance within capitalism, only to lose that position in the speculative crashes that followed. In the present phase, however, it is not so much the concentration of power in financial institutions that matters, as the explosion in new financial instruments and markets, coupled with the rise of highly sophisticated systems of financial coordination on a global scale. It is through this financial system that much of the geographical and temporal flexibility of capital accumulation has been achieved. The nation state, though seriously weakened as an autonomous power, nevertheless retains important powers of labour disciplining as well as of intervention in financial flows and markets, while becoming itself much more vulnerable to fiscal crisis and the discipline of international money. I am therefore tempted to see the flexibility achieved in production, labour markets, and consumption more as an outcome of the search for financial solutions to the crisis-tendencies of capitalism, rather than the other way round. This would imply that the financial system has achieved a degree of autonomy from real production unprecedented in capitalism's history, carrying capitalism into an era of equally unprecedented financial dangers.

The emphasis on financial and monetary solutions derives, of course, from the inflationary rather than deflationary nature of the way the crisis was manifest from the mid-1960s on. What is surprising is the way in which indebtedness and fictitious capital formation have accelerated since then, at the same time as massive defaults and devaluations have been absorbed, not without trauma to be sure, within the financial apparatus of overall regulation (see figures 2.12 and 2.13). In the United States, for example, the banking system went into the red, for the first time since 1934, in the first half of 1987 with scarcely a murmur of panic. The pace of bank failures has likewise picked up dramatically since 1980 (figure 2.14). And we need only take the secondary market value of third world debt, and multiply it by the obligations outstanding, to get a rough estimate of the volume of devaluation current within the financial system (see figure 2.16 and table 2.9). Compared to all of this, the extraordinary fluctuations manifest in stock and currency markets appear more as epiphemonena rather than as fundamental structural problems.

It is tempting, of course, to see this all as some prelude to a financial crash that would make 1929 look like a footnote in history.

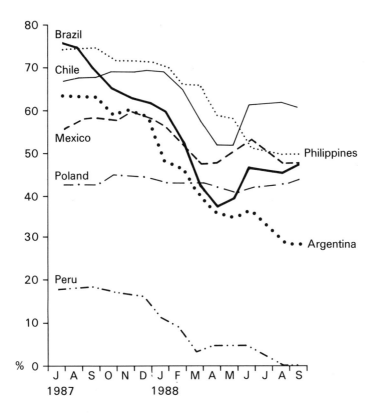

Figure 2.16 The changing secondary market value of the debt obligations of selected countries
(Source: The Economist)

While it would be foolish to rule that out as a very real possibility, particularly in the light of the heavy losses in world stock markets in October 1987 (see table 2.10), circumstances do indeed appear radically different this time around. Consumer, corporate, and governmental debts are much more tightly tied in with each other (figure 2.13), permitting the simultaneous regulation of both consumption and production magnitudes through speculative and fictitious financing. It is also much easier to deploy strategies of temporal and geographical displacement together with sectoral change under the hegemonic umbrella of burgeoning financial markets. Innovation within the financial systems appears to have been a necessary prerequisite to overcoming the general rigidities as well as the distinctive temporal,

*Table 2.9   The outstanding debt of selected third world countries
and an estimate of devaluation, measured by secondary market value of
the debt at the end of 1987*

Country	Outstanding debt, end of 1987 (US $bns)	Secondary market value, end 1987 (% of face value)	Estimated devaluation (US $bns)
Argentina	49.4	34	22.5
Brazil	114.5	45	63.2
Chile	20.5	62	11.8
Mexico	105.0	52	50.4
Peru	16.7	96	16.0
Total devaluation measure (5 countries, US $bns)			174.0

Source: World Bank Debt Tables and *The Economist*

geographical, and even geopolitical crisis into which Fordism had fallen by the late 1960s.

Two basic (though tentative) conclusions then follow. First, that if we are to look for anything truly distinctive (as opposed to 'capitalism as usual') in the present situation, then it is upon the financial aspects of capitalist organization and on the role of credit that we should concentrate our gaze. Secondly, if there is to be any medium-term stability to the present regime of accumulation, then it is in the realms of new rounds and forms of temporal and spatial fixes that these will most likely be found. It may, in short, prove possible to 're-schedule the crisis' by re-scheduling (for example) third world and other debt repayments until the twenty-first century, while simultaneously provoking a radical reconstitution of spatial configurations in which a diversity of systems of labour control may prevail along with new products and patterns in the international division of labour.

I want to stress the tentative nature of these conclusions. Yet it does seem important to emphasize to what degree flexible accumulation has to be seen as a particular and perhaps new combination of mainly old elements within the overall logic of capital accumulation. Furthermore, if I am right that the crisis of Fordism was in large part a crisis of temporal and spatial form, then we should pay rather more attention to these dimensions of the problem than is customary in either radical or conventional modes of analysis. We look more

Table 2.10 *The losses in world stock markets, October 1987*

Country	Per cent change from 1987 high point of share values
Australia	-29
Austria	-6
Belgium	-16
Canada	-25
Denmark	-11
France	-25
West Germany	-17
Hong Kong	-16
Ireland	-25
Italy	-23
Japan	-15
Malaysia	-29
Mexico	-30
Netherlands	-24
New Zealand	-22
Norway	-25
Singapore	-28
South Africa	-18
Spain	-12
Sweden	-15
Switzerland	-20
UK	-23
USA	-26

Source: *Financial Times*, 24 October 1987

closely at them in Part III, since it also transpires that the changing experience of time and space underlies, at least in part, the impulsive turn to postmodernist cultural practices and philosophical discourses.

Part III

The experience of space and time

I hear the ruin of all space, shattered glass and toppling masonry, and time one livid final flame.   *James Joyce*

12

Introduction

Marshall Berman (1982) equates modernity (among other things) with a certain mode of experience of space and time. Daniel Bell (1978, 107–11) argues that the various movements that brought modernism to its apogee had to work out a new logic in the conception of space and motion. He suggests, furthermore, that the organization of space has 'become the primary aesthetic problem of mid-twentieth century culture as the problem of time (in Bergson, Proust, and Joyce) was the primary aesthetic problem of the first decades of this century.' Frederic Jameson (1984b) attributes the postmodern shift to a crisis in our experience of space and time, a crisis in which spatial categories come to dominate those of time, while themselves undergoing such a mutation that we cannot keep pace. 'We do not yet possess the perceptual equipment to match this new kind of hyperspace,' he writes, 'in part because our perceptual habits were formed in that older kind of space I have called the space of high modernism.'

In what follows, I shall accept these statements at their face value. But since few trouble to explain exactly what they mean by them, I shall give an account of space and time in social life so as to highlight material links between political–economic and cultural processes. This will allow me to explore the link between postmodernism and the transition from Fordism to more flexible modes of capital accumulation via the mediations of spatial and temporal experiences.

Space and time are basic categories of human existence. Yet we rarely debate their meanings; we tend to take them for granted, and give them common-sense or self-evident attributions. We record the passage of time in seconds, minutes, hours, days, months, years, decades, centuries, and eras, as if everything has its place upon a single objective time scale. Even though time in physics is a difficult and contentious concept, we do not usually let that interfere with the common-sense of time around which we organize daily routines. We recognize, of course, that our mental processes and perceptions can play tricks, make seconds feel like light years, or pleasurable hours pass by so fast we hardly notice. We may also learn to appreciate how different societies (or even different sub-groups) cultivate quite different senses of time (see table 3.2).

In modern society, many different senses of time get pinned together. Cyclical and repetitive motions (everything from daily breakfast and going to work, to seasonal rituals like festivals, birthdays, vacations, the openings of baseball or cricket seasons) provide a sense of security in a world where the general thrust of progress appears to be ever onwards and upwards into the firmament of the unknown. When the sense of progress is checked by depression or recession, by war or social disruption, we may reassure ourselves (somewhat) either with the idea of cyclical time ('long waves,' 'kondratieff cycles,' etc.) as a natural phenomenon to which we must perforce adapt, or dredge up an even more compelling image of some stable universal propensity (such as innate human quarrelsomeness) as the perpetual counterpoint to progress. At another level we can see how what Hareven (1982) calls 'family time' (the time implicit in raising children and transferring knowledge and assets between generations through kinship networks) may be mobilized to meet the exigencies of 'industrial time' which allocates and reallocates labour to tasks according to powerful rhythms of technological and locational change forged out of the restless search for capital accumulation. And in moments of despair or exaltation, who among us can refrain from invoking the time of fate, of myth, of the Gods? Astrologers, we have learned, peddled their insights even in the corridors of the Reagan White House.

Out of such different senses of time, serious conflicts can arise: should the optimal rate of exploitation of a resource be set by the interest rate, or should we search, as environmentalists insist, for a sustainable development which assures the perpetuation of the ecological conditions suitable for human life into an indefinite future? Such questions are by no means arcane. The time horizon implicated in a decision materially affects the kind of decision we make. If we want to leave something behind, or build a better future for our children, then we do quite different things than would be the case were we simply concerned with our own pleasures in the here and now. For this reason, time gets used in political rhetoric in confusing ways. Failure to defer gratifications is often used by conservative critics, for example, to explain the persistence of impoverishment in an affluent society, even though that society systematically promotes the debt-financing of present gratifications as one of its principal engines of economic growth.

In spite of (or perhaps precisely because of) this diversity of conceptions and the social conflicts that flow therefrom, there is still a tendency to regard the differences as those of perception or interpretation of what should fundamentally be understood as a single, objective yardstick of time's ineluctable arrow of motion. I shall shortly challenge this conception.

Space likewise gets treated as a fact of nature, 'naturalized' through the assignment of common-sense everyday meanings. In some ways more complex than time – it has direction, area, shape, pattern and volume as key attributes, as well as distance – we typically treat of it as an objective attribute of things which can be measured and thus pinned down. We do recognize, of course, that our subjective experience can take us into realms of perception, imagination, fiction, and fantasy, which produce mental spaces and maps as so many mirages of the supposedly 'real' thing. We also discover that different societies or sub-groups possess different conceptions. The Plains Indians of what is now the United States did not hold at all to the same conception of space as the white settlers that replaced them; 'territorial' agreements between the groups were based on such different meanings that conflict was inevitable. Indeed, the conflict in part was precisely over the proper sense of space that should be used to regulate social life and give meaning to concepts such as territorial rights. The historical and anthropological record is full of examples of how varied the concept of space can be, while investigations of the spatial worlds of children, the mentally ill (particularly schizophrenics), oppressed minorities, women and men of different class, rural and urban dwellers, etc. illustrate a similar diversity within outwardly homogeneous populations. Yet some sense of an overarching and objective meaning of space which we must, in the last instance, all acknowledge is pervasive.

I think it important to challenge the idea of a single and objective sense of time or space, against which we can measure the diversity of human conceptions and perceptions. I shall not argue for a total dissolution of the objective–subjective distinction, but insist, rather, that we recognize the multiplicity of the objective qualities which space and time can express, and the role of human practices in their construction. Neither time nor space, the physicists now broadly propose, had existence (let alone meaning) before matter; the objective qualities of physical time–space cannot be understood, therefore, independently of the qualities of material processes. It is, however, by no means necessary to subordinate all objective conceptions of time and space to this particular physical conception, since it, also, is a construct that rests upon a particular version of the constitution of matter and the origin of the universe. The history of the concepts of time, space, and time—space in physics has, in fact, been marked by strong epistemological breaks and reconstructions. The conclusion we should draw is simply that neither time nor space can be assigned objective meanings independently of material processes, and that it is only through investigation of the latter that we can properly ground our concepts of the former. This is not, of course, a new conclusion. It confirms the general thrust of several earlier thinkers, of whom Dilthey and Durkheim are the most prominent.

From this materialist perspective we can then argue that objective conceptions of time and space are necessarily created through material practices and processes which serve to reproduce social life. The Plains Indians or the African Nuer objectify qualities of time and space that are as separate from each other as they are distant from those ingrained within a capitalist mode of production. The objectivity of time and space is given in each case by the material practices of social reproduction, and to the degree that these latter vary geographically and historically, so we find that social time and social space are differentially constructed. Each distinctive mode of production or social formation will, in short, embody a distinctive bundle of time and space practices and concepts.

Since capitalism has been (and continues to be) a revolutionary mode of production in which the material practices and processes of social reproduction are always changing, it follows that the objective qualities as well as the meanings of space and time also change. On the other hand, if advance of knowledge (scientific, technical, administrative, bureaucratic, and rational) is vital to the progress of capitalist production and consumption, then changes in our conceptual apparatus (including representations of space and time) can have material consequences for the ordering of daily life. When, for example, a planner-architect like Le Corbusier, or an administrator like Haussmann, creates a built environment in which the tyranny of the straight line predominates, then we must perforce adjust our daily practices.

This does not mean that practices are determined by built form (no matter how hard the planners may try); for they have the awkward habit of escaping their moorings in any fixed schema of representation. New meanings can be found for older materializations of space and time. We appropriate ancient spaces in very modern ways, treat time and history as something to create rather than to accept. The same concept of, say, 'community' (as a social entity created in space through time) can disguise radical differences in meaning because the processes of community production themselves diverge remarkably according to group capacities and interests. Yet the treatment of communities as if they are comparable (by, say, a planning agency) has material implications to which the social practices of people who live in them have to respond.

Beneath the veneer of common-sense and seemingly 'natural' ideas about space and time, there lie hidden terrains of ambiguity, contradiction, and struggle. Conflicts arise not merely out of admittedly diverse subjective appreciations, but because different objective material qualities of time and space are deemed relevant to social life in different situations. Important battles likewise occur in the realms of scientific, social, and aesthetic theory, as well as in practice. How we represent space and time in theory matters, because it affects how we and others interpret and then act with respect to the world.

Consider, for example, one of the more startling schisms in our intellectual heritage concerning conceptions of time and space. Social theories (and I here think of traditions emanating from Marx, Weber, Adam Smith, and Marshall) typically privilege time over space in their formulations. They broadly assume either the existence of some pre-existing spatial order within which temporal processes operate, or that spatial barriers have been so reduced as to render space a contingent rather than fundamental aspect to human action. Aesthetic theory, on the other hand, is deeply concerned with 'the spatialization of time.'

It is a tribute to the compartmentalizations in Western thought that this disjunction has for so long passed largely unremarked. On the surface, the difference is not too hard to understand. Social theory has always focused on processes of social change, modernization, and revolution (technical, social, political). Progress is its theoretical object, and historical time its primary dimension. Indeed, progress entails the conquest of space, the tearing down of all spatial barriers, and the ultimate 'annihilation of space through time.' The reduction of space to a contingent category is implied in the notion of progress itself. Since modernity is about the experience of progress through modernization, writings on that theme have tended to emphasize temporality, the process of *becoming*, rather than *being* in space and place. Even Foucault (1984, 70), obsessed as he confesses himself to be with spatial metaphors, wonders, when pressed, when and why it happened that 'space was treated as the dead, the fixed, the undialectical, the immobile' while 'time, on the contrary, was richness, fecundity, life, dialectic.'

Aesthetic theory, on the other hand, seeks out the rules that allow eternal and immutable truths to be conveyed in the midst of the maelstrom of flux and change. The architect, to take the most obvious case, tries to communicate certain values through the construction of a spatial form. Painters, sculptors, poets, and writers of all sorts do no less. Even the written word abstracts properties from the flux of experience and fixes them in spatial form. 'The invention of printing embedded the word in *space*,' it has been said, and writing — a 'set of tiny marks marching in neat line, like armies of insects, across pages and pages of white paper' — is, therefore, a definite spatialization (quoted in McHale, 1987, 179–81). Any system of representation, in fact, is a spatialization of sorts which automatically freezes the flow of experience and in so doing distorts what it strives to represent. 'Writing,' says Bourdieu (1977, 156) 'tears practice and discourse out of the flow of time.' For this reason, Bergson, the great theorist of becoming, of time as flux, was incensed that it took the spatializations of the clock to tell the time.

The philosopher Karsten Harries (1982, 59–69) makes much of this idea. Architecture, he maintains, is not only about domesticating space, wresting and shaping a liveable place from space. It is also a deep defence against 'the terror of time'. The 'language of beauty' is 'the language of a timeless reality.' To create a beautiful object 'is to link time and eternity' in such a way as to redeem us from time's tyranny. The urge to 'devaluate time' reappears as the artist's will to redeem through the creation of a work 'strong enough to still time.' Much of the aesthetic thrust of modernism, we saw in Part I, is to strive for this sense of eternity in the midst of flux. But in leaning to the eternal side of Baudelaire's formulation, this emphasizes space rather than time. The aim of spatial constructs is 'not to illuminate temporal reality so that [we] might feel more at home in it, but to be relieved of it: to abolish time within time, if only for a time.' Harries here echoes those famous modernist formulations of Baudelaire, 'one can only forget time by making use of it,' and T. S. Eliot, 'only through time, time is conquered.'

But here arises the paradox. We learn our ways of thinking and conceptualizing from active grappling with the spatializations of the written word, the study and production of maps, graphs, diagrams, photographs, models, paintings, mathematical symbols, and the like. How adequate are such modes of thought and such conceptions in the face of the flow of human experience and strong processes of social change? On the other side of the coin, how can spatializations in general, and aesthetic practices in particular, represent flux and change, particularly if these latter are held essential truths to be conveyed? This was the dilemma that plagued Bergson. It became a central problem for both futurist and Dada art. Futurism sought to shape space in ways that could represent speed and motion. Dadaists viewed art as ephemeral and, renouncing any permanent spatialization, sought eternity by embedding their happenings in revolutionary action. It was perhaps in response to this conundrum that Walter Pater argued that 'all art aspires to the condition of music' − music, after all, contains its aesthetic effect precisely through its temporal movement. But the most obvious means of representation of time was the film. The young Sartre was particularly impressed by its possibilities. 'It is an art which reflects civilization in our time,' he said; it 'will teach you about the beauty of the world you live in, the poetry of speed, machines, and the inhuman splendid inevitability of industry' (Cohen-Solal, 1987). The combination of film and music provides a powerful antidote to the spatial passivity of art and architecture. Yet the very confinement of the film to a depthless screen and a theatre is a reminder that it, too, is space-bound in some curious way.

There is much to be learned from aesthetic theory about how different forms of spatialization inhibit or facilitate processes of social change. Conversely, there is much to be learned from social theory concerning the flux and change with which aesthetic theory has to cope. By playing these two currents of thought off against each other, we can, perhaps, better understand the ways in which political−economic change informs cultural practices.

But let me first illustrate where the political significance of such an argument might lie. In so doing, I shall revert to that conception which Kant advanced (see above, p. 19), of aesthetic judgement as a potential mediator between the worlds of objective science and of subjective moral judgement (without necessarily conceding either the tripartite division of knowledge that Kant proposed or the entirely disinterested satisfaction with which his concept of beauty is associated). Aesthetic judgements (as well as 'redemptive' artistic practices) have entered in as powerful criteria of political, and hence of social and economic, action. If aesthetic judgement prioritizes space over time, then it follows that spatial practices and concepts can, under certain circumstances, become central to social action.

In this regard, the German philosopher Heidegger is an intriguing figure. Rejecting the Kantian dichotomies of subject and object, he proclaimed the permanence of Being over the transitoriness of Becoming (*Metaphysics*, 202). His investigations of Being led him away from the universals of modernism and of the Judaeo-Christian tradition, and back to the intense and creative nationalism of pre-Socratic Greek thought. All metaphysics and philosophy, he declared, are given their meaning only in relation to the destiny of the people

(Blitz, 1981). The geopolitical position of Germany in the inter-war years – squeezed in a 'great pincer' between Russia and America – led to the following reflections:

> From a metaphysical point of view, Russia and America are the same; the same dreary technological frenzy, the same unrestricted organization of the average man. At a time when the furthermost corner of the globe has been conquered by technology and opened to economic exploitation; when any incident whatsoever, regardless of where and when it occurs, can be communicated to the rest of the world at any desired speed; when the assassination of a King in France and a Symphony in Tokyo can be 'experienced' simultaneously; when time has ceased to be anything other than velocity, instantaneousness and simultaneity, and time as history has vanished from the lives of all peoples ... then, yes, then, through all this turmoil a question still haunts us like a spectre: What for? Whither? What then?

The sense of time–space transformation and the anguish it provoked, could hardly be stronger. Heidegger's response is explicit:

> All this implies that this nation, as a historical nation, must move itself and thereby the history of the West beyond the centre of their future 'happening' and into the primordial realm of the powers of being. If the great decision regarding Europe is not to bring annihilation, that decision must be made in terms of new spiritual energies unfolding historically from out of the centre.

Herein, for Heidegger, lay the 'inner truth and greatness of the National Socialist movement' (understood as the 'encounter between global technology and modern man'). In support of Germany's withdrawal from the League of Nations, he sought a knowledge that does not 'divide the classes' but binds and unites them 'in the great will of the state.' By such means he hoped that the German people might 'grow in its unity as a work people, finding again its simple worth and genuine power, and procuring its duration and greatness as a work state. To the man of this unheard of will, our Fuhrer Adolf Hitler, a three-fold Sieg-Heil!' (quoted in Blitz, 1981, 217).

That a great twentieth-century philosopher (who has incidentally inspired the deconstructionism of Derrida) should so compromise himself politically has been a matter of considerable concern (a concern that has erupted once more into the status of 'scandal' in France as the result of Farias's (1987) documentation of Heidegger's rather long-lasting Nazi links). But I think a number of useful points can be made on the basis of the Heidegger case. He was evidently disturbed by the bland universalisms of technology, the collapse of spatial distinctiveness and identity, and the seemingly uncontrolled acceleration of temporal processes. From this standpoint he exemplifies all the dilemmas of modernity as Baudelaire articulates them. He is deeply influenced by Nietzsche's interventions (see above, p. 15–18) but sees them leading down the path of an unacceptable and total nihilism. It is from such a fate that he seeks to rescue civilization. His search for permanence (the philosophy of Being) connects with a place-bound sense of geopolitics and destiny that was both revolutionary (in the sense of forward looking) and intensely nationalistic. From a metaphysical point of view this entailed rooting himself in classical values (particularly those of pre-Socratic Greek civilization), thereby highlighting a parallel orientation towards classicism in Nazi rhetoric in general and in architecture in particular. The rejection of Platonic and Judaeo-Christian values, of the 'myth' of machine rationality and internationalism, was total, even if the revolutionary side to his thought forced him to compromise with the advances of science and technology in practical affairs. Reactionary modernism of the Nazi sort simultaneously emphasized the power of myth (of blood and soil, of race and fatherland, of destiny and place) while mobilizing all the accoutrements of social progress towards a project of sublime national achievement. The application of this particular aesthetic sense to politics altered the course of history with a vengeance.

The Nazi case is by no means unique. The aestheticization of politics has a long history and poses deep problems for doctrines of untrammelled social progress. It has its left and its right versions (the Sandinistas, after all, aestheticize politics around the figure of Sandino in order to promote adherence to a left political programme of national liberation and social justice). The clearest form the problem takes is the shift in emphasis from historical change towards national cultures and destinies, sparking geographical conflicts between different spaces in the world economy. Geopolitical conflicts invariably imply a certain aestheticization of politics in which appeal to the mythology of place and person has a strong role to play. The rhetoric of national liberation movements is here just as powerful as the counter-rhetoric, imposed through imperialism and colonialism, of manifest destiny, racial or cultural supremacy, paternalism (white man's burden, for example), and doctrines of national superiority.

How and why the world's history (the outcome of struggles between classes in Marxian versions) dissolves into geopolitical conflicts often of a most destructive kind cannot be regarded as a matter of mere accident. It may have its roots in the political–economic processes that force capitalism into configurations of uneven geographical development and make it seek out a series of spatial fixes to the overaccumulation problem. But the aestheticization of politics that accompanies this geopolitical turn must likewise be taken seriously. Herein, I think, lies the significance of conjoining aesthetic and social theoretic perspectives on the nature and meaning of space and time. And it is exactly from this sort of perspective that Eagleton (1987) launches his most virulent polemic against the postmodernism of Lyotard:

> Modernity for Lyotard would seem *nothing but* a tale of terroristic reason and Nazism little more than the lethal terminus of totalizing thought. This reckless travesty ignores the fact that the death camps were among other things the upshot of a barbarous irrationalism which, like some aspects of postmodernism itself, junked history, refused argumentation, aestheticized politics and staked all on the charisma of those who told the stories.

13

Individual spaces and times in social life

The material practices from which our concepts of space and time flow are as varied as the range of individual and collective experiences. The challenge is to put some overall interpretative frame around them that will bridge the gap between cultural change and the dynamics of political economy.

Let me begin with the simplest descriptor of daily practices as set out in the time geography pioneered by Hägerstrand. Individuals are here viewed as purposeful agents engaged in projects that take up time through movement in space. Individual biographies can be tracked as 'life paths in time-space,' beginning with daily routines of movement (from house to factory, to shops, to school, and back home again), and extending to migratory movements over phases of a life-span (for example, youth in the country, professional training in the large city, marriage and movement to the suburbs, and retirement to the country). Such life paths can be portrayed diagrammatically (see figure 3.1). The idea is to study the principles of time–space behaviour through an examination of such biographies. Finite time resources and the 'friction of distance' (measured in time or cost taken to overcome it) constrain daily movement. Time for eating, sleeping, etc. has to be found, and social projects always encounter 'coupling constraints,' specified as the need to have the time–space paths of two or more individuals intersect to accomplish any social transaction. Such transactions typically occur within a geographical pattern of available 'stations' (places where certain activities like working, shopping, etc. occur) and 'domains' where certain social interactions prevail.

Hägerstrand's schema is a useful descriptor of how the daily life of individuals unfolds in space and time. But it tells us nothing about how 'stations' and 'domains' are produced, or why the 'friction of distance' varies in the way it palpably does. It also leaves aside the

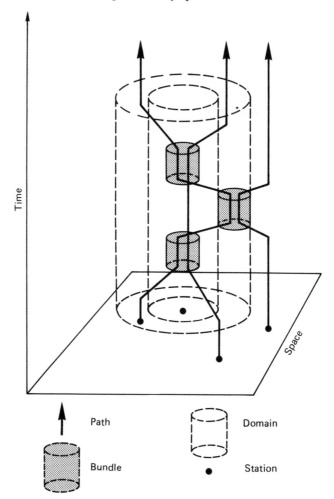

Figure 3.1 Diagrammatic representation of daily time—space paths according to Hägerstrand (1970).

question of how and why certain social projects and their characteristic 'coupling constraints' become hegemonic (why, for example, the factory system dominates, or is dominated by dispersed and artisanal forms of production), and it makes no attempt to understand why certain social relations dominate others, or how meaning gets assigned to places, spaces, history, and time. Unfortunately, assembling massive empirical data on time—space biographies does not get at the answers to these broader questions, even though the record of such biographies forms a useful datum for considering the time—space dimension of social practices.

Consider, by way of contrast, the socio-psychological and phenomenological approaches to time and space that have been put forward by writers such as de Certeau, Bachelard, Bourdieu, and Foucault. The latter treats the space of the body as the irreducible element in our social scheme of things, for it is upon that space that the forces of repression, socialization, disciplining, and punishing are inflicted. The body exists in space and must either submit to authority (through, for example, incarceration or surveillance in an organized space) or carve out particular spaces of resistance and freedom — 'heterotopias' — from an otherwise repressive world. That struggle, the centrepiece of social history for Foucault, has no necessary temporal logic. But Foucault does see particular historical transitions as important and he pays great attention to the periodization of experience. The power of the *ancien régime* was undermined by the Enlightenment only to be replaced by a new organization of space dedicated to the techniques of social control, surveillance, and repression of the self and the world of desire. The difference lies in the way state power in the modern era becomes faceless, rational, and technocratic (and hence more systematic), rather than personalized and arbitrary. The irreducibility (for us) of the human body means that it is only from that site of power that resistance can be mobilized in the struggle to liberate human desire. Space, for Foucault, is a metaphor for a site or container of power which usually constrains but sometimes liberates processes of *Becoming*.

Foucault's emphasis upon imprisonment within spaces of social control has more than a little literal (as opposed to metaphorical) relevance to the way modern social life is organized. The entrapment of impoverished populations in inner city spaces is a theme that has, for example, long captured the attention of urban geographers. But Foucault's exclusive concentration on the spaces of organized repression (prisons, the 'panopticon,' hospitals, and other institutions of social control) weakens the generality of his argument. De Certeau provides an interesting corrective. He treats social spaces as more open to human creativity and action. Walking, he suggests, defines a 'space of enunciation.' Like Hägerstand, he begins his story at ground level, but in this case 'with footsteps' in the city. 'Their swarming mass is an innumerable collection of singularities. Their intertwined paths give their shape to spaces. They weave places together,' and so create the city through daily activities and movements. 'They are not localized; it is rather that they spatialize' (note how different the sentiment is from that conveyed in Hägerstand's work). The particular spaces of the city are created by myriad actions, all of which bear the stamp of human intent. Answering Foucault, de Certeau sees a daily substitution 'for the technological system of a coherent and totalizing space' by a 'pedestrian rhetoric' of trajectories that have 'a mythical structure' understood as 'a story jerry-built out of elements taken from common sayings, an allusive and fragmentary story whose gaps mesh with the social practices it symbolizes.'

De Certeau here defines a basis for understanding the ferment of popular, localized street cultures, even as expressed within the framework imposed by some overarching repressive order. 'The goal,' he writes, 'is not to make clear how the violence of order is trans- muted into a disciplinary technology, but rather to bring to light the clandestine forms taken by the dispersed, tactical and makeshift creativity of groups or individuals already caught in the nets of "discipline."' The 'resurgence of "popular" practices within industrial and scientific modernity,' he writes, 'cannot be confined to the past, the countryside or primitive peoples' but 'exists at the heart of the contemporary economy.' Spaces can be more easily 'liberated' than Foucault imagines, precisely because social practices spatialize rather than becoming localized within some repressive grid of social control.

De Certeau, as we shall see, recognizes that the practices of every- day life can and do get converted into the 'totalizations' of rationally ordered and controlled space and time. But he tells us little of why and how the rationalizations take the forms they do. In some in- stances it seems as if the Enlightenment project (or even capitalism) has something to do with it, although in other instances he points to the symbolic orderings of space and time which give profounder continuity (by no means necessarily freedom-giving) to social prac- tices. On this latter point, de Certeau draws some sustenance from Bourdieu.

Symbolic orderings of space and time provide a framework for experience through which we learn who or what we are in society. 'The reason why submission to the collective rhythms is so rigorously demanded,' writes Bourdieu (1977, 163), 'is that the temporal forms or the spatial structures structure not only the group's representation of the world but the group itself, which orders itself in accordance with this representation.' The common-sense notion that 'there is a time and a place for everything' gets carried into a set of prescriptions which replicate the social order by assigning social meanings to spaces and times. This was the sort of phenomenon that Hall (1966) saw as the root of a lot of intercultural conflict, precisely because different groups signalled quite different meanings by their use of space and time. Through studies of the internal world of the Kabyle house and of the external worlds of fields, markets, gardens, and the like in relation to the annual calendar and divisions between night and day, Bourdieu shows how 'all the divisions of the group are projected at every moment into the spatio-temporal organization which assigns each category its place and time: it is here that the fuzzy logic of practice works wonders in enabling the group to achieve as much social and logical integration as is compatible with the diversity imposed by the division of labour between the sexes, the ages, and the "occupations" (smith, butcher).' It is, suggests Bourdieu, through the 'dialectical relationship between the body and a structured organization of space and time that common practices and representations are determined.' And it is precisely out of such experiences (in the home, in particular) that durable schemes of perception, thought, and action get imposed (see figure 3.2). Even more profoundly, 'the organization of time and the group in accordance with mythical structures leads collective practice to appear as "realized myth."'

Findings of this sort have been replicated in many anthropological studies in recent years (through without necessarily accepting all of Bourdieu's interpretative apparatus). The more general question, however, concerns the degree to which similar kinds of social

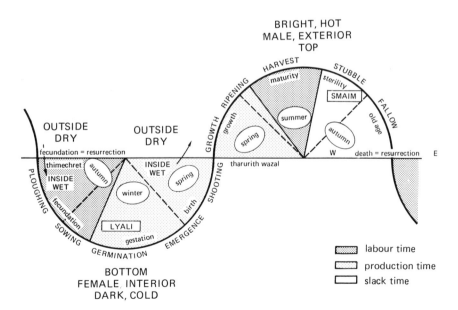

Figure 3.2 The annual calendar of the Kabyle, according to Bourdieu (1977) (reproduced by permission of Cambridge University Press)

meanings can be signalled through spatial and temporal organization in contemporary capitalist culture. Certainly, it is not hard to spot examples of such processes at work. The organization of spaces within a household, for example, still says much about gender and age relations. The organized spatio-temporal rhythms of capitalism provide abundant opportunities for socialization of individuals to distinctive roles. The common-sense notion that there is 'a time and a place for everything' still carries weight, and social expectations attach to where and when actions occur. But while the mechanisms to which Bourdieu points may be omni-present in capitalist society, they do not easily conform to the broadly static picture of social reproduction which he evokes in the case of the Kabyles. Modernization entails, after all, the perpetual disruption of temporal and spatial rhythms, and modernism takes as one of its missions the production of new meanings for space and time in a world of ephemerality and fragmentation.

Bourdieu provides the barest hint of how the search for money power might undermine traditional practices. Moore (1986), in her study of the Endo, elaborates on that idea, and in so doing sheds further insight on the complex relations between spatializations and social reproduction. Value and meaning 'are not inherent in any spatial order,' she insists, 'but must be invoked.' The idea that there is some 'universal' language of space, a semiotics of space independent of practical activities and historically situated actors, has to be rejected. Yet within the context of specific practices, the organization of space can indeed define relationships between people, activities, things, and concepts. 'The organization of space amongst the Endo can be conceived of as a text; as such, it "talks about" or "works over" states of affairs which are imaginary' but nonetheless important, because they represent social concerns. Such spatial representations are 'both product and producer.' Under pressures of monetization and the introduction of wage labour, the representations shift. In the case of the Endo, 'modernism' is displayed by the replacement of the traditional round house with a square house, coupled with an overt display of wealth, the separation of the cooking area from the main house, and other spatial reorganizations that signal a shift in social relations.

The potentiality for such processes to become wrapped in myth and ritual tells us much about the dilemmas of modernism and postmodernism. We have already noted, in Part I as well as in the introduction to Part III, how modernism was so often to flirt with mythology. We here encounter the fact that spatial and temporal practices can themselves appear as 'realized myth' and so become an essential ideological ingredient to social reproduction. The difficulty under capitalism, given its penchant for fragmentation and ephemerality in the midst of the universals of monetization, market exchange, and the circulation of capital, is to find a stable mythology expressive of its inherent values and meanings. Social practices may invoke certain myths and push for certain spatial and temporal representations as part and parcel of their drive to implant and reinforce their hold on society. But they do so in such an eclectic and ephemeral fashion that it is hard to speak of 'realized myth' under capitalism with the same certitude that Bourdieu achieves for the Kabyles. This does not prevent the deployment of powerful mythologies (as with the case of Nazism or the myth of the machine) as vigorous provocations to historical–geographic change. Moreover, mythology is presented in mild enough forms (the evocation of tradition, of collective memory, of locality and place, of cultural identity) to make of it a more subtle affair than the raucous claims of Nazism. But it is hard to find examples of its workings in contemporary society that do not in some way evoke a very specific sense of what a 'time and a place for everything' means. Hence the significance of spatializing practices in architecture and urban design, of historical evocation, and the struggles that go on over the definition of what exactly is the right time and right place for what aspects of social practice.

Bachelard (1964), for his part, focuses our attention on the space of imagination – 'poetic space.' Space 'that has been seized upon by the imagination cannot remain indifferent space subject to the measures and estimates of the surveyor' any more than it can be exclusively represented as the 'affective space' of the psychologists. 'We think we know ourselves in time,' he writes, 'when all we know is a sequence of fixations in the spaces of the being's stability.' Memories 'are motionless, and the more securely they are fixed in space, the sounder they are.' The echoes of Heidegger are strong here. 'Space contains compressed time. That is what space is for.' And the space which is paramount for memory is the house – 'one of the greatest powers of integration of the thoughts, memories and dreams of mankind.' For it is within that space that we learned how to dream and imagine. There

> Being is already a value. Life begins well, it begins enclosed, protected, all warm in the bosom of the house.... This is the environment in which the protective beings live. ... In this remote region, memory and imagination remain associated, each one working for their mutual deepening.... Through dreams,

the various dwelling-places in our lives co-penetrate and retain the treasures of former days. And after we are in the new house, when memories of other places we have lived in come back to us, we travel to the land of Motionless Childhood, motionless the way all Immemorial things are.

Being, suffused with immemorial spatial memory, transcends Becoming. It founds all those nostalgic memories of a lost childhood world. Is this the foundation for collective memory, for all those manifestations of place-bound nostalgias that infect our images of the country and the city, of region, milieu, and locality, of neighbourhood and community? And if it is true that time is always memorialized not as flow, but as memories of experienced places and spaces, then history must indeed give way to poetry, time to space, as the fundamental material of social expression. The spatial image (particularly the evidence of the photograph) then asserts an important power over history (see chapter 18).

Spatial and temporal practices, in any society, abound in subtleties and complexities. Since they are so closely implicated in processes of reproduction and transformation of social relations, some way has to be found to depict them and generalize about their use. The history of social change is in part captured by the history of the conceptions of space and time, and the ideological uses to which those conceptions might be put. Furthermore, any project to transform society must grasp the complex nettle of the transformation of spatial and temporal conceptions and practices.

I shall try to capture some of the complexity through construction of a 'grid' of spatial practices (table 3.1). Down the left hand side I range three dimensions identified in Lefebvre's *La production de l'espace*:

1   Material spatial practices refer to the physical and material flows, transfers, and interactions that occur in and across space in such a way as to assure production and social reproduction.

2   Representations of space encompass all of the signs and significations, codes and knowledge, that allow such material practices to be talked about and understood, no matter whether in terms of everyday common-sense or through the sometimes arcane jargon of the academic disciplines that deal with spatial practices (engineering, architecture, geography, planning, social ecology, and the like).

3   Spaces of representation are mental inventions (codes, signs, 'spatial discourses,' utopian plans, imaginary landscapes, and even

material constructs such as symbolic spaces, particular built environments, paintings, museums, and the like) that imagine new meanings or possibilities for spatial practices.

Lefebvre characterizes these three dimensions as the experienced, the perceived, and the imagined. He regards the dialectical relations between them as the fulcrum of a dramatic tension through which the history of spatial practices can be read. The spaces of representation, therefore, have the potential not only to affect representation of space but also to act as a material productive force with respect to spatial practices. But to argue that the relations between the experienced, the perceived, and the imagined are dialectically rather than causally determined leaves things much too vague. Bourdieu (1977) provides a clarification. He explains how 'a matrix of perceptions, appreciations, and actions' can at one and the same time be put to work flexibly to 'achieve infinitely diversified tasks' while at the same time being 'in the last instance' (Engels's famous phrase) engendered out of the material experience of 'objective structures,' and therefore 'out of the economic basis of the social formation in question.' The mediating link is provided by the concept of 'habitus' – a 'durably installed generative principle of regulated improvisations' which 'produces practices' which in turn tend to reproduce the objective conditions which produced the generative principle of habitus in the first place. The circular (even cumulative?) causation is obvious. Bourdieu's conclusion is, however, a very striking depiction of the constraints to the power of the imagined over the experienced:

> Because the habitus is an endless capacity to engender products – thoughts, perceptions, expressions, actions – whose limits are set by the historically and socially situated conditions of its production, the conditioning and conditional freedom it secures is as remote from a creation of unpredictable novelty as it is from a simple mechanical reproduction of the initial conditionings. (Bourdieu, 1977, 95)

That theorization, though not in itself complete, is of considerable interest. I shall return to examine its implications for cultural production later.

Across the top of the grid (table 3.1) I list four other aspects to spatial practice drawn from more conventional understandings:

1 Accessibility and distanciation speak to the role of the 'friction of distance' in human affairs. Distance is both a barrier to, and a

Table 3.1 A 'grid' of spatial practices

	Accessibility and distanciation	Appropriation and use of space	Domination and control of space	Production of space
Material spatial practices (experience)	flows of goods, money, people labour power, information, etc.; transport and communications systems; market and urban hierarchies; agglomeration	land uses and built environments; social spaces and other 'turf' designations; social networks of communication and mutual aid	private property in land; state and administrative divisions of space; exclusive communities and neighbourhoods; exclusionary zoning and other forms of social control (policing and surveillance)	production of physical infrastructures (transport and communications; built environments; land clearance, etc.); territorial organization of social infrastructures (formal and informal)

Representations of space (perception)	social, psychological and physical measures of distance; map-making; theories of the 'friction of distance' (principle of least effort, social physics, range of a good, central place and other forms of location theory)	personal space; mental maps of occupied space; spatial hierarchies; symbolic representation of spaces; spatial 'discourses'	forbidden spaces; 'territorial imperatives'; community; regional culture; nationalism; geopolitics; hierarchies	new systems of mapping, visual representation, communication, etc.; new artistic and architectural 'discourses'; semiotics.
Spaces of representation (imagination)	attraction/repulsion; distance/desire; access/denial; transcendence 'medium is the message'.	familiarity; hearth and home; open places; places of popular spectacle (streets, squares, markets); iconography and graffiti; advertising	unfamiliarity; spaces of fear; property and possession; monumentality and constructed spaces of ritual; symbolic barriers and symbolic capital; construction of 'tradition'; spaces of repression	utopian plans; imaginary landscapes; science fiction ontologies and space; artists' sketches; mythologies of space and place; poetics of space spaces of desire

Source: in part inspired by Lefebvre (1974)

defence against, human interaction. It imposes transaction costs upon any system of production and reproduction (particularly those based on any elaborate social division of labour, trade, and social differentiation of reproductive functions). Distanciation (cf. Giddens, 1984, 258–9) is simply a measure of the degree to which the friction of space has been overcome to accommodate social interaction.

2   The appropriation of space examines the way in which space is occupied by objects (house, factories, streets, etc.), activities (land uses), individuals, classes, or other social groupings. Systematized and institutionalized appropriation may entail the production of territorially bounded forms of social solidarity.

3   The domination of space reflects how individuals or powerful groups dominate the organization and production of space through legal or extra-legal means so as to exercise a greater degree of control either over the friction of distance or over the manner in which space is appropriated by themselves or others.

4   The production of space examines how new systems (actual or imagined) of land use, transport and communications, territorial organization, etc. are produced, and how new modes of representation (e.g. information technology, computerized mapping, or design) arise.

These four dimensions to spatial practice are not independent of each other. The friction of distance is implicit in any understanding of the domination and appropriation of space, while the persistent appropriation of a space by a particular group (say the gang that hangs out on the street corner) amounts to a *de facto* domination of that space. The production of space, insofar as it reduces the friction of distance (capitalism's 'annihilation of space through time,' for example) alters distanciation and the conditions of appropriation and domination.

My purpose in setting up such a grid is not to attempt any systematic exploration of the positions within it, though such an examination would be of considerable interest (I have penned in a few controversial positionings within the grid for purposes of illustration, and would like to suggest that the different authors we have so far examined concentrate on different facets of it). My purpose is to find some point of entry that will allow a deeper discussion of the shifting experience of space in the history of modernism and postmodernism.

The grid of spatial practices can tell us nothing important by itself. To suppose so would be to accept the idea that there is some universal spatial language independent of social practices. Spatial practices derive their efficacy in social life only through the structure of social relations within which they come into play. Under the social relations of capitalism, for example, the spatial practices portrayed in the grid become imbued with class meanings. To put it this way is not, however, to argue that spatial practices are derivative of capitalism. They take on their meanings under specific social relations of class, gender, community, ethnicity, or race and get 'used up' or 'worked over' in the course of social action. When placed in the context of capitalist social relations and imperatives (see chapter 14 below), the grid helps unravel some of the complexity that prevails in understanding the transformation of spatial experience associated with the shift from modernist to postmodernist ways of thinking.

Gurvitch (1964) suggests an analogous framework for thinking about the meaning of time in social life. He addresses the issue of the social content of temporal practices directly, however, while avoiding issues of materiality, representation, and imagination of the sort that Lefebvre insists upon. His primary thesis is that particular social formations (listed in the right-hand column of table 3.2) associate with a specific sense of time. Out of that study comes an eightfold classification of the types of social time that have existed historically. This typology proves rather interesting in its implications.

To begin with, it inverts the proposition that there is a time for everything and proposes that we think, instead, of every social relation containing its own sense of time. It is tempting, for example, to think of 1968 as an 'explosive' time (in which quite different behaviours were suddenly deemed acceptable) emerging out of the 'deceptive' time of Fordism−Keynesianism and giving way in the late 1970s to the world of 'time in advance of itself' populated by speculators, entrepreneurs, and debt-peddling finance capitalists. It is also possible to use the typology to look at different senses of time at work contemporaneously, with academics and other professionals perpetually condemned (it seems) to 'retarded time,' perhaps with a mission to avert 'explosive' and 'erratic' times, and so restore to us some sense of 'enduring' time (a world also populated by ecologists and theologians). The potential mixes are intriguing, and I shall come back to them later, since they shed light, I think, on the confused transition in the sense of time implied in the shift from modernist to postmodernist cultural practices.

If there were an independent language (or semiotic) of time or space (or time−space) we could at this point reasonably abandon social concerns and enquire more directly into the properties of space−time languages as means of communication in their own right. But since it is a fundamental axiom of my enquiry that time and

Table 3.2 Gurvich's typology of social times

Type	Level	Form	Social formations
Enduring time	ecological	continuous time in which past is projected in the present and future; easily quantifiable	kinships and locality groupings (particularly rural peasant societies and patriarchal structures)
Deceptive time	organized society	long and slowed down duration masking sudden and unexpected crises and ruptures between past and present	large cities and political 'publics'; charismatic and theocratic societies
Erratic time	social roles, collective attitudes (fashion) and technical mixes	time of uncertainty and accentuated contingency in which present prevails over past and future	non-political 'publics' (social movements and fashion-followers); classes in process of formation
Cyclical time	mystical unions	past, present and future projected into each other accentuating continuity within change; diminution of contingency	astrology-followers; archaic societies in which mythological, mystical and magical beliefs prevail
Retarded time	social symbols	future becomes present so late as to be outmoded as soon as it is crystallized	community and its social symbols; guilds, professions etc. feudalism

Table 3.2 cont.

Type	Level	Form	Social formations
Alternating time	rules, signals, signs and collective conduct	past and future compete in the present; discontinuity without contingency	dynamic economic groups; transition epochs (inception of capitalism)
Time in advance of itself (rushing forward)	collective transformative action and innovation	discontinuity, contingency; qualitative change triumphant; the future becomes present	competitive capitalism; speculation
Explosive time	revolutionary ferment and collective creation	present and past dissolved into a transcendent future	revolutions and radical transformations of global structures

Source: Gurvitch (1964)

space (or language, for that matter) cannot be understood independently of social action, I shall now shift the focus to a consideration of how power relations are always implicated in spatial and temporal practices. This will then permit us to put these rather passive typologies and possibilities into the more dynamic frame of historical materialist conceptions of capitalist modernization.

14

Time and space as sources of social power

We owe the idea that command over space is a fundamental and all-pervasive source of social power in and over everyday life to the persistent voice of Henri Lefebvre. How that form of social power articulates with control over time, as well as with money and other forms of social power, requires further elaboration. The general argument I shall explore is that in money economies in general, and in capitalist society in particular, the intersecting command of money, time, and space forms a substantial nexus of social power that we cannot afford to ignore. 'Time measurement,' Landes (1983, 12) declares in his authoritative study of the subject, 'was at once a sign of new-found creativity and an agent and catalyst in the use of knowledge for wealth and power.' Accurate timekeepers and accurate maps have long been worth their weight in gold, and command over spaces and times is a crucial element in any search for profit. For example, the property speculator who has the money to wait while controlling development on adjacent spaces is in a much better situation to make pecuniary gains compared to someone who lacks power in any one of these dimensions. Furthermore, money can be used to command time (our own or that of others) and space. Conversely, command of time and space can be converted back into command over money.

Two very general questions then emerge. First, those who define the material practices, forms, and meanings of money, time, or space fix certain basic rules of the social game. I do not wish to imply by this that those who define the rules always win any contest that may ensue. There are too many examples of unintended consequences (in which those in power define rules that undermine their own power base), and of oppositional groups learning and using the rules to overwhelm those who devised them, for such a simple equation to be credible. It is nevertheless the case that ideological and political hegemony in any society depends on an ability to control the material context of personal and social experience. For this reason, the materializations and meanings given to money, time, and space have more than a little significance for the maintenance of political power. The immediate problem, however, is to understand the social processes whereby their objective qualities are established. That way we can better evaluate the claim that something vital has happened to our experience of space and time since the 1970s so as to provoke the turn to postmodernism.

Interior to that general question lies another: to consider how well-established spatial and temporal practices and 'discourses' are 'used up' and 'worked over' in social action. How, for example, does the grid of spatial practices or the typology of social time acquire a class, gender, or other social content in a given historical situation? The common-sense rules which define the 'time and place for everything' are certainly used to achieve and replicate particular distributions of social power (between classes, between women and men, etc.). This question is not, however, independent of the first. Frustrated power struggles (on the part of women, workers, colonized peoples, ethnic minorities, immigrants, etc.) within a given set of rules generate much of the social energy to change those rules. Shifts in the objective qualities of space and time, in short, can be, and often are, effected through social struggle.

It is against this background that I shall take a cursory look (drawing heavily upon materials already published in Harvey, 1985a, chapter 2, and 1985b, chapter 1) at the relations between money, space, and time as interlocking sources of social power. I begin with the simplest connection. Money measures value, but if we ask what constitutes value in the first instance, we find it impossible to define value without saying something about how the time of social labour is allocated. 'Economy of time,' says Marx (1973, 173), 'to this all economy ultimately reduces itself.' Conversely, though money represents social labour time, the rise of the money form shaped the meaning of time in important and specific ways. Le Goff (1980) points out, for example, that the enlargement of the monetary sphere of circulation, and the organization of commercial networks over space in the early mediaeval period, forced the merchant to construct 'a more adequate and predictable measure of time for the orderly conduct of business.' But notice the implication of space in this argument. The mediaeval merchant discovered the fundamental concept of 'the price of time' only in the course of exploring space. Because trade and exchange entail spatial movement, it was the time taken up by this spatial movement which taught the merchant to attach prices, and hence the money form itself, to working time (cf. Landes, 1983, 72).

Two general implications then follow. First, progressive monetization of relations in social life transforms the qualities of time and space. The definition of a 'time and a place for everything' necessarily changes and constitutes a new framework for promoting new kinds of social relations. The mediaeval merchants, for example, in constructing a better measure of time 'for the orderly conduct of business' promoted a 'fundamental change in the measurement of time which was indeed a change in time itself.' Symbolized by clocks and bells that called workers to labour and merchants to market, separated from the 'natural' rhythms of agrarian life, and divorced from religious significations, merchants and masters created a new 'chronological net' in which daily life was caught. The new definition of time did not pass undisputed by religious authority any more than by the workers called upon to accept the new rules of temporal discipline. 'These evolving mental structures and their material expression,' Le Goff concludes, 'were deeply implicated in the mechanisms of class struggle.' Ironically, the explorations of the calendar and time measurement that had been promoted by the monastic orders in order to impose religious discipline were appropriated by the nascent bourgeoisie as a means to organize and discipline the populations of mediaeval towns to a new-found and very secular labour discipline. 'Equal hours' in the city, comments Landes (1983, 78), 'announced the victory of a new cultural and economic order.'

By the same token, the mapping of the world opened up a way to look upon space as open to appropriation for private uses. Mapping also turned out to be far from ideologically neutral. Helgerson (1986), for example, argues that Christopher Saxton's collection of county maps of Britain, published in 1579, not only allowed the English, for the first time, to take 'effective visual and conceptual possession of the physical kingdom in which they lived,' but also strengthened the sense of individual and local powers within a framework of national loyalties, all 'at the expense of identity based on dynastic loyalty.' But if the dynastic powers looked to trade as a source of the money power which they needed to pursue their political and military objectives (as well as their passion for consumption), then they had to initiate the rational representation of space and time that supported the power of that class (the merchants) which would ultimately supplant them. In the long run, of course, the state authorities had little option. The cost of cartographic ignorance – militarily as well as in trade and commerce – was so enormous that the incentive to procure good maps overwhelmed any other reservations. 'In the international contest for access to the riches of the Indies,' Landes (1983, 110) notes, 'maps were money, and secret agents of aspiring powers paid gold for good copies of the carefully guarded Portuguese *padrons*'.

A second, and in some respects more difficult implication is that modifications of the qualities of space and time can result from the pursuit of monetary objectives. If money has no meaning independent of time and space, then it is always possible to pursue profit (or other forms of advantage) by altering the ways time and space are used and defined. This thesis can be most cogently explored in the context of the profit-seeking that occurs within the standard form of circulation of capital. Material commodity exchange entails change of location and spatial movement. Any complicated system of production entails spatial organization (even if only of the shop floor or office). Overcoming these spatial barriers takes time and money. Efficiency of spatial organization and movement is therefore an important issue for all capitalists. The time of production together with the time of circulation of exchange make up the concept of 'the turnover time of capital.' This, too, is an extremely important magnitude. The faster the capital launched into circulation can be recuperated, the greater the profit will be. The definitions of 'efficient spatial organization' and of 'socially necessary turnover time' are fundamental norms against which the search for profit is measured. And both are subject to change.

Consider, first, the turnover time of capital. There is an omnipresent incentive for individual capitalists to accelerate their turnover time *vis-à-vis* the social average, and in so doing to promote a social trend towards faster average turnover times. Capitalism, as we shall see, has for this reason been characterized by continuous efforts to shorten turnover times, thereby speeding up social processes while reducing the time horizons of meaningful decision-making. There are, however, a number of barriers to this tendency – barriers in the rigidity of production and labour skills, fixed capital that must be amortized, marketing frictions, consumption lags, bottlenecks to money circulation, and the like. There is a whole history of technical and organizational innovation applied to the reduction of such barriers – everything from assembly-line production (of cars or battery hens), acceleration of physical processes (fermentation, genetic engineering), to planned obsolescence in consumption (the mobilization of fashion and advertising to accelerate change), the credit system, electronic banking, and the like. It is in this context that the adaptability and flexibility of workers become vital to capitalist development. Workers, instead of acquiring a skill for life, can now look forward to at least one if not multiple bouts of de-skilling and re-skilling in a lifetime. The accelerated destruction and reconstruction of workers' skills have been, as we saw in Part II, a central feature in the turn from Fordist to flexible modes of accumulation.

The general effect, then, is for capitalist modernization to be very much about speed-up and acceleration in the pace of economic processes and, hence, in social life. But that trend is discontinuous, punctuated by periodic crises, because fixed investments in plant and machinery, as well as in organizational forms and labour skills, cannot easily be changed. The implantation of new systems has either to await the passing of the 'natural' lifetime of the factory and the worker, or to engage in that process of 'creative destruction' which rests on the forced devaluation or destruction of past assets in order to make way for the new. Since the latter implies a loss of value even for the capitalists, strong social forces are ranged against it. When the conditions of accumulation are relatively easy, the incentive to apply such innovations is relatively weak. But at times of economic difficulty and intensifying competition, individual capitalists are forced to accelerate the turnover of their capital; those who can best intensify or speed up production, marketing, etc. are in the best position to survive. Modernizations that affect turnover time are not, therefore, deployed at a uniform rate. They tend to bunch together mainly in periods of crisis. I shall later explore (chapter 17) this thesis in the context of speed-up as a response to capitalist crisis since 1972.

Since 'moments' are 'the elements of profit' (Marx, 1967, vol. 1, 233), it is command over the labour time of others, however, that gives capitalists the initial power to appropriate profit as their own. Struggles between owners of labour and of capital over the use of time and the intensity of labour have been endemic. They go back, as both Le Goff and E. P. Thompson (1967) agree, to at least the mediaeval period. Marx notes that the struggle over the length of the working day arose in Elizabethan England when the state legislated an increase in the length of the customary working day for labourers freshly released from the land by violent expropriation, and consequently prone to be unstable, undisciplined, and itinerant. The incarceration of the unemployed with the mad (which Marx highlights and Foucault erects into a whole book) was but one of many means to bring the labour force to heel. 'New labour habits were formed, and a new time-discipline imposed,' Thompson confirms, over several generations, forged under the pressure to synchronize both the social and the detail division of labour and to maximize the extraction of the labourer's surplus labour time (the basis of profit).

Thus came into being 'the familiar landscape of industrial capitalism, with the time-sheet, the timekeeper, the informers and the fines.' The battle over minutes and seconds, over the pace and intensity of work schedules, over the working life (and rights of retirement), over the working week and day (with rights to 'free time'), over the working year (and rights to paid vacations), has been, and continues to be, right royally fought. Workers learned to fight back within the confines of the newly internalized sense of time:

> The first generation of factory workers were taught by their masters the importance of time; the second generation formed their short-time work committees in the ten-hour movement; the third generation struck for overtime or time-and-a-half. They had accepted the categories of their employers and learned to fight back within them. They had learned their lesson, that time is money, only too well. (Thompson, 1967, 90)

It is still very much the case that attempts to speed up or intensify labour processes spark some of the strongest and bitterest of struggles between labour and management. Stratagems such as piece-work or production bonuses can only ever be counted partial successes from the standpoint of management, because workers frequently establish their own work norms that in turn regulate the rate for the job. Direct confrontations over speed-up and intensity, over break times and schedules, are too often destructive to be engaged in with ease. The speed of assembly-line movement, robotization, and automated control systems provide more insidious means of indirect control, but rarely can be altered except marginally without sparking worker protest. Yet in spite of this resistance, most work schedules are extremely tightly ordered, and the intensity and speed of production have largely been organized in ways that favour capital rather than labour. Telephone operators working for AT&T are expected to deal with one call every 28 seconds as a condition of contract, lorry drivers push themselves to extremes of endurance and court death by taking pills to keep awake, air traffic controllers suffer extremes of stress, assembly-line workers take to drugs and alcohol, all part and parcel of a daily work rhythm fixed by profit-making rather then by the construction of humane work schedules. Compensations, such as paid vacations, higher wages, shorter working weeks, early retirement, are all too often, as Marx long ago observed, recuperated by capital in the form of even greater intensity and speed-up on the job. The balance of class forces is not easily struck, however. When the General Motors plant at Lordstown was set up in the early 1970s, a young and restive labour force fought speed-up and automated control tooth and nail. By the end of the 1970s, however, much of the resistance had crumbled under the pressures of widespread local unemployment, fears of plant closure, and co-optation into new rhythms of work.

We can track similar processes and arrive at similar conclusions with respect to the experience of space. The incentive to create the world market, to reduce spatial barriers, and to annihilate space through time is omni-present, as is the incentive to rationalize spatial organization into efficient configurations of production (serial organization of the detail division of labour, factory systems, and assembly line, territorial division of labour, and agglomeration in large towns), circulation networks (transport and communications systems), and consumption (household and domestic layout, community organization, and residential differentiation, collective consumption in cities). Innovations dedicated to the removal of spatial barriers in all of these respects have been of immense significance in the history of capitalism, turning that history into a very geographical affair — the railroad and the telegraph, the automobile, radio and telephone, the jet aircraft and television, and the recent telecommunications revolution are cases in point.

But here, too, capitalism encounters multiple contradictions. Spatial barriers can be reduced only through the production of particular spaces (railways, highways, airports, teleports, etc.). Furthermore, a spatial rationalization of production, circulation, and consumption at one point in time may not be suited to the further accumulation of capital at a later point in time. The production, restructuring, and growth of spatial organization is a highly problematic and very expensive affair, held back by vast investments in physical infrastructures that cannot be moved, and social infrastructures that are always slow to change. The continuous incentive for individual capitalists to relocate in lower-cost or higher-profit locations is likewise checked by the costs of movement. Consequently the intensification of competition and the onset of crises tend to accelerate the pace of spatial restructuring through selective and place-specific devaluation of assets.

These general trends and tensions have to be set, however, against the background of divergent interests and class struggle, since it is almost invariably the case that shifts in tempo or in spatial ordering redistribute social power by changing the conditions of monetary gain (in the form of wages, profits, capital gains, and the like). Superior command over space has always been a vital aspect of class (and intra-class) struggle. In 1815, for example, Nathan Rothschild used his unrivalled information network to get the first news of Wellington's victory over Napoleon at Waterloo, promptly sold, and triggered such a market panic that he could then move in to pick up all manner of market bargains, so earning 'the quickest unearned fortune on record' (Davidson and Rees-Mogg, 1988). Capitalists, furthermore, are not averse to using spatial strategies in competition with each other. The struggle between diverse railroad interests in the nineteenth century provides abundant examples of this practice, while Tarbell (1904, 146) depicts Rockefeller 'bent over a map and with military precision [planning] the capture of strategic locations on the map of East Coast oil refineries.' Domination of marketing networks and spaces remains a fundamental corporate aim, and many a bitter struggle for market share is fought out with the precision of a military campaign to capture territory and space. Accurate geographical information (including inside information on everything from political development to crop yields or labour struggles) becomes a vital commodity in such struggles.

For these reasons also, the ability to influence the production of space is an important means to augment social power. In material terms this means that those who can affect the spatial distribution of investments in transport and communications, in physical and social infrastructures, or the territorial distribution of administrative, political, and economic powers can often reap material rewards. The range of phenomena to be considered here is vast indeed – it varies all the way from one neighbour inciting another to help improve local property values by painting the porch, through systematic pressures by land and property developers to put in water and sewer connections that will improve the value of the lands they hold, to the interest of military contractors in exacerbating geopolitical tensions (such as the Cold War) as a means to ensure bigger and better armaments contracts. Influence over the ways of representing space, as well as over the spaces of representation, can also be important. If workers can be persuaded, for example, that space is an open field of play for capital but a closed terrain for themselves, then a crucial advantage accrues to the capitalists. Workers, in conceding greater powers of mobility to capital (see Part II), might be more liable to concede before the threat of capital flight than would be the case if they were convinced that capitalists could not move. If, to take an example from the field of spatial representation, geopolitical threats can be partially manufactured with the help of the appropriate kinds of map projection' (which merge the image of an 'evil empire' like Russia with a threatening geopolitical position), then considerable power goes to those who command the techniques of representation. If a picture or map is worth a thousand words, then power in the realms of representation may end up being as important as power over the materiality of spatial organization itself.

Such considerations have long entered in as crucial determinants in the dynamics of class struggle. We can here, I think, invoke a simple rule: that those who command space can always control the politics of place even though, and this is a vital corollary, it takes control of some place to command space in the first instance. The relative powers of working-class movements and the bourgeoisie to command space had long been an important constituent element in the power relations between them. John Foster, in *Class struggle in the industrial revolution*, for example, recounts several incidents in which local mill owners found it difficult to control their work-force because the local forces of law and order were prone to sympathize (if only through kinship connections) with the militants, and because it was difficult to summon external assistance with the requisite speed. In the massive railroad strike that shook the East Coast of the United States, on the other hand, a different story was to unfold. The railroad owners likewise found themselves facing a local militia reluctant to act. But the telegraph not only allowed federal assistance to be summoned with great dispatch, but also facilitated the transmission of false messages to the effect that workers had returned to work in St Louis or Baltimore, and that the strike was collapsing at different points along the line. Even though the press played an important progressive role during this incident (being rather more pro-labour then than now), the superior power to command space gave the capitalists an added advantage in what was an uneven but tense power struggle.

The differential powers of geographical mobility for capital and labour have not remained constant over time, nor are they evenly available to different factions of capital and labour. When either capitalists or workers have important assets fixed and immobile in space, then neither side is in a good position to use powers of geographical mobility against the other. The skilled roving craft-workers in, say, the iron industry in the early years of the industrial revolution moved far and wide across Europe and used their superior powers of geographical mobility to their own financial advantage. Modern, debt-encumbered homeowners in weak housing market situations, with strong social interests in staying in a particular milieu, are much more vulnerable. While some capitalists are plainly more mobile than others, they are all forced to some degree or other to 'put down roots,' and many can ill afford to change locations as a result. There are, however, various facets of the capitalists' condition that often force their hand. Accumulation provides them with the wherewithal for expansion, and the options are always to expand *in situ* or to set up a branch plant elsewhere. The incentive to go for the latter increases over time simply by virtue of the congestion costs associated with expansion on original sites. Inter-capitalist competition and the fluidity of money capital over space also force geographical rationalizations in location as part of the accumulation dynamic. Such processes frequently get caught up in the dynamics of class struggle. Gordon (1978) records, for example, cases of suburbanization of industry in New England at the beginning of the century for the direct purpose of avoiding the stronger labour organization in the larger cities. More recently, under conditions of heightened competition, technological change and rapid restructuring, innumerable cases can be cited of industrial relocation decisions taken with an eye to achieving better labour discipline. If capitalists wish to avoid unionization in the United States, a recent consultant's report advised, they should try to split their labour process into components employing no more than fifty workers, and locate the units at least two hundred miles apart from each other. The conditions of flexible accumulation make the exploration of such options more, rather than less, possible.

Prior to the coming of the railroad and the telegraph, the powers of capital and labour in terms of the ability to command space were not radically different. The bourgeoisie plainly feared the revolutionary threat of that power. When, for example, the Luddites took to machine-breaking in many disparate incidents, or agricultural labourers simultaneously took to rick-burning and other forms of protest in many different locales in England in 1830, the bourgeoisie became only too ready to accept the theory that mysterious figures such as Ned Ludd or Captain Swing were passing undetected through the land, fomenting discontent and revolutionary sentiments as they went. The bourgeoisie soon learned to use its superior trading connections and command over space as a means to establish social control. In 1848, for example, the French bourgeoisie used its commercial ties to mobilize a *petit bourgeois* militia from provincial France in order to crush the revolution in Paris (a tactic that was to be repeated with even more horrendous effects in the suppression of the Paris Commune). Selective control over the rapid means of communication was deployed to great advantage to counter the Chartist movement in Britain in the 1840s and to suppress working-class discontent in France after the *coup d'état* of 1851. 'The supreme glory of Napoleon III,' wrote Baudelaire, 'will have been to prove that anybody can govern a great nation as soon as they have got control of the telegraph and the national press.'

The working-class movement, for its part, accumulated similar insights. Not only did the First International seek to unite workers from many different places and industries, working under quite different social relations, into a common cause, but it also began, in the 1860s, to transfer funds and material aid from one space of class struggle to another. If the bourgeoisie could command space for its own class purposes, then the workers' movement could do the same. And to the degree that the First International appeared to command genuine power, the bourgeoisie had every reason to fear it (as indeed they did) in exactly the same way that they had feared the mysterious roamings of Captain Swing decades before. The capacity to link workers in united action across space has always been an important variable in class struggle. To some degree Marx seemed to believe that the massing of workers in the factories and the cities of industrial capitalism would by itself provide a sufficient geopolitical power base for class action. But the whole thrust of First International geopolitics was to broaden that base in as systematic a way as possible.

It is rare indeed for class action not to have to face up to its specific geographical constraints. In the prolonged miners' strike in Britain in 1984, for example, the so-called 'flying pickets' moving quickly from one pit-head to another posed an acute problem for the state powers, which had to devise equally mobile tactics in response. Legislation to outlaw secondary industrial action and flying pickets was designed to curb working-class power over space and to weaken the potential for coherent class action by confining it to place.

The crushing of the Paris Commune, and the 1877 railroad strike in the United States, demonstrated early on, however, that superior command over space would usually lie with the bourgeoisie. Nevertheless, the workers' movement persisted in its internationalist vision (though with weak actual organization) up until the eve of the First World War, when the Second International split essentially on the question of loyalty to nation (space) versus loyalty to class (historical) interests. The victory of the former current not only had workers fighting on both sides of what most recognized as a war between capitalists, but initiated a phase of workers' movement history in which proletarian interests always ended up, no matter what the rhetoric, serving at the feet of national interests.

Working-class movements are, in fact, generally better at organizing in and dominating *place* than they are at commanding *space*. The various revolutions that broke out in Paris in the nineteenth century foundered on the inability to consolidate national power through a spatial strategy that would command the national space. Movements such as the Seattle general strike of 1918 (when workers effectively took control of the city for nearly a week), the St Petersburg uprising of 1905, coupled with a long and detailed history of municipal socialism, community organization around strike action (such as the Flint strike of 1933), through to the urban uprisings of the United States of the 1960s, all illustrate the point. On the other hand, simultaneity of revolutionary upsurges in different locations, as in 1848 or 1968, strikes fear into any ruling class precisely because its superior command over space is threatened. It is exactly in such situations that international capitalism raises the spectre of an international conspiracy, deeply offensive to national interests, and often invokes the power of the latter to preserve its ability to command space.

What is even more interesting is the political response to this latent power of revolutionary and worker mobilization in place. One of the principal tasks of the capitalist state is to locate power in the spaces which the bourgeoisie controls, and disempower those spaces which oppositional movements have the greatest potentiality to command. This was the principle that led France to deny self-government to Paris until the total *embourgeoisement* of the city allowed it to become the fiefdom of Chirac's right-wing politics. This was the same strategy that lay behind Thatcher's abolition of metropolitan governments like the Greater London Council (controlled by a Marxist left during the period 1981–85). It was also manifest in the slow erosion of municipal and urban powers in the United States during the 'progressive era' when municipal socialism appeared as a real possibility, thus making a federalization of state powers more acceptable to the large-scale capitalists. It is in such a context that class struggle also assumes its global role. Henri Lefebvre puts it this way:

> Today, more than ever, the class struggle is inscribed in space. Indeed, it is that struggle alone which prevents abstract space from taking over the whole planet and papering over all differences. Only the class struggle has the capacity to differentiate, to generate differences which are not intrinsic to economic growth ... that is to say, differences which are not either induced by or acceptable to that growth.

The whole history of territorial organization (see Sack, 1987), colonization and imperialism, of uneven geographical development, of urban and rural contradictions, as well as of geopolitical conflict testifies to the importance of such struggles within the history of capitalism.

If space is indeed to be thought of as a system of 'containers' of social power (to use the imagery of Foucault), then it follows that the accumulation of capital is perpetually deconstructing that social power by re-shaping its geographical bases. Put the other way round, any struggle to reconstitute power relations is a struggle to re-organize their spatial bases. It is in this light that we can better understand 'why capitalism is continually reterritorializing with one hand what it was deterritorializing with the other' (Deleuze and Guattari, 1984).

Movements of opposition to the disruptions of home, community, territory, and nation by the restless flow of capital are legion. But then so too are movements against the tight constraints of a purely monetary expression of value and the systematized organization of space and time. What is more, such movements spread far beyond the realms of class struggle in any narrowly defined sense. The rigid discipline of time schedules, of tightly organized property rights and other forms of spatial determination, generate widespread resistances on the part of individuals who seek to put themselves outside these hegemonic constraints in exactly the same way that others refuse the discipline of money. And from time to time these individual resistances can coalesce into social movements with the aim of liberating space and time from their current materializations and constructing an alternative kind of society in which value, time, and money are understood in new and quite different ways. Movements of all sorts – religious, mystical, social, communitarian, humanitarian, etc. – define themselves directly in terms of an antagonism to the power of money and of rationalized conceptions of space and time over daily life. The history of such utopian, religious, and communitarian movements testifies to the vigour of exactly this antagonism. Indeed, much of the colour and ferment of social movements, of street life and culture, as well as of artistic and other cultural practices, derives precisely from the infinitely varied texture of oppositions to the materializations of money, space, and time under conditions of capitalist hegemony.

Yet all such social movements, no matter how well articulated their aims, run up against a seemingly immovable paradox. For not only does the community of money, coupled with a rationalized space and time, define them in an oppositional sense, but the movements have to confront the question of value and its expression as well as the necessary organization of space and time appropriate to their own reproduction. In so doing, they necessarily open themselves to the dissolving power of money as well as to the shifting definitions of space and time arrived at through the dynamics of capital circulation. Capital, in short, continues to dominate, and it does so in part through superior command over space and time, even when opposition movements gain control over a particular place for a time. The 'othernesses' and 'regional resistances' that postmodernist politics emphasize can flourish in a particular place. But they are all too often subject to the power of capital over the co-ordination of universal fragmented space and the march of capitalism's global historical time that lies outside of the purview of any particular one of them.

A number of general conclusions can now be ventured. Spatial and temporal practices are never neutral in social affairs. They always express some kind of class or other social content, and are more often than not the focus of intense social struggle. That this is so becomes doubly obvious when we consider the ways in which space and time connect with money, and the way that connection becomes even more tightly organized with the development of capitalism. Time and space both get defined through the organization of social practices fundamental to commodity production. But the dynamic force of capital accumulation (and overaccumulation), together with conditions of social struggle, renders the relations unstable. As a consequence, nobody quite knows what 'the right time and place for everything' might be. Part of the insecurity which bedevils capitalism as a social formation arises out of this instability in the spatial and temporal principles around which social life might be organized (let alone ritualized in the manner of traditional societies). During phases of maximal change, the spatial and temporal bases for reproduction of the social order are subject to the severest disruption. In subsequent chapters I shall show that it is exactly at such moments that major shifts in systems of representation, cultural forms, and philosophical sentiment occur.

15

The time and space of the Enlightenment project

In what follows I shall make frequent reference to the concept of 'time—space compression.' I mean to signal by that term processes that so revolutionize the objective qualities of space and time that we are forced to alter, sometimes in quite radical ways, how we represent the world to ourselves. I use the word 'compression' because a strong case can be made that the history of capitalism has been characterized by speed-up in the pace of life, while so overcoming spatial barriers that the world sometimes seems to collapse inwards upon us. The time taken to traverse space (plate 3.1) and the way we commonly represent that fact to ourselves (plate 3.2) are useful indicators of the kind of phenomena I have in mind. As space appears to shrink to a 'global village' of telecommunications and a 'spaceship earth' of economic and ecological interdependencies — to use just two familiar and everyday images — and as time horizons shorten to the point where the present is all there is (the world of the schizophrenic), so we have to learn how to cope with an over-whelming sense of *compression* of our spatial and temporal worlds.

The experience of time—space compression is challenging, exciting, stressful, and sometimes deeply troubling, capable of sparking, therefore, a diversity of social, cultural, and political responses. 'Compression' should be understood as relative to any preceding state of affairs. In what follows, I shall consider the matter historically, using the European case (somewhat ethnocentrically) as an example. In this chapter, I shall look briefly at the long transition that prepared the way for Enlightenment thinking about space and time.

In the relatively isolated worlds (and I use the plural advisedly) of European feudalism, place assumed a definite legal, political, and social meaning indicative of a relative autonomy of social relations and of community inside roughly given territorial boundaries. Within each knowable world, spatial organization reflected a confused

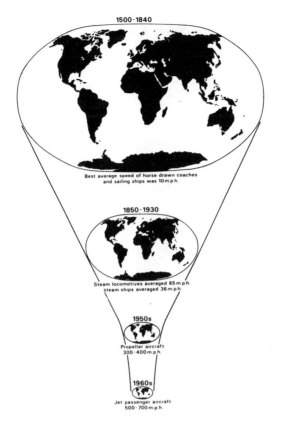

1500-1840

Best average speed of horse-drawn coaches
and sailing ships was 10 m.p.h.

1850-1930

Steam locomotives averaged 65 m.p.h.
steam ships averaged 36 m.p.h.

1950s

Propeller aircraft
300-400 m.p.h.

1960s

Jet passenger aircraft
500-700 m.p.h.

Plate 3.1 The shrinking map of the world through innovations in transport which 'annihilate space through time'.

overlapping of economic, political, and legal obligations and rights. External space was weakly grasped and generally conceptualized as a mysterious cosmology populated by some external authority, heavenly hosts, or more sinister figures of myth and imagination. The finite centred qualities of place (an intricate territory of interdependence, obligation, surveillance, and control) matched time-honoured routines of daily life set in the infinity and unknowability of 'enduring time' (to use Gurvitch's term). Mediaeval parochialism and superstition were paralleled by an 'easy and hedonistic psychophysiological' approach to spatial representation. The mediaeval artist 'believed that he could render what he saw before his eyes convincingly by representing what it felt like to walk about, experiencing structures, almost tactilely, from many different sides, rather than from a single overall vantage' (Edgerton, 1976). Mediaeval art and

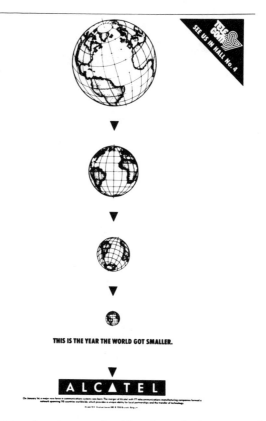

Plate 3.2 A 1987 advertisement by Alcatel emphasizes a popular image of the shrinking globe.

cartography, interestingly, seem to match the sensibility portrayed in de Certeau's 'spatial stories' (see plate 3.3).

There were, of course, disruptive forces at work in this feudal world – class conflicts, disputes over rights, ecological instabilities, and population pressures, doctrinal conflicts, Saracen invasions and the crusades, and the like. Above all, the progress of monetization (with its disruptive effect on the traditional community) and commodity exchange, in the first instance between communities but later through more independent forms of merchant trading, suggested an entirely different conception of time and space (see above, pp. 227–9) from that which dominated the feudal order.

The Renaissance, however, saw a radical reconstruction of views of space and time in the Western world. From an ethnocentric

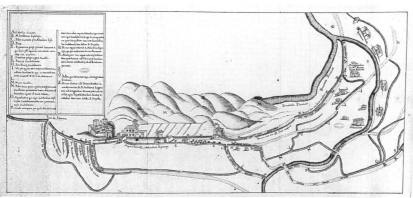

Plate 3.3 The tradition of medieval mapping typically emphasizes the sensuous rather than the rational and objective qualities of spatial order: (above) Plan des dimes de Champeaux from the XVth century and (below) the Vue de Cavaillon et ses environs from the XVIIth century.

viewpoint, the voyages of discovery produced an astounding flow of knowledge about a wider world that had somehow to be absorbed and represented. They indicated a globe that was finite and potentially knowable. Geographical knowledge became a valued commodity in a society that was becoming more and more profit-conscious. The accumulation of wealth, power, and capital became linked to personalized knowledge of, and individual command over, space. By the same token, each place became vulnerable to the direct influence of that wider world through trade, intra-territorial competition, military action, the inflow of new commodities, of bullion, and the like. But by virtue of the piecemeal development of the processes shaping it, the revolution in conceptions of space and time was slow to unfold.

Fundamental rules of perspective – rules that broke radically with the practices of mediaeval art and architecture, and which were to dominate until the beginning of the twentieth century – were elaborated in mid-fifteenth-century Florence by Brunelleschi and Alberti. This was a fundamental achievement of the Renaissance; it shaped ways of seeing for four centuries. The fixed viewpoint of perspective maps and paintings 'is elevated and distant, completely out of plastic or sensory reach.' It generates a 'coldly geometrical' and 'systematic' sense of space which nevertheless gives 'a sense of harmony with natural law, thereby underscoring man's moral responsibility within God's geometrically ordered universe' (Edgerton, 1976, 114). A conception of infinite space allowed the globe to be grasped as a finite totality without challenging, at least in theory, the infinite wisdom of the deity. 'Infinite space is endowed with infinite quality,' wrote Giordano Bruno at the end of the Renaissance, 'and in the infinite quality is lauded the infinite act of existence' (cited in Kostof, 1985, 537). The chronometer, which gave strength and measure to the idea of time's arrow, was likewise rendered theoretically compatible with God's infinite wisdom by attributing infinite qualities to time analogous to those which attached to space. The attachment was of immense importance. It meant that the idea of time as 'becoming' – a very human sense of time which is also contained in the idea of time's arrow – was separated from the analytical and 'scientific' sense of time which rested on a conception of infinity that was preferred (though not by the authorities in Rome) broadly for religious reasons. The Renaissance separated scientific and supposedly factual senses of time and space from the more fluid conceptions that might arise experientially.

Giordano Bruno's conceptions, which prefigured those of Galileo and Newton, were in practice so pantheistic that Rome burned him at the stake as a threat to centralized authority and dogma. In so doing, the Church was recognizing a rather significant challenge that infinite time and space posed to hierarchically conceived systems of authority and power based in a particular place (Rome).

Perspectivism conceives of the world from the standpoint of the 'seeing eye' of the individual. It emphasizes the science of optics and the ability of the individual to represent what he or she sees as in some sense 'truthful,' compared to superimposed truths of mythology or religion. The connection between individualism and perspectivism is important. It provided an effective material foundation for the Cartesian principles of rationality that became integrated into the Enlightenment project. It signalled a break in artistic and architectural practice from artisan and vernacular traditions towards intellectual activity and the 'aura' of the artist, scientist, or entrepreneur as a creative individual. There is also some evidence to connect the formulation of perspectivist rules with the rationalizing practices emerging in commerce, banking, book-keeping, trade, and agricultural production under centralized land management (Kostof, 1985, 403−10).

The story of Renaissance maps, which took on entirely new qualities of objectivity, practicality, and functionality, is particularly revealing (see plate 3.4). Objectivity in spatial representation became a valued attribute because accuracy of navigation, the determination of property rights in land (as opposed to the confused system of legal rights and obligations that characterized feudalism), political boundaries, rights of passage and of transportation, and the like, became economically as well as politically imperative. Many special-purpose map representations, such as the portolan charts used by navigators and estate maps used by landowners, already existed, of course, but the importation of the Ptolemaic map from Alexandria to Florence around 1400 appears to have played a crucial role in the Renaissance discovery and use of perspectivism:

The portolans did not furnish a geometrical framework for comprehending the whole world. The Ptolemaic grid, on the other hand, posed an immediate mathematical unity. The most far-flung places could all be precisely fixed in relation to one another by unchanging coordinates so that their proportionate distance, as well as their directional relationships, would be apparent.... The Ptolemaic system gave the Florentines a perfect, expandable cartographic tool for collecting, collating, and correcting geographical knowledge. Above all, it supplied to geography the same aesthetic principles of geometrical harmony which Florentines demanded of all their art. (Edgerton, 1976)

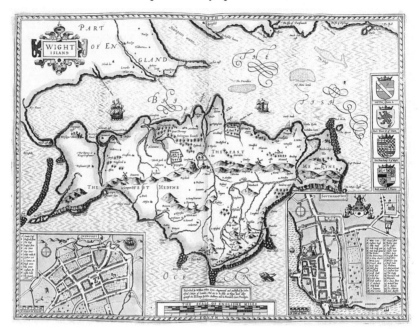

Plate 3.4 The rational ordering of space in the renaissance maps of England played an important role in affirming the position of individuals in relation to territory: John Speed's map of the Isle of Wight, 1616.

The connection with perspectivism lay in this: that in designing the grid in which to locate places, Ptolemy had imagined how the globe as a whole would look to a human eye looking at it from outside. A number of implications then follow. The first is an ability to see the globe as a knowable totality. As Ptolemy himself put it, the goal 'of chorography is to deal separately with a part of the whole,' whereas 'the task of geography is to survey the whole in its just proportion.' Geography rather than chorography became a Renaissance mission. A second implication is that mathematical principles could be applied, as in optics, to the whole problem of representing the globe on a flat surface. As a result, it seemed as if space, though infinite, was conquerable and containable for purposes of human occupancy and action. It could be appropriated in imagination according to mathematical principles. And it was exactly in such a context that the revolution in natural philosophy, so brilliantly described by Koyré (1957), which went from Copernicus to Galileo and ultimately to Newton, was to occur.

Perspectivism had reverberations in all aspects of social life and in all fields of representation. In architecture, for example, it allowed the replacement of Gothic structures 'spun from arcane geometrical formulae jealously guarded by the lodge' with a building conceived of and built 'on a unitary plan drawn to measure' (Kostof, 1985, 405). This way of thinking could be extended to encompass the planning and construction of whole cities (like Ferrara) according to a similar unitary plan. Perspectivism could be elaborated upon in innumerable ways, as, for example, in the baroque architecture of the seventeenth century which expressed 'a common fascination with the idea of the infinite, of movement and force, and the all-embracing but expansive unity of things.' While still religious in ambition and intent, such architecture would have been 'unthinkable in the earlier, simpler days before projective geometry, calculus, precision clocks, and Newtonian optics' (Kostof, 1985, 523). Baroque architecture and Bach fugues are both expressive of those concepts of infinite space and time which post-Renaissance science elaborated upon with such zeal. The extraordinary strength of spatial and temporal imagery in the English literature of the Renaissance likewise testifies to the impact of this new sense of space and time on literary modes of representation. The language of Shakespeare, or of poets like John Donne and Andrew Marvell, is rife with such imagery. It is intriguing to note, furthermore, how the image of the world as a theatre ('all the world's a stage' played in a theatre called 'The Globe') was reciprocated in the titles commonly given to atlases and maps (such as John Speed's *Theatre of the Empire of Great Britain* and the French atlas, *Théâtre français* of 1594). The construction of land-scapes (both rural and urban) according to principles of theatrical design soon followed suit.

If spatial and temporal experiences are primary vehicles for the coding and reproduction of social relations (as Bourdieu suggests), then a change in the way the former get represented will almost certainly generate some kind of shift in the latter. This principle helps explain the support that the Renaissance maps of England supplied to individualism, nationalism, and parliamentary democracy at the expense of dynastic privilege (see plate 3.5). But, as Helgerson points out, maps could just as easily function 'in untroubled support of a strongly centralized monarchic regime,' though Philip II of Spain thought his maps sufficiently subversive to keep them under lock and key as a state secret. Colbert's plans for a rational spatial integration of the French nation state (focused as much upon the enhancement of trade and commerce as upon administrative efficiency) are typical of the deployment of the 'cold rationality' of maps used for instrumental ends in support of centralized state power. It was,

Plate 3.5 Dynasty versus the map: the Ditchley Portrait of Queen Elizabeth emphasizing the power of dynasty over individual and nation as represented by the Renaissance map

after all, Colbert, in the age of French Absolutism, who encouraged the French Academy of Sciences (set up in 1666) and the first of the great map-making family, Jean Dominique Cassini, to produce a coherent and well-ordered map of France.

The Renaissance revolution in concepts of space and time laid the conceptual foundations in many respects for the Enlightenment project. What many now look upon as the first great surge of modernist thinking, took the domination of nature as a necessary condition of human emancipation. Since space is a 'fact' of nature, this meant that the conquest and rational ordering of space became an integral part of the modernizing project. The difference this time was that space and time had to be organized not to reflect the glory of God, but to celebrate and facilitate the liberation of 'Man' as a free and active individual, endowed with consciousness and will. It was in this image that a new landscape was to emerge. The twisting perspectives and intense force fields constructed to the glory of God in baroque architecture had to give way to the rationalized structures of an architect like Boulée (whose project, see plate 3.6, for a cenotaph for Isaac Newton is a visionary piece of modernism). There is a continuous thread of thought from Voltaire's concern with rational city planning through to Saint-Simon's vision of associated capitals unifying the earth by way of vast investments in transport and communications, and Goethe's heroic invocation in Faust – 'let me open spaces for many millions/ to dwell in, though not secure, yet active and free' – and the ultimate realization of exactly such projects as part and parcel of the capitalist modernization process in the nineteenth century. Enlightenment thinkers similarly looked to command over the future through powers of scientific prediction, through social engineering and rational planning, and the institutionalization of rational systems of social regulation and control. They in effect appropriated and pushed Renaissance conceptions of space and time to their limit in the search to construct a new, more democratic, healthier, and more affluent society. Accurate maps and chronometers were essential tools within the Enlightenment vision of how the world should be organized.

Maps, stripped of all elements of fantasy and religious belief, as well as of any sign of the experiences involved in their production, had become abstract and strictly functional systems for the factual ordering of phenomena in space. The science of map projection, and techniques of cadastral surveying, made them mathematically rigorous depictions. They defined property rights in land, territorial boundaries, domains of administration and social control, communication routes, etc. with increasing accuracy. They also allowed the whole

*Plate 3.6 Boulée's eighteenth-century design for Newton's Cenotaph
pioneered the rational and ordered sense of architectural space later taken up
by modernism.*

population of the earth, for the first time in human history, to be
located within a single spatial frame (see plate 3.7). The grid that the
Ptolemaic system had provided as a means to absorb the inflow of
new information had by now been corrected and filled out, so that a
long line of thinkers, from Montesquieu to Rousseau, could begin to
speculate on the material and rational principles that might order the
distribution of populations, ways of life, and political systems on the
surface of the globe. It was within the confines of such a totalizing
vision of the globe that environmental determinism and a certain
conception of 'otherness' could be admitted, even flourish. The diversity of peoples could be appreciated and analysed in the secure
knowledge that their 'place' in the spatial order was unambiguously
known. In exactly the same way that Enlightenment thinkers believed
that translation from one language to another was always possible
without destroying the integrity of either language, so the totalizing
vision of the map allowed strong senses of national, local, and
personal identities to be constructed in the midst of geographical
differences. Were not the latter after all entirely compatible with the
division of labour, commerce, and other forms of exchange? Were
they not also explicable in terms of different environmental conditions? I do not want to idealize the qualities of thought that

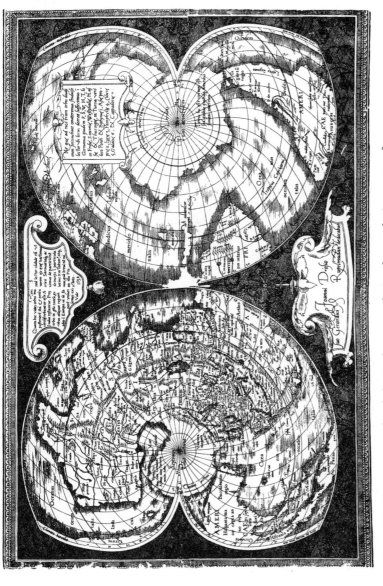

Plate 3.7 *Mercator completed the Ptolemaic ambition by producing maps of the world, such as this effort of 1538, that ever more accurately represented the physical spatial relationships of all places on the globe's surface.*

resulted. The environmentalist explanations of difference put forward
by Montesquieu and Rousseau hardly appear enlightened, while the
sordid facts of the slave trade and the subjugation of women passed
Enlightenment thinkers by with hardly a murmur of protest. Nevertheless, I do want to insist that the problem with Enlightenment
thought was not that it had *no* conception of 'the other' but that it
perceived 'the other' as necessarily having (and sometimes 'keeping
to') a specific *place* in a spatial order that was ethnocentrically
conceived to have homogeneous and absolute qualities.

The recording of time by the chronometer was no less totalizing in
its implication for thought and action. Increasingly seen as a mechanical division fixed by the swing of the pendulum, time's arrow was
conceived to be linear both forwards and backwards. The conception
of past and future as linearly connected by the ticking away of the
clock allowed all manner of scientific and historical conceptions to
flourish. On such a temporal schema it was possible to see retro-
diction and prediction as symmetrical propositions, and to formulate
a strong sense of potentiality to control the future. And even though
it took many years for geological and evolutionary time scales to be
accepted, there is a sense in which such time scales were already
implicit in the very acceptance of the chronometer as the way of
telling time. Even more important, perhaps, was the significance of
such a conception of homogeneous and universal time to conceptions
of the rate of profit (return on stock of capital over time, said Adam
Smith), the rate of interest, the hourly wage, and other magnitudes
fundamental to capitalist decision-making. What all this adds up to is
the by now well accepted fact that Enlightenment thought operated
within the confines of a rather mechanical 'Newtonian' vision of the
universe, in which the presumed absolutes of homogeneous time and
space formed limiting containers to thought and action. The breakdown in these absolute conceptions under the stress of time–space
compression was the central story of the birth of nineteenth- and
early twentieth-century forms of modernism.

I think it useful, however, to pave the path to understanding the
break into modernist ways of seeing after 1848 with a consideration
of the tensions that lay within Enlightenment conceptions of space.
The theoretical, representational, and practical dilemmas are also
instructive in interpreting the subsequent move towards postmodernism.

Consider, as a starting point, de Certeau's contemporary critique
of the map as a 'totalizing device.' The application of mathematical
principles produces 'a formal ensemble of abstract places' and 'col-
lates on the same plane heterogeneous places, some received from

tradition and others produced by observation.' The map is, in effect, a homogenization and reification of the rich diversity of spatial itineraries and spatial stories. It 'eliminates little by little' all traces of 'the practices that produce it.' While the tactile qualities of the mediaeval map preserved such traces, the mathematically rigorous maps of the Enlightenment were of quite different qualities. Bourdieu's arguments also apply. Since any system of representation is itself a fixed spatial construct, it automatically converts the fluid, confused, but nonetheless objective spaces and time of work and social reproduction into a fixed schema. 'Just as the map replaces the discontinuous patchy space of practical paths by the homogeneous, continuous space of geometry, so the calendar substitutes a linear, homogeneous, continuous time for practical time, which is made up of incommensurable islands of duration each with its own rhythm.' The analyst, Bourdieu continues, may win 'the privilege of totalization' and secure 'the means for apprehending the logic of the system which a partial or discrete view would miss,' but there is also 'every likelihood that he will overlook the change in status to which he is subjecting practice and its product,' and consequently 'insist on trying to answer questions which are not and cannot be questions for practice.' By treating certain idealized conceptions of space and time as real, Enlightenment thinkers ran the danger of confining the free flow of human experience and practice to rationalized configurations. It is in these terms that Foucault detects the repressive turn in Enlightenment practices towards surveillance and control.

This provides a useful insight into 'postmodernist' criticism of the 'totalizing qualities' of Enlightenment thought and the 'tyranny' of perspectivism. It also highlights a recurring problem. If social life is to be rationally planned and controlled so as to promote social equality and the welfare of all, then how can production, consumption, and social interaction be planned and efficiently organized except through the incorporation of the ideal abstractions of space and time as given in the map, the chronometer, and the calendar? Beyond this there lies another problem. If perspectivism, for all its mathematical rigour, constructs the world from a given individual viewpoint, then from whose perspective is the physical landscape to be shaped? The architect, designer, planner could not preserve the tactile sense of mediaeval representations. Even when not directly dominated by class interests, the producer of space could only produce 'alien art' from the standpoint of its inhabitants. Insofar as the social planning of high modernism reincorporated these elements into its practical applications, it likewise stood to be accused of the 'totalizing vision' of space and time to which Enlightenment thinking was heir. The mathematical unities given by Renaissance perspectivism could, from this standpoint, be regarded as just as totalizing and repressive as the maps.

Let me follow this line of argument a bit further in order to capture the central dilemma of defining a proper spatial frame for social action.

The conquest and control of space, for example, first requires that it be conceived of as something usable, malleable, and therefore capable of domination through human action. Perspectivism and mathematical mapping did this by conceiving of space as abstract, homogeneous, and universal in its qualities, a framework of thought and action which was stable and knowable. Euclidean geometry provided the basic language of discourse. Builders, engineers, architects, and land managers for their part showed how Euclidean representations of objective space could be converted into a spatially ordered physically landscape. Merchants and landowners used such practices for their own class purposes, while the absolutist state (with its concern for taxation of land and the definition of its own domain of domination and social control) likewise relished the capacity to define and produce spaces with fixed spatial co-ordinates. But these were islands of practice within a sea of social activities in which all manner of other conceptions of space and place — sacred and profane, symbolic, personal, animistic — could continue to function undisturbed. It took something more to consolidate the actual use of space as universal, homogeneous, objective, and abstract in social practice. In spite of the plethora of utopian plans, the 'something more' that came to dominate was private property in land, and the buying and selling of space as a commodity.

This brings us to the heart of the dilemmas of the politics of space in any kind of project to transform society. Lefebvre (1974, 385) observes, for example, that one of the ways in which the homogeneity of space can be achieved is through its total 'pulverization' and fragmentation into freely alienable parcels of private property, to be bought and traded at will upon the market. This was, of course, exactly the strategy that so forcefully transformed the British landscape through the enclosure movements of the eighteenth and early nineteenth centuries, and which demanded systematic mapping as one of its accoutrements. There is, Lefebvre suggests, a permanent tension between the free appropriation of space for individual and social purposes, and the domination of space through private property, the state, and other forms of class and social power. Out of Lefebvre's proposition we can extract five explicit dilemmas:

1   If it is true that the only way that space can be controlled and organized is through its 'pulverization' and fragmentation, then it behoves us to establish the principles of that fragmentation. If space, as Foucault would have it, is always a container of social power, then the reorganization of space is always a reorganization of the framework through which social power is expressed. Political economists of the Enlightenment period debated this problem quite explicitly under the opposed doctrines of mercantilism (in which the state was the relevant geographical unit around which spatial policy should be formulated) and liberalism (in which it was the rights of individualized private property that were paramount). Turgot, French minister of state and an eminent economist with physiocratic and liberal leanings, commissioned the accurate cadastral mapping of much of France precisely because he sought to support private property relations, the dispersal of economic and political power, and to facilitate the free circulation of commodities both within and without France. Colbert, on the other hand, had earlier tried to organize the French space to concentrate on Paris, the capital, because of his interest in supporting the absolute state and monarchical power. Both were concerned to enhance the fiscal basis of state power, but saw quite different spatial policies as necessary to meet that goal, because they envisaged quite different relations of power between private property and the state (Dockès, 1969).

2   What Enlightenment thinkers began to grapple with was the whole problem of 'the production of space' as a political and economic phenomenon. The production of turnpikes, canals, systems of communication and administration, cleared lands, and the like put the question of the production of a space of transport and communications clearly on the agenda. Any change in space relations wrought by such investments, after all, affected the profitability of economic activity unevenly, and therefore led to a redistribution of wealth and power. Any attempt to democratize and disperse political power likewise entailed some kind of spatial strategy. One of the first initiatives of the French Revolution was to devise a rational system of administration through a highly rational and egalitarian division of the French national space into 'departments' (see plate 3.8). Perhaps the clearest example of this politics in action is the design of the homesteading system and the spatial grid for land settlement in the United States (a product of Jeffersonian democratic and Enlightenment thinking). The pulverization and fragmentation of the space of the United States along such rationalistic lines was

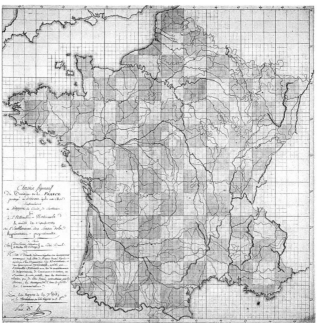

Plate 3.8 *The French Revolution emphasized Enlightenment concerns for both the rational mapping of space and its rational division for purposes of administration: (above) a 1780 prospectus for a 'Nouvelle Topographie' of France and (below) a 1789 map drawn up by the National Assembly to facilitate proportional representation.*

thought to (and in some respects indeed did) imply maximum individual liberty to move and settle in a reasonably egalitarian way in the spirit of a property-owning and agrarian democracy. The Jeffersonian vision was ultimately subverted, but at least up until the Civil War there was enough truth in its practical meaning to give some credence to the idea that the United States, precisely because of its open spatial organization, was the land where the utopian visions of the Enlightenment might be realized.

3   There can be no politics of space independent of social relations. The latter give the former their social content and meaning. This was the rock upon which the innumerable utopian plans of the Enlightenment foundered. The pulverization of space, which Jeffersonian land politics presumed would open the way to an egalitarian democracy, ended up being a means that facilitated the proliferation of capitalist social relations. It provided a remarkably open framework within which money power could operate with few of the constraints encountered in Europe. In the European context it was the ideas of Saint-Simon, with his associated capitals conquering and subduing space in the name of human welfare, that similarly got subverted. After 1848, credit bankers such as the Péreire brothers in Second Empire France, promoted a highly profitable even if speculative 'spatial fix' to the dilemmas of overaccumulation and capitalist crisis, through a vast wave of investments in railways, canals, and urban infrastructures.

4   The homogenization of space poses serious difficulties for the conception of place. If the latter is the site of Being (as many theorists were later to suppose), then Becoming entails a spatial politics that renders place subservient to transformations of space. Absolute space yields, as it were, to relative space. It is precisely at this point that the incipient tension between place and space can get transformed into an absolute antagonism. The reorganization of space to democratic ends challenged dynastic power embedded in place. 'The beating down of gates, the crossing of castle moats, walking at one's ease in places where one was once forbidden to enter: the appropriation of a certain space, which had to be opened and broken into, was the first delight of the [French] Revolution.' Moreover, as 'good sons of the Enlightenment,' Ozouf (1988, 126–37) goes on to report, the revolutionaries 'saw space and time as an occasion' to construct a ceremonial space that was the equivalent of 'the time of the Revolution'. But the subversion of that democratizing project by money power and capital led to the commodification of space and

the production of new but equally oppressive geographical systems for the containerization of power (as in the United States).

5 This leads us back to the most serious dilemma of all: the fact that space can be conquered only through the production of space. The specific spaces of transport and communications, of human settlement and occupancy, all legitimized under some legal system of rights to spaces (of the body, of land, of home, etc.) which guarantees security of place and access to the members of society, form a fixed frame within which the dynamics of a social process must unfold. When placed in the context of capital accumulation this fixity of spatial organization becomes heightened into an absolute contradiction. The effect is to unleash capitalism's powers of 'creative destruction' upon the geographical landscape, sparking violent movements of opposition from all kinds of quarters.

This last point is sufficiently important to warrant generalization. Not only does it take the production of a specific, fixed, and immovable space to pursue the 'annihilation of space through time,' but it also takes long-term investments of slow turnover time (automated plants, robots, etc.) in order to accelerate the turnover time of the mass of capitals. How capitalism confronts and periodically succumbs to this nexus of contradictions is one of the major untold stories in the historical geography of capitalism. Time—space compression is a sign of the intensity of forces at work at this nexus of contradiction and it may well be that crises of overaccumulation as well as crises in cultural and political forms are powerfully connected to such forces.

Enlightenment thinkers sought a better society. In so doing they had to pay attention to the rational ordering of space and time as prerequisites to the construction of a society that would guarantee individual liberties and human welfare. The project meant the reconstruction of the spaces of power in radically new terms, but it proved impossible to specify exactly what those terms might be. State, communitarian, and individualistic ideas were associated with different spatial landscapes, just as differential command over time posed crucial problems of class relations, of the rights to the fruits of one's labour, and of capital accumulation. Yet all Enlightenment projects had in common a relatively unified common-sense of what space and time were about and why their rational ordering was important. This common basis in part depended on the popular availability of watches and clocks, and on the capacity to diffuse cartographic knowledge by cheaper and more efficient printing techniques. But it also rested upon the link between Renaissance perspectivism and a conception of the individual as the ultimate source and container of social power, albeit assimilated within the nation state as a collective system of authority. The economic conditions of the European Enlightenment contributed in no uncertain measure to the sense of common objectives. Increased competition between states and other economic units created pressure to rationalize and co-ordinate the space and time of economic activity, be it within a national space of transport and communications, of administration and military organization, or the more localized spaces of private estates and municipalities. All economic units were caught up in a world of increasing competition in which the stakes were ultimately economic success (measured in the bullion so dear to the mercantilists, or by the accumulation of individualized money, wealth, and power as lauded by the liberals). The practical rationalization of space and time throughout the eighteenth century – a progress marked by the rise of the Ordnance Survey or of systematic cadastral mapping in France at the end of the eighteenth century – formed the context in which Enlightenment thinkers formulated their projects. And it was against this conception that the second great turn of modernism after 1848 revolted.

16

Time–space compression and the rise of modernism as a cultural force

The depression that swept out of Britain in 1846–7 and which quickly engulfed the whole of what was then the capitalist world, can justly be regarded as the first unambiguous crisis of capitalist overaccumulation. It shook the confidence of the bourgeoisie and challenged its sense of history and geography in profound ways. There had been many economic and political crises before, but most could reasonably be attributed to natural calamities (such as harvest failures) or wars and other geopolitical struggles. But this one was different. Though there were bad harvests here and there, this crisis could not easily be attributed to God or nature. Capitalism had matured by 1847–8 to a sufficient degree, so that even the blindest bourgeois apologist could see that financial conditions, reckless speculation, and over-production had something to do with events. The outcome, in any case, was a sudden paralysis of the economy, in which surpluses of capital and labour lay side by side with apparently no way to reunite them in profitable and socially useful union.

There were, of course, as many explanations of the crisis as there were class positions (and a good few more besides). The craft workers from Paris to Vienna tended to view it as the inevitable outcome of a rampant capitalist development process that was changing employment conditions, raising the rate of exploitation, and destroying traditional skills, while progressive elements in the bourgeoisie could view it as a product of the recalcitrant aristocratic and feudal orders who refused the course of progress. The latter, for their part, could attribute the whole affair to the undermining of traditional values and social hierarchies by the materialist values and practices of both workers and an aggressive class of capitalists and financiers.

The thesis I want to explore here, however, is that the crisis of 1847–8 created a crisis of representation, and that this latter crisis itself derived from a radical readjustment in the sense of time and space in economic, political, and cultural life. Before 1848, progressive elements within the bourgeoisie could reasonably hold to the Enlightenment sense of time ('time pressing forward' as Gurvitch would put it), recognizing that they were fighting a battle against the 'enduring' and ecological time of traditional societies and the 'retarded time' of recalcitrant forms of social organization. But after 1848, that progressive sense of time was called into question in many important respects. Too many people in Europe had fought on the barricades, or been caught up in the maelstrom of hopes and fears, not to appreciate the stimulus that comes with participant action in 'explosive time.' Baudelaire, for one, could never forget the experience, and came back to it again and again in his explorations of a modernist language. In retrospect, it became easier to invoke some cyclical sense of time (hence the growing interest in the idea of business cycles as necessary components to the capitalist growth process that would connect back to the economic troubles of 1837, 1826, and 1817). Or, if people were mindful enough of class tensions, they might invoke, as Marx did in *The eighteenth brumaire of Louis Bonaparte*, a sense of 'alternating time' in which the outcome of bitter struggles must always be seen as a precarious balance between class forces. But I think it true to say that the question 'What time are we in?' came in upon the philosophical agenda after 1848 in ways that challenged the simple mathematical presuppositions of Enlightenment thinking. The sense of physical and social time, so recently brought together in Enlightenment thought, began once more to diverge. It then became possible for the artist and the thinker to explore the nature and meaning of time in new ways.

The events of 1847–8 also challenged certainties as to the nature of space and the meaning of money. Events proved that Europe had achieved a level of spatial integration in its economic and financial life that was to make the whole continent vulnerable to simultaneous crisis formation. The political revolutions that erupted at once across the continent emphasized the synchronic as well as the diachronic dimensions to capitalist development. The certainty of absolute space and place gave way to the insecurities of a shifting relative space, in which events in one place could have immediate and ramifying effects in several other places. If, as Jameson (1988, 349) suggests, 'the truth of experience no longer coincides with the place in which it takes place,' but is spreadeagled across the world's spaces, then a situation arises 'in which we can say that if individual experience is authentic, then it cannot be true; and that if a scientific or cognitive mode of the same content is true, then it escapes individual experience.' Since individual experience always forms the raw material of works of art, this condition posed deep problems for artistic production. But this was not the only arena of confusion. Diverse local workers' movements suddenly found themselves swept up in a series of events and political shifts which had no obvious boundaries. Nationalist workers could exhibit xenophobia in Paris yet sympathize with Polish or Viennese workers struggling, like them, for political and economic emancipation in their particular spaces. It was in such a context that the universalist propositions of *The communist manifesto* made more than a little sense. How to reconcile the perspective of place with the shifting perspectives of relative space became a serious issue to which modernism was to address itself with increasing vigour up until the shock of the First World War.

European space was becoming more and more unified precisely because of the internationalism of money power. 1847−8 was a financial and monetary crisis which seriously challenged received ideas as to the meaning and role of money in social life. The tension between the functions of money as a measure and store of value, and money as a lubricant of exchange and investment had long been evident. But it was now registered as a downright antagonism between the financial system (the whole structure of credit moneys and 'fictitious capitals') and its monetary base (gold and other tangible commodities that give a clear physical meaning to money). Credit money in effect came crashing down, leaving a shortage of 'real money' and specie in 1847−8. Those who controlled specie controlled a vital source of social power. The Rothschilds used that power to great effect and, through their superior command over space, came to dominate the finances of the whole European continent. Yet the question of the true nature and meaning of money was not so easily resolved. The tension between credit and specie money loomed large in the subsequent years, eventually bringing even the Rothschilds into a banking world in which the credit system and 'fictitious capital formation' became paramount. This in turn altered the meaning of time (investment times, rate of return, etc.) and other vital magnitudes to capitalism's dominant mode of conducting business. It was only after 1850, after all, that stock and capital markets (markets for 'fictitious capital') were systematically organized and opened to general participation under legal rules of incorporation and market contract.

All of these shifts created a crisis of representation. Neither literature nor art could avoid the question of internationalism, synchrony, insecure temporality, and the tension within the dominant measure of value between the financial system and its monetary or commodity base. 'Around 1850,' writes Barthes (1967, 9), 'classical writing therefore disintegrated, and the whole of literature, from Flaubert to the present day, became the problematics of language.' It is no accident that the first great modernist cultural thrust occurred in Paris after 1848. The brushstrokes of Manet that began to decompose the traditional space of painting and to alter its frame, to explore the fragmentations of light and colour; the poems and reflections of Baudelaire that sought to transcend ephemerality and the narrow politics of place in the search for eternal meanings; and the novels of Flaubert with their peculiar narrative structures in space and time coupled with a language of icy aloofness; all of these were signals of a radical break of cultural sentiment that reflected a profound questioning of the meaning of space and place, of present, past and future, in a world of insecurity and rapidly expanding spatial horizons.

Flaubert, for example, explores the question of representation of heterogeneity and difference, of simultaneity and synchrony, in a world where both time and space are being absorbed under the homogenizing powers of money and commodity exchange. 'Everything should sound simultaneously,' he wrote; 'one should hear the bellowing of the cattle, the whispering of the lovers, and the rhetoric of the officials all at the same time.' Unable to represent this simultaneity with the requisite effect, Flaubert 'dissolves the sequence by cutting back and forth (the cinematographic analogy is quite deliberate)' and in the final crescendo to a scene in *Madame Bovary* juxtaposes two sequences 'in a single sentence to reach a unified effect' (Bell, 1978, 114). Frédéric Moreau, the hero of Flaubert's *L'Éducation sentimentale*, moves from space to space in Paris and its suburbs, collecting experiences of quite different qualities as he goes. What is special is the way that he glides in and out of the differentiated spaces of the city, with the same sort of ease that money and commodities change hands. The whole narrative structure of the book likewise gets lost in perpetual postponements of decisions precisely because Frédéric has enough inherited money to enjoy the luxury of not deciding, even in the midst of revolutionary turmoil. Action is reduced to a set of paths that might have been but were not taken. 'The thought of the future torments us, and the past is holding us back,' Flaubert (1979, 134) later wrote, adding, 'that is why the present is slipping from our grasp.' Yet it was the possession of money that allowed the present to slip through Frédéric's grasp, while opening social spaces to casual penetration. Evidently, time, space, and money could be invested with rather different significances, depending upon the conditions and possibilities of trade-off between them. Flaubert had to find a new language to speak of such possibilities.

These explorations of new cultural forms occurred in an economic and political context which in many respects belied that of the economic collapse and revolutionary upsurge of 1848. Even though, for example, excessive speculation in railroad construction triggered the first European-wide crisis of overaccumulation, the resolution to that crisis after 1850 rested heavily upon further exploration of temporal and spatial displacement. New systems of credit and corporate forms of organization, of distribution (the large department stores), coupled with technical and organizational innovations in production (increasing fragmentation, specialization, and de-skilling in the division of labour for example), helped speed up the circulation of capital in mass markets. More emphatically, capitalism became embroiled in an incredible phase of massive long-term investment in the conquest of space. The expansion of the railway network, accompanied by the advent of the telegraph, the growth of steam shipping, and the building of the Suez Canal, the beginnings of radio communication and bicycle and automobile travel at the end of the century, all changed the sense of time and space in radical ways. This period also saw the coming on stream of a whole series of technical innovations. New ways of viewing space and motion (derived from photography and exploration of the limits of perspectivism) began to be thought out and applied to the production of urban space (see Lefaivre, 1986). Baloon travel and photography from on high changed perceptions of the earth's surface, while new technologies of printing and mechanical reproduction allowed a dissemination of news, information, and cultural artefacts throughout ever broader swathes of the population.

The vast expansion of foreign trade and investment after 1850 put the major capitalist powers on the path of globalism, but did so through imperial conquest and inter-imperialist rivalry that was to reach its apogee in World War I − the first global war. En route, the world's spaces were deterritorialized, stripped of their preceding significations, and then reterritorialized according to the convenience of colonial and imperial administration. Not only was the relative space revolutionized through innovations in transport and communications, but what that space contained was also fundamentally re-ordered. The map of domination of the world's spaces changed out of all recognition between 1850 and 1914. Yet it was possible, given the flow of information and new techniques of representation, to sample a wide range of simultaneous imperial adventures and conflicts with a mere glance at the morning newspaper. And if that was not enough, the organization of a series of World Exhibitions, beginning with the Crystal Palace in 1851 and passing through several French efforts to the grand Columbian Exhibition in Chicago in 1893, celebrated the fact of globalism while providing a framework within which what Benjamin calls 'the phantasmagoria' of the world of commodities and competition between nation states and territorial production systems might be understood.

So successful was this project of subduing space and rekindling capitalist growth that the economist Alfred Marshall could confidently assert in the 1870s that the influence of time is 'more fundamental than that of space' in economic life (thus consolidating that privileging of time over space in social theory which we have already noted). Yet this transformation also undermined the cogency and meaning of realist fiction and painting. Zola predicted the end of his own genre, as well as that of a self-contained peasantry in France, in *La Terre* when he has the school teacher articulate the idea that the import of cheap American wheat that then appeared imminent was bound to bury locality (its parochial politics and culture) within a flood of internationalist influences. Frank Norris, on the other side of the Atlantic, sensed the same problem in *The octopus* – the wheat farmers of California had to recognize that they were 'merely a part of an enormous whole, a unit in the vast agglomeration of wheat land the world around, feeling the effects of causes thousands of miles distant.' How was it possible, using the narrative structures of realism, to write anything other than a parochialist and hence to some degree 'unrealistic' novel in the face of all this spatial simultaneity? Realist narrative structures assumed, after all, that a story could be told as if it was unfolding coherently, event after event, in time. Such structures were inconsistent with a reality in which two events in quite different spaces occurring at the same time could so intersect as to change how the world worked. Flaubert, the modernist, pioneered a path that Zola, the realist, found it impossible to emulate.

It was in the midst of this rapid phase of time–space compression that the second great wave of modernist innovation in the aesthetic realm began. To what degree, then, can modernism be interpreted as a response to a crisis in the experience of space and time? Kern's (1983) study of *The culture of time and space, 1880–1918* makes such a supposition more than a little plausible.

Kern accepts that 'the telephone, wireless-telegraph, X-ray, cinema, bicycle, automobile and airplane established the material foundation' for new modes of thinking about and experiencing time and space. While he is anxious to maintain the independence of cultural developments, he does argue that 'the interpretation of phenomena such

as class structure, diplomacy, and war tactics in terms of modes of
time and space makes possible the demonstration of their essential
similarity to explicit considerations of time and space in literature,
philosophy, science, and art' (pp.1–5). Lacking any theory of technological innovation, of capitalist dynamics across space, or of cultural production, Kern offers only 'generalizations about the essential
cultural developments of the period.' But his descriptions highlight
the incredible confusions and oppositions across a spectrum of possible reactions to the growing sense of crisis in the experience of time
and space, that had been gathering since 1848 and seemed to come to
a head just before the First World War. I note in parenthesis that
1910–14 is roughly the period that many historians of modernism
(beginning with Virginia Woolf and D. H. Lawrence) point to as
crucial in the evolution of modernist thinking (see above p. 28;
Bradbury and McFarlane, 1976, 31). Henri Lefebvre agrees:

> Around 1910 a certain space was shattered. It was the space of
> common sense, of knowledge, of social practice, of political
> power, a space hitherto enshrined in everyday discourse, just as
> in abstract thought, as the environment of and channel for
> communication... Euclidean and perspectivist space have dis-
> appeared as systems of reference, along with other former
> 'common places' such as town, history, paternity, the tonal
> system in music, traditional morality, and so forth. This was a
> truly crucial moment. (Lefebvre, 1974)

Consider a few aspects of this crucial moment set, significantly
enough, between Einstein's special theory of relativity of 1905 and
the general theory of 1916. Ford, we recall, set up his assembly line
in 1913. He fragmented tasks and distributed them in space so as to
maximize efficiency and minimize the friction of flow in production.
In effect, he used a certain form of spatial organization to accelerate
the turnover time of capital in production. Time could then be
accelerated (speed-up) by virtue of the control established through
organizing and fragmenting the spatial order of production. In that
very same year, however, the first radio signal was beamed around
the world from the Eiffel tower, thus emphasizing the capacity to
collapse space into the simultaneity of an instant in universal public
time. The power of wireless had been clearly demonstrated the year
before with the rapid diffusion of news about the sinking of the
Titanic (itself a symbol of speed and mass motion that came to grief
in much the same way that the *Herald of Free Enterprise* was to keel
over to speedy disaster some seventy-five years later). Public time

was becoming ever more homogeneous and universal across space. And it was not only commerce and railways, for the organization of large-scale commuting systems and all the other temporal co-ordinations that made metropolitan life bearable also depended upon establishing some universal and commonly accepted sense of time. The more than 38 billion telephone calls made in the United States in 1914 emphasized the power of intervention of public time and space in daily and private life. Indeed, it was only in terms of such a public sense of time that reference to private time could make sense. De Chirico appropriately celebrated these qualities by conspicuously placing clocks (an unusual gesture in art history) in his paintings of 1910–14 (see plate 3.9).

The reactions pointed in many directions. James Joyce, for one, began his quest to capture the sense of simultaneity in space and time during this period, insisting upon the present as the only real location of experience. He had his action take place in a plurality of spaces, Kern (p. 149) notes, 'in a consciousness that leaps about the universe and mixes here and there in defiance of the ordered diagramming of the cartographers.' Proust, for his part, tried to recover past time and to create a sense of individuality and place that rested on a conception of experience across a space of time. Personal conceptions of time became a matter of public commentary. 'The two most innovative novelists of the period,' Kern continues, 'transformed the stage of modern literature from a series of fixed settings in homogeneous space' (of the sort that realist novelists typically deployed) 'into a multitude of qualitatively different spaces that varied with the shifting moods and perspectives of human consciousness.'

Picasso and Braque, for their part, taking their cue from Cézanne who had begun to break up the space of painting in new ways in the 1880s, experimented with cubism, thus abandoning 'the homogeneous space of linear perspective' that had dominated since the fifteenth century. Delaunay's celebrated work of 1910–11 depicting the Eiffel Tower (plate 3.10) was perhaps the most startling public symbol of a movement that tried to represent time through a fragmentation of space; the protagonists were probably unaware that this paralleled the practices on Ford's assembly line, though the choice of the Eiffel Tower as symbol reflected the fact that the whole movement had something to do with industrialism. It was in 1912, also, that Durkheim's *Elementary forms of the religious life* was published with its explicit recognition that 'the foundation of the category time is the rhythm of social life,' and that the social origin of space likewise necessarily entailed the existence of multiple spatial visions. Ortega y Gasset, following Nietzsche's injunction that 'there is *only*

Plate 3.9 De Chirico's The Philosopher's Conquest *(1914) explores modernist themes of time and space explicitly. (The Art Institute of Chicago, Joseph Winterbotham Collection)*

a perspective seeing, *only* a proper perspective knowing,' formulated a new version of the theory of perspectivism in 1910 which insisted that 'there were as many spaces in reality as there were perspectives on it,' and that 'there are as many realities as points of view.' This

Plate 3.10 Delaunay's Eiffel Tower *(transfer lithograph, 1926), first exhibited in 1911, uses a familiar image of construction to examine the fragmentation and break up of space typical of cubism. (Collection, The Museum of Modern Art, New York, Purchase Fund)*

put a philosophical nail in the coffin of rationalist ideals of homogeneous and absolute space (Kern, 1983, 150−1).

I have cited just a few of the incidents that Kern records in order
to convey a sense of the confusions rampant in social and cultural
thought in the period 1910−14. But matters can, I think, be taken a
step further, hinging an argument on an idea that Kern launches but
makes very little of: 'One response was a growing sense of unity
among people formerly isolated in distance and lack of communication. This was not, however, unambiguous, because proximity also
generated anxiety − apprehension that the neighbours were seen as
getting a bit too close' (p. 88). How was this 'ambiguity' expressed?
Two broad and rather distinctive currents of thought can be identified
depending upon the emphasis upon unity or difference.

Those who emphasized the unity between peoples also accepted
the 'unreality of place' within a fragmented relative space. Celebrating
the annihilation of space through time, the task was to re-launch the
Enlightenment project of universal human emancipation in a global
space bound together through mechanisms of communication and
social intervention. Such a project implied, however, spatial fragmentation through planned co-ordination. And how could that be
done except through 'pulverizing' pre-existing spaces in some manner?
Ford had shown how social processes could be speeded up, and
productive forces augmented, by the spatialization of time. The
problem was to harness this capacity to human emancipation rather
than to some narrow set of interests, such as those of capital. A
German group proposed in 1911, for example, the creation of a
'world office' that would 'unify all the humanitarian tendencies that
run in parallel but disorderly directions, and bring about a concentration and a promotion of all creative activities' (quoted in Tafuri,
1985, 122). It was only in such a context of rationalized and totally
organized external and public space, that interior and very private
senses of time and space could properly flourish. The space of the
body, of consciousness, of the psyche − spaces kept too long repressed, given the absolute suppositions of Enlightenment thought,
but now opening up as a consequence of psychological and philosophical findings − could be liberated only through the rational
organization of exterior space and time. But rationality now meant
something more than planning with the aid of the map and the
chronometer, or subjecting all of social life to time and motion
study. New senses of relativism and perspectivism could be invented
and applied to the production of space and the ordering of time. This
kind of reaction, which many were later to dub as exclusively modernist, typically entailed a whole set of accoutrements. Despising

history, it sought entirely new cultural forms that broke with the past and solely spoke the language of the new. Holding that form followed function and that spatial rationality should be imposed on the external world in order to maximize individual liberty and welfare, it took efficiency and function (and hence the image of the metropolis as a well-oiled machine) as its central motif. It had a deep concern for purity of language, no matter whether it was in architecture, music, or literature.

It is an open question, of course, whether this response was a pure bowing down to the force of spatial and temporal restructuring of the period (see above, pp. 28−31). Fernand Léger, the French cubist painter, certainly thought so, observing in 1913 that life was 'more fragmented and faster moving than in previous periods' and that it was essential to devise a dynamic art to depict it (quoted in Kern, 1983, 118). And Gertrude Stein certainly interpreted cultural events, such as the advent of cubism, as a response to the time−space compression to which everyone was exposed and sensitized. This in no way detracts, of course, from the importance of grappling with that experience in the field of representation in such a way as to enhance, support, and perhaps even command the processes that seemed to be escaping from all forms of collective control (as they were indeed set to do in World War I). But it does re-focus our attention on the practical ways in which that might be done. Le Corbusier was, in effect, merely following the Jeffersonian principles of land partition when he argued that the way to individual liberty and freedom lay through the construction of a highly ordered and rationalized space. His project was internationalist, and emphasized the kind of unity in which a socially conscious notion of individual difference could be fully explored.

The other kind of reaction bundled together a host of seemingly divergent responses built, however, around one central principle which I shall later have frequent cause to invoke: that the more unified the space, the more important the qualities of the fragmentations become for social identity and action. The free flow of capital across the surface of the globe, for example, places strong emphasis upon the particular qualities of the spaces to which that capital might be attracted. The shrinkage of space that brings diverse communities across the globe into competition with each other implies localized competitive strategies and a heightened sense of awareness of what makes a place special and gives it a competitive advantage. This kind of reaction looks much more strongly to the identification of place, the building and signalling of its unique qualities in an increasingly homogeneous but fragmented world (see above, pp. 88−92).

We can spot this 'other side' to modernism's explorations in a number of contexts. Foucault's perceptive remark (quoted in Crimp, 1983, 47) that 'Flaubert is to the library what Manet is to the museum' underlines how the innovators of modernism in literature and painting, while in one sense breaking with all past conventions, still had to situate themselves historically and geographically somewhere. Both the library and the museum have the effect of recording the past and depicting geography while breaking with it. The reduction of the past to a representation organized as a display of artefacts (books, paintings, relics, etc.) is just as formalistic as the reduction of geography to a set of displays of things from far-off places. Modernist artists and writers painted for the museums or wrote for the libraries precisely because to work this way allowed them to break with the constraints of their own place and time.

Yet the museum, the library, and the exhibition usually aspire to some kind of coherent ordering. The ideological labour of inventing tradition became of great significance in the late nineteenth century precisely because this was an era when transformations in spatial and temporal practices implied a loss of identity with place and repeated radical breaks with any sense of historical continuity. Historical preservation and the museum culture experienced strong bursts of life from the late nineteenth century on, while the international expositions not only celebrated the world of international commodification but also exhibited the geography of the world as a series of artefacts for all to see. It was out of such a climate that one of the most sensitive of modernist writers, Simmel, could write so persuasively on the significance of ruins. They were, he said, places where 'the past with its destinies and transformations has been gathered into this instant of an aesthetically perceptible present' (quoted in Kern, 1983, 40). Ruins helped ground our shaken identity in a rapidly transforming world. This was also an age when the artefacts of the past or from afar began to trade as valued commodities. The emergence of an active antique and foreign craft market (the latter symbolized by the Japanese prints that Manet inserted into his portrait of Zola, and which to this day adorn Monet's house in Giverny) are indicative of a trend that was consistent, also, with the revival of the craft tradition pushed by William Morris in Britain, by the craftwork movement of Vienna, and in the art noveau style that swamped France in the early years of the century. Architects like Louis Sullivan in Chicago and Gaudemar in Paris likewise searched for new and local vernacular styles that could satisfy the new functional needs but also celebrate the distinctive qualities of the places they occupied. The identity of place was reaffirmed in the midst of the growing abstractions of space.

This trend to privilege the spatialization of time (Being) over the annihilation of space by time (Becoming) is consistent with much of what postmodernism now articulates; with Lyotard's 'local determinisms', Fish's 'interpretive communities', Frampton's 'regional resistances', and Foucault's 'heterotopias.' It evidently offers multiple possibilities within which a spatialized 'otherness' can flourish. Modernism, seen as a whole, explored the dialectic of place versus space, of present versus past, in a variety of ways. While celebrating universality and the collapse of spatial barriers, it also explored new meanings for space and place in ways that tacitly reinforced local identity.

By enhancing links between place and the social sense of personal and communal identity, this facet of modernism was bound, to some degree, to entail the aestheticization of local, regional, or national politics. Loyalties to place then take precedence over loyalties to class, spatializing political action. At the end of the process lies the restoration of the Hegelian notion of the state and the resurrection of geopolitics. Marx, of course, had restored historical time (and class relations) to primacy of place in social theory, in part as a reaction to Hegel's spatialized conception of the 'ethical state' as the end-point of a teleological history. The introduction of the state – a spatialization – poses intriguing questions for social theory for as Lefebvre (1974) points out, 'the state crushes time by reducing differences to repetitions of circularities (dubbed "equilibrium", "feedback", "self-regulation", etc.).' If 'this modern state imposes itself as the stable centre – definitively – of [national] societies and spaces,' then geopolitical argument has to resort, as has in fact always been the case, to aesthetic rather than to social values in its search for legitimacy.

It is, therefore, a readily understandable paradox that in an age when the annihilation of space through time was proceeding at a furious pace, geopolitics and the aestheticization of politics underwent a strong revival.

Nietzsche captured the essential thrust philosophically in *The will to power*. Nihilism – a condition in which 'the highest values devaluate themselves' – stands at our door as 'the uncanniest of guests.' European culture, he asserts, 'has been moving as toward a catastrophe, with a tortured tension that is growing from decade to decade: restlessly, violently, headlong, like a river that wants to reach the end, that no longer reflects, that is afraid to reflect.' The dissolution of 'unalienable landed property, honouring the old (origin of the belief in gods and heroes as ancestors)' in part arises, he suggests (prefiguring Heidegger's arguments exactly, see above pp. 207–9), with the collapse of space: 'newspapers (in place of daily prayers), railway, telegraph.' The consequent 'centralization of a tremendous number of different interests in a single soul,' means that individuals must now be 'very strong and protean.' It is in such a circumstance that the will to power – 'an attempt at a revolution of all values' – must assert itself as a guiding force in the quest for a new morality:

> And do you know what 'the world' is to me? Shall I show it to you in my mirror? This world: a monster of energy, without beginning, without end; . . . enclosed by 'nothingness' as by a boundary; not something blurry or wasted, not something end-lessly extended, but set in a definite space as a definite force, and not a space that might be 'empty' here or there, but rather as force throughout, as a play of forces and waves of forces, at the same time one and many, increasing here, and at the same time decreasing there; a sea of forces flowing and rushing to-gether, eternally changing, eternally flooding back, with tremen-dous years of recurrence, with an ebb and a flood of its forms; out of the simplest forms striving toward the most complex, out of the stillest, most rigid, coldest forms toward the hottest, most turbulent, most self-contradictory, and then again returning home to the simple out of this abundance, out of the play of contradictions back to the joy of concord, still affirming itself in this uniformity of its courses and its years, blessing itself as that which must return eternally, as a becoming that knows no satiety, no disgust, no weariness: this, my Dio-nysian world of the eternally self-creating, the eternally self-destroying, this mystery world of the twofold voluptuous delight, my 'beyond good and evil,' without goal, unless the joy of the circle is itself a goal; without will, unless a ring feels good will toward itself – do you want a *name* for this world? A *solution* for all its riddles? A *light* for you, too, you best-concealed, strongest, most intrepid, most midnightly men? – *This world is the will to power – and nothing besides*! And you yourselves are also this will to power – and nothing besides!

The extraordinary imagery of space and time, of successive waves of compression and implosion, in passages such as this suggests that Nietzsche's powerful intervention in the modernity debate (see above, pp. 15–20) had an experiential basis in the world of late nineteenth-century time–space transformation.

The search for this new morality of power and the charisma of 'very strong and protean' individuals lay at the heart of the new science of geopolitics. Kern pays close attention to the rising significance of such theories at the turn of the century. Friedrich Ratzel in Germany, Camille Vallaux in France, Halford Mackinder in Britain, and Admiral Mahan in the United States all recognized the significance of command over space as a fundamental source of military, economic, and political power. Were there, they asked, strategic spaces within the new globalism of trade and politics, the command of which would confer favoured status upon particular peoples? If there was some Darwinian struggle for survival of the different peoples and nations of the earth, then what principles governed that struggle and what would its outcome probably be? Each tilted his answer towards a national interest, and in so doing conceded the right of a particular people to command its own particular place and, if survival, necessity, or moral certitudes impelled it, to expand in the name of 'manifest destiny' (USA), the 'white man's burden' (Britain), the *'mission civilisatrice'* (France) or the need for *'Lebensraum'* (Germany). In Ratzel's case in particular, we find a philosophical predisposition to insist upon a unity between a people and its land as the basis of cultural sophistication and political power, a union that can be dissolved only through violence and dispossession. This union formed the basis of a national culture and civilizing influence, whose sources were radically different from those given by the universals of Enlightenment thinking or of the confused but universalist modernism that formed the other major current in late nineteenth-century thought.

It would be wrong to consider these two wings of thought — the universalism and the particularism — as separate from each other. They should be regarded, rather, as two currents of sensibility that flowed along side by side, often within the same person, even when one or other sensibility became dominant in a particular place and time. Le Corbusier started his life paying close attention to vernacular styles even while recognizing the importance of rationalizing a homogeneous space in ways proposed by utopian planners. The fascination of cultural movements in Vienna, particularly before World War I, derives, I suspect, precisely from the confused ways in which the two currents I have identified mixed in time, place, and person almost without restraint. The free-flowing sensuality of Klimt, the agonized expressionism of Egon Schiele, the rigorous rejection of ornament and the rational shaping of space of Adolf Loos ... all clinging together in the midst of a crisis of bourgeois culture, caught in its own rigidities but faced with whirlwind shifts in the experience of space and time.

While modernism always ostensibly asserted the values of internationalism and universalism, it could never properly settle its account with parochialism and nationalism. It either defined itself in opposition to these all too familiar forces (strongly identified, though by no means exclusively so, with the so-called 'middle classes') or else it took the elitist and ethnocentric road by presuming that Paris, Berlin, New York, London, or wherever, was indeed the intellectual fount of all representational and aesthetic wisdom. In the latter case, modernism stood to be accused of cultural imperialism in much the same way that abstract expressionism became caught up with national interests in the United States after World War II (see above, pp. 36–8). In putting things this way I am, to some degree, departing from the normal conception of what modernism was supposed to be about. But unless we are prepared to see even its universal aspirations as the outcome of a perpetual dialogue with localism and nationalism, I think we shall miss some of its more important features.

Since this opposition is important, I shall take up one example brilliantly exploited in Carl Schorske's *Fin-de-siècle Vienna*: the contrast between Camillo Sitte's and Otto Wagner's approaches to the production of urban space. Sitte, rooted in the craftworker tradition of late nineteenth-century Vienna, and abhorring the narrow and technical functionalism that seemed to attach to the lust for commercial profit, sought to construct spaces that would make the city's people feel 'secure and happy.' This meant that 'city building must be not just a technical question but an aesthetic one in the highest sense.' He therefore set out to create interior spaces – plazas and squares – that would promote the preservation and even re-creation of a sense of community. He sought 'to overcome fragmentation and provide a "community life-outlook"' for the people as a whole. This deployment of art in the shaping of space to create a real sense of community was, to Sitte, the only possible response to modernity. As Schorske (p. 72) summarizes it: 'In the cold traffic-swept modern city of the slide-rule and the slum, the picturesque comforting square can reawaken memories of the vanished burgher past. This spatially dramatic memory will inspire us to create a better future, free of philistinism and utilitarianism.' To what coherent values could Sitte appeal? Needing a new ideal 'beside and above the real world,' Sitte 'exalted Richard Wagner as the genius who recognized this redemptive, future-oriented work as the special task of the artist. The world that the rootless seeker of science and trade destroyed, leaving the suffering Volk without a vital myth to live by, the artist must create anew' (p. 69).

Sitte's ideas (which parallel those of an anti-modernist like Jane Jacobs, and which are quite popular with urban planners today) can be seen as a specific reaction to commercialization, utilitarian rationalism, and the fragmentations and insecurities that typically arise under conditions of time−space compression. They also definitely attempt to spatialize time, but in so doing cannot help but aestheticize politics, in Sitte's case through appeal to the Wagnerian myth and its notion of a rooted community. Sitte was here conceding, however, to a whole set of political, cultural, and spatial practices that sought to reinforce local community solidarity and tradition in the face of the universalism and globalism of money power, commodification, and capital circulation. Kern, for example, reports that 'national festivals in Germany in this period were staged in spaces around national monuments where masses of people could sing and dance.' These were the kinds of spaces that Sitte set out to provide.

What is terrifying about the subsequent history of this sort of spatial practice is the way that so many of the Viennese artisans whom Sitte championed (along with their German counterparts) were later to mass in the squares, piazzas, and living spaces that Sitte wanted to create, in order to express their virulent opposition to internationalism, turning to anti-semitism (attacking the ethnic and religious group most representative of internationalism, of both capital and labour, by virtue of its condition of diaspora) and the place-specific myths of Nazism in opposition to the rational utilitarianism of Enlightenment thought. The dramatic spectacles of the sort the Nazis organized certainly brought space alive and managed to appeal to a deep mythology of place, symbolizing 'community,' but community of a most reactionary sort. Under conditions of mass un-employment, the collapse of spatial barriers, and the subsequent vulnerability of place and community to space and capital, it was all too easy to play upon sentiments of the most fanatical localism and nationalism. I am not even indirectly blaming Sitte or his ideas for this history. But I do think it important to recognize the potential connection between projects to shape space and encourage spatial practices of the sort that Sitte advocated, and political projects that can be at best conserving and at worst downright reactionary in their implications. These were, after all, the sorts of sentiments of place, Being, and community that brought Heidegger into the embrace of national socialism.

Otto Wagner, a contemporary of Sitte's, accepted the universality of modernity with much more *élan*. Building his ideas upon the motto 'necessity is art's only mistress,' he set out to impose order upon chaos, to rationalize the organization of movement on the basis of 'efficiency, economy, and the facilitation of the pursuit of business.' But he too had to appeal to some kind of dominant aesthetic sense in order to surmount the 'painful uncertainty' that arose in a 'fast

moving world of time and motion' (Schorske, 1981, 85). That uncertainty could be overcome only by a clean break with the past,
taking to the image of the machine as the ultimate form of efficient
rationality, and exploring every nook and cranny of modern techniques and materials. Wagner was, in short, a late nineteenth-century
pioneer of the 'heroic' forms of modernism that became fashionable
in the 1920s with Le Corbusier, Gropius, Mies van der Rohe, and
the like.

These two lines – internationalist and localized – of coping with
the phenomena of time–space compression collided violently in the
global war of 1914–18. How that war was actually triggered rather
than contained is of interest precisely because it illustrates how
conditions of time–space compression, in the absence of a proper
means for their representation, make national lines of conduct impossible to determine, let alone follow. The new systems of transportation
and communication, Kern (1983, 260–1)˙notes, 'tightened the skein
of internationalism and facilitated international co-operation' at the
same time as they 'divided nations as they all grabbed for empire and
clashed in a series of crises.' It is, he suggests, 'one of the great
ironies of the period that a world war became possible only after the
world had become so highly united.' Even more disturbing is his
account of the July crisis that led into war. In the summer of 1914,
'the men in power lost their bearings in the hectic rush paced by
flurries of telegrams, telephone conversations, memos, and press
releases; hard-boiled politicians broke down and seasoned negotiators
cracked under the pressure of tense confrontations and sleepless
nights, agonizing over the probable disastrous consequence of their
snap judgements and hasty actions.' Newspapers fed popular anger,
swift military mobilizations were set in motion, thus contributing to
the frenzy of diplomatic activity that broke down simply because
enough decisions could not be made fast enough in enough locations
to bring the warlike stresses under collective control. Global war was
the result. It seemed, to both Gertrude Stein and Picasso, a *cubist*
war and was fought on so many fronts and in so many spaces that
the denotation appears reasonable even on a global scale.

It is hard, even in retrospect, to assess the impact of that event on
thinking about space and time (see above, pp. 30–1). Some credence
must be given to Kern's judgement that 'in four years the belief in
evolution, progress, and history itself was wiped out' as the war
'ripped up the historical fabric and cut everyone off from the past
suddenly and irretrievably.' The breakdown echoed the stresses of
1848 almost exactly and shook up perceptions of space and time.

Taylor's (1987, 126) account of what happened to the German artist
Beckmann is instructive here:

> Before the war Beckmann had defended a sensuous, painterly
> style of rounded volumes and rich gradations of space....
> Then, in the war itself, his style changed completely. Beckmann
> is billeted near the front line in some of the fiercest fighting of
> the war, but continues to draw and paint the harrowing ex-
> periences around him with almost compulsive interest.... His
> allegorical style falls away ... to be replaced by a more shallow,
> splintered and crowded manner. He writes late in 1914 of the
> fascinated horror he was developing for 'space, distance, in-
> finity.' By 1915 he speaks of '... this infinite space, the fore-
> ground of which one must even fill again with some sort of
> rubbish, so that one will not see its terrible depth ... thus to
> cover up to some extent that dark black hole....' Beckmann
> then suffered a breakdown after which his art soon took on an
> almost unimaginably strange dimension ... quasi-mystical
> works of transcendent generality which responded to no actual
> events.

But there was also something quite consistent with the modernist
impulse in creating and exploring such a radical break with the past.
The advent of the Russian Revolution allowed some, at least, to see
rupture as an opportunity for progression and new creation. Unfortunately, the socialist movement itself divided, internalizing the tension between international and national aims (as evidenced by the
famous debates of the period between Lenin, Luxemburg, and many
others on the national question and the prospects for socialism in
one country). The very advent of revolution, however, allowed the
overwhelmingly nationalist strains of the Second International to be
challenged by a new sense of connection between the aims of modernism and those of socialist revolution and internationalism.

'Heroic' modernism after 1920 can then be interpreted as a dogged
fight of the universalist against localist sensibility within the arena of
cultural production. The 'heroism' derived from the extraordinary
intellectual and artistic attempt to come to terms with and dominate
the crisis in the experience of space and time that had built up before
the First World War, and to fight off the nationalist and geopolitical
sentiments the war expressed. The heroic modernists sought to show
how the accelerations, fragmentations, and imploding centralization
(particularly in urban life) could be represented and thereby contained

within a singular image. They sought to show how localism and nationalism could be overcome and how some sense of a global project to advance human welfare could be restored. This entailed a definite change of stance with respect to space and time. The shift that occurred in Kandinsky's painting style between 1914 and 1930 is illustrative. Before the war, Kandinsky is painting extraordinary canvases in which violent swirls of brilliant colour seem to implode simultaneously upon the canvas and explode beyond the edges of a frame that seems powerless to contain them. Ten years later we find Kandinsky at the Bauhaus (one of the key centres of modernist thought and practice) painting controlled pictures of spaces neatly organized within a secure frame, in some cases clearly taking the form of diagrammed city plans viewed from a perspective high above the earth (see plates 3.11 and 3.12). If modernism meant, among other things, the subjugation of space to human purposes, then the rational ordering and control of space as part and parcel of a modern culture founded on rationality and technique, the suppression of spatial barriers and difference, had to be merged with some kind of historical project. Picasso's evolution is also instructive. Abandoning cubism after the 'cubist war,' he turned to classicism for a brief period after 1919, probably out of some search to rediscover humanist values. But he returns shortly thereafter to his explorations of interior spaces through their total pulverization, only to recoup the destruction in a creative masterpiece, *Guernica*, in which the modernist style is used as a 'flexible instrument for the connection of multiple temporal and spatial viewpoints within the scope of the rhetorically powerful image' (Taylor, 1987, 150).

Enlightenment thinkers had postulated human welfare as their goal. That objective was never far from the surface of the rhetoric of inter-war modernism. The problem was to find practical circumstances and the financial resources to realize such goals. The Russians, obviously attracted to the modernist ethos of a radical break with the past for ideological reasons, provided a space within which a whole set of experiments — Russian formalism and constructivism being by far the most important — could unfold, and out of which came wideranging initiatives in cinema, painting, literature, and music as well as architecture. But the breathing space for such experimentation was relatively short, and the resources were hardly munificent, even for those most committed to the cause of the revolution. On the other hand, this connection between socialism and modernism, however slender, placed a cloud over modernism's reputation in the capitalist West, where the turn to surrealism (also with political overtones) did not help matters. In societies where the accumulation of capital —

Plate 3.11 Kandinsky's paintings of the pre-1914 war period, such as the Jugement Dernier *of 1912, exhibit such an explosive sense of space that they appear to spill off the canvas with an uncontrollable dynamism*

that 'historical mission of the bourgeoisie' as Marx called it — remained the effective pivot of action, there was only place for machine-style modernism of the Bauhaus sort.

Modernism's travails were also internal. To begin with, it could never escape the problem of its own aesthetic as a spatialization of sorts. However flexible Otto Wagner's or Le Corbusier's plans were in their capacity to absorb future developments and expansions, they necessarily fixed space in the midst of a historical process that was highly dynamic.

How to contain flowing and expanding processes in a fixed spatial frame of power relations, infrastructures and the like could not easily be resolved. The result was a social system that was all too prone to creative destruction of the sort that unfolded mercilessly after the capitalist crash of 1929. As spatializations, the artefacts produced by the moderns (with exceptions, of course, such as the Dadaists) conveyed some permanent if not monumental sense of supposedly universal human values. But even Le Corbusier recognized that such an

Plate 3.12 After the trauma of World War I, Kandinsky shifts to a much more controlled and rationalized imagery of spatial organization, as in Les Deux *of 1924 which bears more than a casual resemblance to a stylized urban map.*

act had to invoke the power of myth. And here the real tragedy of modernism begins. Because it was not the myths favoured by Le Corbusier or Otto Wagner or Walter Gropius that in the end dominated matters. It was either the worship of Mammon or, worse still, the myths stirred up by an aestheticized politics that called the tune. Le Corbusier flirted with Mussolini and compromised with Pétain's France, Oscar Niemeyer planned Brasilia for a populist president but built it for ruthless generals, the insights of the Bauhaus were mobilized into the design of the death camps, and the rule that form follows profit as well as function dominated everywhere. It was, in the end, the aestheticizations of politics and the power of money capital that triumphed over an aesthetic movement that had shown how time–space compression could be controlled and responded to rationally. Its insights, tragically, were absorbed for purposes that were not, by and large, its own. The trauma of World War II showed, if further proof were needed of such a proposition, that it was all too easy for Hegel's spatializations to subvert the Enlightenment's (and Marx's) historical project. Geopolitical and aesthetic interventions always seem to imply nationalist, and hence unavoidably reactionary, politics.

The opposition between Being and Becoming has been central to modernism's history. That opposition has to be seen in political terms as a tension between the sense of time and the focus of space. After 1848, modernism as a cultural movement struggled with that opposition, often in creative ways. The struggle was warped in all sorts of respects by the overwhelming power of money, profit, capital accumulation, and state power as frames of reference within which all forms of cultural practice had to unfold. Even under conditions of widespread class revolt, the dialectic of Being and Becoming has posed seemingly intractable problems. Above all, the changing meaning of space and time which capitalism has itself wrought, has forced perpetual re-evaluations in representations of the world in cultural life. It was only in an era of speculation on the future and fictitious capital formation that the concept of an avant-garde (both artistic and political) could make any sense. The changing experience of space and time had much to do with the birth of modernism and its confused wanderings from this to that side of the spatial–temporal relation. If this is indeed the case, then the proposition that postmodernism is some kind of response to a new set of experiences of space and time, a new round of 'time–space compression,' is well worth exploring.

17

Time—space compression and the postmodern condition

How have the uses and meanings of space and time shifted with the transition from Fordism to flexible accumulation? I want to suggest that we have been experiencing, these last two decades, an intense phase of time—space compression that has had a disorienting and disruptive impact upon political—economic practices, the balance of class power, as well as upon cultural and social life. While historical analogies are always dangerous, I think it no accident that postmodern sensibility evidences strong sympathies for certain of the confused political, cultural, and philosophical movements that occurred at the beginning of this century (in Vienna for example) when the sense of time—space compression was also peculiarly strong. I also note the revival of interest in geopolitical theory since around 1970, the aesthetics of place, and a revived willingness (even in social theory) to open the problem of spatiality to a general reconsideration (see, e.g., Gregory and Urry, 1985, and Soja, 1988).

The transition to flexible accumulation was in part accomplished through the rapid deployment of new organizational forms and new technologies in production. Though the latter may have originated in the pursuit of military superiority, their application had everything to do with bypassing the rigidities of Fordism and accelerating turnover time as a solution to the grumbling problems of Fordism—Keynesianism that erupted into open crisis in 1973. Speed-up was achieved in production by organizational shifts towards vertical disintegration — sub-contracting, outsourcing, etc. — that reversed the Fordist tendency towards vertical integration and produced an increasing roundaboutness in production even in the face of increasing financial centralization. Other organizational shifts — such as the 'just-in-time' delivery system that reduces stock inventories — when coupled with the new technologies of electronic control, small-batch production, etc., all reduced turnover times in many sectors of production (electronics, machine tools, automobiles, construction, clothing, etc.). For the labourers this all implied an intensification (speed-up) in labour processes and an acceleration in the de-skilling and re-skilling required to meet new labour needs (see Part II).

Accelerating turnover time in production entails parallel accelerations in exchange and consumption. Improved systems of communication and information flow, coupled with rationalizations in techniques of distribution (packaging, inventory control, containerization, market feed-back, etc.), made it possible to circulate commodities through the market system with greater speed. Electronic banking and plastic money were some of the innovations that improved the speed of the inverse flow of money. Financial services and markets (aided by computerized trading) likewise speeded up, so as to make, as the saying has it, 'twenty-four hours a very long time' in global stock markets.

Of the many developments in the arena of consumption, two stand out as being of particular importance. The mobilization of fashion in mass (as opposed to elite) markets provided a means to accelerate the pace of consumption not only in clothing, ornament, and decoration but also across a wide swathe of life-styles and recreational activities (leisure and sporting habits, pop music styles, video and children's games, and the like). A second trend was a shift away from the consumption of goods and into the consumption of services – not only personal, business, educational, and health services, but also into entertainments, spectacles, happenings, and distractions. The 'lifetime' of such services (a visit to a museum, going to a rock concert or movie, attending lectures or health clubs), though hard to estimate, is far shorter than that of an automobile or washing machine. If there are limits to the accumulation and turnover of physical goods (even counting the famous six thousand pairs of shoes of Imelda Marcos), then it makes sense for capitalists to turn to the provision of very ephemeral services in consumption. This quest may lie at the root of the rapid capitalist penetration, noted by Mandel and Jameson (see above, p. 63), of many sectors of cultural production from the mid-1960s onwards.

Of the innumerable consequences that have flowed from this general speed-up in the turnover times of capital, I shall focus on those that have particular bearing on postmodern ways of thinking, feeling, and doing.

The first major consequence has been to accentuate volatility and ephemerality of fashions, products, production techniques, labour processes, ideas and ideologies, values and established practices. The sense that 'all that is solid melts into air' has rarely been more pervasive (which probably accounts for the volume of writing on that theme in recent years). The effect of this on labour markets and skills has already been considered (see Part II). My interest here is to look at the more general society-wide effects.

In the realm of commodity production, the primary effect has been to emphasize the values and virtues of instantaneity (instant and fast foods, meals, and other satisfactions) and of disposability (cups, plates, cutlery, packaging, napkins, clothing, etc.). The dynamics of a 'throwaway' society, as writers like Alvin Toffler (1970) dubbed it, began to become evident during the 1960s. It meant more than just throwing away produced goods (creating a monumental waste-disposal problem), but also being able to throw away values, life-styles, stable relationships, and attachments to things, buildings, places, people, and received ways of doing and being. These were the immediate and tangible ways in which the 'accelerative thrust in the larger society' crashed up against 'the ordinary daily experience of the individual' (Toffler, p. 40). Through such mechanisms (which proved highly effective from the standpoint of accelerating the turn-over of goods in consumption) individuals were forced to cope with disposability, novelty, and the prospects for instant obsolescence. 'Compared to the life in a less rapidly changing society, more situations now flow through the channel in any given interval of time – and this implies profound changes in human psychology.' This transcience, Toffler goes on to suggest, creates 'a temporariness in the structure of both public and personal value systems' which in turn provides a context for the 'crack-up of consensus' and the diversification of values within a fragmenting society. The bombardment of stimuli, simply on the commodity front, creates problems of sensory overload that makes Simmel's dissection of the problems of modernist urban living at the turn of the century seem to pale into insignificance by comparison. Yet, precisely because of the relative qualities of the shift, the psychological responses exist roughly within the range of those which Simmel identified – the blocking out of sensory stimuli, denial, and cultivation of the blasé attitude, myopic specialization, reversion to images of a lost past (hence the importance of mementoes, museums, ruins), and excessive simplification (either in the presentation of self or in the interpretation of events). In this regard, it is instructive to see how Toffler (pp. 326–9), at a much later moment of time–space compression, echoes the thinking of Simmel, whose ideas were shaped at a moment of similar trauma more than seventy years before.

The volatility, of course, makes it extremely difficult to engage in any long-term planning. Indeed, learning to play the volatility right is now just as important as accelerating turnover time. This means either being highly adaptable and fast-moving in response to market shifts, or masterminding the volatility. The first strategy points mainly towards short-term rather than long-term planning, and cultivating the art of taking short-term gains wherever they are to be had. This has been a notorious feature of US management in recent times. The average tenure of company executive officers has come down to five years, and companies nominally involved in production frequently seek short-term gains through mergers, acquisitions, or operations in financial and currency markets. The tension of managerial performance in such an environment is considerable, producing all kinds of side-effects, such as the so-called 'yuppie flu' (a psychological stress condition that paralyses the performance of talented people and produces long-lasting flu-like symptoms) or the frenzied life-style of financial operators whose addiction to work, long hours, and the rush of power makes them excellent candidates for the kind of schizophrenic mentality that Jameson depicts.

Mastering or intervening actively in the production of volatility, on the other hand, entails manipulation of taste and opinion, either through being a fashion leader or by so saturating the market with images as to shape the volatility to particular ends. This means, in either case, the construction of new sign systems and imagery, which is itself an important aspect of the postmodern condition – one that needs to be considered from several different angles. To begin with, advertising and media images (as we saw in Part I) have come to play a very much more integrative role in cultural practices and now assume a much greater importance in the growth dynamics of capitalism. Advertising, moreover, is no longer built around the idea of informing or promoting in the ordinary sense, but is increasingly geared to manipulating desires and tastes through images that may or may not have anything to do with the product to be sold (see plate 1.6). If we stripped modern advertising of direct reference to the three themes of money, sex, and power there would be very little left. Furthermore, images have, in a sense, themselves become commodities. This phenomenon has led Baudrillard (1981) to argue that Marx's analysis of commodity production is outdated because capitalism is now predominantly concerned with the production of signs, images, and sign systems rather than with commodities themselves. The transition he points to is important, though there are in fact no serious difficulties in extending Marx's theory of commodity production to cope with it. To be sure, the systems of production and marketing of images (like markets for land, public goods, or labour power) do exhibit some special features that need to be taken into account. The consumer turnover time of certain images can be very short indeed (close to that ideal of the 'twinkling of an eye' that Marx saw as optimal from the standpoint of capital circulation). Many images can also be mass-marketed instantaneously over space. Given the pressures to accelerate turnover time (and to overcome spatial barriers), the commodification of images of the most ephemeral sort would seem to be a godsend from the standpoint of capital accumulation, particularly when other paths to relieve over-accumulation seem blocked. Ephemerality and instantaneous communicability over space then become virtues to be explored and appropriated by capitalists for their own purposes.

But images have to perform other functions. Corporations, governments, political and intellectual leaders, all value a stable (though dynamic) image as part of their aura of authority and power. The mediatization of politics has now become all pervasive. This becomes, in effect, the fleeting, superficial, and illusory means whereby an individualistic society of transients sets forth its nostalgia for common values. The production and marketing of such images of permanence and power require considerable sophistication, because the continuity and stability of the image have to be retained while stressing the adaptability, flexibility, and dynamism of whoever or whatever is being imaged. Moreover, image becomes all-important in competition, not only through name-brand recognition but also because of various associations of 'respectability,' 'quality,' 'prestige,' 'reliability,' and 'innovation.' Competition in the image-building trade becomes a vital aspect of inter-firm competition. Success is so plainly profitable that investment in image-building (sponsoring the arts, exhibitions, television productions, new buildings, as well as direct marketing) becomes as important as investment in new plant and machinery. The image serves to establish an identity in the market place. This is also true in labour markets. The acquisition of an image (by the purchase of a sign system such as designer clothes and the right car) becomes a singularly important element in the presentation of self in labour markets and, by extension, becomes integral to the quest for individual identity, self-realization, and meaning. Amusing yet sad signals of this sort of quest abound. A California firm manufactures imitation car telephones, indistinguishable from the real ones, and they sell like hot cakes to a populace desperate to acquire such a symbol of importance. Personal image consultants have become big business in New York City, the *International Herald Tribune* has reported, as a million or so people a year in the city region sign up for courses with firms called Image Assemblers, Image Builders, Image Crafters, and Image Creators. 'People make up their minds about you in around one tenth of a second these days,' says one image consultant. 'Fake it till you make it,' is the slogan of another. It has always been the case, of course, that symbols of wealth, status, fame, and power as well as of class have been important in bourgeois society, but probably nowhere near as widely in the past as now. The increasing material affluence generated during the post-war Fordist boom posed the problem of converting rising incomes into an effective demand that satisfied the rising aspirations of youth, women, and the working class. Given the ability to produce images as commodities more or less at will, it becomes feasible for accumulation to proceed at least in part on the basis of pure image production and marketing. The ephemerality of such images can then be interpreted in part as a struggle on the part of the oppressed groups of whatever sort to establish their own identity (in terms of street culture, musical styles, fads and fashions made up for themselves) and the rush to convert those innovations to commercial advantage (Carnaby Street in the late 1960s proved an excellent pioneer). The effect is to make it seem as if we are living in a world of ephemeral created images. The psychological impacts of sensory overload, of the sort that Simmel and Toffler identify, are thereby put to work with a redoubled effect.

The materials to produce and reproduce such images, if they were not readily to hand, have themselves been the focus for innovation – the better the replication of the image, the greater the mass market for image making could become. This is in itself an important issue and it brings us more explicitly to consider the role of the 'simulacrum' in postmodernism. By 'simulacrum' is meant a state of such near perfect replication that the difference between the original and the copy becomes almost impossible to spot. The production of images as simulacra is relatively easy, given modern techniques. Insofar as identity is increasingly dependent upon images, this means that the serial and recursive replications of identities (individual, corporate, institutional, and political) becomes a very real possibility and problem. We can certainly see it at work in the realm of politics as the image makers and the media assume a more powerful role in the shaping of political identities. But there are many more tangible realms where the simulacrum has a heightened role. With modern building materials it is possible to replicate ancient buildings with such exactitude that authenticity or origins can be put into doubt. The manufacture of antiques and other art objects becomes entirely possible, making the high-class forgery a serious problem in the art collection business. We not only possess, therefore, the capacity to pile images from the past or from other places eclectically and simultaneously upon the television screen, but even to transform those images into material simulacra in the form of built environments, events and spectacles, and the like, which become in many respects indistinguishable from the originals. What happens to cultural forms when the imitations become real, and the real takes on many of the qualities of an imitation, is a question to which we shall return.

The organization and conditions of labour prevailing within what we might broadly refer to as the 'image production industry' are also quite special. An industry of this sort has to rely, after all, upon the innovative powers of the direct producers. The latter have an insecure existence, tempered by very high rewards for the successful and at least a semblance of command over their own labour process and creative powers. The growth of cultural output has in fact been phenomenal. Taylor (1987, 77) contrasts the art market condition in New York in 1945, when there were a handful of galleries and no more than a score of artists regularly exhibiting, and the two thousand or so artists who practised in or around Paris in the mid-nineteenth century, with the 150,000 artists in the New York region who claim professional status, exhibiting at some 680 galleries, producing more than 15 million art-works in a decade (compared to 200,000 in late nineteenth-century Paris). And this is only the tip of an iceberg of cultural production that encompasses local entertainers and graphic designers, street and pub musicians, photographers, as well as the more established and recognized schools for teaching art, music, drama, and the like. Dwarfing all of this, however, is what Daniel Bell (1978, 20) calls 'the cultural mass' defined as:

> not the creators of culture but the transmitters: those working in higher education, publishing, magazines, broadcast media, theater, and museums, who process and influence the reception of serious cultural products. It is in itself large enough to be a market for culture, purchase books, prints and serious music recordings. And it is also the group which, as writers, magazine editors, movie-makers, musicians, and so forth, produce the popular materials for the wider mass-culture audience.

This whole industry specializes in the acceleration of turnover time through the production and marketing of images. This is an industry where reputations are made and lost overnight, where big money talks in no uncertain terms, and where there is a ferment of intense, often individualized, creativity poured into the vast vat of serialized and recursive mass culture. It is the organizer of fads and fashions and, as such, it actively produces the very ephemerality that has always been fundamental to the experience of modernity. It becomes a social means to produce that sense of collapsing time horizons which it in turn so avidly feeds upon.

The popularity of a work like Alvin Toffler's *Future shock* lay precisely in its prescient appreciation of the speed with which the future has come to be discounted into the present. Out of that, also, comes a collapse of cultural distinctions between, say, 'science' and 'regular' fiction (in the works of, for example, Thomas Pynchon and Doris Lessing), as well as a merging of the cinema of distraction with the cinema of futuristic universes. We can link the schizophrenic dimension to postmodernity which Jameson emphasizes (above, pp. 53–5) with accelerations in turnover times in production, exchange, and consumption that produce, as it were, the loss of a sense of the future except and insofar as the future can be discounted into the present. Volatility and ephemerality similarly make it hard to maintain any firm sense of continuity. Past experience gets compressed into some overwhelming present. Italo Calvino (1981, 8) reports the effect on his own craft of novel writing this way:

> long novels written today are perhaps a contradiction: the dimension of time had been shattered, we cannot live or think except in fragments of time each of which goes off along its own trajectory and immediately disappears. We can rediscover the continuity of time only in the novels of that period when time no longer seemed stopped and did not yet seem to have exploded, a period that lasted no more than a hundred years.

Baudrillard (1986), never afraid to exaggerate, considers the United States as a society so given over to speed, motion, cinematic images, and technological fixes as to have created a crisis of explanatory logic. It represents, he suggests, 'the triumph of effect over cause, of instantaneity over time as depth, the triumph of surface and of pure objectivization over the depth of desire.' This, of course, is the kind of environment in which deconstructionism can flourish. If it is impossible to say anything of solidity and permanence in the midst of this ephemeral and fragmented world, then why not join in the [language] game? Everything, from novel writing and philosophizing to the experience of labouring or making a home, has to face the challenge of accelerating turnover time and the rapid write-off of traditional and historically acquired values. The temporary contract in everything, as Lyotard remarks (see above, p. 113), then becomes the hallmark of postmodern living.

But, as so often happens, the plunge into the maelstrom of ephemerality has provoked an explosion of opposed sentiments and tendencies. To begin with, all sorts of technical means arise to guard against future shocks. Firms sub-contract or resort to flexible hiring practices to discount the potential unemployment costs of future market shifts. Futures markets in everything, from corn and pork bellies to currencies and government debt, coupled with the 'securitization' of all kinds of temporary and floating debts, illustrate techniques for discounting the future into the present. Insurance hedges of all kinds against future volatility become much more widely available.

Deeper questions of meaning and interpretation also arise. The greater the ephemerality, the more pressing the need to discover or manufacture some kind of eternal truth that might lie therein. The religious revival that has become much stronger since the late sixties, and the search for authenticity and authority in politics (with all of its accoutrements of nationalism and localism and of admiration for those charismatic and 'protean' individuals with their Nietzschian 'will to power') are cases in point. The revival of interest in basic institutions (such as the family and community), and the search for historical roots are all signs of a search for more secure moorings and longer-lasting values in a shifting world. Rochberg-Halton (1986, 173), in a sample study of North Chicago residents in 1977, finds, for example, that the objects actually valued in the home were not the 'pecuniary trophies' of a materialist culture which acted as 'reliable indices of one's socio-economic class, age, gender and so on,' but the artefacts that embodied 'ties to loved ones and kin, valued experiences and activities, and memories of significant life events and people.' Photographs, particular objects (like a piano, a clock, a chair), and events (the playing of a record of a piece of music, the singing of a song) become the focus of a contemplative memory, and hence a generator of a sense of self that lies outside the sensory overloading of consumerist culture and fashion. The home becomes a private museum to guard against the ravages of time−space compression. At the very time, furthermore, that postmodernism proclaims the 'death of the author' and the rise of anti-auratic art in the public realm, the art market becomes ever more conscious of the monopoly power of the artist's signature and of questions of authenticity and forgery (no matter that the Rauschenberg is itself a mere reproduction montage). It is, perhaps, appropriate that the postmodernist developer building, as solid as the pink granite of Philip Johnson's AT & T building, should be debt-financed, built on the basis of fictitious capital, and architecturally conceived of, at least on the outside, more in the spirit of fiction than of function.

The spatial adjustments have been no less traumatic. The satellite communications systems deployed since the early 1970s have rendered the unit cost and time of communication invariant with respect to distance. It costs the same to communicate over 500 miles as it does over 5,000 via satellite. Air freight rates on commodities have likewise come down dramatically, while containerization has reduced the cost of bulk sea and road transport. It is now possible for a large multinational corporation like Texas Instruments to operate plants with simultaneous decision-making with respect to financial, market, input costs, quality control, and labour process conditions in more than fifty different locations across the globe (Dicken, 1986, 110–13). Mass television ownership coupled with satellite communication makes it possible to experience a rush of images from different spaces almost simultaneously, collapsing the world's spaces into a series of images on a television screen. The whole world can watch the Olympic Games, the World Cup, the fall of a dictator, a political summit, a deadly tragedy ... while mass tourism, films made in spectacular locations, make a wide range of simulated or vicarious experiences of what the world contains available to many people. The image of places and spaces becomes as open to production and ephemeral use as any other.

We have, in short, witnessed another fierce round in that process of annihilation of space through time that has always lain at the center of capitalism's dynamic (see plate 3.2). Marshall McLuhan described how he thought the 'global village' had now become a communications reality in the mid–1960s:

> After three thousand years of explosion, by means of fragmentary and mechanical technologies, the Western World is imploding. During the mechanical ages we had extended our bodies in space. Today, after more than a century of electronic technology, we have extended our central nervous system itself in a global embrace, abolishing both space and time as far as our planet is concerned.

In recent years a whole spate of writing has taken this idea on board and tried to explore, as for example Virilio (1980) does in his *Esthétique de la disparition*, the cultural consequences of the supposed disappearance of time and space as materialized and tangible dimensions to social life.

But the collapse of spatial barriers does not mean that the significance of space is decreasing. Not for the first time in capitalism's history, we find the evidence pointing to the converse thesis. Heightened competition under conditions of crisis has coerced capitalists into paying much closer attention to relative locational advantages, precisely because diminishing spatial barriers give capitalists the power to exploit minute spatial differentiations to good effect. Small differences in what the space contains in the way of labour supplies, resources, infrastructures, and the like become of increased significance. Superior command over space becomes an even more important weapon in class struggle. It becomes one of the means to enforce speed-up and the redefinition of skills on recalcitrant work forces. Geographical mobility and decentralization are used against a union power which traditionally concentrated in the factories of mass production. Capital flight, deindustrialization of some regions, and the industrialization of others, the destruction of traditional working-class communities as power bases in class struggle, become leitmotifs of spatial transformation under more flexible conditions of accumulation (Martin and Rowthorn, 1986; Bluestone and Harrison, 1982; Harrison and Bluestone, 1988).

As spatial barriers diminish so we become much more sensitized to what the world's spaces contain. Flexible accumulation typically exploits a wide range of seemingly contingent geographical circumstances, and reconstitutes them as structured internal elements of its own encompassing logic. For example, geographical differentiations in the mode and strengths of labour control together with variations in the quality as well as the quantity of labour power assume a much greater significance in corporate locational strategies. New industrial ensembles arise, sometimes out of almost nothing (as the various silicon valleys and glens) but more often on the basis of some pre-existing mix of skills and resources. The 'Third Italy' (Emilia-Romagna) builds upon a peculiar mix of co-operative entrepreneurialism, artisan labour, and local communist administrations anxious to generate employment, and inserts its clothing products with incredible success into a highly competitive world economy. Flanders attracts outside capital on the basis of a dispersed, flexible, and reasonably skilled labour supply with a deep hostility to unionism and socialism. Los Angeles imports the highly successful patriarchal labour systems of South-East Asia through mass immigration, while the celebrated paternalistic labour control system of the Japanese and Taiwanese is imported into California and South Wales. The story in each case is different, making it appear as if the uniqueness of this or that geographical circumstance matters more than ever before. Yet it does so, ironically, only because of the collapse of spatial barriers.

While labour control is always central, there are many other aspects of geographical organization that have risen to a new prominence under conditions of more flexible accumulation. The need for accurate information and speedy comunication has emphasized the role

of so-called 'world cities' in the financial and corporate system
(centres equipped with teleports, airports, fixed communication links,
as well as a wide array of financial, legal, business, and infrastructural services). The diminution of spatial barriers results in the re-
affirmation and realignment of hierarchy within what is now a global
urban system. The local availability of material resources of special
qualities, or even at marginally lower costs, starts to be ever more
important, as do local variations in market taste that are today more
easily exploited under conditions of small-batch production and flexible design. Local differences in entrepreneurial ability, venture capital, scientific and technical know-how, social attitudes, also enter in,
while the local networks of influence and power, the accumulation
strategies of local ruling elites (as opposed to nation state policies)
also become more deeply implicated in the regime of flexible
accumulation.

But this then raises another dimension to the changing role of
spatiality in contemporary society. If capitalists become increasingly
sensitive to the spatially differentiated qualities of which the world's
geography is composed, then it is possible for the peoples and
powers that command those spaces to alter them in such a way as to
be more rather than less attractive to highly mobile capital. Local
ruling elites can, for example, implement strategies of local labour
control, of skill enhancement, of infrastructural provision, of tax
policy, state regulation, and so on, in order to attract development
within their particular space. The qualities of place stand thereby to
be emphasized in the midst of the increasing abstractions of space.
The active production of places with special qualities becomes an
important stake in spatial competition between localities, cities, regions, and nations. Corporatist forms of governance can flourish in
such spaces, and themselves take on entrepreneurial roles in the
production of favourable business climates and other special qualities.
And it is in this context that we can better situate the striving, noted
in Part I (pp. 88–92), for cities to forge a distinctive image and to
create an atmosphere of place and tradition that will act as a lure to
both capital and people 'of the right sort' (i.e. wealthy and influential).
Heightened inter-place competition should lead to the production of
more variegated spaces within the increasing homogeneity of international exchange. But to the degree that this competition opens up
cities to systems of accumulation, it ends up producing what Boyer
(1988) calls a 'recursive' and 'serial' monotony, 'producing from
already known patterns or molds places almost identical in ambience
from city to city: New York's South Street Seaport, Boston's Quincy
Market, Baltimore's Harbor Place.'

We thus approach the central paradox: the less important the spatial barriers, the greater the sensitivity of capital to the variations of place within space, and the greater the incentive for places to be differentiated in ways attractive to capital. The result has been the production of fragmentation, insecurity, and ephemeral uneven development within a highly unified global space economy of capital flows. The historic tension within capitalism between centralization and decentralization is now being worked out in new ways. Extraordinary decentralization and proliferation of industrial production ends up putting Benetton or Laura Ashley products in almost every serially produced shopping mall in the advanced capitalist world. Plainly, the new round of time—space compression is fraught with as many dangers as it offers possibilities for survival of particular places or for a solution to the overaccumulation problem.

The geography of devaluation through deindustrialization, rising local unemployment, fiscal retrenchment, write-offs of local assets, and the like, is indeed a sorry picture. But we can at least see its logic within the frame of the search for a solution to the overaccumulation problem through the push into flexible and more mobile systems of accumulation. But there are also a priori reasons to suspect (as well as some material evidence to support the idea) that regions of maximum churning and fragmentation are also regions that seem best set to survive the traumas of devaluation in the long run. There is more than a hint that a little devaluation now is better than massive devaluation later in the scramble for local survival in the world of severely constrained opportunities for positive growth. Reindustrializing and restructuring cannot be accomplished without deindustrializing and devaluing first.

None of these shifts in the experience of space and time would make the sense or have the impact they do without a radical shift in the manner in which value gets represented as money. Though long dominant, money has never been a clear or unambiguous representation of value, and on occasion it becomes so muddled as to become itself a major source of insecurity and uncertainty. Under the terms of the postwar settlement, the question of world money was put on a fairly stable basis. The US dollar became the medium of world trade, technically backed by a fixed convertibility into gold, and backed politically and economically by the overwhelming power of the US productive apparatus. The space of the US production system became, in effect, the guarantor of international value. But, as we have seen, one of the signals of the breakdown of the Fordist—Keynesian system was the breakdown of the Bretton Woods agreement, of convertibility of US dollars to gold, and the shift to a global system of floating exchange rates. The breakdown in part occurred because of the shifting dimensionalities of space and time generated out of capital accumulation. Rising indebtedness (particularly within the United States), and fiercer international competition from the reconstructed spaces of the world economy under conditions of growing accumulation, had much to do with undermining the power of the US economy to operate as an exclusive guarantor of world money.

The effects have been legion. The question of how value should now get represented, what form money should take, and the meaning that can be put upon the various forms of money available to us, has never been far from the surface of recent concerns. Since 1973, money has been 'de-materialized' in the sense that it no longer has a formal or tangible link to precious metals (though the latter have continued to play a role as one potential form of money among many others), or for that matter to any other tangible commodity. Nor does it rely exclusively upon productive activity within a particular space. The world has come to rely, for the first time in its history, upon immaterial forms of money – i.e. money of account assessed quantitatively in numbers of some designated currency (dollars, yen, Deutsch Marks, sterling, etc.). Exchange rates between the different currencies of the world have also been extremely volatile. Fortunes could be lost or made simply by holding the right currency during the right phases. The question of which currency I hold is directly linked to which place I put my faith in. That may have something to do with the competitive economic position and power of different national systems. That power, given the flexibility of accumulation over space, is itself a rapidly shifting magnitude. The effect is to render the spaces that underpin the determination of value as unstable as value itself. This problem is compounded by the way that speculative shifts bypass actual economic power and performance, and then trigger self-fulfilling expectations. The de-linking of the financial system from active production and from any material monetary base calls into question the reliability of the basic mechanism whereby value is supposed to be represented.

These difficulties have been most powerfully present in the process of devaluation of money, the measure of value, through inflation. The steady inflation rates of the Fordist–Keynesian era (usually in the 3 per cent range, and rarely above 5 per cent) gave way from 1969 onwards, and then accelerated in all the major capitalist countries during the 1970s into double-digit rates (see figure 2.8). Worse still, inflation became highly unstable, between as well as within countries, leaving everyone in doubt as to what the true value (the buying power) of a particular money might be in the near future.

Money consequently became useless as a means of storing value for any length of time (the real rate of interest, measured as the money rate of interest minus the rate of inflation, was negative for several years during the 1970s, so dispossessing savers of the value they were seeking to store). Alternative means had to be found to store value effectively. And so began the vast inflation in certain kinds of asset prices – collectibles, art objects, antiques, houses, and the like. Buying a Degas or Van Gogh in 1973 would surely outstrip almost any other kind of investment in terms of capital gain. Indeed it can be argued that the growth of the art market (with its concern for authorial signature) and the strong commercialization of cultural production since around 1970 have had a lot to do with the search to find alternative means to store value under conditions where the usual money forms were deficient. Commodity and general price inflation, though to some degree brought under control in the advanced capitalist countries during the 1980s, has by no means diminished as a problem. It is rampant in countries like Mexico, Argentina, Brazil, and Israel (all with recent rates in hundreds of per cent), and the prospect of generalized inflation looms in the advanced capitalist countries, where it is in any case arguable that the inflation of asset prices (housing, works of art, antiques, etc.) has taken over where commodity and labour market inflation left off in the early 1980s.

The breakdown of money as a secure means of representing value has itself created a crisis of representation in advanced capitalism. It has also been reinforced by, and added its very considerable weight to, the problems of time–space compression which we earlier identified. The rapidity with which currency markets fluctuate across the world's spaces, the extraordinary power of money capital flow in what is now a global stock and financial market, and the volatility of what the purchasing power of money might represent, define, as it were, a high point of that highly problematic intersection of money, time, and space as interlocking elements of social power in the political economy of postmodernity.

It is, furthermore, not hard to see how all of this might create a more general crisis of representation. The central value system, to which capitalism has always appealed to validate and gauge its actions, is dematerialized and shifting, time horizons are collapsing, and it is hard to tell exactly what space we are in when it comes to assessing causes and effects, meanings or values. The intriguing exhibition at the Pompidou Centre in 1985 on 'The Immaterial' (an exhibition for which none other than Lyotard acted as one of the consultants) was perhaps a mirror image of the dissolution of the material representations of value under conditions of more flexible accumulation, and of the confusions as to what it might mean to say, with Paul Virilio, that time and space have disappeared as meaningful dimensions to human thought and action.

There are, I would submit, more tangible and material ways than this to go about assessing the significance of space and time for the condition of postmodernity. It should be possible to consider how, for example, the changing experience of space, time, and money has formed a distinctive material basis for the rise of distinctive systems of interpretation and representation, as well as opening a path through which the aestheticization of politics might once more reassert itself. If we view culture as that complex of signs and significations (including language) that mesh into codes of transmission of social values and meanings, then we can at least begin upon the task of unravelling its complexities under present-day conditions by recognizing that money and commodities are themselves the primary bearers of cultural codes. Since money and commodities are entirely bound up with the circulation of capital, it follows that cultural forms are firmly rooted in the daily circulation process of capital. It is, therefore, with the daily experience of money and the commodity that we should begin, no matter if special commodities or even whole sign systems may be extracted from the common herd and made the basis of 'high' culture or that specialized 'imaging' which we have already had cause to comment upon.

The annihilation of space through time has radically changed the commodity mix that enters into daily reproduction. Innumerable local food systems have been reorganized through their incorporation into global commodity exchange. French cheeses, for example, virtually unavailable except in a few gourmet stores in large cities in 1970, are now widely sold across the United States. And if this is thought a somewhat elite example, the case of beer consumption suggests that the internationalization of a product, that traditional location theory always taught should be highly market-oriented, is now complete. Baltimore was essentially a one-beer town (locally brewed) in 1970, but first the regional beers from places like Milwaukee and Denver, and then Canadian and Mexican beers followed by European, Australian, Chinese, Polish, etc. beers became cheaper. Formerly exotic foods became commonplace while popular local delicacies (in the Baltimore case, blue crabs and oysters) that were once relatively inexpensive jumped in price as they too became integrated into long-distance trading.

The market place has always been an 'emporium of styles' (to quote Raban's phrase) but the food market, just to take one example, now looks very different from what it was twenty years ago. Kenyan haricot beans, Californian celery and avocados, North African potatoes, Canadian apples, and Chilean grapes all sit side by side in a British supermarket. This variety also makes for a proliferation of culinary styles, even among the relatively poor. Such styles have always migrated, of course, usually following the migration streams of different groups before diffusing slowly through urban cultures. The new waves of immigrants (such as the Vietnamese, Koreans, Filipinos, Central Americans, etc. that have added to the older groups of Japanese, Chinese, Chicanos, and all the European ethnic groups that have also found their culinary heritage can be revived for fun and profit) make a typical United States city such as New York, Los Angeles, or San Francisco (where the last census showed the majority of the population to be made up of minorities) as much an emporium of culinary styles as it is an emporium of the world's commodities. But here, too, there has been an acceleration, because culinary styles have moved faster than the immigration streams. It did not take a large French immigration to the United States to send the croissant rapidly spreading across America to challenge the traditional doughnut, nor did it take a large immigration of Americans to Europe to bring fast-food hamburgers to nearly all medium-sized European cities. Chinese takeaways, Italian pizza-parlours (run by a US chain), Middle Eastern felafel stalls, Japanese sushi bars ... the list is now endless in the Western world.

The whole world's cuisine is now assembled in one place in almost exactly the same way that the world's geographical complexity is nightly reduced to a series of images on a static television screen. This same phenomenon is exploited in entertainment palaces like Epcot and Disneyworld; it becomes possible, as the US commercials put it, 'to experience the Old World for a day without actually having to go there.' The general implication is that through the experience of everything from food, to culinary habits, music, television, entertainment, and cinema, it is now possible to experience the world's geography vicariously, as a simulacrum. The interweaving of simulacra in daily life brings together different worlds (of commodities) in the same space and time. But it does so in such a way as to conceal almost perfectly any trace of origin, of the labour processes that produced them, or of the social relations implicated in their production.

The simulacra can in turn become the reality. Baudrillard (1986) in *L'Amérique* even goes so far, somewhat exaggeratedly in my view, to suggest that US reality is now constructed as a giant screen: 'the cinema is everywhere, most of all in the city, incessant and marvellous film and scenario.' Places portrayed in a certain way, particularly if they have the capacity to attract tourists, may begin to 'dress themselves up' as the fantasy images prescribe. Mediaeval castles offer mediaeval weekends (food, dress, but not of course the primitive heating arrangements). Vicarious participation in these various worlds has real effects on the ways in which these worlds get ordered. Jencks (1984, 127) proposes that the architect should be an active participant in this:

> Any middle class urbanite in any large city from Teheran to Tokyo is bound to have a well-stocked, indeed over-stocked 'image bank' that is continually restuffed by travel and magazines. His *musée imaginaire* may mirror the pot-pourri of the producers but it is nonetheless natural to his way of life. Barring some kind of totalitarian reduction in the heterogeneity of production and consumption, it seems to be desirable that architects learn to use this inevitable heterogeneity of languages. Besides, it is quite enjoyable. Why, if one can afford to live in different ages and cultures, restrict oneself to the present, the locale? Eclecticism is the natural evolution of a culture with choice.

Much the same can be said of popular music styles. Commenting on how collage and eclecticism have recently come to dominate, Chambers (1987) goes on to show how oppositional and subcultural musics like reggae, Afro-American and Afro-Hispanic have taken their place 'in the museum of fixed symbolic structures' to form a flexible collage of 'the already seen, the already worn, the already played, the already heard.' A strong sense of 'the Other' is replaced, he suggests, by a weak sense of 'the others.' The loose hanging together of divergent street cultures in the fragmented spaces of the contemporary city re-emphasizes the contingent and accidental aspects of this 'otherness' in daily life. This same sensibility exists in postmodern fiction. It is, says McHale (1987), concerned with 'ontologies,' with a potential as well as an actual plurality of universes, forming an eclectic and 'anarchic landscape of worlds in the plural.' Dazed and distracted characters wander through these worlds without a clear sense of location, wondering, 'Which world am I in and which of my personalities do I deploy?' Our postmodern ontological landscape, suggests McHale, 'is unprecedented in human history − at least in the degree of its pluralism.' Spaces of very different worlds seem to collapse upon each other, much as the world's commodities are assembled in the supermarket and all manner of sub-cultures get juxtaposed in the contemporary city. Disruptive spatiality triumphs over the coherence of perspective and narrative in postmodern fiction, in exactly the same way that imported beers coexist with local brews, local employment collapses under the weight of foreign competition, and all the divergent spaces of the world are assembled nightly as a collage of images upon the television screen.

There seem to be two divergent sociological effects of all of this in daily thought and action. The first suggests taking advantage of all of the divergent possibilities, much as Jencks recommends, and cultivating a whole series of simulacra as milieux of escape, fantasy, and distraction:

> All around us − on advertisement hoardings, bookshelves, record covers, television screens − these miniature escape fantasies present themselves. This, it seems, is how we are destined to live, as split personalities in which the private life is disturbed by the promise of escape routes to another reality. (Cohen and Taylor, 1978, quoted in McHale, 1987, 38)

From this standpoint I think we have to accept McHale's argument that postmodern fiction is mimetic of something, much as I have argued that the emphasis upon ephemerality, collage, fragmentation, and dispersal in philosophical and social thought mimics the conditions of flexible accumulation. And it should not be surprising either to see how all of this fits in with the emergence since 1970 of a fragmented politics of divergent special and regional interest groups.

But it is exactly at this point that we encounter the opposite reaction that can best be summed up as the search for personal or collective identity, the search for secure moorings in a shifting world. Place-identity, in this collage of superimposed spatial images that implode in upon us, becomes an important issue, because everyone occupies a space of individuation (a body, a room, a home, a shaping community, a nation), and how we individuate ourselves shapes identity. Furthermore, if no one 'knows their place' in this shifting collage world, then how can a secure social order be fashioned or sustained?

There are two elements within this problem that deserve close consideration. First, the capacity of most social movements to command place better than space puts a strong emphasis upon the potential connection between place and social identity. This is manifest in political action. The defensiveness of municipal socialism, the insistence on working-class community, the localization of the fight against capital, become central features of working-class struggle within an overall patterning of uneven geographical development. The consequent dilemmas of socialist or working-class movements in the face of a universalizing capitalism are shared by other oppositional groups — racial minorities, colonized peoples, women, etc. — who are relatively empowered to organize in place but disempowered when it comes to organizing over space. In clinging, often of necessity, to a place-bound identity, however, such oppositional movements become a part of the very fragmentation which a mobile capitalism and flexible accumulation can feed upon. 'Regional resistances,' the struggle for local autonomy, place-bound organization, may be excellent bases for political action, but they cannot bear the burden of radical historical change alone. 'Think globally and act locally' was the revolutionary slogan of the 1960s. It bears repeating.

The assertion of any place-bound identity has to rest at some point on the motivational power of tradition. It is difficult, however, to maintain any sense of historical continuity in the face of all the flux and ephemerality of flexible accumulation. The irony is that tradition is now often preserved by being commodified and marketed as such. The search for roots ends up at worst being produced and marketed as an image, as a simulacrum or pastiche (imitation communities constructed to evoke images of some folksy past, the fabric of traditional working-class communities being taken over by an urban gentry). The photograph, the document, the view, and the reproduction become history precisely because they are so overwhelmingly present. The problem, of course, is that none of these are immune from tampering or downright faking for present purposes. At best, historical tradition is reorganized as a museum culture, not necessarily of high modernist art, but of local history, of local production, of how things once upon a time were made, sold, consumed, and integrated into a long-lost and often romanticized daily life (one from which all trace of oppressive social relations may be expunged). Through the presentation of a partially illusory past it becomes possible to signify something of local identity and perhaps to do it profitably.

The second reaction to the internationalism of modernism lies in the search to construct place and its meanings qualitatively. Capitalist hegemony over space puts the aesthetics of place very much back on the agenda. But this, as we have seen, meshes only too well with the idea of spatial differentiations as lures for a peripatetic capital that values the option of mobility very highly. Isn't this place better than that place, not only for the operations of capital but also for living in, consuming well, and feeling secure in a shifting world? The construction of such places, the fashioning of some localized aesthetic image, allows the construction of some limited and limiting sense of identity in the midst of a collage of imploding spatialities.

The tension in these oppositions is clear enough but it is hard to appreciate their intellectual and political ramifications. Here, for example, is Foucault (1984, 253) addressing the issue from his own perspective:

> Space is fundamental in any form of communal life; space is fundamental in any exercise of power. . . . I recall having been invited in 1966, by a group of architects, to do a study of space, of something that I called at the time 'heterotopias,' those singular spaces to be found in some given social spaces whose functions are different or even the opposite of others. The architects worked on this, and at the end of the study someone spoke up – a Sartrean psychologist – who firebombed me, saying that *space* is reactionary and capitalist but *history* and *becoming* are revolutionary. This absurd discourse was not at all unusual at the time. Today everyone would be convulsed with laughter at such a pronouncement, but not then.

The proposition the Sartrean critic offers is, though crude and oppositional, nowhere near as laughable as Foucault avers. On the other hand, postmodernist sentiment definitely leans towards Foucault's position. Whereas modernism looked upon the spaces of the city, for example, as 'an epiphenomenon of social functions,' postmodernism 'tends to disengage urban space from its dependence on functions, and to see it as an autonomous formal system' incorporating 'rhetorical and artistic strategies, which are independent of any simple historical determinism' (Colquhoun, 1985). It is precisely this disengagement that permits Foucault to deploy spatial metaphors so extensively in his studies of power. Spatial imagery, liberated from its roots in any social determination, becomes a means to depict the forces of social determination. It is a short step, however, from Foucault's metaphors to reinforcement of a political ideology that sees place and *Being* with all its associated aesthetic qualities as a proper basis for social action. Geopolitics and the Heideggerian trap come not too far behind. Jameson (1988, 351), for his part, views the

> spatial peculiarities of post-modernism as symptoms and expressions of a new and historically original dilemma, one that involves our insertion as individual subjects into a multidimensional set of radically discontinuous realities, whose frames range from the still surviving spaces of bourgeois private life all

the way to the unimaginable decentering of global capitalism itself. Not even Einsteinian relativity, or the multiple subjective worlds of the older modernists, is capable of giving any adequate figuration to this process, which in lived experience makes itself felt by the so-called death of the subject, or, more exactly, the fragmented and schizophrenic decentering and dispersion of this last.... And although you may not have realized it, I am talking about practical politics here: since the crisis of socialist internationalism, and the enormous strategic and tactical difficulties of coordinating local and grassroots or neighborhood political actions with national or international ones, such urgent political dilemmas are all immediately functions of the enormously complex new international space I have in mind.

Jameson exaggerates somewhat with respect to the uniqueness and newness of this experience. Stressful though the current condition undoubtedly is, it is qualitatively similar to that which led to Renaissance and various modernist reconceptualizations of space and time. Nevertheless, the dilemmas which Jameson depicts are exact and capture the drift of postmodern sensibility as to the meaning of space in contemporary political and cultural as well as economic life. If, however, we have lost the modernist faith in becoming, as Foucault's Sartrean critic argued, is there any way out except via the reactionary politics of an aestheticized spatiality? Are we sadly destined to end up on the track that Sitte began with, in his turn to Wagnerian mythology as support for his assertion of the primacy of place and community in a world of changing spaces? Worse still, if aesthetic production has now been so thoroughly commodified and thereby become really subsumed within a political economy of cultural production, how can we possibly stop that circle closing onto a produced, and hence all too easily manipulated, aestheticization of a globally mediatized politics?

This should alert us to the acute geopolitical dangers that attach to the rapidity of time—space compression in recent years. The transition from Fordism to flexible accumulation, such as it has been, ought to imply a transition in our mental maps, political attitudes, and political institutions. But political thinking does not necessarily undergo such easy transformations, and is in any case subject to the contradictory pressures that derive from spatial integration and differentiation. There is an omni-present danger that our mental maps will not match current realities. The serious diminution of the power of individual nation states over fiscal and monetary policies, for example, has not been matched by any parallel shift towards an internationalization of politics. Indeed, there are abundant signs that localism and nationalism have become stronger precisely because of the quest for the security that place always offers in the midst of all the shifting that flexible accumulation implies. The resurgence of geopolitics and of faith in charismatic politics (Thatcher's Falklands War, Reagan's invasion of Grenada) fits only too well with a world that is increasingly nourished intellectually and politically by a vast flux of ephemeral images.

Time–space compression always exacts its toll on our capacity to grapple with the realities unfolding around us. Under stress, for example, it becomes harder and harder to react accurately to events. The erroneous identification of an Iranian airbus, ascending within an established commercial flight corridor, with a fighter-bomber descending towards a targeted US warship – an incident that resulted in many civilian deaths – is typical of the way that reality gets created rather than interpreted under conditions of stress and time–space compression. The parallel with Kern's account of the outbreak of World War I (cited above, p. 278) is instructive. If 'seasoned negotiators cracked under the pressure of tense confrontations and sleepless nights, agonizing over the probable disastrous consequences of their snap judgements and hasty actions,' then how much more difficult must decision-making now be? The difference this time is that there is not even time to agonize. And the problems are not confined to the realms of political and military decision-making, for the world's financial markets are on the boil in ways that make a snap judgement here, an unconsidered word there, and a gut reaction somewhere else the slip that can unravel the whole skein of fictitious capital formation and of interdependency.

The conditions of postmodern time–space compression exaggerate in many respects the dilemmas that have from time to time beset capitalist procedures of modernization in the past (1848 and the phase just before the First World War spring particularly to mind). While the economic, cultural, and political responses may not be exactly new, the range of those reponses differs in certain important respects from those which have occurred before. The intensity of time–space compression in Western capitalism since the 1960s, with all of its congruent features of excessive ephemerality and fragmentation in the political and private as well as in the social realm, does seem to indicate an experiential context that makes the condition of postmodernity somewhat special. But by putting this condition into its historical context, as part of a history of successive waves of time–space compression generated out of the pressures of capital accumulation with its perpetual search to annihilate space through time and reduce turnover time, we can at least pull the condition of postmodernity into the range of a condition accessible to historical materialist analysis and interpretation. How to interpret and react to it will be taken up in Part IV.

18

Time and space in the postmodern cinema

Postmodern cultural artefacts are, by virtue of the eclecticism of their conception and the anarchy of their subject matter, immensely varied. I think it useful, however, to illustrate how the themes of time—space compression that have been elaborated on here get represented in postmodern works. For this purpose I choose to look at the cinema, in part because this is an art form which (together with photography) arose in the context of the first great burst of cultural modernism, but also because, of all the art forms, it has perhaps the most robust capacity to handle intertwining themes of space and time in instructive ways. The serial use of images, and the ability to cut back and forth across space and time, free it from many of the normal constraints, even though it is, in the final analysis, a spectacle projected within an enclosed space on a depthless screen.

The two films I shall consider are *Blade Runner* and *Himmel über Berlin* (called *Wings of Desire* in English). Ridley Scott's *Blade Runner* is a popular science fiction movie, considered an excellent example of its genre by many, and a film that still circulates in the late-night cinemas of large metropolitan areas. It is a piece of pop art that nevertheless explores important themes. I am particularly indebted to Giuliana Bruno's perceptive analysis of its postmodern aesthetics. Wim Wenders's *Wings of Desire*, on the other hand, is a piece of 'highbrow' cinema, very favourably received by the critics (a 'bittersweet masterpiece' one critic wrote), but hard to grasp at first viewing. It is the kind of film that has to be worked at to be understood and appreciated. However, it explores similar themes to those set out in *Blade Runner*, though from a rather different perspective and in a very different style. Both films exemplify many of the characteristics of postmodernism, and in addition pay particular attention to the conceptualization and meanings of time and space.

The story of *Blade Runner* concerns a small group of genetically produced human beings, called 'replicants,' who return to face their makers. The film is set in Los Angeles in the year 2019 and hinges around the search of the 'blade runner' Deckard to uncover the presence of the replicants and to eliminate or 'retire' them (as the film has it) as a serious danger to the social order. The replicants have been created for the specific purpose of working on highly skilled tasks in particularly difficult environments at the frontiers of space exploration. They are endowed with strengths, intelligence, and powers that are at the limit of, or even beyond that of, ordinary human beings. They are also endowed with feelings; only in this way, it seems, can they adapt to the difficulty of their tasks in such a way as to make judgements consistent with human requirements. However, fearing that they might at some point pose a threat to the established order, their makers have given them a life-span of only four years. If they escape control during these four years they have to be 'retired.' But to retire them is both dangerous and difficult precisely because of their superior endowments.

The replicants are, it should be noted, not mere imitations but totally authentic reproductions, indistinguishable in almost all respects from human beings. They are simulacra rather than robots. They have been designed as the ultimate form of short-term, highly skilled and flexible labour power (a perfect example of a worker endowed with all of the qualities necessary to adapt to conditions of flexible accumulation). But like all workers faced with the threat of a shortened working life, the replicants do not take kindly to the restrictions of their four-year life-span. Their purpose in returning to their makers is to try to find ways to prolong their life, by infiltrating to the heart of the productive apparatus that made them, and there persuading or forcing their makers to re-programme their genetic make-up. Their designer, Tyrell (head of a vast corporate empire of that name), points out to Roy, the leader of the replicants, who ultimately penetrates into his inner sanctum, that the replicants have more than adequate recompense for the brevity of their life-span – they live, after all, with the most incredible intensity. 'Revel in it,' says Tyrell, 'a flame that burns twice as intensely lives half as long.' The replicants exist, in short, in that schizophrenic rush of time that Jameson, Deleuze and Guattari, and others see as so central to postmodern living. The also move across a breadth of space with a fluidity that gains them an immense fund of experience. Their persona matches in many respects the time and space of instantaneous global communications.

In revolt against their conditions of 'slave labour' (as Roy, the leader of the replicants, calls it) and seeking to prolong their lifespans, four replicants fight and kill their way back into Los Angeles, where the 'blade runner' Deckard, an expert in methods of detecting and retiring escaped replicants, is summoned to deal with them. Though tired of all the killing and violence, Deckard is forced out of retirement and given no option by the authorities except to undertake the task, on pain of his own reduction in status to that of 'little person.' Both Deckard and the replicants, therefore, exist in a similar relation to the dominant social power in society. This relation defines a hidden bond of sympathy and understanding between the hunted and the hunter. During the film, Deckard's life is twice saved by a replicant, while he, in turn, saves the life of a fifth, a recently created and even more sophisticated replicant called Rachel, with whom Deckard eventually falls in love.

The Los Angeles to which the replicants return is hardly a utopia. The flexibility of the replicants' capacity to labour in outer space is, as we have recently come to expect, matched in Los Angeles by a decrepit landscape of deindustrialization and post-industrial decay. Empty warehouses and abandoned industrial plant drip with leaking rain. Mist swirls, rubbish piles up, infrastructures are in a state of disintegration that makes the pot-holes and failing bridges of contemporary New York look mild by comparison. Punks and scavengers roam among the garbage, stealing whatever they can. J. F. Sebastian, one of the genetic designers who will eventually provide access to Tyrell for the replicants (and who himself suffers from a disease of premature aging called 'accelerated decrepitude') lives alone in such an empty space (actually a deserted version of the Bradbury building built in Los Angeles in 1893), surrounding himself with a fantastic array of mechanical and talking toys and dolls for company. But above the scenes of street-level and interior chaos and decay, there soars a high-tech world of zooming transporters, of advertising ('a chance to buy again in a golden land,' proclaims one advertisement circulating in the sky of mist and pouring rain), of familiar images of corporate power (Pan Am, surprisingly still in business in 2019, Coca-Cola, Budweiser, etc.), and the massive pyramidal building of the Tyrell Corporation that dominates one part of the city. The Tyrell Corporation specializes in genetic engineering. 'Commerce,' says Tyrell, 'more human than human, that's our business.' Opposed to these images of overwhelming corporate power, however, is another street-level scene of seething small-scale production. The city streets are full of all sorts of people − Chinese and Asiatics seem predominant, and it is the smiling face of a Japanese woman that advertises the Coca-Cola. A 'city-speak' language has emerged, a hybrid of Japanese, German, Spanish, English, etc. Not only has the 'third world' come to Los Angeles even more than at present, but signs of third world systems of labour organization and informal labour practices are everywhere. The scales for a genetically produced snake are produced in a tiny workshop, and human eyes are produced in another (both run by Orientals), indicating intricate relations of sub-contracting between highly disaggregated firms as well as with the Tyrell Corporation itself. The sense of the city at street level is chaotic in every respect. Architectural designs are a postmodern mish-mash – the Tyrell Corporation is housed in something that looks like a replica of an Egyptian pyramid, Greek and Roman columns mix in the streets with references to Mayan, Chinese, Oriental, Victorian and contemporary shopping mall architecture. Simulacra are everywhere. Genetically reproduced owls fly, and snakes slither across the shoulders of Zhora, a genetically reproduced replicant, as she performs in a cabaret that looks like a perfect 1920s imitation. The chaos of signs, of competing significations and messages, suggests a condition of fragmentation and uncertainty at street level that emphasizes many of those facets of postmodern aesthetics that were described in Part I. The aesthetic of *Blade Runner*, says Bruno, is the result 'of recycling, fusion of levels, discontinuous signifiers, explosion of boundaries, and erosion.' Yet there is also an overwhelming sense of some hidden organizing power – the Tyrell Corporation, the authorities who commission Deckard to his task without offering any choice, the rapid descent of the powers of law and order when necessary to establish street control. The chaos is tolerated, precisely because it seems so unthreatening to overall control.

Images of creative destruction are everywhere. They are most powerfully present, of course, in the figure of the replicants themselves, created with marvellous powers only to be prematurely destroyed, and most certainly to be 'retired' should they actually engage their own feelings and try to develop their own capacities in their own way. The images of decay everywhere in the landscape reinforce exactly that same structure of feeling. The sense of shattering and fragmentation in social life is highlighted in an incredible sequence in which Deckard pursues one of the women replicants, Zhora, through the crowded, incoherent, and labyrinth-like spaces of the city. Finally tracking her down in an arcade full of stores exhibiting their commodities, he shoots her in the back as she goes crashing though layer after layer of glass doors and windows, dying as she sends shards of glass flying in a million and one directions in the final plunge through a huge window.

The search for the replicants depends upon a certain technique of interrogation, which rests on the fact that they have no real history; they have, after all, been genetically created as full adults and lack the experience of human socialization (a fact which also renders them potentially dangerous should they evade control). The key question that exposes one of the replicants, Leon, is 'Tell me about your feelings around your mother?' To which Leon replies, 'Let me tell you about my mother,' and shoots his interrogator dead. Rachel, the most sophisticated of the replicants, tries to convince Deckard of her authenticity as a person (after she suspects that Deckard has seen through her other defences) by producing a photograph of a mother and a little girl which she claims is her. The point here, as Bruno perceptively observes, is that photographs are now construed as evidence of a real history, no matter what the truth of that history may have been. The image is, in short, proof of the reality, and images can be constructed and manipulated. Deckard discovers a whole range of photographs in Leon's possession, presumably meant to document that he has a history too. And Rachel, seeing Deckard's photographs of his family (and it is interesting that the only sense of history that we have for Deckard is provided by his photographs), tries to integrate with them. She puts her hair in the style of the photographs, plays the piano as if in a picture, and acts as if she knows what home means. It is this willingness to search for identity, home, and history (the match with Bachelard's views on the poetics of space is almost perfect here) that ultimately leads to her reprieve from 'retirement.' Deckard is certainly touched by it. But she can re-enter the symbolic realm of a truly human society only by acknowledging the overwhelming power of the Oedipal figure, the father. That is the only route she can take in order to be able to respond to the question, 'Tell me about your mother?' In submitting to Deckard (trusting him, deferring to him, and ultimately submitting to him physically), she learns the meaning of human love and the essence of ordinary sociality. In killing the replicant Leon as he is about to kill Deckard, she provides the ultimate evidence of the capacity to act as Deckard's woman. She escapes the schizoid world of replicant time and intensity to enter the symbolic world of Freud.

I do not think Bruno is correct, however, when she contrasts Roy's with Rachel's fate as hinging upon Rachel's willingness to submit to the symbolic order and Roy's refusal so to do. Roy is programmed to die shortly, and no reprieve or salvation is possible. His demand to overcome all the waste of his own condition simply cannot be met. His anger, as well as that of the other replicants, is huge. Gaining access to Tyrell, Roy first kisses him before tearing out Tyrell's eyes and killing his maker. Bruno quite reasonably interprets this as a reversal of the Oedipal myth and a clear sign that the replicants do not live within the frame of the Freudian symbolic order. This does not mean, however, that replicants have no human feelings. We have already seen something of Roy's capacity to feel, in his moving and deeply affectionate response to the death of the woman replicant Pris, shot down by Deckard in the midst of J. F. Sebastian's replicas. Roy's subsequent pursuit by Deckard, which quickly reverses into the hunted pursuing the hunter, culminates with Roy at the last minute rescuing Deckard from falling into the canyon of a street below. And it is almost exactly at that moment that Roy reaches his own programmed end.

But before he dies, Roy recounts something of the wondrous events he has participated in and the sights he has seen. He voices his anger at his condition of enslavement, and the waste that allows all his incredible intensity of experience to be 'washed away in time like tears in rain.' Deckard acknowledges the power of those aspirations. The replicants, he reflects, are just like most of us. They simply want to know 'where they have come from, where they are going to and how much time they've got.' And it is with Rachel, who has not been programmed to die in the four years, that Deckard escapes, after the four other replicants are dead, into a natural landscape of forests and mountains where the sun, never seen in Los Angeles, shines. The replicant has become the simulacrum to such perfection that she and the human can set off into their own futures, though with both of them 'wondering how much time we've got.'

Blade Runner is a science fiction parable in which postmodernist themes, set in a context of flexible accumulation and time–space compression, are explored with all the imaginary power that the cinema can command. The conflict is between people living on different time scales, and seeing and experiencing the world very differently as a result. The replicants have no real history, but can perhaps manufacture one; history for everyone has become reduced to the evidence of the photograph. Though the socialization is still important to personal history, that too, as Rachel shows, can be replicated. The depressing side of the film is precisely that, in the end, the difference between the replicant and the human becomes so unrecognizable that they can indeed fall in love (once both get on the same time scale). The power of the simulacrum is everywhere. The strongest social bond between Deckard and the replicants in revolt – the fact that they are both controlled and enslaved by a dominant corporate power – never generates the slightest hint that a coalition of the oppressed might be forged between them. While Tyrell's eyes are indeed torn out during his killing, this is an individual rather than a class act of rage. The finale of the film is a scene of sheer escapism (tolerated, it should be noted, by the authorities) that leaves unchanged the plight of replicants as well as the dismal conditions of the seething mass of humanity that inhabits the derelict streets of a decrepit, deindustrialized, and decaying postmodernist world.

In *Wings of Desire*, we similarly encounter two groups of actors living on different time scales. Angels live in enduring and eternal time, and humans live in their own social time, and, of course, they each see the world very differently. The film articulates that same sense of fragmentation that suffuses *Blade Runner*, while the question of the relations between time, space, history, and place is directly rather than indirectly posed. The problem of image, particularly that implied by the photograph, versus the telling of a story in real time, is central to the construction of the film.

The film begins with a fairy-tale-like narration of what it was like when children were children. It was a time, we are told, when children thought everything was full of life and life was as one, when they had no opinion on anything (including, presumably, having opinions, which would be totally acceptable to a postmodernist philosopher like Rorty), and when they were not even disturbed by photographs. Nevertheless, children ask important questions such as: 'Why am I me and not you?' 'Why am I here and not there?' and, 'When did time begin and where does space end?' These questions are repeated at several key points in the film, and frame the thematic material. Children, at various points in the film, look upwards or around them as if they are partially aware of the angels' presence in ways that the preoccupied and self-referential adults seem incapable of doing. The questions children ask are, of course, fundamental questions of identity, and the film explores two parallel tracks for defining answers.

The place is Berlin. In a sense it is a pity that Berlin disappears from the English title because the film is a wonderful and sensitive evocation of the sense of that place. We are quickly given to understand, however, that Berlin is one city among many in a global interactive space. Peter Falk, an instantly identifiable international media star (many will recognize him as the detective Columbo in a media series of that name, and that role is directly referenced several times) flies in by air. His thoughts go 'Tokyo, Kyoto, Paris, London, Trieste, ... Berlin!' as he locates the place for which he is bound. Shots of airliners leaving or arriving punctuate the film at various key points. People think their thoughts in German, French, and English, with other languages occasionally used (language has not yet degenerated to the condition of 'city-speak' in *Blade Runner*).

References to the international space of the media are everywhere. Berlin is, evidently, just one place of many, and it exists in a cosmopolitan world of internationalism. Yet Berlin is still the distinctive place to be explored. A moment before we listen in to Falk's thoughts, we overhear a young girl thinking about how to draw the space of home. The relation between space and place is early put straight onto the agenda.

The first part of the film examines Berlin through the monochromatic eyes of a pair of angels. Outside the human time of becoming, they exist in the realm of pure spirit, in infinite and eternal time. They can also move effortlessly and instantaneously in space. For them, time and space just are, an infinite present in an infinite space which reduces the whole world to a monochromatic state. Everything seems to float in the same undifferentiated present, much as contemporary social life floats in the undifferentiated and homogenizing stream of international money. The angels cannot, however, get inside the problem of human decision-making. They cannot resonate with 'here' and 'now' precisely because they live in a world of 'always' and 'forever.'

The picture of Berlin that emerges from their perspective is an extraordinary landscape of fragmented spaces and ephemeral incidents that has no binding logic. The opening shots take us from on high, down into the inner courtyards and divided spaces of nineteenth-century worker housing. From there we go into labyrinth-like interior spaces, listening in with the angels, to people's inner thoughts. Isolated spaces, isolated thoughts, and isolated individuals are all we can see. A youth in a room contemplates suicide over a lost love, while his father and mother think quite disparate thoughts about him. In the underground, on a bus, in cars, in an ambulance racing with a pregnant woman, on the street, on a bicycle, everything appears as fragmented and ephemeral, each incident recorded in the same monotone and monochrome as the other. Being outside human space and time, all the angels can do is to offer some spiritual comfort, try to soothe the fragmented and often shattered feelings of the individuals whose thoughts they monitor. They sometimes succeed, and just as often fail (the youth commits suicide, and the high school student taking to prostitution is inconsolable at the loss of her dead boy friend). As angels, one of them complains, we can never really participate, only pretend.

This extraordinary evocation of an urban landscape, of alienated individuals in fragmented spaces caught in an ephemera of unpatterned incidents, has a powerful aesthetic effect. The images are stark, cold, but endowed with all of the beauty of old-style still photography, though set in motion through the camera lens. It is a selective landscape that we see. The facts of production, and the necessary class relations that attach thereto, are noticeable by their absence. We are treated to a picture of the urban that is, in the fashion of postmodern sociology, entirely *déclassé*, much closer to Simmel (in his 'Metropolis and Mental Life' essay) than to Marx. Death, birth, anxiety, pleasure, loneliness are all aestheticized on the same plane, empty of any sense of class struggle or of ethical or moral commentary.

The identity of this place called Berlin is constituted through this alien but quite beautiful imagery. The distinctive organization of space and time is, moreover, seen as the framework within which individual identities are forged. The image of divided spaces is particularly powerful, and they are superimposed upon each other in the fashion of montage and collage. The Berlin Wall is one such divide, and it is again and again evoked as a symbol of overarching division. Is this where space now ends? 'It is impossible to get lost in Berlin,' someone says, 'because you can always find the wall.' More fine-grained divisions exist, however. Germany, the driver of a car reflects as he tracks through street scenes that conjure up images of war-time destruction, has become fragmented to the point where every individual constitutes a mini-state, where each street has its barriers surrounded by a no man's land through which one can pass only if one has the right password. Even access from any one individual to another demands payment of a toll. Not only may this extreme condition of alienated and isolated individualism (of the sort that Simmel described) be considered a good thing (compared with the collective life of Nazism that had gone before) but individuals may seek it out. 'Get a good costume, that's half the battle,' says Falk thinking about the part he is to play, and, in a wonderfully humorous scene he tries on hat after hat in order, he says, to be able to pass unrecognized among the crowd and achieve the anonymity he desires. The hats he puts on turn into virtual masks of characters, in much the same way that Cindy Sherman photographs mask the person. This hat makes him look like Humphrey Bogart, this one is for going to the races, that one for going to the opera, and another is for getting married in. The act of masking and disguising connects with spatial fragmentation and alienated individualism.

This landscape bears all the marks of high postmodernist art as Pfeil (1988, 384) for one has recently described it. 'One is confronted not with a unified text, much less by the presence of a distinct personality and sensibility, but by a discontinuous terrain of heterogeneous discourses uttered by anonymous, unplaceable tongues, a chaos different from that of the classic texts of high modernism precisely insofar as it is not recontained or recuperated within an overarching mythic framework.' The quality of utterance is 'deadpan, indifferent, depersonalized, effaced,' so as to cancel out 'the possibility of traditional audience participation.' Only the angels have an overall view, and they, when they perch on high, hear only a babble of intersecting voices and whispers, and see nothing but a monochromatic world.

How can some sense of identity be forged and sustained in such a world? Two spaces assume a peculiar significance in this regard. The library − a repository of historical knowledge and collective memory − is a space into which many are evidently drawn (even angels seem to take their rest there). An old man enters the library. He is to play an extremely important, though ambiguous role. He sees himself as the story-teller, the muse, the potential guardian of collective memory and history, the representative of 'everyman.' But he is disturbed at the thought that the tight circle of listeners who used to gather round him has been broken up and dispersed, he knows not where, as readers who do not communicate with each other. Even language, the meanings of words and sentences, he complains, seem to slip and slide into incoherent fragments. Forced now to live 'from day to day,' he uses the library to try and recuperate a proper sense of the history of this distinctive place called Berlin. He wants to do it not from the standpoint of leaders and kings, but as a hymn of peace. The books and photographs, however, conjure up images of the death and destruction wrought in World War II, a trauma to which the film again and again makes reference, as if this was indeed when this time began and when the spaces of the city were shattered. The old man, surrounded by model globes in the library, spins a wheel, thinking that the whole world is disappearing in the dusk. He leaves the library and walks in search of the Potsdamer Platz (one of those urban spaces that Sitte would surely have admired), the heart of old Berlin, with its Café Josti where he used to take coffee and a cigar and watch the crowd. Walking alongside the Berlin Wall, all he can find is an empty weed-strewn lot. Puzzled, he collapses into an abandoned armchair, insisting that his quest is neither hopeless nor unimportant. Even though he feels like a poet ignored and mocked on the edge of no man's land, he cannot give up, he says, because if mankind loses its story-teller then it loses its childhood. Even though the story may in parts be ugly − and he recalls how when flags appeared in the Potsdamer Platz the crowd turned unfriendly and the police brutish − it still has to be told. Besides, he feels personally protected, saved, he says, 'from present and future troubles by the tale.' His search to reconstruct and tell this tale of salvation and protection is a subtle sub-plot throughout the film that assumes its importance only at the very end.

But there is a second site where a fragile sense of identity prevails. The circus, a spectacle held together within the enclosed space of a tent, offers a venue of special interaction within which some kind of human relating can go on. It is within this space that the trapeze artist, Marion, acquires some sense of herself, a possibility of achieving and belonging. But the news that the circus is out of money and has to close shows immediately how ephemeral and contingent that identity is. The short-term contract prevails here too. Yet Marion, while plainly distressed at this news, insists she has a story, and that she is going to go on creating one, though not in the circus. She even imagines going into a photo-automat and emerging with a new identity (the power of the photo image, once more), taking up a job as waitress or whatever. Her own history, we are reminded as one of the angels watches her in her caravan, can in any case be collapsed (like that of Deckard) into family photographs pinned to the wall, so why not build a new history with the aid of photographs? These fantasies are suffused, however, with a powerful aura of desire to become a whole rather than a fragmented and alienated person. She longs to be complete, but recognizes that this can come to be only through a relation with another. After the tent is down and the circus is gone, she stands alone on the empty site, feeling herself a person without roots, without history, or without country. Yet that very emptiness seems to hold out the possibility of some radical transformation. 'I can become the world,' she says, as she watches a jet airliner cruise across the sky.

One of the angels, Damiel, already chafing at his powerlessness to resonate with the here and now, is attracted by Marion's energy and beauty, particularly in the performance of her trapeze act. He becomes caught up in her inner longings to become rather than just to be. For the first time he gets a glimpse of what the world would look like in colour, and he is increasingly drawn to the idea of entering the flow of human time, leaving behind the time of the spirit and of eternity. Two catalytic moments trigger his decision. She dreams of him as the resplendent 'other,' and he sees himself reflected in her dream. Invisible still, he follows Marion into a night club and, as she dances dreamily by herself, he touches her thoughts. She responds with a sense of rapturous well-being, as if, she says, a hand is softly tightening within her body. The second catalytic moment is with Peter Falk who, it later transpires, is an angel come to ground some time ago. He senses the presence of the invisible Damiel as he takes a cup of coffee at a street stall. 'I can't see you, but I know you're there,' he says to a surprised Damiel, and then goes on to speak with warmth and humour of how good it is to live in the flow of human time, to feel material events, and take tangible account of the whole range of human sensations.

Damiel's decision to come inside is taken in the no man's land between two lines of the Berlin Wall, patrolled by soldiers. Fortunately, his fellow angel has the power to place him on the western side. There Damiel wakes up to a world of rich and vibrant colours. He has to navigate the city in real physical terms, and in so doing experiences the exhilaration that comes with creating a spatial story (in the manner of de Certeau) simply by traversing the city, which then no longer seems as fragmented but which assumes a more coherent structure. This human sense of space and motion contrasts with that of angels, earlier depicted as a hyper-space of speeding flashes, each image like a cubist painting, suggesting a totally different mode of spatial experience. Damiel shifts from one mode to the other as he enters the flow of time. But he needs money, now, to survive. He borrows enough from a passer-by to buy a cup of coffee and trades in a piece of ancient armour (which we subsequently learn is the initial endowment of all angels who come to earth) and emerges from the shop with a colourful set of clothes and a watch which he inspects with the greatest interest. He comes across the set where Peter Falk is filming, and here experiences a major check because the guard will not let him enter. Cursing the guard, he has to shout to Falk through a chain link fence. Falk, who guesses immediately who he is, asks him, 'How long?' Damiel replies, 'Minutes, hours, days, weeks, . . . TIME!' to which Falk immediately responds, with kind and gentle humour, 'Here, let me give you some dollars!' Damiel's entry into this human world is now firmly located within the co-ordinates of social space, social time, and the social power of money.

The coming together of Damiel and Marion is clearly meant as the climactic point of the film. The two circle each other in the same night-club she had been in before, watched tiredly by Damiel's earlier angel companion, before coming together in the bar close by. There they meet in an almost ritualistic way, she ready and determined to make her history, to supersede being with becoming, he determined to learn the meaning of the flow of human experience in space and time. In the lengthy monologue that follows, she insists on the seriousness of their common project even though the times themselves may not be serious. She insists on doing away with coincidence and contingency. The temporary contracts are over. She tries to define a way of coming together that has a universal meaning beyond this particular place and time. There may not be any destiny, she says, but there is certainly decision. And it is a decision in which all the people of the city, even of the world, can participate. She imagines a square full of people, and that she and Damiel are so full of that place that they can make a decision for all. It is a decision to forge a bond between a man and a woman around a common project of becoming, in which a woman can say 'my man' in such a way as to open up a whole world to fresh insight and interpretation. It means entering the labyrinth of happiness through the transformation of desire into love, so that she can finally be truly alone with herself, because to be truly alone presupposes a wholeness that can come only through a non-contingent relation to another. It seems she now has answers to the compelling questions: 'Why am I me and not you?' 'Why am I here and not there?' and 'Where did time begin and where does space end?' What is born of their coming together, reflects Damiel as he helps her to practise her trapeze act after their first night together, is not a child but an immortal image that all can share and live by.

It is hard to prevent this ending slipping into banality (presaged by the kitschy dream sequence in which the angel comes to Marion in resplendent silver costume). Are we to conclude, after all, that it is merely romantic love that makes the world go round? A charitable reading might be that we should not let our jaded experience of kitsch and pastiche stand in the way of liberating romantic desire and undertaking major projects. But the final shots are portentous indeed. The film switches back into the monochrome of enduring time. The old man, with whom we have lost all contact in the coloured sequences of the film, shuffles towards the Berlin Wall, saying, 'Who will look for me, their story-teller? They need me more than ever.' The camera suddenly zooms past him and up into the clouds, as if taking off in flight. 'We are on our way,' says Marion. More is to follow, the final credit assures us.

I read this second part of the film as an attempt to resurrect something of the modernist spirit of human communication, togetherness, and becoming, out of the ashes of a monochromatic and dead-pan postmodernist landscape of feeling. Wenders is plainly mobilizing all his artistic and creative powers in a project of redemption. He proposes, in effect, a romantic myth that can redeem us 'from the formless universe of contigency' (see above, p. 206). The fact that many angels, according to Falk, have chosen to come to earth, suggests that it is better always to be inside than outside the flow of human time, that becoming always has the potential to break with the stasis of being. Space and time are constituted in radically different ways in the two parts of the film, and the presence of colour, creativity, and, we should not forget, money as a form of social bonding, provides the necessary framework within which some sense of common purpose can be found.

Yet there are serious dilemmas to be resolved. Damiel has no history, and Marion is cut off from her roots, her history reduced to a set of photographs and a few other 'objects of memory' of the sort that now constitute the sense of history both in the home (see above, p. 292) and in the museum (see above, p. 62). Is it possible to set about the project of becoming a-historically? The old man's persistent voice seems to question the viability of that. The sheer romanticism of the ending, he seems to say, has to be tempered by a real sense of history. Indeed, Marion's image of a whole 'Platz' of people participating in their decision, raises the spectre of when the Potsdamer Platz turned ugly as it filled with flags. Put more formally, there is a tension in the film between the power of spatial images (photographs, the film itself, the striving of Damiel and Marion at the end to make an image the world can live by) and the power of the story. The old man (described as Homer, the story-teller in the credits) is in many respects marginalized within the film, and complains explicitly at that very fact. Becoming, according to him, has to be more than creating just another set of depthless images. It has to be situated and understood historically. But that presupposes that history can be captured without the use of images. The old man leafs through a book of photographs, wanders into the Potsdamer Platz trying to reconstitute its sense of place from memory, and remembers it when it turned ugly, not conducive to that epic of peace that he seeks. This dialogue between image and story provides an underlying dramatic tension in the film. Powerful images (of the sort that Wenders and his brilliant cameraman, Henri Alekan, know how to wield only too well) can both illuminate and obscure stories. In the film they overwhelm the verbal messages the old man tries to communicate. It is almost as if the film gets caught in the circularity (known in the postmodernist lexicon as 'intertextuality') of its own images. Within this tension lies the whole issue of how to handle the aesthetic qualities of space and time in a postmodern world of monochromatic fragmentation and ephemerality. 'Perhaps,' says Marion, 'time itself is the sickness,' leaving us to wonder, as in the final sequence of *Blade Runner*, 'how much time we've got.' But whatever that may mean to the participants, the monochromatic landscape of eternal time and infinite but fragmented space plainly will not do.

It is both intriguing and interesting that two films otherwise so disparate should depict such similar conditions. I do not believe the similarity is accidental or contingent. It supports the idea that the experience of time—space compression in recent years, under the pressures of the turn to more flexible modes of accumulation, has generated a crisis of representation in cultural forms, and that this is a subject of intense aesthetic concern, either *in toto* (as I think is the case in *Wings of Desire*) or in part (as would be true of everything from *Blade Runner* to Cindy Sherman's photographs and the novels of Italo Calvino or Pynchon). Such cultural practices are important. If there is a crisis of representation of space and time, then new ways of thinking and feeling have to be created. Part of any trajectory out of the condition of postmodernity has to embrace exactly such a process.

The distressing side of both films, in spite of the overt optimism of Wenders's ending, is the inability to go much further than romanticism (individualized and strongly aestheticized) as a solution to the conditions that both film makers so brilliantly portray. It seems as if the film makers are unable to break free from the power of the images they themselves create. Marion and Damiel seek an image to replace images, and seem to see that as an adequate conception of how to change the world. The turn in both cases to romanticism is, from this standpoint, dangerous precisely because it presages the continuation of a condition in which aesthetics predominates over ethics. The qualities of the romanticism on offer vary of course. The tired machismo of Deckard and the submission of Rachel are entirely different from the meeting of minds and of souls in the case of Marion and Damiel (both of whom are set to learn from each other). Yet even here there is a sense that *Blade Runner* speaks with a rather more authentic (though not necessarily praiseworthy) voice, because it is at least concerned with what nature of symbolic order we might be in (a question that Wenders evades). Wenders likewise evades the question of class relations and consciousness entirely by casting the social problem as the unmediated relationship between individuals and collectivity (the state). While signs of objective class relations abound in *Blade Runner*, the participants in the action evidently see no purpose in relating to them even if they are, like Deckard, vaguely aware of their existence. Brilliant portrayals though both films are of the conditions of postmodernity, and in particular of the conflictual and confusing experience of space and time, neither has the power to overturn established ways of seeing or transcend the conflictual conditions of the moment. This must, in part, be attributed to the contradictions inherent in the cinematic form itself.

Cinema is, after all, the supreme maker and manipulator of images for commercial purposes, and the very act of using it well always entails reducing the complex stories of daily life to a sequence of images upon a depthless screen. The idea of a revolutionary cinema has always run aground on the rocks of exactly this difficulty. Nevertheless, the *malaise* lies rather deeper than that. Postmodern art forms and cultural artefacts by their very nature must self-consciously embrace the problem of image creation, and necessarily turn inwards upon themselves as a result. It then becomes difficult to escape being what is being imaged within the art form itself. Wenders, I think, really struggles with that problem and the fact that he does not, in the end, succeed, is perhaps most clearly signalled in the final caption that 'more is to follow.' Within these limits, however, the mimetic qualities of cinema of this sort are extraordinarily revealing. Both *Wings of Desire* and *Blade Runner* hold up to us, as in a mirror, many of the essential features of the condition of post-modernity.

Part IV

The condition of postmodernity

The new value placed on the transitory, the elusive and the ephemeral, the very celebration of dynamism, discloses a longing for an undefiled, immaculate and stable present.   *Jurgen Habermas*

The Enlightenment is dead, Marxism is dead, the working class movement is dead ... and the author does not feel very well either.   *Neil Smith*

19

Postmodernity as a historical condition

Aesthetic and cultural practices are peculiarly susceptible to the changing experience of space and time precisely because they entail the construction of spatial representations and artefacts out of the flow of human experience. They always broker between Being and Becoming.

It is possible to write the historical geography of the experience of space and time in social life, and to understand the transformations that both have undergone, by reference to material and social conditions. Part III proposed an historical sketch of how that might be done with respect to the post-Renaissance Western world. The dimensions of space and time have there been subject to the persistent pressure of capital circulation and accumulation, culminating (particularly during the periodic crises of overaccumulation that have arisen since the mid-nineteenth century) in disconcerting and disruptive bouts of time–space compression.

The aesthetic responses to conditions of time–space compression are important and have been so ever since the eighteenth-century separation of scientific knowledge from moral judgement opened up a distinctive role for them. The confidence of an era can be assessed by the width of the gap between scientific and moral reasoning. In periods of confusion and uncertainty, the turn to aesthetics (of whatever form) becomes more pronounced. Since phases of time–space compression are disruptive, we can expect the turn to aesthetics and to the forces of culture as both explanations and *loci* of active struggle to be particularly acute at such moments. Since crises of overaccumulation typically spark the search for spatial and temporal resolutions, which in turn create an overwhelming sense of time–space compression, we can also expect crises of overaccumulation to be followed by strong aesthetic movements.

The crisis of overaccumulation that began in the late 1960s and which came to a head in 1973 has generated exactly such a result. The experience of time and space has changed, the confidence in the association between scientific and moral judgements has collapsed, aesthetics has triumphed over ethics as a prime focus of social and intellectual concern, images dominate narratives, ephemerality and fragmentation take precedence over eternal truths and unified politics, and explanations have shifted from the realm of material and pol-itical—economic groundings towards a consideration of auto-nomous cultural and political practices.

The historical sketch I have here proposed suggests, however, that shifts of this sort are by no means new, and that the most recent version of it is certainly within the grasp of historical materialist enquiry, even capable of theorization by way of the meta-narrative of capitalist development that Marx proposed.

Postmodernism can be regarded, in short, as a historical—geo-graphical condition of a certain sort. But what sort of condition is it and what should we make of it? Is it pathological or portentous of a deeper and even wider revolution in human affairs than those already wrought in the historical geography of capitalism? In this conclusion I sketch in some possible answers to those questions.

20

Economics with mirrors

'Voodoo economics' and 'economics with mirrors' said George Bush and John Anderson respectively of Ronald Reagan's economic programme to revive a flagging economy in the primary and presidential election campaigns of 1980. A sketch on the back of a napkin by a little-known economist called Laffer purported to show that tax cuts were bound to increase tax yields (at least up to a certain point) because they stimulated growth and, hence, the base upon which taxes were assessed. So was the economic policy of the Reagan years to be justified, a policy that indeed worked wonders with mirrors even if it brought the United States several steps closer to international bankruptcy and fiscal ruin (see figures 2.13 and 2.14). The strange and puzzling thing is that such a simplistic idea could gain the purchase it did and seem to work so well politically for so long. Even stranger, is the fact that Reagan was re-elected when all the polls showed that the majority of the US electorate (to say nothing of the majority of eligible voters, who did not vote) disagreed fundamentally with him on almost all major issues of social, political, and even foreign policy. Strangest of all is how such a President could leave office riding so high on the wave of public affection, even though more than a dozen senior members of his administration had either been accused or been found guilty of serious infringement of legal procedures and blatant disregard for ethical principles. The triumph of aesthetics over ethics could not be plainer.

Image-building in politics is nothing new. Spectacle, pomp and circumstance, demeanour, charisma, patronage, and rhetoric have long been part of the aura of political power. And the degree to which these could be bought, produced, or otherwise acquired has also long been important to the maintenance of that power. But something has changed qualitatively about that in recent times. The mediatization of politics was given a new direction in the Kennedy–

Nixon television debate, in which the latter's loss of a presidential election was attributed by many to the untrustworthy look of his five o'clock shadow. The active use of public relations firms to shape and sell a political image quickly followed (the careful imaging of Thatcherism by the now all-powerful firm of Saatchi and Saatchi is a recent example, illustrating how Americanized in this regard European politics is becoming).

The election of an ex-movie actor, Ronald Reagan, to one of the most powerful positions in the world put a new gloss on the possibilities of a mediatized politics shaped by images alone. His image, cultivated over many years of political practice, and then carefully mounted, crafted, and orchestrated with all the artifice that contemporary image production could command, as a tough but warm, avuncular, and well-meaning person who had an abiding faith in the greatness and goodness of America, built an aura of charismatic politics. Carey McWilliams, an experienced political commentator and long-time editor of the *Nation*, described it as 'the friendly face of fascism.' The 'teflon president,' as he came to be known (simply because no accusation thrown at him, however true, ever seemed to stick), could make mistake after mistake but never be called to account. His image could be deployed, unfailingly and instantaneously, to demolish any narrative of criticism that anyone cared to construct. But the image concealed a coherent politics. First, to exorcize the demon of the defeat in Vietnam by taking assertive action in support of any nominally anti-communist struggle anywhere in the world (Nicaragua, Grenada, Angola, Mozambique, Afghanistan, etc.). Second to expand the budget deficit through defence spending and force a recalcitrant Congress (and nation) to cut again and again into the social programmes that the rediscovery of poverty and of racial inequality in the United States in the 1960s had spawned.

This open programme of class aggrandizement was partially successful. Attacks upon union power (led by the Reagan onslaught upon the air traffic controllers), the effects of deindustrialization and regional shifts (encouraged by tax breaks), and of high unemployment (legitimized as proper medicine in the fight against inflation), and all the accumulated impacts of the shift from manufacturing to service employment, weakened traditional working-class institutions sufficiently to render much of the population vulnerable. A rising tide of social inequality engulfed the United States in the Reagan years, reaching a post-war high in 1986 (see figure 2.15); by then the poorest fifth of the population, which had gradually improved its share of national income to a high of point of nearly 7 per cent in the early 1970s, found itself with only 4.6 per cent. Between 1979 and 1986, the number of poor families with children increased by 35 per cent, and in some large metropolitan areas, such as New York, Chicago, Baltimore, and New Orleans, more than half the children were living in families with incomes below the poverty line. In spite of surging unemployment (cresting at over 10 per cent by official figures in 1982) the percentage of unemployed receiving any federal benefit fell to only 32 per cent, the lowest level in the history of social insurance since its inception in the New Deal (see figure 2.9). An increase in homelessness signalled a general state of social dis-location, marked by confrontations (many of them with racist or ethnic overtones). The mentally ill were returned to their communities for care, which consisted largely of rejection and violence, the tip of an iceberg of neglect which left nearly 40 million citizens in one of the richest nations of the world with no medical insurance cover whatsoever. While jobs were indeed created during the Reagan years, many of them were low-wage and insecure service jobs, hardly sufficient to offset the 10 per cent decline in the real wage from 1972 to 1986. If family incomes rose, that simply signified that more and more women were entering the workforce (see figures 2.2 and 2.9).

Yet for the young and the rich and the educated and the privileged things could not have been better. The world of real estate, finance, and business services grew, as did the 'cultural mass' given over to the production of images, knowledge, and cultural and aesthetic forms (see above, p. 290). The political—economic base and, with it, the whole culture of cities were transformed. New York lost its traditional garment trade and turned to the production of debt and fictitious capital instead. 'In the last seven years,' ran a report by Scardino (1987) in the *New York Times*,

New York has constructed 75 new factories to house the debt production and distribution machine. These towers of granite and glass shine through the night as some of this generation's most talented professionals invent new instruments of debt to fit every imagined need: Perpetual Floating Rate Notes, Yield Curve Notes and Dual Currency Notes, to name a few, now traded as casually as the stock of the Standard Oil Company once was.

The trade is as vigorous as that which once dominated the harbour. But 'today, the telephone lines deliver the world's cash to be remixed as if in a bottling plant, squirted into different containers, capped and shipped back out.' The biggest physical export from New York

City is now waste paper. The city's economy in fact rests on the production of fictitious capital to lend to the real estate agents who cut deals for the highly paid professionals who manufacture fictitious capital. Likewise, when the image production machine of Los Angeles came to a grinding halt during the Writers' Guild strike, people suddenly realized 'how much of its economic structure is based on a writer telling a producer a story, and that finally it's the weaving of that tale (into images) that pays the wages of the man who drives the van that delivers the food that's eaten in the restaurant that feeds the family who make the decisions that keep the economy running' (report of Scott Meek in *The Independent*, 14 July 1988).

The emergence of this casino economy, with all of its financial speculation and fictitious capital formation (much of it unbacked by any growth in real production) provided abundant opportunities for personal aggrandizement (plate 4.1 and figure 4.1). Casino capitalism had come to town, and many large cities suddenly found they had command of a new and powerful business. On the back of this boom in business and financial services, a whole new Yuppie culture formed, with its accoutrements of gentrification, close attention to symbolic capital, fashion, design, and quality of urban life.

The obverse side of this affluence was the plague of homelessness, disempowerment, and impoverishment that engulfed many of the central cities. 'Otherness' was produced with a vengeance and a vengefulness unparalleled in the post-war era. The forgotten voices and unforgettable dreams of New York's homeless were recorded this way (Coalition For the Homeless, 1987):

> I am 37 years old. I look like 52 years old. Some people say that street life is free and easy.... It's not free and it's not easy. You don't put no money down. Your payment is your health and mental stability.

> My country's name is apathy. My land is smeared with shame. My sightscape moves its homeless hordes through welfare's turgid flame. The search goes on for rooms and warmth, some closet hooks, a drawer; a hot place just for one's soup – what liberty is for.

Just before Christmas 1987, the United States Government cut $35 million from the budget for emergency help to the homeless. Meanwhile personal indebtedness continued to accelerate, and presidential candidates began to fight over who could enunciate the pledge of

Plate 4.1 This Lloyds Bank advertisement on accumulation-speculation promotes acceptance of the world of fictions capital formation and voodoo economics as a normal basis for daily life.

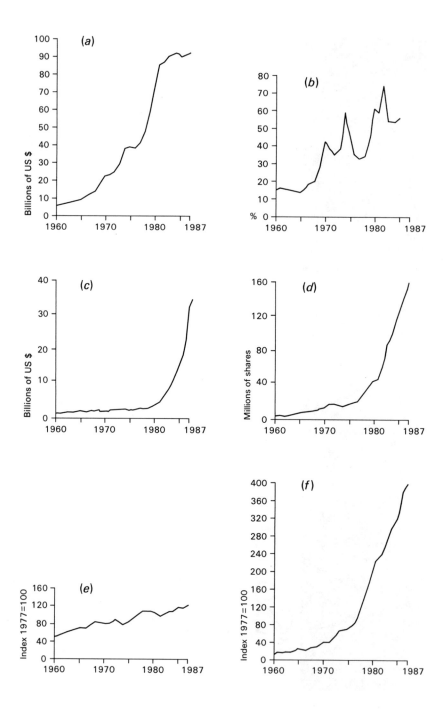

allegiance in more convincing tones. The voices of the homeless sadly went unheard in a world 'cluttered with illusion, fantasy and pretence.'

Figure 4.1 The speculative world of voodoo economics 1960–1987:
(a) nominal interest payments for US non-financial corporations
(Source: Department of Commerce)
(b) nominal interest payments as percentage of pre-tax profits in the United States
(Source: Department of Commerce)
(c) total capital of New York Stock Exchange firms
(Source: New York Times)
(d) daily trading volume on the New York Stock Exchange
(Source: New York Times)
(e) index of US manufacturing production (after Harrison and Bluestone, 1988)
(f) index of futures trading volume in New York (after Harrison and Bluestone, 1988)

21

Postmodernism as the mirror of mirrors

One of the prime conditions of postmodernity is that no one can or should discuss it as a historical–geographical condition. It is never easy, of course, to construct a critical assessment of a condition that is overwhelmingly present. The terms of debate, description, and representation are often so circumscribed that there seems to be no escape from evaluations that are anything other than self-referential. It is conventional these days, for example, to dismiss out of hand any suggestion that the 'economy' (however that vague word is understood) might be determinant of cultural life even in (as Engels and later Althusser suggested) 'the last instance.' The odd thing about postmodern cultural production is how much sheer profit-seeking is determinant in the first instance.

Postmodernism has come of age in the midst of this climate of voodoo economics, of political image construction and deployment, and of new social class formation. That there is some connection between this postmodernist burst and the image-making of Ronald Reagan, the attempt to deconstruct traditional institutions of working-class power (the trade unions and the political parties of the left), the masking of the social effects of the economic politics of privilege, ought to be evident enough. A rhetoric that justifies homelessness, unemployment, increasing impoverishment, disempowerment, and the like by appeal to supposedly traditional values of self-reliance and entrepreneurialism will just as freely laud the shift from ethics to aesthetics as its dominant value system. The street scenes of impoverishment, disempowerment, graffiti and decay become grist for the cultural producers' mill, not, as Deutsche and Ryan (1984) point out, in the muckraking reformist style of the late nineteenth century, but as a quaint and swirling backdrop (as in *Blade Runner*) upon which no social commentary is to be made. 'Once the poor become aestheticized, poverty itself moves out of our field of social vision', except as a passive depiction of otherness, alienation and contingency within the human condition. When 'poverty and home-lessness are served up for aesthetic pleasure', then ethics is indeed submerged by aesthetics, inviting, thereby, the bitter harvest of charismatic politics and ideological extremism.

If there is a meta-theory with which to embrace all these gyrations of postmodern thinking and cultural production, then why should we not deploy it?

22

Fordist modernism versus flexible postmodernism, or the interpenetration of opposed tendencies in capitalism as a whole

Collage, though pioneered by the modernists, is a technique that postmodernism has very much made its own. The juxtaposition of diverse and seemingly incongruous elements can be fun and occasionally instructive. In this spirit I have taken the oppositions provided by Ihab Hassan (table 1.1) and by Halal, Lash and Urry, and Swyngedouw (tables 2.6, 2.7, and 2.8) and jumbled up their terms (adding in a few of my own for good measure) to produce a collage of terms in table 4.1.

Down the left-hand side are ranged a series of intersecting terms to describe the condition of 'Fordist modernity,' while the right-hand column represents 'Flexible postmodernism.' The table suggests amusing associations. But it also indicates how two rather different regimes of accumulation and their associated modes of regulation (including the materializations of cultural habits, motivations, and styles of representation) might hang together, each as a distinctive and relatively coherent kind of social formation. Two reservations to that idea immediately come to mind. First, the oppositions, highlighted for didactic purposes, are never so clear-cut, and the 'structure of feeling' in any society is always a synthetic moment somewhere between the two. Second, associations are no proof of historical causation or even of necessary or integral relations. Even if the associations look plausible – and many of them do – some other way has to be found to establish that they form a meaningful configuration.

The oppositions within each profile are noteworthy. Fordist modernity is far from homogeneous. There is much here that is about relative fixity and permanence – fixed capital in mass production, stable, standardized, and homogeneous markets, a fixed configuration of political—economic influence and power, easily identifiable authority and meta-theories, secure grounding in materiality and technical—scientific rationality, and the like. But all of this is ranged around a social and economic project of Becoming, of growth and transformation of social relations, of auratic art and originality, of renewal and avant-gardism. Postmodernist flexibility, on the other hand, is dominated by fiction, fantasy, the immaterial (particularly of money), fictitious capital, images, ephemerality, chance, and flexibility in production techniques, labour markets and consumption niches; yet it also embodies strong commitments to Being and place, a penchant for charismatic politics, concerns for ontology, and the stable institutions favoured by neo-conservatism. Habermas's judgement that the value placed on the transitory and the ephemeral 'discloses a longing for an undefiled, immaculate and stable present' is everywhere in evidence. It seems as if postmodernist flexibility merely reverses the dominant order to be found in Fordist modernity. The latter achieved relative stability in its political—economic apparatus in order to produce strong social and material change, whereas the former has been dogged by disruptive instability in its political—economic apparatus, but sought compensation in stable places of being and in charismatic geopolitics.

But what if the table as a whole itself constitutes a structural description of the totality of political—economic and cultural—ideological relations within capitalism? To view it this way requires that we see the oppositions across as well as within the profiles as internal relations within a structured whole. That idea, outrageous by postmodernism's own standards (because it resurrects the ghost of Marxist thinkers like Lukacs and appeals to a theory of internal relations of the sort that Bertell Ollman advances) makes more than a little sense. It helps explain how it is that Marx's *Capital* is so rich in insights into what the current status of thinking is all about. It also helps us understand how the cultural forces at work in, say, *fin de siècle* Vienna constituted such a complex mix that it is almost impossible to tell where the modernist impulse begins or ends. It helps us dissolve the categories of both modernism and postmodernism into a complex of oppositions expressive of the cultural contradictions of capitalism. We then get to see the categories of both modernism and postmodernism as static reifications imposed upon the fluid interpenetration of dynamic oppositions. Within this matrix of internal relations, there is never one fixed configuration, but a swaying back and forth between centralization and decentralization, between authority and deconstruction, between hierarchy and anarchy, between permanence and flexibility, between the detail and the

Table 4.1 *Fordist modernity versus flexible postmodernity, or the interpenetration of opposed tendencies in capitalist society as a whole*

Fordist modernity	Flexible postmodernity
economies of scale/master code/hierarchy homogeneity/detail division of labour	economies of scope/idiolect/anarchy diversity/social division of labour
paranoia/alienation/symptom public housing/monopoly capital	schizophrenia/decentering/desire homelessness/entrepreneurialism
purpose/design/mastery/determinacy production capital/universalism	play/chance/exhaustion/indeterminacy fictitious capital/localism
state power/trade unions state welfarism/metropolis	financial power/individualism neo-conservatism/counterurbanization
ethics/money commodity God the Father/materiality	aesthetics/moneys of account The Holy Ghost/immateriality
production/originality/authority blue collar/avant-gardism interest group politics/semantics	reproduction/pastiche/eclecticism white collar/commercialism charismatic politics/rhetoric
centralization/totalization synthesis/collective bargaining	decentralization/deconstruction antithesis/local contracts

operational management/master code
phallic/single task/origin

strategic management/idiolect
androgynous/multiple tasks/trace

metatheory/narrative/depth
mass production/class politics
technical-scientific rationality

language games/image/surface
small-batch production/social
movements/pluralistic otherness

utopia/redemptive art/concentration
specialized work/collective consumption

heterotopias/spectacle/dispersal
flexible worker/symbolic capital

function/representation/signified
industry/protestant work ethic
mechanical reproduction

fiction/self-reference/signifier
services/temporary contract
electronic reproduction

becoming/epistemology/regulation
urban renewal/relative space

being/ontology/deregulation
urban revitalization/place

state interventionism/industrialization
internationalism/permanence/time

laissez-faire/deindustrialization
geopolitics/ephemerality/space

social division of labour (to list but a few of the many oppositions that can be identified). The sharp categorical distinction between modernism and postmodernism disappears, to be replaced by an examination of the flux of internal relations within capitalism as a whole.

But why the flux? This brings us back to the problem of causation and historical trajectory.

23

The transformative and speculative logic of capital

Capital is a process and not a thing. It is a process of reproduction of social life through commodity production, in which all of us in the advanced capitalist world are heavily implicated. Its internalized rules of operation are such as to ensure that it is a dynamic and revolutionary mode of social organization, restlessly and ceaselessly transforming the society within which it is embedded. The process masks and fetishizes, achieves growth through creative destruction, creates new wants and needs, exploits the capacity for human labour and desire, transforms spaces, and speeds up the pace of life. It produces problems of overaccumulation for which there are but a limited number of possible solutions.

Through these mechanisms capitalism creates its own distinctive historical geography. Its developmental trajectory is not in any ordinary sense predictable, precisely because it has always been based on speculation — on new products, new technologies, new spaces and locations, new labour processes (family labour, factory systems, quality circles, worker participation), and the like. There are many ways to make a profit. *Post hoc* rationalizations of speculative activity depend on a positive answer to the question: 'Was it profitable?' Different entrepreneurs, whole spaces of the world economy, generate different solutions to that question, and new answers overtake the old as one speculative wave engulfs another.

There are laws of process at work under capitalism capable of generating a seemingly infinite range of outcomes out of the slightest variation in initial conditions or of human activity and imagination. In the same way that the laws of fluid dynamics are invariant in every river in the world, so the laws of capital circulation are consistent from one supermarket to another, from one labour market to another, from one commodity production system to another, from one country to another and from one household to another. Yet

New York and London are as different from each other as the Hudson is from the Thames.

Cultural life is often held to be outside rather than within the embrace of this capitalist logic. People, it is said, make their own history in these realms in very specific and quite unpredictable ways, depending upon their values and aspirations, their traditions and norms. Economic determination is irrelevant, even in the famous last instance. I hold this argument to be erroneous in two senses. First, I see no difference in principle between the vast range of speculative and equally unpredictable activities undertaken by entrepreneurs (new products, new marketing stratagems, new technologies, new locations, etc.) and the equally speculative development of cultural, political, legal, and ideological values and institutions under capitalism. Secondly, while it is indeed possible that speculative development in these latter domains would not be reinforced or discarded according to the *post hoc* rationalizations of profit-making, profitability (in either the narrow or the broader sense of generating and acquiring new wealth) has long been implicated in these activities, and with the passing of time the strength of this connection has increased rather than diminished. Precisely because capitalism is expansionary and imperialistic, cultural life in more and more areas gets brought within the grasp of the cash nexus and the logic of capital circulation. To be sure, this has sparked reactions varying from anger and resistance to compliance and appreciation (and there is nothing predictable about that either). But the widening and deepening of capitalist social relations with time is, surely, one of the most singular and undisputable facts of recent historical geography.

The oppositional relations depicted in table 4.1 are always subject to the restless transformative activity of capital accumulation and speculative change. Exact configurations cannot be predicted in advance, even though the law-like behaviour of the transformative force can. Put more concretely, the degree of Fordism and modernism, or of flexibility and postmodernism, is bound to vary from time to time and from place to place, depending on which configuration is profitable and which is not. Behind all the ferment of modernity and postmodernity, we can discern some simple generative principles that shape an immense diversity of outcomes. Yet the latter strikingly fail (as in the case of the serially produced downtown renewals) to create unpredictable novelty, even though the seemingly infinite capacity to engender products feeds all the illusions of freedom and of open paths for personal fulfilment. Wherever capitalism goes, its illusory apparatus, its fetishisms, and its system of mirrors come not far behind.

It is here that we can invoke, once more, Bourdieu's thesis (above, p. 219) that we each of us possess powers of regulated improvisation, shaped by experience, which allow us 'an endless capacity to engender products — thoughts, perceptions, expressions, actions — whose limits are set by the historically situated conditions' of their production; the 'conditioned and conditional freedom' this secures 'is as remote from the creation of unpredictable novelty as it is from simple mechanical reproduction of the initial conditionings.' It is, Bourdieu suggests, through mechanisms of this sort that every established order tends to produce 'the naturalization of its own arbitrariness' expressed in the 'sense of limits' and the 'sense of reality' which in turn form the basis for an 'ineradicable adherence to the established order'. The reproduction of the social and symbolic order through the exploration of difference and 'otherness' is all too evident in the climate of postmodernism.

So where, then, can real change come from? To begin with, the contradictory experiences acquired under capitalism — many of which are set out in table 4.1 — render the novelty a little less thoroughly predictable than was the case in Bourdieu's encounter with the Kabyles. Mechanical reproduction of value systems, beliefs, cultural preferences, and the like is impossible, not in spite of but precisely because of the speculative grounding of capitalism's inner logic. The exploration of contradictions always lies at the heart of original thought. But it is also evident that the expression of such contradictions in the form of objective and materialized crises plays a key role in breaking the powerful link 'between the subjective structures and the objective structures' and thereby lay the groundwork for a critique that 'brings the undiscussed into discussion and the unformulated into formulation'. While crises in the experience of space and time, in the financial system, or in the economy at large, may form a necessary condition for cultural and political changes, the sufficient conditions lie more deeply embedded in the internalized dialectics of thought and knowledge production. For it is ever the case that, as Marx (1967, 178) has it, 'we erect our structure in imagination before we erect it in reality'.

24

The work of art in an age of electronic reproduction and image banks

'In principle a work of art has always been reproducible,' wrote Walter Benjamin, but mechanical reproduction 'represents something new.' It made concrete the poet Paul Valéry's prediction: 'Just as water, gas, and electricity are brought into our houses from far off to satisfy our needs in response to minimal effort, so we shall be supplied with visual or auditory images, which will appear and disappear at a simple movement of the hand.' The consequences that Benjamin foresaw have been emphasized many times over by the advances in electronic reproduction and the capacity to store images, torn out of their actual contexts in space and time, for instantaneous use and retrieval on a mass basis.

The increased role of the masses in cultural life has had both positive and negative consequences. Benjamin feared their desire to bring things closer spatially and humanly, because it inevitably led to transitoriness and reproducibility as hallmarks of a cultural production system that had hitherto explored uniqueness and permanence. The ease with which fascism could make use of that was a signal warning that the democratization of working-class culture was not necessarily an unmitigated blessing.

What is really at stake here, however, is an analysis of cultural production and the formation of aesthetic judgements through an organized system of production and consumption mediated by sophisticated divisions of labour, promotional exercises, and marketing arrangements. And these days the whole system is dominated by the circulation of capital (more often than not of a multinational sort).

As a production, marketing, and consumption system, it exhibits many peculiarities in the form its labour process takes, and in the manner of linkage between production and consumption. The one thing that cannot be said of it is that the circulation of capital is absent, and that the practitioners and agents at work within it are unaware of the laws and rules of capital accumulation. And it is certainly not democratically controlled and organized, even though consumers are highly dispersed and have more than a little say in what is produced and what aesthetic values shall be conveyed.

This is not the place to launch into any extensive discussion of the various modes of organization of this sector of economic activity, or of the ways in which aesthetic and cultural trends get woven into the fabric of daily life. Such topics have been thoroughly investigated by others (Raymond Williams providing a host of thoughtful insights). But two important issues do stand out as directly relevant to understanding the condition of postmodernity as a whole.

First, the class relations prevailing within this system of production and consumption are of a peculiar sort. What stands out here is sheer money power as a means of domination rather than direct control over the means of production and wage labour in the classic sense. One side-effect has been to rekindle a lot of theoretical interest in the nature of money (as opposed to class) power and the asymmetries that can arise therefrom (cf. Simmel's extraordinary treatise on *The philosophy of money*). Media stars, for example, can be highly paid yet grossly exploited by their agents, the record companies, the media tycoons, and the like. Such a system of asymmetrical money relations relates to the need to mobilize cultural creativity and aesthetic ingenuity, not only in the production of a cultural artefact but also in its promotion, packaging, and transformation into some kind of successful spectacle. But asymmetrical money power does not necessarily promote class consciousness. It is conducive to demands for individual liberty and entrepreneurial freedom. The conditions prevailing within what Daniel Bell calls 'the cultural mass' of producers and consumers of cultural artefacts shape attitudes different from those that arise out of conditions of wage labour. This cultural mass adds yet another layer to that amorphous formation known as 'the middle class.'

The political identity of such a social stratum has always been notoriously shaky, varying from the white-collar workers who formed the backbone of German Nazism (see Speier, 1986) to those who played such an important role in re-shaping the cultural and political life of late nineteenth-century Paris. While it is dangerous to advance any general rules in this regard, such strata tend to lack 'the reassuring support of a moral tradition that they could call their own' (Speier). They either become 'value parasites' — drawing their consciousness from association with one or other of the dominant classes in society — or cultivate all manner of fictitious marks of their own identity. It is in these strata that the quest for symbolic capital is most marked, and for them that movements of fashion, localism, nationalism, language, and even religion and myth can be of the greatest significance. What I am proposing here is to look carefully at the kind of circularity within the cultural mass which brings together producers held in thrall by pure money power on the one hand, and on the other hand relatively affluent consumers, themselves part of the cultural mass, who look for a certain kind of cultural output as a clear mark of their own social identity. In the same way that the new social layers provided the mass audience to which the Paris Impressionists, themselves part of that social formation, could appeal, so the new social layers that came into existence with the formation of the cultural mass and the rise of new white-collar occupations in finance, real estate, law, education, science, and business services provided a powerful source of demand for new cultural forms based on fashion, nostalgia, pastiche, and kitsch – in short, all that we associate with postmodernism.

The politics of the cultural mass are, however, important, since they are in the business of defining the symbolic order through the production of images for everyone. The more it turns in upon itself, or the more it sides with this or that dominant class in society, the more the prevailing sense of the symbolic and moral order tends to shift. I think it fair to say that the cultural mass drew heavily upon the working-class movement for its cultural identity in the 1960s, but that the attack upon, and decline of, the latter from the early 1970s onwards cut loose the cultural mass, which then shaped its own identity around its own concerns with money power, individualism, entrepreneurialism, and the like (the changing politics of a newspaper like *Libération* in France, which began as an iconoclastic but left-wing newspaper in the 1960s, and now represents an equally iconoclastic cultural entrepreneurialism, is a perfect example). The imaging of politics by the public relations agencies matched the politics of imaging in powerful ways.

Second, the development of cultural production and marketing on a global scale has itself been a primary agent in time–space compression in part because it projected a *musée imaginaire*, a jazz club, or a concert hall into everyone's living room, but also for a set of other reasons that Benjamin considered:

> Our taverns and our metropolitan streets, our offices and furnished rooms, our railroad stations and our factories appeared to have us locked up hopelessly. Then came the film and burst this prison-world asunder by the dynamite of a tenth of a second, so that now, in the midst of its far-flung ruins and

debris, we calmly and adventurously go travelling. With the close-up space expands, with slow motion, movement is extended .... Evidently a different nature opens itself to the camera than opens to the naked eye – if only because an unconsciously penetrated space is substituted for a space consciously explored. (Benjamin, 1969, 236)

25

Responses to time–space compression

There have been various responses to the travails of time–space compression. The first line of defence is to withdraw into a kind of shell-shocked, blasé, or exhausted silence and to bow down before the overwhelming sense of how vast, intractable, and outside any individual or even collective control everything is. Excessive information, it transpires, is one of the best inducements to forgetting. The qualities of postmodern fiction – 'the flattest possible characters in the flattest possible landscape rendered in the flattest possible diction' (above, p. 58) – are suggestive of exactly that reaction. The personal world that Wenders depicts in *Paris, Texas* does likewise. *Wings of Desire*, though more optimistic, still replies in the affirmative to the other question which Newman poses: 'Have the velocities of recent change been so great that we do not know how to trace their lines of force, that no sensibility, least of all narrative, has been able to articulate them?'

This aspect of postmodernism has been reinforced by the activities of the deconstructionists. In their suspicion of any narrative that aspires to coherence, and in their rush to deconstruct anything that even looks like meta-theory, they challenged all basic propositions. To the degree that all the narrative accounts on offer contained hidden presuppositions and simplifications, they deserved critical scrutiny, if only to emerge the stronger for it. But in challenging all consensual standards of truth and justice, of ethics, and meaning, and in pursuing the dissolution of all narratives and meta-theories into a diffuse universe of language games, deconstructionism ended up, in spite of the best intentions of its more radical practitioners, by reducing knowledge and meaning to a rubble of signifiers. It thereby produced a condition of nihilism that prepared the ground for the re-emergence of a charismatic politics and even more simplistic propositions than those which were deconstructed.

The second reaction amounts to a free-wheeling denial of the complexity of the world, and a penchant for the representation of it in terms of highly simplified rhetorical propositions. Slogans abound, from left to right of the political spectrum, and depthless images are deployed to capture complex meanings. Travel, even imaginary and vicarious, is supposed to broaden the mind, but it just as frequently ends up confirming prejudices.

The third response has been to find an intermediate niche for political and intellectual life which spurns grand narrative but which does cultivate the possibility of limited action. This is the progressive angle to postmodernism which emphasizes community and locality, place and regional resistances, social movements, respect for otherness, and the like (above, p.113). It is an attempt to carve out at least one knowable world from the infinity of possible worlds which are daily shown to us on the television screen. At its best it produces trenchant images of possible other worlds, and even begins to shape the actual world. But it is hard to stop the slide into parochialism, myopia, and self-referentiality in the face of the universalizing force of capital circulation. At worst, it brings us back to narrow and sectarian politics in which respect for others gets mutilated in the fires of competition between the fragments. And, it should not be forgotten, this was the path that allowed Heidegger to reach his accommodation with Nazism, and which continues to inform the rhetoric of fascism (witness the rhetoric of a contemporary fascist leader like Le Pen).

The fourth response has been to try and ride the tiger of time–space compression through construction of a language and an imagery that can mirror and hopefully command it. I place the frenetic writings of Baudrillard and Virilio in this category, since they seem hell-bent on fusing with time–space compression and replicating it in their own flamboyant rhetoric. We have seen this kind of response before, most specifically in Nietzsche's extraordinary evocations in *The will to power* (above, p.274). Compared to that, however, it seems as if Baudrillard reduces Nietzsche's tragic sense to farce (but then postmodernism always has trouble in taking itself seriously). Jameson, for all his brilliance, likewise loses his hold on both the reality he is seeking to represent and on the language that might properly be deployed to represent it in his more protean writings.

Indeed, the hyper-rhetoric of this wing of the postmodern reaction can dissolve into the most alarming irresponsibility. In reading Jameson's account of schizophrenia, for example, it is hard not to impute euphoric qualities to the hallucinogenic rush of intoxicating experience behind the surface appearance of anxiety and neurosis. But as Taylor (1987, 67) points out, Jameson's selective quotations from the autobiography of a schizophrenic girl eliminate the terror that attaches to her unreality states, making it all seem like a well-controlled LSD trip rather than a succession of states of guilt, lethargy, and helplessness coupled with anguished and sometimes tempestuous dislocation. Deleuze and Guattari, applauded by Foucault, likewise recommend that we accommodate to the fact that 'everywhere capitalism sets in motion schizo-flows that animate "our" arts and "our" sciences, just as they congeal into the production of "our own" sick, the schizophrenics.' Revolutionaries, they advise, 'should carry out their undertakings along the lines of the schizo process,' because the schizophrenic 'has become caught up in a flux of desire that threatens the social order.' If this is indeed the case, then I am left contemplating the following account from the Associated Press, 27 December 1987, as a possible epitaph on 'our' civilization:

> Mr Dobben had been diagnosed as a schizophrenic.... On Thanksgiving Day, the police say, Mr Dobben took his two sons, Bartley Joel, 2 years old, and Peter David, 15 months old, to the Cannon—Muskegon Corporation foundry where he worked and put them inside a giant ladle used to carry molten metal. He then heated it to 1,300 degrees while his wife, unknowing, waited outside in the car. Now Bartley James Dobben, 26, sits under suicide surveillance.

In case this be thought a too extreme vision, I quote also Kenny Scharf (an East Village 'Day-Glo' painter) whose sequence of paintings of Estelle escaping time—space compression with a one-way ticket to outer space has her, in the final picture, 'just kind of having fun by herself, floating and watching the world blow up' (Taylor, 1987, 123). And if that is judged too imaginary, then I quote Alan Sugar, Chairman of the Amstrad Corporation: 'If there was a market in mass-produced portable nuclear weapons then we'd market them too.'

26

The crisis of historical materialism

The odd thing is how radical some of these diverse responses appeared, and how difficult it has been for the left, as opposed to the right, to cope with them. On reflection, the oddity disappears easily enough. A mode of thought that is anti-authoritarian and iconoclastic, that insists on the authenticity of other voices, that celebrates difference, decentralization, and democratization of taste, as well as the power of imagination over materiality, has to have a radical cutting edge even when indiscriminately used. In the hands of its more responsible practitioners, the whole baggage of ideas associated with postmodernism could be deployed to radical ends, and thereby be seen as part of a fundamental drive towards a more liberatory politics, in exactly the same way that the turn to more flexible labour processes could be seen as an opening to a new era of democratic and highly decentralized labour relations and co-operative endeavours.

From the standpoint of the traditionalist right, the excesses of the 1960s and the violence of 1968 appeared subversive in the extreme. Perhaps for that reason, Daniel Bell's description in *The cultural contradictions of capitalism*, though launched entirely from a right-wing perspective that sought the restoration of respect for authority, was probably more accurate than many of the left attempts to grasp what was happening. Other writers, like Toffler and even McLuhan, saw the significance of time–space compression and the confusions it generated in ways that the left could not see, precisely because it was so deeply embroiled in creating the confusion. Only recently has the left come to terms with some of these issues, and I think it significant that Berman's book, published in 1982, recuperates some of these themes only by treating Marx as the first great modernist writer rather than as a Marxist who could see through what modernism was all about.

The New Left was preoccupied with a struggle to liberate itself from the dual shackles of old left politics (particularly as represented by traditional communist parties and 'orthodox' Marxism) and the repressive powers of corporate capital and bureaucratized institutions (the state, the universities, the unions, etc.). It saw itself from the very outset as a cultural as well as a political—economic force, and helped force the turn to aesthetics that postmodernism has been about.

But there were unintended consequences of such a line of action. The push into cultural politics connected better with anarchism and libertarianism than with traditional Marxism, and set the New Left against traditional working-class attitudes and institutions. The New Left embraced the new social movements which were themselves agents of fragmentation of old left politics. To the degree that the latter were at best passive, and at worst reactionary, in their treatment of race and gender issues, of difference, and of the problems of colonized peoples and repressed minorities, of ecological and aesthetic issues, some kind of political shift of the sort that the New Left proposed was surely justified. But in making its move, the New Left tended to abandon its faith both in the proletariat as an instrument of progressive change and in historical materialism as a mode of analysis. André Gorz proclaimed farewell to the working class, and Aronowitz announced the crisis of historical materialism.

The New Left thereby cut itself off from its own ability to have a critical perspective on itself or on the social processes of transformation that underlay the surge into postmodernist ways of thought. In insisting that it was culture and politics that mattered, and that it was neither reasonable nor proper to invoke economic determination even in the last instance (let alone invoke theories of capital circulation and accumulation, or of necessary class relations in production), it was unable to stop its own drift into ideological positions that were weak in contest with the new-found strength of the neo-conservatives, and which forced it to compete on the same terrain of image production, aesthetics, and ideological power when the means of communication lay in its opponents' hands. In a 1983 symposium, *Marxism and the interpretation of culture*, for example, most of the authors paid far more attention to Foucault and Derrida than they did to Marx (Nelson and Grossberg, 1988). Ironically, it was an old left figure (noticeably absent from that symposium), Raymond Williams, a long-time student of working-class cultural forms and values, who crossed the tracks of the New Left and tried to re-establish the material groundings of what cultural practices might be about. Williams not only rejected modernism as a valid category but, by extension, saw postmodernism as itself a mask for the deeper transformations in the culture of capitalism which he sought to identify.

The interrogation of 'orthodox' Marxian formulations (by writers in the tradition of Fanon or Simone de Beauvoir as well as by the deconstructionists) was both necessary and positive in its implications. Important transitions were indeed afoot in political economy, in the nature of state functions, in cultural practices, and in the time–space dimension across which social relations had to be assessed (the relation between, say, apartheid in South Africa and working-class movements in Europe or North America became even more significant as a political issue than it had been at the high point of direct imperialism). It took a properly dynamic rather than static conception of both theory and historical materialism to grasp the significance of these shifts. Of the areas of greatest development I would list four:

1   The treatment of difference and 'otherness' not as something to be added on to more fundamental Marxist categories (like class and productive forces), but as something that should be omni-present from the very beginning in any attempt to grasp the dialectics of social change. The importance of recuperating such aspects of social organization as race, gender, religion, within the overall frame of historical materialist enquiry (with its emphasis upon the power of money and capital circulation) and class politics (with its emphasis upon the unity of the emancipatory struggle) cannot be overestimated.

2   A recognition that the production of images and of discourses is an important facet of activity that has to be analysed as part and parcel of the reproduction and transformation of any symbolic order. Aesthetic and cultural practices matter, and the conditions of their production deserve the closest attention

3   A recognition that the dimensions of space and time matter, and that there are real geographies of social action, real as well as metaphorical territories and spaces of power that become vital as organizing forces in the geopolitics of capitalism, at the same time as they are the sites of innumerable differences and othernesses that have to be understood both in their own right and within the overall logic of capitalist development. Historical materialism is finally beginning to take its geography seriously.

4   Historical–geographical materialism is an open-ended and dialectical mode of enquiry rather than a closed and fixed body of understandings. Meta-theory is not a statement of total truth but an attempt to come to terms with the historical and geographical truths that characterize capitalism both in general as well as in its present phase.

27

Cracks in the mirrors, fusions at the edges

'We feel that postmodernism is over,' a major United States developer told the architect Moshe Safdie (*New York Times*, 29 May 1988). 'For projects which are going to be ready in five years, we are now considering new architectural appointments.' He said this, reported Safdie, 'with the naturalness of a clothing manufacturer who tells you that he does not want to be stuck with a line of blue coats when red is in.' Perhaps for this very reason, Philip Johnson has put his considerable weight behind the new movement of 'deconstructivism' with all its high-brow appeal to theory. If this is where the developers are heading, can the philosophers and literary theorists be far behind?

On 19 October 1987, someone peeked behind the reflecting mirrors of US economic policy and, frightened at what they saw there, plunged the world's stock markets into such a fearful crash that nearly a third of the paper value of assets worldwide was written off within a few days (see table 2.10). The event provoked ugly memories of 1929, pushed most finance houses to draconian economies, others into hasty mergers. Fortunes made overnight by the young, the aggressive, and the ruthless traders in the hyper-space of instant financial dealing were lost even more speedily than they had been acquired. The economy of New York City and other major financial centres was threatened by the rapid fall in the volume of trading. Yet the rest of the world remained strangely unmoved. 'Different worlds' was the headline in the *Wall Street Journal*, as it compared the 'eerily detached' view from Main Street, USA, with that of Wall Street. 'The crash aftermath is the tale of two cultures — processing different information, operating on different time horizons, dreaming different dreams. . . . The financial community — living by the minute and trading by the computer — operates on one set of values,' while 'the rest of America — living by the decade, buying and holding — has a different code' which might be called 'the ethic of those who have their hands on shovels.'

Main Street may feel justified in its indifference because the dire predictions in the aftermath of the crash have not as yet materialized. But the mirrors of accelerating indebtedness (personal, corporate, governmental) continue to work overtime (see figure 2.13). Fictitious capital is even more hegemonic than before in its influence. It creates its own fantastic world of booming paper wealth and assets. Asset inflation takes over where the commodity inflation of the 1970s left off until the mass of funds thrown into the markets to ward off the crash in October 1987 works its way through the economy to produce a resurgence of wage and commodity inflation two years later. Debts get re-scheduled and rolled over at ever faster rates, with the aggregate effect of re-scheduling the crisis-tendencies of capitalism into the twenty-first century. Yet cracks in the reflecting mirrors of economic performance abound. US banks write off billions of dollars of bad loans, governments default, international currency markets remain in perpetual turmoil.

On the philosophical front, deconstructionism has been put on the defensive by the controversies over the Nazi sympathies of Heidegger and Paul de Man. That Heidegger, the inspiration of deconstruction, should have had such an unrepentant attachment to Nazism, and that Paul de Man, one of deconstructionism's most accomplished practitioners, should have had such a murky past of anti-semitic writing, has proved a major embarrassment. The charge that deconstruction is neo-fascist is not in itself interesting, but the manner of defence against the charge is.

Hillis Miller (1988), for example, appeals to the 'facts' (a positivist argument), to principles of fairness and reasonableness (liberal humanist argument), and to historical context (an historical materialist argument) in his defence of de Man's 'appalling' interventions. The irony, of course, is that these are all ways of arguing that Hillis Miller had pulled apart in the work of others. Rorty, on the other hand, takes his own position to its logical conclusion, declaring that the political opinions of a great philosopher do not have to be taken any more seriously than philosophy itself (which is hardly at all), and that any relationship between ideas and reality, moral positions and philosophical writings is purely contingent. The flagrant irresponsibility of that position is almost as embarrassing as the transgressions that set the whole debate rolling.

The cracks in an intellectual edifice that opens the way to the empowerment of aesthetics over ethics are important. Deconstructionism, like any system of thought and any definition of an overwhelming symbolic order, internalizes certain contradictions which at a certain point become more and more self-evident. When Lyotard, for example, seeks to keep his radical hopes alive by appeal to some pristine and unsullied concept of justice, he proposes a truth statement that lies above the mêlée of interest groups and their cacophony of language games. When Hillis Miller is forced to appeal to liberal and positivist values to defend his mentor Paul de Man against what he considers the calumny of false accusations, then he, too, invokes universals.

And at the edges of these trends there are all sorts of fusions of the fragments in progress. Jesse Jackson employs charismatic politics in a political campaign which nevertheless begins to fuse some of the social movements in the United States that have long been apathetic to each other. The very possibility of a genuine rainbow coalition defines a unified politics which inevitably speaks the tacit language of class, because this is precisely what defines the common experience within the differences. US trade union leaders finally begin to worry that their support for foreign dictatorships in the name of anti-communism since 1950, has promoted the unfair labour practices and low wages in many countries which now compete for jobs and investment. And when British Ford car workers struck and stopped car production in Belgium and West Germany, they suddenly realized that spatial dispersal in the division of labour is not entirely to the capitalists' advantage and international strategies are feasible as well as desirable. Signs of a new internationalism in the ecological sphere (forced by events for the bourgeoisie, sought out actively by many ecological groups) and in the fight against racism, apartheid, world hunger, uneven geographical development, are everywhere, even if much of it still lies in the realm of pure image making (like Band Aid) rather than in political organization. The geopolitical stress between East and West also undergoes a notable amelioration (again, no thanks to the ruling classes in the West, but more because of an evolution in the East).

The cracks in the mirror may not be too wide, and the fusions at the edges may not be too striking, but the fact that all are there suggests that the condition of postmodernity is undergoing a subtle evolution, perhaps reaching a point of self-dissolution into something different. But what?

Answers to that cannot be rendered in abstraction from the political–economic forces currently transforming the world of labour, finance, uneven geographical development, and the like. The lines of tension are clear enough. Geopolitics and economic nationalism, localism and the politics of place, are all fighting it out with a new internationalism in the most contradictory of ways. The fusion of the European Economic Community as a commodity trading block takes place in 1992; takeovers and merger manias will sweep the continent; yet Thatcherism still proclaims itself as a distinctive national project resting upon the peculiarities of the British (a proposition which both left and right politics tend to accept). International control over finance capital looks inevitable, yet it seems impossible to arrive at that through the collectivity of national interests. In the intellectual and cultural spheres similar oppositions can be identified.

Wenders seems to propose a new romanticism, the exploration of global meanings and the prospects for Becoming through the release of romantic desire out of the stasis of Being. There are dangers in releasing an unknown and perhaps uncontrollable aesthetic power into an unstable situation. Brandon Taylor favours a return to realism as a means to bring cultural practices back into a realm where some kind of explicit ethical content can be expressed. Even some of the deconstructionists seem to be reverting to ethics.

Beyond that there is a renewal of historical materialism and of the Enlightenment project. Through the first we can begin to understand postmodernity as an historical–geographical condition. On that critical basis it becomes possible to launch a counter-attack of narrative against the image, of ethics against aesthetics, of a project of Becoming rather than Being, and to search for unity within difference, albeit in a context where the power of the image and of aesthetics, the problems of time–space compression, and the significance of geopolitics and otherness are clearly understood. A renewal of historical-geographical materialism can indeed promote adherence to a new version of the Enlightenment project. Poggioli (1968, 73) captures the difference thus:

> In the consciousness of the classical epoch, it is not the present that brings the past into culmination, but the past that culminates in the present, and the present is in turn understood as a new triumph of ancient and eternal values, as a return to the principle of the true and the just, as a restoration or re-birth of those principles. But for the moderns, the present is valid only by virtue of the potentialities of the future, as the matrix of the future, insofar as it is the forge of history in continued metamorphosis, seen as a permanent spiritual revolution.

There are some who would have us return to classicism and others who seek to tread the path of the moderns. From the standpoint of the latter, every age is judged to attain 'the fullness of its time, not by being but by becoming.' I could not agree more.

References

Aglietta, M. (1979): *A theory of capitalist regulation*. London.
Arac, J. (ed.) (1986): *Postmodernism and politics*. Manchester.
Aragon, L. (1971): *Paris peasant*. London.
Archives Nationales (1987): *Espace français*. Paris.
Armstrong, P., Glyn, A., and Harrison, J. (1984): *Capitalism since World War II*. London.
Aronowitz, S. (1981): *The crisis of historical materialism*. New York.
Bachelard, G. (1964): *The poetics of space*. Boston, Mass.
Banham, R. (1986): *A concrete Atlantis: U.S. industrial building and European modern architecture*. Cambridge, Mass.
Barthes, R. (1967): *Writing degree zero*. London.
Barthes, R. (1975): *The pleasure of the text*. New York.
Baudelaire, C. (1981): *Selected writing on art and artists*. London.
Baudrillard, J. (1981): *For a critique of the political economy of the sign*. St Louis, Mo.
Baudrillard, J. (1986): *L'Amérique*. Paris.
Bell, D. (1978): *The cultural contradictions of capitalism*. New York.
Benjamin, W. (1969): *Illuminations*. New York.
Berman, M. (1982): *All that is solid melts into air*. New York.
Bernstein, R. (ed.) (1985): *Habermas and modernity*. Oxford.
Blitz, M. (1981): *Heidegger's Being and Time: and the possibility of political philosophy*. Ithaca, NY.
Block, F. (1977): *The origins of international economic disorder: a study of the United States international policy since World War II to the present*. Berkeley, Calif.
Bluestone, B. and Harrison, B. (1982): *The deindustrialization of America*. New York.
Borges, J. (1972): *The chronicles of Bustos-Domecq*. New York.
Bourdieu, P. (1977): *Outline of a theory of practice*. Cambridge.
Bourdieu, P. (1984): *Distinction: a social critique of the judgement of taste*. London.
Bove, P. (1986): 'The ineluctability of difference: scientific pluralism and the critical intelligence.' In Arac (ed.)

Boyer, M. (1988): 'The return of aesthetics to city planning.' *Society*, 25 (4), 49–56.

Boyer, R. (1986a): *La flexibilité du travail en Europe.* Paris.

Boyer, R. (1986b): *La théorie de la régulation: une analyse critique.* Paris.

Bradbury, M. and McFarlane, J. (1976): *Modernism, 1890–1930.* Harmondsworth.

Braverman, H. (1974): *Labor and monopoly capital.* New York.

Bruno, G. (1987): 'Ramble city: postmodernism and *Blade Runner.*' *October* 41, 61–74.

Burawoy, M. (1979): *Manufacturing consent: changes in the labor process under monopoly capitalism.* Chicago, Ill.

Bürger, P. (1984): *Theory of the avant-garde.* Manchester.

Calvino, I. (1981): *If on a winter's night a traveler.* New York.

Caro, R. (1974): *The power broker: Robert Moses and the fall of New York.* New York.

Cassirer, E. (1951): *The philosophy of the Enlightenment.* Princeton, NJ.

Chambers, I. (1986): *Popular culture: the metropolitan experience.* London.

Chambers, I. (1987): 'Maps for the metropolis: a possible guide to the present.' *Cultural Studies*, 1, 1–22.

Clark, T. J. (1985): *The painting of modern life: Paris in the art of Manet and his followers.* New York.

Coalition for the Homeless, New York City (1987): *Forgotten voices, unforgettable dreams.* New York.

Cohen, S. and Taylor, L. (1978): *Escape attempts: the theory and practice of resistance to everyday life.* Harmondsworth.

Cohen-Solal, A. (1987): 'The lovers' contract.' *The Observer*, 11 October 1987.

Collins, G. and Collins, C. (1986): *Camillo Sitte: the birth of modern city planning.* New York.

Colquhoun, A. (1985): 'On modern and post-modern space.' In Princeton Architectural Press.

Crimp, D. (1983): 'On the museum's ruins.' In H. Foster (ed.).

Crimp, D. (1987): 'Art in the 80s: the myth of autonomy.' *PRECIS* 6, 83–91.

Dahrendorf, R. (1987): 'The erosion of citizenship and its consequences for us all.' *New Statesman*, 12 June 1987.

Daniels, P. (1985): *Service industries: a geographical appraisal.* London.

Davidson, J. D. and Rees-Mogg, W. (1988): *Blood in the streets.* London.

Davis, M. (1986): *Prisoners of the American dream.* London.

de Certeau, M. (1984): *The practice of everyday life.* Berkeley, Calif.

de Vroey, M. (1984): 'A regulation approach interpretation of the contemporary crisis.' *Capital and Class*, 23, 45–66.

Debord, G. (1983): *Society of the spectacle.* Detroit, Mich.

Deleuze, G. and Guattari, F. (1984): *Anti-Oedipus: capitalism and schizophrenia.* London.

Deutsche, R. and Ryan, C. (1984): 'The fine art of gentrification.' *October*, 31, 91–111.

Deyo, F. (1987): 'Labor systems, segmentation and the politics of labor: the East Asian NIC's in the transnational division of labor.' Paper presented to the American Sociological Association, Chicago.

Dicken, P. (1986): *Global shift: industrial change in a turbulent world.* London.

Dockès, P. (1969): *L'espace dans la pensée économique du XVIe au XVIIIe siècle.* Paris.

Durkheim, E. (1915): *The elementary forms of the religious life.* London.

Eagleton, T. (1987): 'Awakening from modernity.' *Times Literary Supplement*, 20 February 1987.

Eco, U. (1986): 'Function and the sign: an introduction to urban semiotics.' In M. Gottdiener and A. Lagopoulos (eds): *The city and the sign: an introduction to urban semiotics.* New York.

Edgerton, S. (1976): *The renaissance re-discovery of linear perspective.* New York.

Edwards, R. (1979): *Contested terrain: the transformation of the workplace in the twentieth century.* New York.

Farias, V. (1987): *Heidegger et le nazisme.* Paris.

Fayol, H. (1916): *Administration industrielle et générale.* Paris.

Ferry, L. and Renault, A. (1988): *Heidegger et les modernes.* Paris.

Feyerabend, P. (1975): *Against method.* London.

Fish, S. (1980): *Is there a text in this class? The authority of interpretive communities.* Cambridge, Mass.

Fishman, R. (1982): *Urban utopias in the twentieth century.* Cambridge, Mass.

Flaubert, G. (1964): *Sentimental education.* Harmondsworth.

Flaubert, G. (1979): *Letters, 1830–57.* London.

Foster, H. (1985): *Recodings: art, spectacle, cultural politics.* Port Townsend, Washington.

Foster, H. (ed.) (1983): *The anti-aesthetic: essays on postmodern culture.* Port Townsend, Washington.

Foster, J. (1974): *Class struggle in the industrial revolution.* London.

Foucault, M. (1972): *Power/knowledge.* New York.

Foucault, M. (1984): *The Foucault reader* (ed. P. Rabinow). Harmondsworth.

Frampton, K. (1980): *Modern architecture: a critical history.* London.

Frisby, D. (1985): *Fragments of modernity.* Cambridge.

Giddens, A. (1984): *The constitution of society.* Oxford.

Giedion, S. (1941): *Space, time and architecture.* New York.

Gilligan, C. (1982): *In a different voice: psychological theory and women's development.* Cambridge, Mass.

Giovannini, J. (1988): 'Breaking all the rules.' *New York Times Magazine*, 12 June 1988.

Goldberger, P. (1988): 'Theories as the building blocks for a new style.' *New York Times*, 26 June 1988.

Goldthorpe, J., et al. (1969): *The affluent worker in the class structure.* Cambridge.

Gordon, D. (1978): 'Capitalist development and the history of American cities.' In W. Tabb and L. Sawers (eds), *Marxism and the metropolis*. New York.

Gordon, D. (1988): 'The global economy: new edifice or crumbling foundations?' *New Left Review*, 168, 24–65.

Gramsci, A. (1971): *Selections from the prison notebooks*. London.

Gregory, D. and Urry, J. (eds) (1985): *Social relations and spatial structures*. London.

Guilbaut, S. (1983): *How New York stole the idea of modern art*. Chicago.

Gurvitch, G. (1964): *The spectrum of social time*. Dordrecht.

Habermas, J. (1983): 'Modernity: an incomplete project.' In H. Foster (ed.).

Habermas, J. (1987): *The philosophical discourse of modernity*. Oxford.

Hägerstrand, T. (1975): 'Survival and arena: on the life history of individuals in relation to their geographical environment.' In T. Carlstein, D. Parkes, and M. Thrift (eds), *Human activity and time geography*, vol. 2. London.

Halal, W. (1986): *The new capitalism*. New York.

Hall, E. (1966): *The hidden dimension*. New York.

Hareven, T. (1982): *Family time and industrial time*. London.

Harries, K. (1982): 'Building and the terror of time.' *Perspecta: the Yale Architectural Journal*, 19, 59–69.

Harrington, M. (1960): *The other America*. New York.

Harrison, B. and Bluestone, B. (1988): *The great U-turn: capital restructuring and the polarizing of America*. New York.

Hartsock, N. (1987): 'Rethinking modernism: minority versus majority theories.' *Cultural Critique*, 7, 187–206.

Harvey, D. (1982): *The limits to capital*. Oxford.

Harvey, D. (1985a): *The urbanization of capital*. Oxford.

Harvey, D. (1985b): *Consciousness and the urban experience*. Oxford.

Harvey, D. (1985c): 'The geopolitics of capitalism.' In D. Gregory and J. Urry (eds), *Social relations and spatial structures*. London.

Harvey, D. (1989): *The urban experience*. Oxford.

Hassan, I. (1975): *Paracriticisms: seven speculations of the times*. Urbana, Ill.

Hassan, I. (1985): 'The culture of postmodernism.' *Theory, Culture and Society*, 2 (3), 119–32.

Heidegger, M. (1959): *An introduction to Metaphysics*. New Haven, Conn.

Helgerson, R. (1986): 'The land speaks: cartography, chorography, and subversion in Renaissance England.' *Representations*, 16, 51–85.

Herf, J. (1984): *Reactionary modernism*. Cambridge.

Hewison, R. (1987): *The heritage industry*. London.

Horkheimer, M. and Adorno, T. (1972): *The dialectic of Enlightenment*. New York.

Hunt Commission Report (1971): *Financial structure and regulation*. Washington, DC.

Huyssens, A. (1984): 'Mapping the post-modern.' *New German Critique*, 33, 5–52.

Institute of Personnel Management (1986): *Flexible patterns of work*. London.

Jager, M. (1986): 'Class definition and the esthetics of gentrification.' In N. Smith and P. Williams (eds). *The gentrification of the city*. London.

Jacobs, J. (1961): *The death and life of great American cities.* New York.

Jameson, F. (1984a): 'The politics of theory: ideological positions in the post-modernism debate.' *New German Critique,* 33, 53–65.

Jameson, F. (1984b): 'Postmodernism, or the cultural logic of late capitalism.' *New Left Review,* 146, 53–92.

Jameson, F. (1988): 'Cognitive mapping.' In Nelson and Grossberg (eds).

Jencks, C. (1984): *The language of post-modern architecture.* London.

Jessop, B. (1982): *The capitalist state.* Oxford.

Jessop, B. (1983): 'Accumulation strategies, state forms, and hegemonic projects.' *Kapitalistate,* 10/11, 89–112.

Kern, S. (1983): *The culture of time and space, 1880–1918.* London.

Klotz, H. (ed.) (1985): *Post-modern visions.* New York.

Kostof, S. (1985): *A history of architecture: settings and rituals.* Oxford.

Koyré, A. (1968): *From the closed world to the infinite universe.* Baltimore, Md.

Krier, R. (1987): 'Tradition-modernity-modernism: some necessary explanations.' *Architectural Design Profile,* 65. London.

Kroker, A. and Cook, D. (1986): *The postmodern scene: excremental culture and hyper-aesthetics.* New York.

Kuhn, T. (1962): *The structure of scientific revolutions.* Chicago, Ill.

Landes, D. (1983): *Revolution in time: clocks and the making of the modern world.* Cambridge, Mass.

Lane, B. (1985): *Architecture and politics in Germany, 1918–1945.* Cambridge, Mass.

Lash, S. and Urry, J. (1987): *The end of organised capitalism.* Oxford.

Le Corbusier (1929): *The city of tomorrow and its planning.* London.

Le Goff, J. (1980): *Time, work and culture in the middle ages.* Chicago, Ill.

Lee, D. (1973): 'Requiem for large-scale planning models.' *Journal of the American Institute of Planners,* 39, 117–42.

Lees, A. (1985): *Cities perceived: urban society in European thought, 1820–1940.* New York.

Lefaivre, M. (1986): *Representing the city: Daniel Hudson Burnham and the making of an urban strategy.* Unpublished Ph.D. dissertation, Johns Hopkins University, Baltimore, Md.

Lefebvre, H. (1974): *La production de l'espace.* Paris.

Lipietz, A. (1986): 'New tendencies in the international division of labour: regimes of accumulation and modes of regulation.' In A. Scott and M. Storper (eds), *Production, work, territory; the geographical anatomy of industrial capitalism.* London.

Lukacs, G. (1969): *Goethe and his age.* London.

Lunn, E. (1985): *Marxism and modernism.* London.

Lyotard, J. (1984): *The postmodern condition.* Manchester.

Maddison, A. (1982): *Phases of capitalist development.* Oxford.

Mandel, E. (1975): *Late capitalism.* London.

Martin, R. and Rowthorn, B. (eds) (1986): *The geography of deindustrialisation.* London.

Marx, K. (1963): *The eighteenth brumaire of Louis Bonaparte.* New York.

Marx, K. (1964): *The economic and philosophic manuscripts of 1844*. New York.

Marx, K. (1967): *Capital* (3 volumes). New York.

Marx, K. (1973): *Grundrisse*. Harmondsworth.

Marx, K. and Engels, F. (1952): *The communist manifesto*. Moscow.

McHale, B. (1987): *Postmodernist fiction*. London.

McLuhan, M. (1966): *Understanding media: the extensions of man*. New York.

Miller, J. Hillis (1988): 'De Man.' *Times Literary Supplement*, 17 June 1988.

Moore, B. (1986): *Space, text and gender*. Cambridge.

Murray, R. (1987): 'Flexible specialization in the "Third Italy".' *Capital and Class*, 33, 84–95.

Nash, J. and Fernandez-Kelly, P. (eds) (1983): *Women, men and the international division of labor*. Albany, NY.

Nelson, C. and Grossberg, L. (eds) (1988): *Marxism and the interpretation of culture*. Urbana, Ill.

Newman, C. (1984): 'The postmodern aura: the act of fiction in an age of inflation.' *Salmagundi*, 63–4, 3–199.

Nietzsche, F. (1968): *The will to power*. New York.

Noble, D. (1977): *America by design*. New York.

Noyelle, T. and Stanback, T. (1984): *The economic transformation of American cities*. Totawa, NJ.

O'Connor, J. (1973): *The fiscal crisis of the state*. New York.

Offe, C. (1985): *Disorganized capitalism*. Oxford.

Ollman, B. (1971): *Alienation*. Cambridge.

Ozouf, M. (1988): *Festivals and the French Revolution*. Cambridge, Mass.

Pfeil, F. (1988): 'Postmodernism as a "structure of feeling".' In Nelson and Grossberg (eds).

Piore, M. and Sabel, C. (1984): *The second industrial divide*. New York.

Poggioli, R. (1968): *The theory of the avant-garde*. Cambridge, Mass.

Pollert, A. (1988): 'Dismantling flexibility.' *Capital and Class*, 34, 42–75.

PRECIS 6 (1987): *The culture of fragments*. Columbia University Graduate School of Architecture, New York.

Princeton Architectural Press (1985): *Architecture, criticism, ideology*. Princeton, NJ.

Raban, J. (1974): *Soft city*. London.

Raphael, M. (1981): *Proudhon, Marx, Picasso: essays in Marxist aesthetics*. London.

Reich, R. (1983): *The next American frontier*. Baltimore, Md.

Relph, E. (1987): *The modern urban landscape*. Baltimore, Md.

Rochberg-Halton, E. (1986): *Meaning and modernity: social theory in the pragmatic attitude*. Chicago, Ill.

Rohatyn, F. (1983): *The twenty-year century*. New York.

Rorty, R. (1979): *Philosophy and the mirror of nature*. Princeton, NJ.

Rorty, R. (1985): 'Habermas and Lyotard on postmodernity.' In Bernstein (ed.).

Rossi, A. (1982): *Architecture and the city*. Cambridge, Mass.

Rowe, C. and Koetter, F. (n.d.): *Collage city*. Cambridge, Mass.

Sabel, C. (1982): *Work and politics; the division of labour in industry*. London.

Sack, R. (1986): *Human territoriality: its theory and history*. Cambridge.

Sayer, A. (1989): 'Post-Fordism in question.' *International Journal of Urban and Regional Research*, forthcoming.

Scardino, A. (1987): 'What, New York City worry?' *New York Times*, 3 May 1987.

Schorske, C. (1981): *Fin-de-siècle Vienna: politics and culture*. New York.

Schumpeter, J. (1934): *The theory of economic development*. Cambridge, Mass.

Scott, A. (1988): *New industrial spaces: flexible production, organisation and regional development in North America and Western Europe*. London.

Shaiken, H. (1984): *Work transformed: automation and labour in the computer age*. New York.

Simmel, G. (1971): 'The metropolis and mental life.' In D. Levine (ed.), *On individuality and social form*. Chicago, Ill.

Simmel, G. (1978): *The philosophy of money*. London.

Smith, N. (1984): *Uneven development*. New York.

Soja, E. (1988): *Postmodern geographies: the reassertion of space in critical social theory*. London.

Sorel, G. (1974): *Reflections on violence*. London.

Speier, H. (1986): *German white collar workers and the rise of Hitler*. New Haven, Conn.

Spufford, P. (1988): *Money and its uses in medieval Europe*. Cambridge.

Stein, G. (1938): *Picasso*. New York.

Swyngedouw, E. (1986): 'The socio-spatial implications of innovations in industrial organisation,' Working Paper, No. 20, Johns Hopkins European Center For Regional Planning and Research. Lille.

Tafuri, M. (1976): *Architecture and utopia*. Cambridge, Mass.

Tafuri, M. (1985): 'USSR−Berlin 1922; from populism to constructivist international.' In Princeton Architectural Press.

Tarbell, I. (1904): *The history of the Standard Oil Company*, vol. 1. New York.

Taylor, B. (1987): *Modernism, post-modernism, realism: a critical perspective for art*. Winchester.

Taylor, F. W. (1911): *The principles of scientific management*. New York.

Therborn, G. (1984): *Why some people are more unemployed than others*. London.

Thompson, E. P. (1967): 'Time, work discipline, and industrial capitalism.' *Past and Present*, 38, 56−97.

Tichi, C. (1987): *Shifting gears: technology, literature, culture in modernist America*. Chapel Hill.

Timms, E. and Kelley, D. (eds) (1985): *Unreal city: urban experience in modern European literature and art*. Manchester.

Toffler, A. (1970): *Future shock*. New York.

Tomlins, C. (1985): *The state and the unions: labor relations, law and the organized labor movement in America, 1880—1960.* Cambridge.

Trilling, L. (1966): *Beyond culture: essays in literature and learning.* London.

Tuan, Yi Fu (1977): *Space and place.* Minneapolis, Minn.

Venturi, R., Scott-Brown, D., and Izenour, S. (1972): *Learning from Las Vegas.* Cambridge, Mass.

Virilio, P. (1980): *L'esthétique de la disparition.* Paris.

Walker, R. A. (1985): 'Is there a service economy? The changing capitalist division of labor.' *Science and Society,* 49 42—83.

Walton, J. (1987): 'Urban protest and the global political economy: the IMF riots.' In M. P. Smith and J. R. Feagin (eds), *The capitalist city.* Oxford.

Wilson, W. (1987): *The truly disadvantaged.* Chicago, Ill.

Zukin, S. (1982): *Loft living.* Baltimore, Md.

Index

Subject index